TRADE UNIONISM IN THE UNITED STATES

TRADE UNIONISM IN THE UNITED STATES

BY

ROBERT FRANKLIN HOXIE, Ph.D.

WITH AN INTRODUCTION
BY
E. H. DOWNEY, Ph.D.

AND A SUPPLEMENT
BY
MOLLIE RAY CARROLL, Ph.D.

NEW YORK / RUSSELL & RUSSELL

1966

REPRODUCED FROM THE SECOND, REVISED EDITION OF 1923
AND REISSUED, 1966, BY RUSSELL & RUSSELL
A DIVISION OF ATHENEUM HOUSE, INC.
L.C. CATALOG CARD NO: 66—13234

PRINTED IN THE UNITED STATES OF AMERICA

The main reason for teaching, to me, is to open the students' minds to the possibility of questioning the fundamentals of current thinking. I want to turn out men who cannot be led naïvely by current judgments but who will subject these judgments to tests based on the validity of their underlying assumptions—in short, socially sophisticated, thinking men.

R. F. H.

PREFACE

The book here presented is the result of an effort to reproduce as faithfully as possible the notes and lectures on Trade Unionism used by Robert F. Hoxie during his last year of teaching in the University of Chicago, and to combine them with some of his chapters previously published.

This material had been prepared by him without thought of publication in this form. Only lack of time prevented the reorganization of it and much rewriting before it was again used in the classroom when in the fall of 1915 he resumed teaching after a year of study and investigation of the relations of labor and scientific management. In view of these facts it was a question whether the notes could be published without injustice to one in whom the love of thoroughness and perfection was a ruling passion. But doubt on this point was set at rest by those to whom a first copy of the manuscript was submitted, who were unanimously of the opinion that notwithstanding its incompleteness and the fact that its author would have made great changes before embodying any portion of it in the book on Trade Unionism, to which he looked forward as the main work of coming years, there was in the notes value which altogether justified their publication.

Largely owing to the method of study and teaching which Mr. Downey, in the Introduction, has described and to the nature of the social laboratory which Trade Unionism offers, it has not been possible to use all the notes, nor to present without gaps the systematic treatment of the subject and its whole foundation of evidence which the class received and which a reader of the completed text would have had. Nevertheless, no attempt has been made to fill in the gaps by introducing material worked out by another hand.

The work of preparing the manuscript for the printer has consisted mainly in bringing the material together into chapters, using for this purpose the author's course outline and titles. There were many pages in the form of speaker's notes. Where these were full enough t be used they were drawn together by a word, or, rarely, a sentence for the sake of clearness and form. The major portion of the book, however, is a word for word transcription.

Certain omissions were necessary. It was found impossible to use in Chapter IV some of the historical notes which had been gathered for the verification of the hypothesis of functional types in Chapter III. Some notes concerning men and situations in the union movement it was necessary to omit as of a nature too intimate or personal for publication; also those on the discussion of the current events of unionism, of little importance in themselves. As far as possible, repetitions due to pedagogical requirements have been left out, but in several cases, such as in the reconsideration of the functional group theory in "Social Control" after its statement in the "Problem," or the statement of the classical economic theory of society first in "Employers' Associations," and again in "Social Control," the restatement has been too closely interwoven with the fabric of the chapter to be dispensed with.

On the other hand there have been some additions to the material of the Trade Union course proper. Preceding the work on Trade Unions in 1915, Mr. Hoxie gave a course on Labor Conditions and Problems, which served as an introduction for the trade union work. From the notes on this course have been included the discussion of social theories found in the chapter on "Social Control." A course on Scientific Management and Labor Welfare in the spring of 1916 carried forward the consideration of the theory of unionism and the attitude of organized labor into the field of "the latest phase of capitalistic industrial development," and showed the program of unionism in action. For this purpose the lecture on the "Economic Program" was written. The ground of the remaining notes on this course was covered by Mr. Hoxie's last articles, "Scientific Management and Labor Welfare," *Journal of Political Economy,* vol. XXIV, pp. 833-854, and "Why Organized Labor Opposes Scientific Management," *Quarterly Journal of Economics,* vol. XXXII, pp. 62-85. These have been used as Chapters XII and XIII.

In Chapter VI, for the notes on the Industrial Workers of the World and Syndicalism, have been substituted "The Truth About the I. W. W.," *Journal of Political Economy,* vol. XXI, pp. 785-797, and a portion of a discussion of Mr. J. G. Brooks' paper on Syndicalism before the American Economic Association, *American Economic Review Supplement,* IV, no. 1, 136-144. The last part of this chapter, the discussion of revolutionary unionism, is one of three lectures delivered in the spring of 1914 at the University of Michigan. Chapters II and III, "General Character and Types," and "The Essence of Unionism and the Interpretation of Union Types," are from the *Journal of Political Economy,* vol. XXII, pp. 201-217, 464-487, and were the first articles of the projected series on "Trade Unionism in the United States," begun in 1914. Finally, there have been added "Notes on Method." The first of these, "Historical Method *vs.* Historical Narrative," *Journal of Political Economy,* vol. XIV., pp. 568-572, was uniformly used in the consideration of the method to be followed in the study of unionism. Mr. Hoxie's own writing was a "practical application of the methods outlined in it," and he evidently regarded it, Professor Hamilton thinks (*Journal of Political Economy,* vol. XXIV, p. 878), "as the first article of his trade union series."

While the body of the trade union notes is a growth of

several years, the larger part of the book is the product of the last two or three. Chapters XI to XIV inclusive are the work of 1915-1916. Chapters II, III, IV, and part of Chapter VI were written in 1914. The notes themselves were reorganized and partly rewritten in 1913.

In the preparation of these notes and lectures for publication many have borne a part. For encouragement and for varied assistance most cordial thanks are due to several of the author's friends, to officers of the University, to his colleagues in the department of Economics and his students. Professors Henry W. Stuart, Walton H. Hamilton, Harry A. Millis and Mr. E. H. Downey have given the manuscript careful reading and offered valuable advice; Professor Addison W. Moore has given helpful suggestions on the chapter on "Employers' Associations," and Mr. John P. Frey on "Present Union Groups," and "Leaders and the Rank and File;" Miss Leona M. Powell, Mr. Dwight Sanderson, Miss Frieda Miller, and Miss Mollie Ray Carroll, former students, have been consulted on some points. Miss Powell's class notes have been used for reference throughout the work and Miss Carroll has coöperated in the preparation of "The Trade Union Program."

Especial and grateful acknowledgment must be made of the generous assistance and helpful advice in the work of editing given by Professor John R. Commons, who has also read the manuscript in its final form, and by Professor Alvin S. Johnson, who has assisted in the revision of the proof.

Permission to use material already in print has been kindly granted by the editors of the *Journal of Political Economy*, of the *Quarterly Journal of Economics*, and of the *American Economic Review*.

Lucy B. Hoxie.
Nathan Fine.

PREFATORY NOTE TO THE SECOND EDITION

The years since the publication of this book have left much unaccounted for in its pages. In response to numerous requests that it be enlarged to take account of the developments of the post-war period, Professor Mollie Ray Carroll, Chairman of the Social Science Department of Goucher College, has added a supplement indicating the main tendencies of the period, together with an extensive bibliography in the compilation of which Miss Laura D. Thompson, Librarian of the U. S. Department of Labor Library, has generously aided.

It is hoped that this additional material, which the publishers agree is, in the circumstances, the only form of revision to which the text could properly be subjected, will maintain the proved usefulness of the book for the purpose for which it was written.

LUCY B. HOXIE

INTRODUCTION[1]

Like all social movements which excite the hopes and fears of men, trade unionism has more often been the object of passionate denunciation or defense than of scientific inquiry. It is not simply that unionism counts some three million adherents in the United States alone and directly affects the wages and working conditions of perhaps an equal number who stand outside its official membership; nor simply that it interferes with the profits of employers and with their assumed right to manage business enterprises in their own way; it touches intimately the life and work of millions of families; it is able to create profound disturbances in that intricate web of economic relationships wherein the tissue of business life consists, amounting upon occasion to a dramatic interruption in the flow of goods and services without which no modern community can subsist; more than all else, it calls in question some of the most fundamental presuppositions of present day law and order. For ours is, in great part, a business man's government, and our codes of law embody the business man's rules of the game. The business man's right to employ or discharge whom he will, to fix the rate and mode of payment and the hours and conditions of work at his own discretion, to set industry in motion or break off the productive process whenever he sees his own advantage in so doing, and without responsibility for the livelihood of the industrial population—these rights are involved in the legal

[1] The extent of the writer's indebtedness to Professors Hoxie and Veblen, in respect to general standpoint and even phraseology, will be obvious to all.

xiii

conceptions of private property and free enterprise; they are recognized by the common law and the constitution; in support of them the business man can appeal to the courts, the police and even the military arm of the state. A challenge to these prerogatives of business enterprise is in some sort a challenge to the existing social organization; by traversing them unionism moves the passionate opposition, not alone of those whose pecuniary interests are directly at stake, but of social groups who are only remotely affected and whose attachment to the capitalistic system derives mainly from tradition. Disinterestedness in such a question is not the same thing as the absence of bias; the received institutions of any society are so charged with emotional content that an impartial view of them can only be attained by those who are acquainted with institutional history. Hence we see, not alone the thoughtless multitude, but lawyers and clergymen, economists and social workers, take sides for or against unionism accordingly as their training and associations have given them more of the wage earner's or of the business man's point of view. [1]

Even those who are able to dissociate themselves from class prejudices and from the fundamental assumptions of the existing social order find it no easy matter to ascertain so much as the objective facts of unionism. The American labor movement has a history of above one hundred years. It is diffused through thousands of local units and presents a bewildering variety of structure, policies, aims and ideals. The original sources of information, personal and documentary, union and anti-union, are fragmental, contradictory, widely scattered, often difficult of access, nearly always strongly partisan, sometimes even willfully misleading. Much of the record—and that by no means the least important part—was never committed to paper; most of what has been preserved consists of ephemeral

[1] For illustrations see the various pamphlets of the National Manufacturers' Association.

pamphlets and news items, commonly of a propagandist character. To sift out the significant facts from this mass of *ex parte* evidence, to distinguish the typical from the exceptional, and to arrange the whole in just order and proportion, is a task which the combined labor of many scholars has not sufficed to accomplish. Least of all has the obscurity been cleared away from that elusive mass of beliefs, sentiments, ideals and aspirations touching economic relationships which go to make up the social philosophy of unionism and which account for much of its significance to unionists themselves and to society at large.

Yet it is not enough to obtain a dispassionate view or even to ascertain the objective facts. Fruitful understanding of any social movement depends not alone upon knowledge of the features peculiar to it, but upon the ability to relate those features to social phenomena of a more general character, to disentangle the relevant circumstances out of which the particular movement arose, to set forth the efficient causes which shaped its growth and to show what it is becoming under the influence of forces which are currently at work within it or which impinge upon it. For group action is conditioned by group thought and group thought depends in turn upon group experience, so that any useful study of a social movement, more particularly of a class movement, necessarily becomes a genetic inquiry into group psychology. Such an inquiry, however, is at once confronted by all those obstacles which derive from the present rudimentary state of social science. The student of unionism, of political parties or of business enterprise, must make use of many generalizations which have yet to be established—among them the origin and functioning of social classes, the rôle of class conflict in the life of communities and the relative weight of heredity and choice, of tradition and personal experience, and of economics and general social environment in determining institutional growth and decay. Where so little can be taken as securely given, the labor of research is multiplied many fold, for the investigator of each special field must needs formulate even the general social theories in terms of which the phenomena under his immediate observation are to be interpreted.

For all these reasons the making of many books has afforded comparatively little insight into the nature and causes of American trade unionism. Those who know most about the subject can scarcely be expected to furnish a detached view or to interpret the concrete facts in terms of social science at large. Of those who have surveyed the movement from without, many have been disqualified by want of knowledge or trammeled by narrowing preconceptions. Some have poured forth a flood of pious sentiment, often effective as homiletics but not particularly illuminating; some have given a purely economic interpretation and been thereby constrained to ignore important elements of their problem; others have thought it sufficient to show that certain trade union activities do not jump with orthodox economic theory or with received notions of property and free contract. Others, still, have thought to achieve a purely objective treatment by eschewing all interpretation. The result of this last endeavor is a mass of narrative and descriptive literature, useful enough as the raw material of scientific inquiry, but, in its present form, valueless as a basis for social action. Few, out of patient research, have brought forth even a partial interpretation in causal terms. Among this elect number Professor Hoxie will hold a high and secure place.

To the baffling subject with which his best work is so closely identified, Professor Hoxie brought a very exceptional equipment. Trained originally in the straitest sect of cloister economics, he had the good fortune to escape its influence before his teachers had succeeded in dulling his appetite for reality. In the net result, indeed, he profited even from the metaphysicians, for they did but sharpen a keenly analytic mind upon the subtleties of marginal utilitarianism. Falling next under the potent spell of Thorstein Veblen, he acquired the genetic standpoint, a wide acquaintance with cultural history and an abiding interest in institutional development. After this varied apprenticeship he devoted himself for the space of more than ten years to an intensive study of American trade unionism. The literature of the subject, propagandist and scientific, union and anti-union, he made his own; but it was the living movement that chiefly held his interest. By painstaking analysis of documentary sources, by persistent attendance at union and employers' meetings, by personal interviews with scores of union and employers' leaders, above all by long continued and intimate contact with unionists of many types, he strove to ascertain the objective facts of unionism, to explain the causes which have shaped the movement and which are progressively changing it, to determine its drift, and to define its meaning for the community life of which it is a part. In the course of this study he was led into many fields of inquiry—wage theory, socialism, pragmatic philosophy, social psychology, employers' associations and scientific management. But unionism remained always his central problem; to it he returned with fresh zest after each excursus, and upon it all his other studies were made to bear.

To expound Professor Hoxie's trade union views at length, or attempt a detailed appraisal, would far overpass the reasonable limits of an introduction. It may be worth while, however, to indicate his outlook and the main results to which it led him. It has already been said that he approached his subject from the genetic standpoint, by which is meant that he aimed at a reasoned explanation of trade unionism in terms of the efficient causes which have made the movement what it is, and is becoming. Seen from this point of view a union is not so much an outward organization as a like-minded group. The effectual bond which unites a body of wageworkers is not a constitution and by-laws, a set of officers and a treasury, but a conscious·ness of common needs and aims, a common outlook on life, and a common program for the betterment of their lot. To employ Professor Hoxie's terminology, the essence of unionism is a social philosophy—an interpretation of the social facts and relationships which impinge upon the group in question, and a solution of the practical problems which these present. The interpretation may be wide or narrow, explicitly formulated or implicit and ill defined; the program may concern itself solely with conditions of employment or it may look to the economic and political regeneration of society. Some social philosophy, however, more or less consistent and far-reaching, and some generally accepted scheme of policies and methods, are the *sine qua non* of common action.

This method of approach led Professor Hoxie to a conception of unionism which differs in important respects from the views current in the schools. Others have copiously illustrated the structural details and the narrative history of union organizations, have set forth the environmental, more especially the economic, factors which have contributed to union growth and decay, and have told us much of the social creeds which unions impose upon their members, but they have had little to say of the human materials out of which unions are formed or of the manifold influences which go to shape trade union beliefs, ideals and aspirations. Professor Hoxie early focused his attention upon union functioning and the habits of thought which determine union action. Viewed in this way, he found unionism to be not a single social movement, but an imperfect fusion of several, no one of which can be adequately accounted for in purely economic terms. Shortly expressed, his analysis of unionism is characterized by emphasis upon function, the distinction of fundamental types and a pluralistic causal interpretation.

From a functional standpoint, Professor Hoxie distin-

guishes five types of unionism (not to mention sub-vari-
ants) which differ among themselves in aims, methods, and
attitude toward existing institutions. *Business unionism,*
accepting the wage system as it is, seeks the best obtain-
able terms of employment for its own membership. Its
method is collective bargaining supplemented by mutual insurance and occasional resort to strikes; its outlook is that
of the craft or trade, its aims are somewhat narrowly
economic. The railway brotherhoods furnish the stock illustration, though the type is dominant in the American
Federation of Labor as well. *Uplift unionism* accepts,
along with the wage system, the whole existing social
order. Its mission is the diffusion of leisure-class culture
and *bourgeois* virtues among the workers. Mutual insurance is its main function and homiletics its preoccupation.
There is no representative of the pure type—unless the
Woman's Trade Union League be accepted as such—but
there is a strong infusion of uplift idealism in most unions
that are dominated by the business animus. *Revolutionary
unionism* avowedly aims at the overthrow of the extant
socio-economic order by and for the working class. Its
two variants—socialistic and quasi-anarchistic—are sufficiently represented by the Detroit and Chicago organizations of the I. W. W. *Predatory unionism* practices secret, rather than open, violence. It is lawless, and in so far
anarchistic, but it professes no far-reaching philosophy, nor
does it aim at anything beyond the immediate economic advantage of its own membership. When this ruthless policy
is a counsel of despair, the continuation of a bitter struggle
which has gone against the union and the practical answer
to a policy of extermination on the part of employers,

¹ Professor Hoxie cites the Western Federation of Miners as
a socialistic union. But though the official program of this
union is a synopsis of the Communist Manifesto, its actual
methods in later years are more nearly of the ordinary business
type.

Professor Hoxie terms the resultant subspecies _guerrilla unionism._ The dynamiting career of the Structural Iron Workers is a familiar example. When, on the other hand, predation is deliberately adopted for the aggrandizement of a narrow ring, he applies the more opprobrious epithet of _hold-up unionism._ The term is not altogether happy. Cunning characterizes the type still more than force; its most brilliant successes have been gained by illicit alliance with monopoly-seeking employers. "Skinny" Madden and "Sam" Parks are the beaux ideal of the type. It is fair to add that predatory unionism, in both its forms, is more picturesque than significant. _Dependent unionism_ appears in two forms: that which relies upon the support of unionists outside the group concerned and that which is created by employers for ends of their own. Some "label" unions are at least partially dependent in the former sense; all "yellow" unions are wholly dependent in the latter sense.

Manifestly we have here to do with something more than variants from a single norm. These are so many distinct and conflicting social philosophies in terms of the special needs and problems of wageworkers. Each offers an interpretation of existing law and order and a plan of united action for the attainment of more tolerable conditions of life; each is held by large numbers of wageworkers who carry on an active propaganda for the conversion of their fellows, and each aspires to possess the field. [1] These functional varieties, then, are true union types, as distinct as the industrial and craft forms of organization and far more significant.

No functional type, it must be owned, is precisely represented by any concrete union, past or present; which comes to saying that no union is altogether homogeneous in respect to aims, policies, and attitude. Rival types coex-

---

[1] This statement needs some qualification. The predatory type has shown little tendency to proselytize, and the propaganda of "yellow" unionism is carried on by the employers.

ist and struggle for the mastery within the same organization. As already mentioned, the American Federation of
Labor is dominantly of the business type; nevertheless, a
strong and active socialist minority exists in the federation
itself and in most of the constituent unions. The conflict
of business and revolutionary unionism is waged in the
official publications, in local meetings and general conventions, and in elections and referenda. Even the ultra-rev-
olutionary I. W. W. has been torn by internecine strife
between anarchist and socialist groups.

This want of identity between functional and structural
lines of cleavage has obscured the existence of the former.
The organization has an outward and visible identity. It
adopts constitutions and by-laws, holds conventions, enters
into trade agreements, and conducts strikes; above all, it
bears a proper name as the attestation of its corporeality.
The like-minded group which constitutes a functional type
has not these hall-marks of tangibility. It is probable that
no functional type has ever been able to possess itself absolutely of any important organization or to get itself embodied without admixture in any considerable number of
union programs. None the less, these types do exist and
have persisted for decades. Business and uplift unionism
date from the eighteenth century. Revolutionary unionism
has been present in the American Federation of Labor from
its beginning and was present also in its predecessors. The
struggle of these three types for the mastery (the other
two being of minor consequence) has shaped the internal
history of the labor movement. The functional character
of the leading unions has shifted from period to period as
one or another type has gained a position of dominance, but
no major type has ever wholly disappeared or lost its distinctive character.

The emergence and the persistence of these union types
cannot be explained by work-day environment alone, for
radical divergencies of group viewpoint and attitude are

found among the members of the same trade employed in
the same establishment and such divergencies have endured
for half a century even within a single craft organization--
e. g., the Cigar Makers' International Union. Nor is economic circumstance, however broadly conceived, adequate
to account for the phenomena. On the one hand, the most
diverse types coexist under similar industrial and market
conditions; on the other hand, the same types have survived
the most startling economic transformations.

The social philosophy of unionism relates to the practical (mainly economic) problems which confront wageworkers as such, and it turns upon conditions of work and
livelihood and upon the politico-economic institutions which
govern these conditions. But this philosophy is shaped by
the whole mass of influences—personal and cultural—which
bear upon the workers involved. For man is, after all, a
single person. The several aspects of his life cannot be isolated one from another; the habits of thought which he
has acquired as a citizen, a churchman, or a pleasure-seeker
guide him also in his work-day pursuits. Rejecting, therefore, every attempt to give a monistic explanation, Professor Hoxie has sought to analyze the efficient causes actually observable in the evolution of unionism. These
causes may be grouped under five heads:[1]

1. The work-day environment proper, which operates in
manifold ways to produce solidarity among the workmen of
a given trade or industry. This is the most obvious factor
in the case, the one which is best understood and which has
received the most attention from students of the subject.

2. Union tradition, itself in great part the spiritual distillate of experience and consequently differing from union
to union, but within each organization acting as a consolidating force.

[1] The analysis here given is more detailed than that contained in Professor Hoxie's third chapter, but seems to the
writer fully consonant therewith.

INTRODUCTION xxiii

3. The immediate social *milieu*, comprising those economic, juridical, ethical, aesthetic, religious, and other institutional standards, convictions, and relationships which make up the prevalent civilization. A large part of this cultural complex impinges with a fair degree of uniformity upon the members of the same occupational group at a given time and place, and so favors a group interpretation and program. Another part, however—e. g., aesthetic and religious influences—diversely affects workers of the same occupation, even in the same community, and so makes for the formation of subgroups. The like divergence is, of course, more pronounced as between widely separated localities within the same large cultural situation.

4. What may be loosely termed national characteristics. Workers of the same craft in the United States are gathered from many nations, and, what is more to the point, from widely different cultural situations. They bring to their work and to their unions the most diverse convictions and ideals with respect both to economic and political institutions in general, and to the immediate problems which confront them in their capacity of wageworkers. To mold these diverse elements into a homogeneous group—homogeneous as respects even the immediate problems of work and pay—is a labor of time. It is also in good part a labor of Sisyphus, in that it continually requires to be done anew for fresh comers.

5. Congenital variation of those propensities and aptitudes which form the underlying traits of human nature. Such variations may be of an individual character or they may connote the presence of distinct ethnic types in our mixed population. They cover a wide range and are independent of recent cultural antecedents. Just what part is played by these differences of native endowment, as over against environment, may be a moot point, but few would deny to this factor a very considerable rôle in shaping the lives of men. Whatever its importance, it makes for di-

versity of the raw material and finished product of unionism.

From the varied combinations of these relatively permanent forces unionism receives its form and substance.
"Workers similarly situated economically and socially,
closely associated and not too divergent in temperament
(congenital endowment) and training, will tend to develop a
common interpretation of the social situation, and a common
solution of the problem of living" [1]—that is, will tend to
form a functional type. Obviously there will be as many
such types as there are groups of workers with vitally
different viewpoints and plans of action.[2] The functional
character of any given union is, then, a question of the
psychological groups of which it is composed, and this re-
solves itself into a question of the personal traits and cultural
heritage of its members and of the environmental discipline
to which they have been subjected. The differentiation of
unions, whereby one comes to be dominantly business and
another dominantly socialistic in animus, is doubtless a matter partly of selection and partly of progressive adaptation
to environment. Men of certain characteristics, native and
acquired, choose, and are chosen for, the pursuit of locomotive engineers; thereafter the influences of their daily life
and work mold their habits of thought, in many particulars,
to a common pattern. The members of the I. W. W. come
from a very different social stratum, of other natural en-
dowments and other cultural antecedents, and their training
as "hobos" enforces a very different outlook on life. These
forces of selection and adaptation which, on the one hand,
have produced the arch-type of respectable laborism, and,
on the other hand, have made the I. W. W. a hissing and
a byword among the devotees of "law and order"—these
forces are relatively permanent and they work out their
cumulative effects in permanently different combinations.

[1] Chap. III, p. 58.
[2] Chap. III, p. 61.

Hence the resultant union types have hitherto shown no tendency to merge into one common unionism.

This view of unionism, whether as interpretation or as genetic account, wants definitive verification. Nevertheless, there is sufficient warrant for the acceptance of Professor Hoxie's theory as a working hypothesis. It seems to accord with the known facts, it explains much in unionism that is unintelligible on any other view, and it is supported by the latest results of social psychology. Judicious inquirers have long perceived that a purely economic interpretation of history does not suffice to explain even economic institutions. It may well be that the extant material civilization exercises a selective surveillance over other elements of the cultural complex; it may even be granted that the exigencies of material life furnish the chief, if not the sole, stimulus to that process of adjustment whereby all growth and change of civilization are brought to pass.[1] Since, however, this process of growth is cumulative; since, therefore, the whole cultural situation at any given moment forms the starting-point for the next move, all institutions—juridical, aesthetic, and religious, as well as economic—become in their turn causes as well as effects. In the study of a particular social movement, such as labor unionism, the question is not how these institutions arose, but how they have affected, and have been affected by, the movement concerned. The underlying forces, whether temperamental or institutional, may be taken as data, in the sense that they do not themselves require to be explained for the purpose in hand; but to abstract the economic from other influences in such a case is to study the motions of a puppet.

To sum up: Many have given a structural and narrative account of American labor unionism; Professor Hoxie's analysis is functional and genetic. Seen from the stand-

[1] For a very able statement of this view, see Veblen, "The Theory of the Leisure Class," Chap. VIII.

point of aims, ideals, methods, and theories, there is no normal type to which all union variants approximate, no single labor movement which has progressively adapted itself to progressive change of circumstances, no one set of postulates which can be spoken of as *the* philosophy of unionism. Rather there are competing, relatively stable union types, functional and structural, the outcome of permanent differences in the temperament and situation of different groups of wageworkers.

If this pluralistic interpretation of the union movement meets general acceptance, it will have important consequences for social appraisal and action. It means that unionism cannot be judged and treated as a whole, that what is true of one type of union polity is not true of others, that, consequently, union history points no single moral to the publicist, and that no panacea, whether it be profit-sharing, "welfare work," industrial education, minimum wage, or social insurance, will meet the wishes or allay the discontent of all important groups of wageworkers. It means, further, that the errors and perversities of trade unions—as seen from the middle-class standpoint—are not to be corrected by much preaching. The several types of unionism are the outcome of positive conditions. Unionists are what they are by reason of congenital endowment and the circumstances under which they live and work. There is small likelihood, therefore, that union conviction and attitude will be much affected by any action which does not change the ethnic character of the population nor alter the fundamental conditions of life and work.

To the professed student of social science the special significance of these studies will lie in their viewpoint and method of approach. Economics, above all in the United States, has heretofore stood strangely outside the current of modern scientific development; its postulates are of a preëvolutionary order, its method is highly abstract and, *a priori*, its interest centers in classification quite after the fashion of Linnæan botany.[1] In Europe, though pre-Darwinism still holds the field, the evolutionary standpoint has been accepted by many economists of note,[2] but in this country the few exponents of genetic theory have been as voices crying in the wilderness. The present book will give comfort, therefore, to those whose hope it is that economics also may become an evolutionary science.

Like all genetic studies, this of trade unionism transcends the arbitrary limits of traditional economics. Professor Hoxie, in fact, essayed an inquiry into group psychology. The inquiry is economic, not in the sense of isolating the economic life of the groups in question from the cultural situation in which that life is involved, but in virtue of the fact that the convictions, aims, and aspirations inquired into are such as converge upon the ways and means of livelihood. On the other hand, the study is none the less a contribution to social psychology because it has to do with economic groups. Indeed, it is only through such detailed studies of particular groups that a secure basis can be laid for general sociology. For the community is not aggregated of individuals merely; individuals are associated in all manner of groups, occupational, local, political, religious, and what not, each more or less selective in point of membership, each imposing more or less peculiar canons of conduct, each more or less differently affected by those exigencies making for cultural growth and decay. Useful analysis of social organization and functioning, therefore, must deal with these groups of which the larger society is composed.

Important, however, as are Professor Hoxie's contributions to trade union theory and to sociological method, it is

---

[1] Cf. Veblen, "The Preconceptions of Economic Science," *Quarterly Journal of Economics*, XIII, 121, 396; XIV, 240; "The Limitations of Marginal Utility," *Journal of Political Economy*, XVII, 620.

[2] Gustav Schmoller, Werner Sombart, Tugan-Baranowsky, and Paul Vinogradoff will serve to illustrate the point.

as a teacher that he will be most remembered by those who had the good fortune to be his pupils. Year after year he gave himself unreservedly to his classes, in term time and vacation, devoting to the arrangement of courses, the elaboration of notes, the selection of materials and the perfection of pedagogic methods, that infinite care which is too rarely expended even upon formal writing. He was never satisfied; after a course which any other teacher would have considered brilliantly successful, he sat down to analyze the causes of his "failure." He never relied upon stereotyped materials. Courses which he had repeated time and again were worked over afresh each term to incorporate current developments and the latest results of his own reflections. What with this constant revision of class notes, the daily preparation that he never failed to make, and the time that he gave in unstinted measure to the individual direction of student research, he found scant leisure for formal writing —all the less because he was a frequent sufferer from ill health. But he reaped his reward, if reward it be, in widening the intellectual horizon and quickening the social perception of hundreds of men and women.

Professor Hoxie was wont to lay much stress upon the orientation of his classes because experience had taught him that all phenomena, and more especially social phenomena, are distorted by the preconceptions which adults and adolescents bring to their consideration. Above all, in a subject so beset with passionate interests as trade unionism, he found it indispensable to preface his inquiry by an historical and critical analysis of conventional views which served to open the minds of his hearers to other conceptions of economic relationships. For it lies in the social character of man that the institutions and modes of thought to which we have been accustomed shall seem intrinsically good and beautiful. It is only as we become aware that these institutions themselves are not the immutable order of nature, but the outcome of positive historical processes, that we are able to appreciate other ideals of right and good, not as mere perversities, but as objective institutional facts. Such orientation would be a mere digression in a course concerned primarily with external phenomena; it was fundamental to a course which aimed to interpret the trade union point of view. The orientation was not simply preliminary; the genetic standpoint—explanation of what is in terms of how it came to be—was maintained throughout so that the exposition of contrasting preconceptions became a vital feature of the course. In thus examining the fundamental assumptions both of capitalism and of trade unionism, Professor Hoxie was consciously teleological, for he appreciated that knowledge looks to action and that the end of social knowledge is social control. Only he did not forget, as unconscious teleologists so often do, that effective action is conditioned upon knowledge formulated in causal, genetic terms. He impressed upon his students that the purpose and outcome of their study should be to inform their own action and attitude toward unionism, but that, before this result could be attained, they must first of all understand unionism, what it is and how it came to be, why unionists think and act as they do and how union policies are being modified by current socio-economic changes. Upon this objective, causal understanding of the labor movement his whole attention was focused. Looking always to social control of labor relationships, he yet never formulated a social program, much less sought to persuade others of its validity. Program making he willingly left to others, both because he had not sufficiently mastered the complex facts in the case and because he did not deem himself competent to define the social ends toward which a comprehensive labor program should be directed. His was the more modest, and for the present perhaps more useful, rôle of causal explanation.

This explicit recognition of ultimate teleological interest and this insistence upon rigorous causal analysis combined to give the course in trade unionism a quite peculiar objectivity. Professor Hoxie escaped, on the one hand, the sterility of those social scientists who deny all interest in social values—to whom the evolution of a sleeve button has the same importance as the genesis of private property —and, on the other hand, avoided the pitfalls of those who allow meliorative programs to predetermine their conclusions in matters of fact. His consciousness that social science should contribute to human weal helped him to distinguish that which is vital from that which is merely curious or picturesque, while his freedom from all propagandist bent kept him open-minded to every new fact or impression. Having no program of his own to advocate, he could view dispassionately the proposals of anarchists, socialists or uplifters, syndicalists or anti-union employers, and bring them all alike to the test of consonance with those causal relationships which these several meliorists seek to modify.

Pedagogically, Professor Hoxie employed the problem method. His, however, was not the caricature of that method which has been popularized by quiz books, outlines and formal exercises. He set before his classes real problems of interpretation, of *what, how* and *why*, which arose spontaneously out of their reading and class discussion. Most of these problems had to do with current aspects of the labor movement, for Professor Hoxie cared little for labor history as ordinarily conceived. He was interested in the past, indeed, but only in so far as it served to explain the present. What he sought was genetic, as opposed to narrative, history.[1] His concern was with the present and the future of unionism, because his interest was pragmatic, and it is the present and the future alone that are amenable to social control. From the manifold phenomena of the existing movement he raised innumerable

[1] See Appendix I, "Historical Method versus Historical Narrative," p. 377.

questions and he followed these questions whithersoever
they led; into social psychology, it might be, or the opposed
institutional influence of machine discipline and religious
tradition, or the early history of the cordwainers' union.
He led his students by the same paths, sending them to
history only for the answers to concrete questions. The
genetic method, as he conceived it, was thus the pedagogic
also, carrying the student from existing interests to new
problems and giving definite direction and purpose to his
reading.

The problems so set increased in complexity with the
student's advancement; at first merely the meaning and
purpose of particular clauses in trade agreements, of specific working rules or of certain restrictions upon local
autonomy, progressing thence by gradual steps to the formulation of the trade union program and philosophy and to
such recondite questions as the validity of Webb's doctrine
of uniformity, Veblen's view of the relationship of machine
technology to class conflict or Hoxie's own theory of functional union types. The sources drawn upon, aside from
standard works of reference, comprised original docu-
ments of every sort, more especially the trade agreements
and working rules which, not being designed for public
consumption, are exceptionally free from affectation, and,
above all, first-hand contact with union and anti-union
leaders of many types, for which the vast field laboratory
of Chicago afforded so great facilities. Before the trade
union class within a single term appeared the militant
chiefs of the National Manufacturers' Association and the
Metal Trades' Council, the walking delegates of the building trades, the head of the American Federation of Labor,
spokesmen of the building contractors and the railway
brotherhoods, the distinguished editor of the Iron Molders' Journal and the secretary of the I. W. W. Conversely,
teacher and pupils attended the Sunday meetings of the
Chicago Federation of Labor and meetings of local unions,

followed current labor news in the daily press and inter-viewed many individuals in the lower ranks of leadership. Nor were these mere aimless excursions or diverting breaks in the class routine. Speakers before that class did not escape with a set apologia; they were called upon to answer a running fire of questions from both ends of the room— questions suggested as much by previous reading and dis-cussion as by the speaker's own statements. Every visit to a labor meeting was followed by a lively discussion of its significant occurrences; every interview was designed to throw light upon some definite question. In the same spirit were conceived the assigned readings, the class re-ports and the term papers. Each student was expected to become specially familiar with some particular union in its several ways and works, to report before the class on questions which he had investigated in the library or the field, and to embody his own findings upon some limited problem in a final theme. Problem discussion was thus the life of the course; the formal lectures served merely to give orientation and a connected view. As Professor Hoxie sometimes said, "the class taught itself"; indeed, he was frequently in the back row rather than behind the desk.

These methods were carried furthest in the research course for graduate students wherein teacher and class engaged in a joint examination of fundamental theories. The results obtained by the research class also led to important modifications of Professor Hoxie's own views, particularly as respects class conflict and the relations there-to of machine technology. But, indeed, Professor Hoxie's teaching, whether of graduates or undergraduates, always partook of the character of a joint enterprise in the dis-covery of truth. No man was ever more open to sug-gestions from whatever source or more thorough in follow-ing out each suggestion until he had ascertained its final value and incorporated it into the general body of his theory. His maturest conclusions were never more than provisional. Hence his views underwent, not only continuous growth, but continuous change as well. This characteristic is nowhere better seen than in his treatment of class conflict. Professor Veblen's persuasive and brilliant theory was at one time taught by him, not, indeed, as final, but as sufficient for the purpose in hand. Gradually, however, he came to see that class lines in the concrete are less sharp than the contrasting disciplines of business enterprise and machine industry would apparently produce if acting alone, and that, correlatively, political, religious and educational influences are more important than he had at first supposed. He thus found himself more and more in sympathy with Professor Commons' conceptions of social control.

This singular open-mindedness found constant expression in the classroom. No teacher was ever less dogmatic or less given to *ex cathedra* moralizing. As he was always modifying his own views in the light of fuller knowledge, so he led his students to formulate their conclusions, not from *ipse dixit*, but from the evidence before them. The same quality of mind made him signally devoid of partisanship. Conventional moral judgments found no place in his spoken or written words, because he was concerned with the explanation of institutions, not with their justification. For that very reason his influence upon his students was profound and lasting. The teacher who attacks or defends the existing social order will better please the groundlings and will attract the larger immediate following, for he appeals directly to the passionate enthusiasm of youth, but he who raises heart-searching questions, awakens intellectual interests, and lays the foundation for future thought and inquiry, will contribute more to "the increase and diffusion of knowledge—and of character—among men."

E. H. Downey.

CONTENTS

CONTENTS

CONTENTS

TRADE UNIONISM IN THE UNITED STATES

CHAPTER I

THE PROBLEM

The field of American trade unionism is practically virgin soil for the serious student of social affairs. No one knows much about it except, perhaps, trade unionists themselves and employers of organized labor, and their knowledge is admittedly special, narrow, scrappy and altogether biased. A great deal, indeed, has been written about it but this is either fragmentary or hopelessly superficial or hopelessly partisan. Academically, little attempt has been made at a serious, general and scientific study of it.

The study has never been standardized, therefore. There are no adequate textbooks or syllabi available as guides. We cannot get references that cover concisely and adequately even special topics. In short, as students of unionism we are left to fight our way through an intricate jungle of diffused and apparently contradictory facts, misguided at every step by the passion and partisanship of interested parties and prejudiced observers. Besides, unionism is in essence one of the most complex, diffuse and protean of modern social phenomena. There is not one local union, but probably 30,000; there is not

1

one national union, but about 130, each with its own
problems to solve and its own aims, policies, attitudes and
methods. These unions do not amalgamate into a single
general organization and movement but there are many
independent unions and several groups and general associations with vitally different viewpoints, fundamental
purposes, and ways of attaining them. What is true of
one union or group may not be true at all of another.
No judgments may be rendered nor generalizations made
in regard to unionism as such from the study of any
union or any small number of unions or any group. And,
moreover, in the realm of unionism everything is in a
state of flux, of constant change and development. Positive conclusions, therefore, are almost impossible to secure, and tentative generalizations can be made only as
the result of the most broad and painstaking examination
of the facts and an ability to get beneath appearances,
to discount deliberately false and prejudiced statements,
for almost all sources are partisan, meant to mislead the
unwary. We can form even such generalizations only if
we can free ourselves from passion and prejudice.

It is generally conceded that, not only in the study of
trade unionism but in the study of any subject, we need
—if the results are to be worth while—a definitely formulated problem or series of problems for solution, and
if we are to accomplish something worth while we must
get at the outset a clear conception of the nature of the
problem, the attitude of mind necessary to the successful interpretation of the material and the proper method
of attack upon it. A mere indiscriminate study of facts,
a mere accumulation of information without definite
purpose, is not justifiable as a piece of university work
in a time when individual group competition is so keen

and there is such a crying need for the development of social resources and the betterment of the opportunities for decent living and development for a great portion of our people. The knowledge of facts is only worth while when it has a use value, when it can serve a vital social or human purpose. But facts can have no definite use values when they are not carefully selected and for this selection it is necessary to have a definite problem in view which concerns vital social interests, and whose solution is capable of throwing light on some vital human or social end or ends.

From this point of view why should we study trade unionism? What must we get out of the study of it if it is to justify itself? What is the vital problem which it presents to us as individuals and which we must strive to solve through its study? We can perhaps get at this matter best by asking: What vital human and social interests does unionism touch and affect through its aims, principles, policies, demands, methods and attitudes? One way of doing this and at the same time of getting some concrete conception of the thing, unionism, itself, is through a review of the functions which unionism has assumed. From a study of the list of aims, principles, policies, demands, methods and attitudes, it would appear that unionism affects:

(1) Production in almost an immeasurable number of ways, through limitation of hours, overtime, Sunday and holiday time; character of machinery, tools and materials; new machinery and processes; speed of work; bargaining; hiring and discharging; closed shop; promotion; amount of work; who shall work—whether carpenters or sheet metal workers in a jurisdictional strike or dispute; etc.

(2) Established rights, through interferences at every point with the right of the employer to run his business to suit himself; with the assured right of the individual worker to work where, when, for whom, and for what he pleases.

(3) Distribution and capital, at the point of wages and profits, by nonrecognition of profit rates and by demands for more, more, more, now.

(4) Law and order in the matters of legal theory; natural order, free competition, joint combinations, injunctions, contempts, etc.

(5) Ethical standards, through the building up by trade unions of standards in conflict with those commonly held; class loyalty as against individualism; minimizing property rights; setting up life as against property; the theory that might makes right;[1] the right to work; opposition to vested interests: use of physical violence; use of ostracism; etc.

(6) General power over social welfare; power over fuel and transportation; ability to paralyze social action at any time through a strategical hold; "hunting together" in the building trades.

In short, it would appear that unionism has its finger in practically every social pie that is baking. It concerns itself in innumerable ways with the processes of production and distribution and with the welfare of the consumer. Where it is strategically located it can, if it will, paralyze our whole economic activity as such. It is a force affecting definitely the number, training and general efficiency of our productive laborers, the organization of the labor market, the shop, the problems of

[1] An extreme illustration is furnished by the Industrial Workers of the World.

living, discipline, promotion and discharge, the hours of labor, the employment of women and children, the organization of industrial enterprise and the general and specific methods of production, the use or neglect of new industrial machinery and processes, the quantity and quality of the productive output, the modes of payment which may be employed, the cost of production of commodities and the prices which we must pay for them, the problems of industrial accident, disease and death, and the method and extent of compensation which society shall pay therefor, the certainty and continuity of employment, the community problems of housing, cleanliness, health, and recreation, the character of our educational system, the standards of political honesty and efficiency, the character of our legislation, not only on industrial but on all social matters, the enforcement and legal interpretation of our laws, the extent of drunkenness and vice, the general ethical and religious standards of the community, and hundreds of other matters with which the community and every individual in it is vitally concerned.

In fact, unionism is one of those group forces whose influence is effective in a greater or less degree in determining every feature and standard in our industrial, political, social, ethical and religious life. The business man, even though he may employ nonunion men, must understand it, if he is not to become involved in harassing and ruinous difficulty, for unionism has ways of making its force felt far beyond the realm of its membership. The consumer is never free from its influence and effect; the politician must seek its support or find a way to escape from its influence; the lawyer must know its purpose, contentions and force, if he is to serve his clients effectively; the social worker cannot proceed, apart from consideration of its aims and attitudes; the preacher must consider it in working out his plans and prophecies if he is to be more than a mere exhorter; even the teacher finds himself forced to work with or against it. There is apparently no occupation into which any individual may enter where unionism may not appear as a factor that must be taken account of. In view of this we are moved to ask: Is there a single social interest which is not thus affected? Is there a single individual or social right which unionism may not challenge or affect? Is there anything in politics, morals, ethics, or religion upon which it does not have its influence? Apparently then, if we are to study unionism, we shall study, not a narrow slice of reality, but society as a whole from one particular aspect or with some particular problem or series of problems in mind.

This is one view of unionism and the problem which it presents. There is another statement of the matter equally and perhaps more suggestive. This is the contribution of social psychology. The social psychological view of unionism and its relation to society may be stated somewhat as follows: Modern realistic social science has pretty definitely reached the conclusion that society is made up of a great complex of interacting and interlocking social groups. Each of these groups is composed of individuals holding a common viewpoint in regard to some vital social matter or series of such matters. For example, there is something in the nature of a general group of employers and a general group of laborers, but both the laboring and employing groups are again split into an indefinite number of smaller groups, each with its peculiar viewpoint opposed to that of any other group. In general, each occupation and profession is likely to constitute, for certain purposes, a distinct group with a definite point of view. There are religious groups, ethical groups, political groups, and social groups in the narrower sense of the term, such as, for example, the leisure class, the criminal class, etc. As has been said, however, each of these groups is to be distinguished by the fact that it is composed of individuals holding a common viewpoint in regard to some vital social matter or series of such matters. The possession of this common viewpoint welds the individual members of such a group into a more or less permanent social force.

Each of these groups has its own peculiar aims, social motives and attitudes, social principles, theories and program of action more or less clearly formulated, which it is struggling consciously and unconsciously to realize and put into effect in society. Or, to put it in another way, each group has its standards of right, justice, rights and welfare, with respect to the matters with which it is most vitally concerned, and each is attempting to have these standards recognized and established in and by society. The social will and social action in regard to any matter—as, for example, wage rates, hours of labor, woman and child labor, the system of education, religious freedom, the character of the law and the functions of the state—are at any moment the outcome of the struggle between these groups, each attempting to realize its own ideals and ends, subject always, of course, to the great underlying conditioning factors of physical nature and long established social institutions and conditions which themselves constitute determinants of group viewpoints and social will, and set the limits to what society can do.

To make this matter clearer, let us state it in a little different way. Social ideals are formed and social action takes place at any time within a definite and relatively permanent physical and institutional framework or environment, the product partly of physical laws and partly of historical development. This environment very largely molds human nature and desires, sets limits to social accomplishment, and at any time determines what can be done by society and how the fundamental environing forces must be dealt with in order to accomplish the socially possible. Within this fundamental environment and subject to its molding and limiting influence, the social will in regard to any matter is determined by the interaction of a complex of social groups, each with its particular viewpoint and ends, and each struggling for their attainment.

If the position thus taken by modern realistic social science be accepted, it is evident that social conditions in general, and labor conditions in particular, cannot be understood without a thorough study and comprehension of at least the most effective social groups of which society is composed, and that a thorough understanding of these groups is necessary also if we are to know what ought to and can be done toward the betterment of social conditions generally, and of labor conditions in particular. In short, these important social groups must be intimately known in all their varied aspects if we are to take any decided steps toward the effective solution of the multitude of harassing social and labor problems which confront us.

Organizations of labor—trade unions, using the term in its common and most extensive sense—constitute one or rather one great series of these interacting groups of which society is composed. As such, they are an important determining factor, not only of the living conditions and problems that confront the workers, but also of those which confront society as a whole in its struggle for stability and betterment. As such, they affect vitally every active individual in his effort to work toward the accomplishment of his own particular end in life.

The ultimate problem which the student of unionism is fitting himself to solve is evidently that of control—what ought to and can be done to control unionism in the interest of social welfare and of the purposes and welfare of each individual. He must arrive at judgments of it as good or bad and decide whether it should be destroyed, suffered, strengthened, or modified, and how. But none of these things is what should engage him directly in this study of unionism. The trouble is the fog of partisanship and insufficient knowledge. The need is to dispel the fog, for before any judgment can be passed upon unionism, before any intelligent formulations can be made for its control, a purely scientific, unbiased study of what unionism is, and why it is what it is, is necessary. To prove this, to show why this is the case, and farther, what knowledge must be had and how to go about it in order to solve the purely scientific problem, is the object of this preliminary discussion. The first question in this connection is: What must be known in advance to make it possible to say what ought to and can be done to control this thing unionism? What kind of information must be possessed before, with any show of reason or hope of practical success, rules can be laid down or plans formulated for the treatment of unionism? Is it principles of political econ-

omy? Is it social theory in general? Will mere study
of facts help much?

To approach the matter in a little different way, consider what steps the solution of the problem involves and
then the knowledge necessary to take each step. What
then is involved in the problem of union control, in terms
of the interests which we have seen to be involved?
First, the solution involves, obviously, a judgment of
unionism. Before it can be said that anything ought or
ought not to be done, it must be possible to say whether
unionism in its aims, demands, policies, methods, and
effects is good or bad, right or wrong. Secondly, the
solution involves the formulation of practicable modes
and plans of union control, i. e., modes and plans that
will work.

Let us consider these questions separately. First, then,
what must be known in order to say that unionism as a
whole, or in its specific aspects or acts, is right or wrong,
good or bad? One part of the answer to this question
is that nothing can be judged until it is known what
the thing to be judged really *is*. Applied to unionism
this means that before unionism can be judged right or
wrong, good or bad, there must be a thorough knowledge of its real aims, demands, policies, methods, attitudes and results or effects.

The question then arises: Can unionism be known
by reference merely to its objective aims, demands, policies, methods, attitudes and effects—by the mere objective facts of unionism? For example, unionism interferes with the effectiveness of production, but can it be
said, on the basis of this fact alone, that unionism is
opposed to efficiency? Not only what the union rules
and acts are. must be determined, but why the unionists

lay down these rules and do these acts. Unions quite generally attempt to standardize or limit the amount of daily or weekly accomplishment of the individual worker by prohibitions of "rushing," or too rapid work, and by limitation directly of the amount of work per worker. On the basis of these prohibitions and limitations, the statement has often been made dogmatically that unionism is opposed to efficiency of labor; that the unions believe that wages can be raised by decreasing its efficiency. Now these charges may be true. This question will not be settled here. The point is, that, until the objective facts, i.e., these prohibitions and limitations, have been interpreted causally in terms of the peculiar problem and conditions which determine their enactment, it is not possible to say whether or not they bear out the charge that unionism is opposed to efficiency in production. Let us attempt this briefly and note the bearing of the outcome.

The fact is, that the wages of the union workmen are not determined automatically by demand and supply but by a process of bargaining. In determining the outcome of this process of bargaining, the two most important factors are the normal or standard day's work and the standard of living of the workers. These are the standards, practically, of right and justice considered. If the employer can make it appear that under existing conditions the workers are not working or producing up to the standard day's work, he has a strong case to show that wages ought to be lowered or that more work ought to be done for the same pay, which amounts virtually to lowering the wage. If the employer further can make it appear that at the given wage rate, on the basis of the standard day's work, the workers can

secure a standard of living higher than that customary
in their class, he has a strong case to show that the wage
rate should be lowered, or at least that it should not be
increased. In a contest under these circumstances the
employer is fairly sure of the support of public opinion,
arbitrators, police and courts. Now, the workers have
learned by long and bitter experience that if individuals
among them work faster and accomplish more than the
others while receiving the same wage rate, the employers
tend to take the accomplishment of these workers as the
standard day's work and to compare their earnings with
the standard of living of the class, when negotiations
are on to determine wages. Thus, in the case of day
work, the accomplishment of the strongest and the swiftest is the goal which is set for all, if wages are not to be
lowered, while in piece work the wage rate tends to be
lowered because the exceptionally rapid worker at the
given rate can be shown to make more than is necessary
to maintain the customary standard of living. Under
these circumstances the increased efficiency and output
of the few tend to mean less wages for all or more work
for less pay. All this has taught the unionists that if
they wish to prevent wage reductions they must all try to
work at the same pace. Hence, one of the fundamental
principles of their program has come to be uniformity
or standardization. Their specific rule limiting speed
and output is therefore seen to be primarily to establish
and maintain this principle of uniform accomplishment
for a given rate of wages. There is nothing about the
rule thus explained to indicate that the unions would be
unwilling to respond to increased wages for all by increased speed and output by all within normal physiological and social limits, i.e., there is nothing about these

objective facts when causally interpreted to indicate that unionism is opposed to efficiency in general; there is no basis therefore, in this case, for the common judgments rendered.

To take a related case, the charge is made that the unions seek to reduce all the workers of a trade to a dead level of mediocrity because they insist on a uniform wage rate and bring pressure to bear upon the worker who outstrips his fellows or who does more work for the same pay. Again, if we examine the conditions, we find that facts do not necessarily bear out the charge. The workers have found by experience that unregulated competition on their part tends to a progressive lowering of the wage rate. The process is simple. B out of work bids for A's place. A out of work and a weak bargainer bids for C's, C for D's, etc. That is, by this process, the competitive strength of the labor group in fixing wages tends to become the strength of the weakest member and the wage for all tends to sink to what the weakest member could competitively demand. To remedy this evil, unions have found it necessary to make the strength of the weakest member equal the strength of the group by barring out competitive bidding on the part of the workers. Merely establishing a uniform wage rate—so much per hour—does not bar out competitive bidding on the part of the workers. The rate may be lowered as surely by extra exertion, the results of which we have just seen, as by direct underbidding of the rate itself. Hence, the unions strive to make uniform the exertions of the workers as well as to establish a uniform rate of pay. But, having examined even very superficially the underlying conditions and motives, it is seen that to base on this action the charge that the unions seek to reduce all workers to a dead level of mediocrity is absurd.

Or, to take a closely allied example, it is a fact as stated that some unions prohibit piece work, and on this fact also the charge is based that unions are opposed to efficiency. It is true that when unions oppose piece work it is where piece work stimulates to greater effort and longer hours of work, but when we come to ex- amine the circumstances we see that the opposition comes, not because the unions are opposed to greater efficiency as such, but because greater efficiency secured by this means results in a lower rate of pay. The prohibition is primarily to protect the wage rate, rather than to pre- vent increased efficiency. Let us see. The unions have found by experience—and all union notions have a basis in experience—that in determining the wage rate by col- lective bargaining the standard of living is the most im- portant factor. If it can be made apparent, or shown to arbitrators, that the existing wage rate will furnish a daily or weekly wage above the customary standard of living of the trade, as stated above, the strongest argu- ment is made that wages are too high. But, if it can be shown that the wages will not allow living at this stand- ard, a rise in rates can almost always be forced or secured by arbitration. Now, when a rate is established, the stronger men are stimulated to work harder in order to secure a higher wage than the customary one, and, in some cases, the employers by bonuses, secret agreements or threats, attempt to drive the stronger and more ac- tive workers to this extra exertion. As soon as this is successfully accomplished, and these workers are earn- ing a wage above the customary standard, the cry is raised that the piece rate is too high, and the wages of these men are held up as proof. In bargaining and arbitration much is made of the fact that at the old rate an active man can make more than is customary in the trade. This is the strongest sort of argument for lowering the rate and often prevails. The result is a progressive tendency to lower the wage rate. All have to work harder and longer for the old wage, and while the stronger succeed in maintaining the old standard, the weaker are worn out and cast aside.[2]

The opposition to the piece rates, then, in a case of this kind, is seen to be an effort to protect the wage and not any direct objection to efficiency as such. On this evidence it would be absurd to sustain the indictment against unionism and to say that it should be deprived of the right to resist piece work. If the union attitude and action are socially bad, and we wish to change them, we must go behind the act of the union and to its causes. We must change the motives and the conditions which link up piece work with the lowering of the wage rate. But only by a careful study of the underlying conditions can we arrive at this knowledge and conclusion.

Or to take one more illustration—a dangerous one— unionists are condemned as being immoral and antisocial because they sometimes enforce their will by violence; they "slug" the "scab," for example. This shocks all right-minded people, and if every one judged only by effects all would have to join in the condemnation. But consider what effect a little careful analysis will have on our judgment. The unions are trying to raise the

[2] One of the investigators of the Bureau of Labor remarked to the superintendent of a factory that his workers seemed to be tremendously active. "Yes," he replied, "the piece rate is placed so low that the poor devils will have to hustle to make a living."

standard of living and working conditions of the group. It is a most vital matter to them. It means all the difference to them between hardship and comfort, strain and comparative ease, ignorance and leisure for information and education for themselves and for their children. To accomplish this end they find it necessary to establish certain definite rules of the industrial game and to enforce them. To maintain these rules they spend time and money and sacrifice the possibility of individual gain. Now comes the "scab." He has not sacrificed to establish the rules and he now violates them for his own selfish advantage and undoes the painfully established results for which the unionists have sacrificed in the interest of the common good. He is necessarily, from their point of view—the group viewpoint—antisocial, and must be restrained just as the thief is restrained by society. But how restrain him? There is no law to which the organized workers can appeal for the upholding of their working rule against underbidding. They cannot try to fine or imprison the "scab." Moreover, moral suasion will not ordinarily suffice to restrain his underbidding, since he is either driven to it by dire necessity or the struggle for life has made him callous to social considerations—to the welfare of the group. The only effective appeal, then, is to force. In some cases the blow is the only argument that the "scab" can understand. The "slugging" is deplorable, but under similar circumstances it would be resorted to by most men. How would college students, for example, treat one of their number who revealed the signals to the opposing school before an important football contest? The charge of special union immorality is hard to sustain under these circumstances, and again we see how impossible it is to arrive at any conclusion from mere effects without a careful examination of the underlying motives and circumstances.

In order, then, to judge of unionism—whether it is right or wrong, good or bad—to say what ought to be done about it, it is necessary to know, first, just what unionism is and why it is, generally and in each specific case. This means that we must know who the unionists are, what they really want, their ideas and ideals, motives, purposes and aims, what are the forces that mold their ideals and drive them to action, their standards and modes of living, their wages and conditions of employment, what problems they have to meet, what methods are allowed them by custom and law to meet and solve these problems, how adequate these methods are, what alternatives are open to them for action, what opportunities they have for training and advancement, and what their philosophy of life is. In short, before we can judge unionism, and say what ought to be done about it, we must know just what unionism is, and why it is what it is.

There still remains the other half of the question, What can be done, i.e., what must we know in order to formulate methods and plans for union control that *will work?* The point is, when we have judged unionism as good or bad, right or wrong, and decided on the basis of this judgment what ought to be done about it, can what *ought* to be done, always *be* done? And if not, what must be known in order to say what can be done? To get at the matter directly, if unionism is a private group manifestation, can the employers or any other group in society, aside from the unionists, formulate any remedial scheme in relation to unionism that it finds good, and make it work? In other words, society being what it is, can any class do whatever it pleases, regardless of the character and causes of unionism? Can we coerce a social group out of existence while conditions are as they are? If not, why not? For example, looking at unionism as a social group manifestation, would it be possible, just offhand, to destroy unionism, to command unionists to bargain with employers as individuals, or to forbid unionists to strike or quit work? Or, to make a stronger case, can unionists be made to think like employers or uplifters?

The assumption that any remedial action which any group in society may formulate in relation to unionism can be made to work, regardless of the character and causes of unionism, would be valid only in so far as unionism is an arbitrary thing, quite unrelated causally to fundamental economic, legal, and social conditions, a product of the selfish and evil cunning of a few leaders or of some unfounded esoteric theory of social relations. In so far, however, as unionism is indeed a historic development, the outgrowth of living and working conditions or ideals and motives created by these conditions, in so far, in short, as it represents the effort of a social group to meet and solve the everyday problems of living, forced upon it by our system of industry and our legal, moral, and social codes, it is folly to assume that the character and actions of unionism can be changed or controlled merely by the waving of a legal or a moral wand; that anything which, in the view of society, ought to be done, can be done. For, in so far as unionism is of this character, it is the inevitable outgrowth and corollary of our fundamental social and economic institutions and ideals. As long as these institutions and ideals exist, unionism must exist whether we like it or not. It will change only with the change in these, in spite of all our efforts. To attempt to destroy or change it, leaving them what they are, would only mean to have it take the new form necessary to meet the old ends under the new conditions socially created. But no one is now so utopian as to believe that, at will and offhand, we can displace or essentially alter our fundamental institutions. Hence, in so far as unionism is a natural and historical growth, it cannot be arbitrarily affected by social decree.

How then may we, having determined what ought to be done, know what can be done in the control of unionism as it touches upon vital social and economic interests? From all that has been said, the answer should be clear. In so far as unionism is a historical product, it can be changed and controlled only by changing and controlling the conditions that have made it what it is. To know whether this is possible or not, and how to do it, we must know these conditions and their causes. They can be determined only by a genetic study of unionism, only by an understanding of how it came to be what it is.[3]

To the question of what ought to or can be done by society about unionism, no valid answer can be given apart from a most searching causal inquiry. It would be necessary to consider not only the peculiar problem which the union has to solve and the reason why it solves it as it does, but why the problem exists in this form, and why the unionists adopt the particular solution of it. For example, we should have to determine why employers meet increased efficiency and output of individual

[3] *See p.* 376, Historical Method vs. Historical Narrative.

workers with an attempt to lower the wage rate; why the customary standard of living is taken by men and masters as the standard of right and justice in determining wages; why the workers are not satisfied to accept a lower immediate wage—the result of increased efficiency —in the hope of increased prospective wages, the result of increased demand for labor due to increased output, as the orthodox economist would have them do. Only in answering questions of this character could we put ourselves in a position to say what ought to or could be done to alter or better the situation, for it must never be forgotten that men's ideals and actions are the outcome of the circumstances under which they live and act. Society should not and cannot order a man not to do what he must, nor to do what he cannot. If it wishes to change a man's ideals and actions under such circumstances, it must change the conditions which determine his ideals and actions. Hence the necessity, in cases of this kind, of studying the why of the conditions. But this means that, in order to determine what ought to and can be done, in a case of the kind we are considering, we should have to determine not only what the situation institutionally and psychologically is, but how it came to be what it is. For it must never be forgotten that the present is a product of the past, and in a sense is the past; that our ideals, standards and institutions are largely inheritances, undergoing slow modification by present forces; that as individuals and groups we are largely hereditary products—bundles of instincts, habits, propensities, tendencies, preconceptions, prejudices—the product of past struggles with environment. In short, to solve the ultimate problems of unionism, to determine what ought to and can be done about it as it touches and affects our economic, legal, ethical, and general social interests, we must first study what unionism is and why it is what it is, in terms not only of the immediate but of genetic causation. This is the first great task in our study.

With the problem clearly defined, the final question in this orientation confronts us: How shall we go about the study of unionism; what is it necessary for us to do in order to discover the real character of unionism and the conditions and forces which have made it what it is? In this connection I want to emphasize, first, the matter of attitude or spirit. If we hope to get at the truth in regard to unionism it is absolutely necessary that we should approach the subject in a scientific spirit—that we should preserve throughout our study the scientific attitude.

What then is the meaning of the scientific attitude or spirit? It is putting aside as far as possible all passion and prejudice, all preconceived notions in regard to the object of study, all beliefs and feelings; seeking only for the truth and being willing to follow it to whatever conclusions it may lead. Why is this scientific attitude necessary in order to arrive at the truth in general? Because the truth as we apprehend it is not an objective thing. It is a reflex of this thing upon our consciousness; and, therefore, to our apprehension is determined largely by the quality of our mental furniture. Every impression upon the mind is referred to the existent mental furnishings for identification, classification and interpretation. On the quality, therefore, of the existing beliefs, feelings, prejudices, presuppositions, depends the judgment as to the facts. As soon as prejudice enters in, we will slight, or overemphasize, or be unable to see things. Take as illustration the diverse interpretations of natural phenomena by primitive and modern men. Primitive man peopled the world of nature with spirits. Every stick and stone was endowed with consciousness and volition. To him every movement of stick and stone was purposeful, endowed with benevolent or malevolent intent. When the conception of a single God arose, all natural phenomena were expressions of his will—his wrath or his complaisance—and were referred for their causes to the moral quality of man's thoughts or actions. Later, as the scientific conception gained ground, all these natural phenomena have come more and more to be referred to the outworking of blind, impersonal, opaque cause and effect. Applied to the subject of unionism it means that any one who enters upon the study of unionism with any prepossession for or against unionism, with any class bias, is bound to have all his judgments colored and distorted, and to fail to see the truth.

Is there, however, any special reason for emphasizing this matter in connection with the study of unionism? Are we specially prone to prejudice, preconception and partisanship when unionism is in question? Yes. Because unionism is a storm center of the most universal and vital controversy in existence—the struggle for a living. Because, therefore, it not only touches the individual personally in his most vital concerns, but especially arouses group prejudices—the most bitter and the hardest to eradicate, because they are not the result of the thought of the individual, but are inherited and bred in the bone, and are therefore largely unconscious. We are all full of these group prejudices, and for most men they are in the nature of absolute canons of judgment. It is characteristic of almost every man, especially the uneducated, to look upon rules of his group in regard to right and justice, morality and rights, as something fixed, God-given, sacred. There is ordinarily no conception, for example, on the part of the business man—the type of the bourgeois middle class—or the unionist for that matter, that conditions may alter rules of conduct. To him there is only one world—his world—which was, is, and shall be without end. His judgments, therefore, are absolute judgments. He cannot conceive that any one who violates the rules of thought and conduct of his group is not a knave or a fool. Now, unionism does violate many of the canons of right, rights, and justice of the business world and the middle class. It opposes freedom of the individual and free contract, upon which our whole legal structure rests. It has little regard for the sacredness of contract or ordinary property rights. It has little respect for our special code of morality; it sneers at and defies our courts; it stands face to face with a great association of employers engaged in a titanic struggle for supremacy. As the result, the whole atmosphere of union discussion is charged with the most virulent animus; on the one hand unionism is held up as the perfect, the only, social good, in which there is no flaw or stain. Says one of its leaders:

There is not a wrong against which we fail to protest or seek to remedy; there is not a right to which any of our fellows are entitled which it is not our duty, mission, work and struggle to maintain. So long as there shall remain a wrong unrighted or a right denied there will be ample work for the labor movement to do.[4]

The aim of our unions is to improve the standard of life; to foster education, and instill character, manhood, and

[4] President Gompers' Report, Twenty-ninth Annual Convention, American Federation of Labor (1909), p. 1.

an independent spirit among our people; to bring about
a recognition of the interdependence of man upon his fellow
man. We aim to establish a normal workday, to take the
children from the factory and workshop; to give them the
opportunity of the home, the school and the playground.
In a word, our unions strive to lighten toil, educate the
workers, make their homes more cheerful and in every
way contribute the earnest effort to make their life better
worth living.[5]

The trade union movement, true to its history, its traditions and its aspirations, has done, is doing, and will undoubtedly do more in the interests of mankind to humanize
the human family than all other agencies combined.[6]

On the other hand, unionism is denounced as the child
of the devil and the emanation of the pit.

My denunciation [says the President of the National
Association of Manufacturers] was and is of a defiant labor
trust machine representing less than 5 per cent of the wage
earners of the country, every page of whose history is
black with the foulest deeds of inhumanity and injustice,
from dynamiting and murder to throwing egg shells filled
with acids at dumb beasts because their drivers were not
cogs in the wicked labor machine—a machine whose leaders
have indorsed its crimes because its demands could be
enforced through the perpetration of such crimes; a
machine whose leaders have for years striven, and are
today striving to so cripple our courts that no injunctional
interference can prevail in cases of labor disputes to protect peaceful and law-abiding workmen in their God-given
right to labor and enjoy the right to life, liberty and the
purusit of happiness, and who are doing their utmost to

[5] President Gompers' Report, Twenty-eighth Annual Convention, American Federation of Labor (1908), p. 16.

[6] *Ibid.*, p. 27.

secure release from responsibility to the Sherman Law under which some of them have been tried and found guilty.[7]

Every time an employer of labor permits himself to be intimidated or coerced into closing his shop, or other place where labor is performed, to all but those who are members of this organization or that . . . and every time he voluntarily does so, he commits a crime against the Constitution of the United States and a sin against humanity. When he willingly refuses a boy an opportunity to learn a trade because a labor union says the boy shall not have it, that moment he compounds a felony. When he refuses to deal in wares because a labor union has placed its brand of disapproval upon them he brands himself a coward and becomes unworthy of the patronage of decent citizens, and all such citizens should resent his action. To temporize with or yield one jot or one tittle to the demands of organized labor which in any manner helps to increase its power to deprive any man, woman or child of the free untrammeled right to earn their daily bread in such lawful manner as may seem best to them, is to share in the responsibility for the criminal conspiracies in which such organizations are engaged. Conciliating and compromising with crime, and juggling with the principles upon which Christian civilization and justice are based, will never solve the labor question.[8]

This question of belligerent unionism is not one of sentiment. It is not a question to be trifled with or treated with apathy or indifference. . . . The thing in the eye of God is wrong and to attempt to clothe it in the livery of heaven only adds to its wickedness.[9]

But further, even academic and scholarly sources can-

[7] John Kirby, Jr.: "Where Do You Stand?" p. 18.
[8] *Ibid.*, pp. 8, 9.
[9] John Kirby, Jr.: "Disadvantages of Unionism," p. 37.

not always be relied upon for calm and unemotional statements of the truth. They too are prejudiced and the
group which might be supposed to furnish adequate
guidance in the search for the truth about unionism is
not always trustworthy.

Therefore, it is because of what unionism is in its
viewpoint, the interests which it touches, and the nature
of its acts which challenge our habitual way of looking
at things, and because the literature of the subject is
soaked with hidden and open partisanship, that the emphasis put upon the scientific spirit is necessary. We
must consciously attempt to expose our prejudices and
keep in abeyance our inherited and habitual preconceptions and presumptions.

No doubt many may think they have no prejudices on
this subject, conscious or unconscious. Experience has
shown, however, that all have prejudices and those most
sure they have none, have most. Take sabotage, as an
illustration. It is destructive action of the workers applied to the processes of industry, affecting the quantity
and distribution of the product. What is the general
attitude toward it? Absolute condemnation. Ought
there to be the same attitude toward the employer if he
practices sabotage? Is there? The employer practices
sabotage on the consumer through "fake" goods, through
adulterations, patent medicines, etc. How is it regarded?
We say, *caveat emptor*. The employer is right if he
can "get away with it." We are just now waking up to
a different view. We condemn labor for limiting output. It is a matter of course that the manufacturers
should limit output. If it is not immoral for the employer to limit output, to safeguard profits, is it immoral
for the wage earner to limit output, *not* to reduce profits.

but to prevent a cut in wages that will reduce the standard of living? This shows, however, that we are full of unconscious tolerance for things to which we are accustomed. We make the distinction between the natural and right as opposed to the artificial and wrong. Anything is artificial and wrong which interferes with personal liberty, property rights, and free competition (although free competition never existed), or which raises wages by combination. Unionism looked upon as artificial and unnatural is therefore bad.

Most students will have to guard against the tendency to feel that a thing is good because it is the established, legal, ethical or social thing. Some will have to guard against the tendency to feel that a thing is good because it is revolutionary or iconoclastic. Every one must school himself to the view that nothing is absolutely right or sacred; that rights are merely the crystallized will of the group or groups dominant at a particular time, about which there is nothing absolute or sacred; that everything is open to examination and is to be judged solely by its effects. That is, it is for each one to put aside inherited and group prejudices as far as possible, and, imbued solely by the scientific spirit, to search patiently for the truth.

As a final word, and especially to guard against errors into which students might easily fall and which might vitiate the whole study, it is well to specify and make clear some of these errors. They are: (1) Assuming that unionism in some way is easily understood, is definite, fixed, narrow, a consistent thing, everywhere the same and always the same, and can be judged on the basis of economic principles, or of slight or narrow contact. (2) Assuming that it is possible to tell what ought to be done with unionism without the broadest and most intimate first-hand knowledge of the what and why of unionism—an intensive study of unionism as a matter of group psychology and its causes. (3) Assuming that, having decided what ought to be done, it is possible to proceed to action without this study. (4) Assuming a social will and social standards, which we have not, because society is a complex of groups molded by necessity and tradition, differing in standards with, as yet, no social will. (5) Assuming that this study of unionism can amount to anything without combining with it the study of other group psychologies. (6) Mistaking individual standards of good and bad, right and wrong, or the standards of a particular group, for absolute standards on the basis of which unionism can easily be judged. (7) Allowing, therefore, conscious and especially unconscious prejudices to color the facts and warp the judgment.

It is also well to emphasize the necessity of getting into close, first-hand contact with the reality in order to know what unionism is and why it is, and, finally, what ought to and can be done to control it. As has been said, very little that has been written about American unionism is of a scientific and systematic nature. But there is a reason beyond this. Only by coming into direct contact with the unionists themselves, studying their character, realizing their conditions of working and living in detail, studying their problems, their hopes and fears and aspirations, the working of their minds in their efforts to overcome difficulties; only by studying the reports of their conventions, their constitutions and working rules, their pamphlets and journals, only by watching them closely in their formulation of plans and in their actual contests; only by getting them off guard or getting to know them well enough to break down their secrecy and reserve of hostility or to discount or interpret what they say; only, in short, by putting ourselves as nearly as possible into their places can we hope to get at the real character and causes of unionism.

To sum up briefly the main points of this orientation:

1. Trade unionism itself—using the term in its commonly accepted broad sense—is one of the most complex, contradictory, and protean of social problems.

2. The study of unionism is, moreover, beset with peculiar difficulties, in that the subject has never been adequately studied in this country, and consequently there are no adequate texts and guides in the form of syllabi, and not even agreed objects or purposes of study. The materials for the study are inadequate, diffuse and mainly in the raw, obliging us to go for our study chiefly to the original sources. And, finally, the whole subject is involved in the utmost prejudice and partisanship, making it impossible for us to accept what we find at its face value, but requiring, on our part, the exercise of a high degree of keenness and judgment to untangle the true from the false, the real from the seeming.

3. All this means that if we are to avoid confusion, to enter upon and maintain a clear line of endeavor, and to attain results at once valid and significant, three things are necessary: a definite practical problem, a clearly understood method of work, and an attitude of mind which shall guard us as far as possible against the pitfalls of prejudice and partisanship which we shall encounter at every step in our progress.

4. The ultimate problem of unionism, as of the practical study of any other group phenomenon, is control.

This means control not only in the interests of social
welfare, but control in the interest of each individual's
life problems, for we have seen that unionism, in its
aims, principles, policies, demands, methods and attitudes, comes into vital conflict in many ways with efficiency of production, by its various rules hampering the
introduction of new machinery and processes, interfering with the selection of men on the basis of efficiency
and fitness for the task, preventing the speeding of men
and machinery, and in a hundred ways limiting or tending to limit the productive output. It interferes vitally
with current distributive methods and results; it combats
at every point the employers' claims of rights in the management of industry; it conflicts with the legal theory
upon which our social and industrial system is based
and with the established law and order; in many ways
it opposes our conventional ethical standards and notions
of right and justice. But we saw that before this problem of control can be touched, before it is possible to tell
what ought to and can be done about it, we must be able
to judge unionism, and above all, to understand it as a
social group manifestation. Finally, the hope of solving
this problem lies in undertaking the study in a scientific
spirit and applying to it the scientific method, which
means rooting out of our minds all prejudice and partisanship, being willing to follow the truth wherever it
leads, and getting into the closest possible touch with the
facts as they exist, i.e., getting out into the field and
studying at first hand, finding out who the unionists are,
their ideas and ideals, the conditions they have to face,
the problems they have to solve, their actual aims, theories, policies, methods, demands and attitudes, and the
underlying motives and purposes and reasons for them.

CHAPTER II

GENERAL CHARACTER AND TYPES

From the popular viewpoint, trade unionism is a simple, definite phenomenon upon which it is easy and safe to pass positive and sweeping judgments. Almost every one, in fact, who is at all interested in economic or social affairs is inclined to assume that he knows just about what unionism is, and just what ought to be done about it. The man in the street, the lawyer, the economist, the social worker, the teacher, the preacher, each has his positive concept and his positive scheme for union control or regeneration.

Thus the student honestly seeking the truth about unionism is faced at the outset with a mass of confident but contradictory interpretations. He is told that unionism is a narrow group organization designed to benefit certain favored workmen at the expense of all others; that it is an artificial monopoly of labor, an impossible attempt to raise wages by unnatural and therefore socially inimical means; that it is the creation of selfish and unscrupulous leaders primarily for their personal gain and aggrandizement, a thing foisted upon unwilling workers and designed to disrupt the natural harmony of interests between employers and employees; that it is a mere business device for regulating wages and conditions of employment, by means of collective bargaining; that it is a great revolutionary movement, aiming ultimately to overthrow capitalism and our whole legal and moral code; that it is a universal expression of working class idealism whose purpose is to bring to all the toilers hope, dignity, enlightenment, and a reasonable standard of living; that it is, in short, selfish and altruistic, monopolistic and inclusive, artificial and natural, autocratic and democratic, violent and law-abiding, revolutionary and conservative, narrowly economic and broadly social.

And with each of these positive interpretations, a student is commanded to subscribe to an equally positive and final solution of the union problem. He is informed that unionism will cease to be dangerous when it is boldly proceeded against as a trust; that the problem will be solved when once we have guaranties of industrial peace in the shape of universal arbitration schemes, voluntary or compulsory; that unionism is in any form a menace to social welfare and must, therefore, be destroyed by legal enactment and counter-organization; that the trouble with unionism is moral, and the obvious remedy lies, therefore, in moral suasion and the preaching of social obligation; that unionism is the expression of crass ignorance, and hence is to be quietly disregarded while schemes are formulated and put into operation for the welfare of society as a whole; that the real problem is one of encouragement and support since unionism stands for all that is best in human conditions and relationships.

The mutual contradictoriness of these popular interpretations and remedies is sufficient evidence to warrant the rejection of any and all of them, pending the most unbiased and thoroughly scientific investigation of the facts. It must stamp them either as pure fabrications of the imagination or at best as partial truths, the outcome of narrow observation distorted by conscious or unconscious preconceptions derived from tradition, interest, or special environment. To accept them as final truths, therefore, is to block the way to a real comprehension of unionism and the union problem. For such acceptance must mean the coloring of the facts and the warping of the judgment, however sincere and painstaking the student may be. The first step, therefore, toward a scientific understanding of trade unionism and the problems which it presents to us is to rid ourselves of the popular attitude toward it, and to root out of our minds as far as possible these popular conceptions of it. We must start by wiping the slate clean.

The very existence of these numerous contradictory interpretations, nevertheless, carries with it a pregnant suggestion for the student, namely, that trade unionism may be after all, not a simple, consistent entity, but a complex of the utmost diversity, both structurally and functionally. And, indeed, the most obvious facts of union status and history seem to warrant this conclusion, at least as a working hypothesis.

There are in the United States today hundreds of union organizations, each practically independent or sovereign, and each with its own and often peculiar aims, policies, demands, methods, attitudes and internal regulations. Nor is there any visible or tangible bond, however tenuous, that unites these organizations into a single whole. Groups there are indeed with overstructures and declared common aims and methods. But group combats group with the bitterness that can arise only out of the widest diversity of ideals and methods.

A slight acquaintance with the history of organized labor shows that this situation is not unique, and at the same time furnishes the apparent clews to its explanation. It reveals the fact that unionism has not a single genesis, but that it has made its appearance time after time, independently, wherever in the modern industrial era a group of workers, large or small, has developed a strong internal consciousness of common interests. It shows, moreover, that each union and each union group has undergone a constant process of change or development, functionally and structurally, responding apparently to the group psychology and therefore to the changing conditions, needs, and problems of its membership. In short, it reveals trade unionism as above all else essentially an opportunistic phenomenon.

For, if the history of unionism seems to admit of any positive generalizations, they are that unionists have been prone to act first and to formulate theories afterward, and that they have acted habitually to meet the problems thrust upon them by immediate circumstances. Everywhere they have done the thing which under the particular circumstances has seemed most likely to produce results immediately desired. Modes of action which have failed, when measured by this standard, have been rejected and other means sought. Methods that have worked have been preserved and extended, the standards of judgment being always most largely the needs and experiences of the group concerned. So that, prevailingly, whatever theory unionists have possessed has been in the nature of group generalization, slowly developed on the basis of concrete experience.[1]

In making these statements, it is not intended to imply that general economic, political, and social theories have not played a part in the genesis of unions, or in the mold-

[1] In all this, unionism is not unique, but has obeyed the general law of psychological development.

ing of their function and structure. Nor is it intended to deny that some unions have been formed and dominated by individuals and small groups of leaders. Idealism has frequently been a genetic and formative force in union history and the autocrat has played an important rôle in union affairs. But apparently history warrants the general statements that unions, and especially unions that have lived and worked, have arisen mainly in direct response to the immediate needs and problems of specific working groups, and that they have developed characteristically by the trial and error method.

Thus the scope and character of union ideals and methods have been as broad and diverse as the conscious common needs and conditions of the groups of workers entering into organization. Some unions have confined themselves to attempts to deal directly with their immediate employers and their immediate conditions of work and pay; others have emphasized mutual aid and education; still others have enlarged their field of thought and action to include all employers and all conditions— economic, legal, and social. In other words, the union program, taking it with all its mutations and contradictions, comprehends nothing less than all the various economic, political, ethical and social viewpoints and modes of action of a vast and heterogeneous complex of working class groups, molded by diverse environments and actuated by diverse motives; it expresses nothing less than the ideals, aspirations, hopes, and fears, modes of thinking and action of all these working groups. In short, if we can think of unionism as such, it must be as one of the most complex, heterogeneous and protean of modern social phenomena.

But can we thus think of it? If all that has been said

be true, are we not forced to this pregnant conclusion as the basic hypothesis of our study—namely: that there is no such thing as unionism, either in the sense of an abstract unity, or of a concrete, organic, and consistent whole, which can be crowded within the confines of a narrow definition or judged sweepingly as good or bad, right or wrong, socially helpful or harmful? If, then, we dispense with narrow preconceptions and face things as they actually are, and are becoming, it is impossible to say that unionism as such is artificial or natural, revolutionary or conservative, violent or law-abiding, monopolistic or inclusive, boss-ridden or democratic, opposed to industrial progress or favorable to efficiency, the spontaneous outgrowth of legitimate needs or the product and tool of selfish and designing individuals. In short, there is unionism and unionism. But looking at matters concretely and realistically, there is no single thing that can be taken as unionism *per se*.

It follows as a corollary that the union problem is neither simple nor unitary. It is not a mere question of wages and hours, of shop conditions, and of narrow economic rights of employer and employee, and it cannot be solved by a mere resort to economic theory. On the contrary, it is a complex of economic, legal, ethical, and social problems, which can be understood and met only by knowing the facts and the genesis of the viewpoint of organized labor in all its reach, diversity, contradictoriness, and shifting character, and by considering this viewpoint in relation to developing social conditions and social standards.

The study of unionism, therefore, if it is to be fruitful, that is, if it is to assist in the solution of our economic and social problems, must be realistic and scientific.

Unionism is what it is and not what any advocate or opponent would have it to be. It is a matter of fact in the same sense that institutions, animal and plant species, or any other organic manifestations are matters of fact. There is no normal or abnormal unionism; no unionism that is artificial as distinguished from that which is natural. In short, there is no fixed union norm by which any concrete case is to be tested; for all unionism is, and is becoming, by virtue of sufficient causation. The problems which it raises, therefore, like all other problems of a scientific nature, are to be solved, if at all, not through passion and prejudice, and formulations of what ought to be, but through an intimate knowledge of the facts as they exist and a study of causes. It is for the student, then, to put aside his preconceptions and feelings, to get close to the realities, and to be willing to follow the truth to whatever conclusions it may lead. Calmly and dispassionately we must seek to know unionism as it actually appears in all its phases and to search for its underlying causes. Only after we have studied it and its problems thus in the spirit of the biologist or of the student of social psychology and social institutions, shall we be in a position to say positively what unionism really is and what, if anything, should and can be done about it. It is in this spirit that the following tentative analysis is presented.

The master key to the real character of unionism and union problems is to be found apparently in the existence of distinct union types. Though unionism itself is so pragmatic and therefore so protean as to warrant the rejection of all attempts to characterize and judge it as a whole, it has seemingly developed along certain fairly distinct general lines, giving rise thus to types sufficiently definite to allow of legitimate generalization in regard to them. It appears possible to distinguish such types, both as to function and structure. Structural types have, indeed, been recognized quite generally by students. Examination of the history and present status of unionism in the United States appears to reveal four such types, each objectified in a variety of concrete units; while, somewhat akin to these distinct types, may be distinguished other forms which may perhaps be regarded as modes of transition from one to the other.

Naming the structural types in what hypothetically may perhaps be considered their natural sequence of development, we find, first, what is ordinarily called the craft union.[2] This is an organization of wageworkers engaged in a single occupation, as, for example, in glass bottle blowing, horseshoeing, locomotive engineering. The occupation may be limited strictly to one simple task, or may include a number of closely allied tasks or crafts. The strict test of a craft union seems to be that each member of the organization performs or may perform all the tasks included in the occupation Usually a craft union covers but a fraction of the work of a given industry. The craft organization has developed two principal units, or appears in two main forms; the *local craft union,* which usually unites the members of the craft or occupation working in a particular locality—a town, a city, or a section of a city; the *national or international craft union,* which unites into one organization the local

---

[2] The terms "craft union" and "trade union" are often used interchangeably. The writer prefers to make "trade union" the general inclusive term covering all types of unionism, structural and functional. This is the popular usage.

units of a single craft or occupation throughout the country or neighboring countries.[3]

Secondly, there appears what may be termed the *crafts* or *trades union.* This organization is a *federation* of unions in different crafts or industries. It has developed three principal forms or units: the *local trades union,* or *city federation;* the *state federation;* and the *national* or *international federation,*[4] which unite through delegate organizations, respectively, the unions of a locality, a state, or a larger territorial area.[5] Examples are the

[3] Examination of union constitutions reveals a surprising amount of diversity and much individual variation in the matter of structural units. Some organizations, for example, have sub-locals, as in the case of the shop club of the printers, and the pit committee of the miners. There may be also units intermediate between the local and the international, such as district councils, state divisions, etc. There are, moreover, such things as auxiliary organizations. It is not intended here to deal with this matter in detail, but simply to name the most usual and perhaps the most generally important units connected with the different structural types.

[4] These trades unions appear under many different titles. For example, the city federations are known in different localities as trades councils, trades assemblies, trades and labor councils, trades and labor assemblies, trades and labor unions, central trades councils, central labor unions, central labor councils, central federated unions, central trades and labor assemblies, central trades and labor councils, central associated trades councils, labor councils, joint labor councils, united trades and labor assemblies, united trades and labor councils, federations of labor, central federations of labor, etc. The state federations also go locally under different titles, and in the United States and Canada there is more than one national trades union, for example, the Women's Trade Union League, and the Canadian Trades and Labor Assembly.

[5] Trades unions of the same order are not always strictly or exclusively federations of organic units, and unions of the same

Chicago Federation of Labor, The Illinois Federation of Labor, and the American Federation of Labor. The essential characteristic of the trades union is that the constituent organizations retain their individual independence or sovereignty.

Thirdly, we may distinguish the *industrial union*. This type, as the name implies, is organized on the basis of the industry rather than the craft. That is to say, it attempts to unite into one homogeneous organic group all the workers, skilled and unskilled, engaged in turning out and putting on the market a given finished product or series of closely related products. For example, this type of union would unite all the craftsmen in the direct employ of brewing concerns, including not only actual brewers, maltsters, bottlers, and packers, but the engineers, firemen, teamsters, watchmen, etc.; or, again, it would organize into one union all the workmen in and about a coal mine, including actual miners, miners' helpers, shot firers, drivers, spraggers, trappers, trackmen, timbermen, hoisting engineers, check-weighmen, dumpers, etc. The actual connotation of this type of unionism varies in different productive lines and with the integration of productive enterprise, but the essential test of industrial unionism seems to be that the industrial scope or area of the workers' organization shall be coterminous with that of the capitalistic enterprise or series of closely related enterprises. The main forms or units of this type of unionism thus far are: the *local industrial union*, a com-

order may vary considerably in structural character. For example, some trades unions admit individual members and there is great variety in the degree of centralization of authority. Nowhere is the pragmatic character of unionism better illustrated than in such structural variations.

bination of all the employees of a single local industrial plant or of all the industrial enterprises of a like character in a given locality; the *national or international industrial union,* a combination of all the workers in a given industry throughout the nation or the international economic unit; the *district industrial union,* an organization covering an area within which productive and market conditions are essentially similar. Thus, for example, the coal mine workers are organized into local unions at the mines, into an international union including workers in the mines of the United States and Canada, and into district organizations covering adjacent bituminous or anthracite mines or fields.[6]

Fourthly, there exists what is technically known as the *labor union.* This type of unionism proposes the organization of all workers regardless of craft or industrial division into homogeneous groups by localities, by districts, and throughout the nation or largest possible international area. At present the *local labor union* is the only existing unit of importance in the United States which realizes this ideal of organization, though attempts have been made, notably in the case of the Knights of Labor, to establish and maintain labor unionism in all its ideal forms, *local, district,* and *national.*

Besides these four structural types of unionism, there exist in this country at least two varieties which can hardly be designated as distinct types, but which, strictly

[6] The coal-mine workers have also subdistrict organizations. The subdistrict seems to be based on a uniformity of industrial conditions, e. g., thickness of vein, character of roof and floor, etc., while the district represents an area within which market conditions are similar. That is to say, unions may have both territorial and industrial divisions or units.

speaking, are apparently neither craft, trades, industrial, nor labor unions. The first of these varieties may be called the *compound craft* or *crafts union*. It is a centralized, homogeneous organization of the workers in a number of related crafts. It differs from the craft union in that it includes workers who do not engage in the same tasks or occupations. But it is not an industrial union, since it may be one of several labor organizations whose workers are engaged in turning out a given finished product, or are in the employ of a single capitalistic enterprise. On the other hand, it may overlap industrial divisions. It may be the outcome of a formal consolidation of two or more crafts or compound craft unions, in which case it is usually known as an *amalgamated* craft or crafts union. Examples of this variety of unionism are to be found in the Amalgamated Association of Iron, Tin, and Steel Workers of North America, the Amalgamated Meat Cutters and Butcher Workmen of North America, the International Association of Machinists, and the Amalgamated Association of Street and Electrical Employees of America.[7] In fact, a large proportion

[7] The multicraft character of this variety of unionism may be illustrated by the following constitutional quotations:

"The Amalgamated Sheet Metal Workers' International Alliance claims jurisdiction over the following work: all metal roofing, the manufacturing, erection, and finishing of metal cornices, metal skylights, metal furniture, metal lockers, hollow metal doors and trim, metal sash and frames, metal ceilings and sidings (both exterior and interior), all sheet metal work in connection with heating and ventilating, furnace and range work, metal jobbing, assortment work, copper smithing, and all sheet metal work made of No. 10 gauge and lighter; providing, however, this gauge restriction shall not apply to coppersmiths in the working of copper who shall have jurisdiction over copof the unions, *local* and *national,* in the United States are today compound or amalgamated craft unions, whether or not so designated by title. As this variety of union has special representatives in all the intermediate structural stages between strict craft unionism and industrial unionism, it would perhaps be not unreasonable to regard it, provisionally at least, as a mode of transition between these two distinct types. Later considerations, however, must determine the truth of this assumption and, if true, the general direction of the developmental tendency.

The second structural variety of unionism which is difficult to classify may, in the absence of any generally accepted designation, be termed the *quasi industrial federation.* It is generally a federation of industrially related craft and compound craft unions, appearing in *local, district* or *state,* and *national* units. Examples of it are to be seen in local printing trades, and local building trades councils, in state building trades councils and system federations of railway employees, and in the building trades, metal trades and railroad employees' de-

per of any and all gauges." (Constitution [1911], Art. VI, § 2.)

"The Amalgamated Association (Amalgamated Glass Workers' International Association of America) shall consist of an unlimited number of local unions composed of trustworthy and industrious glass workers, consisting of the following branches: glass cutters, lead glazers, metal sash glazers, prism glazers, bevelers, silverers, scratch polishers, embossers, engravers, designers, glass painters, draftsmen, sandblast workers, glass shippers, glass mosaic workers, setters, putty glazers, cementers, benders, flat glass or wheel cutters, glass signmakers, glass packers, plate glass workers, and all wageworkers engaged in the production and handling of glass not already affiliated with a national or international union of glass workers." (Constitution [1905], § 3.)

partments of the American Federation of Labor.[8] This
variety of unionism is one in which the constituent craft
or amalgamated craft unions retain their individual sovereignty, yet appear and act as a single organization with
respect to designated affairs of common interests. It
resembles both the trades union and the industrial union
types, but differs from each essentially. It is a narrower
and closer association than the trades union and is vitally
unlike it in the scope and character of its activities. On
the other hand, it lacks the organic homogeneity and
centralization of the industrial union. As it is in every
case, roughly speaking, an organization within a particular industry, and as its aims and activities approximate—
as far as they go—those of the industrial union type, it
may perhaps be regarded also as an intermediate phase—
a mode of transition between the craft and the industrial
union. Whether it represents thus a continuous evolutionary process, and, if so, what the nature of the process
is, will appear from later considerations.

As we have said, the existence of distinct structural
types and varieties of unionism has quite generally been
recognized, and it has been noted further that union
function tends to vary somewhat with the variation in
structure. It seems possible, however, to go much
further than this in the general functional analysis of
unionism. A penetrating study of the union situation,
past and present, seems, in fact, to warrant the recognition of functional types quite as distinct in their essential
characteristics as the diverse structural manifestations.

[8] This variety shades into the real industrial federation, an
example of which is found in the mining department of the
American Federation of Labor.

It is true that these functional types do not in practice represent exactly and exclusively the ideas and activities of any particular union organization or group. That is to say, no union organization functions strictly and consistently according to type. Yet as representing as fairly distinct alternative programs of union action, and as guides to the essential character and significance of the diverse organizations and groups included in the heterogeneous union complex, these functional types apparently do exist, and are of the most vital concern to the student of unionism. There are seemingly four of these distinct types, two of which present dual variations.

The first and perhaps most clearly recognizable functional type may be termed *business unionism*. Business unionism appears most characteristically in the programs of local and national craft and compound craft organizations. It is essentially trade-conscious, rather than class-conscious. That is to say, it expresses the viewpoint and interests of the workers in a craft or industry rather than those of the working class as a whole. It aims chiefly at more, here and now, for the organized workers of the craft or industry, in terms mainly of higher wages, shorter hours, and better working conditions, regardless for the most part of the welfare of the workers outside the particular organic group, and regardless in general of political and social considerations, except in so far as these bear directly upon its own economic ends. It is conservative in the sense that it professes belief in natural rights, and accepts as inevitable, if not as just, the existing capitalistic organization and the wage system, as well as existing property rights and the binding force of contract. It regards unionism mainly as a bargaining institution and seeks its ends chiefly through collective bargaining, supported by such methods as experience from time to time indicates to be effective in sustaining and increasing its bargaining power. Thus it is likely to be exclusive, that is, to limit its membership, by means of the apprenticeship system and high initiation fees and dues, to the more skilled workers in the craft or industry, or even to a portion of these; though it may, where immediate circumstances dictate, favor a broadly inclusive policy—when, for example, the unregulated competition of the unorganized and the unskilled seriously threatens to sweep aside the trade barriers and break down the standards of wages, hours and shop conditions it has erected. Under these circumstances it tends to develop a broad altruism and to seek the organization of all the workers in the craft or industry. In harmony with its business character it tends to emphasize discipline within the organization, and is prone to develop strong leadership and to become somewhat autocratic in government, though government and leaders are ordinarily held pretty strictly accountable to the pragmatic test. When they fail to "deliver the goods" both are likely to be swept aside by a democratic uprising of the rank and file. In method, business unionism is prevailingly temperate and economic. It favors voluntary arbitration, deprecates strikes, and avoids political action, but it will refuse arbitration, and will resort to strikes and politics when such action seems best calculated to support its bargaining efforts and increase its bargaining power. This type of unionism is perhaps best represented in the program of the railroad brotherhoods, though these organizations, as we shall see later, present some characteristics of a vitally different nature.

The second union functional type seems best designated

by the terms, *friendly* or *uplift unionism*. Uplift unionism, as its name indicates, is characteristically idealistic in
its viewpoint. It may be trade-conscious, or broadly
class-conscious, and at times even claims to think and
act in the interest of society as a whole. Essentially it
is conservative and law-abiding. It aspires chiefly to elevate the moral, intellectual, and social life of the worker,
to improve the conditions under which he works, to
raise his material standards of living, give him a sense
of personal worth and dignity, secure for him the leisure
for culture, and insure him and his family against the
loss of a decent livelihood by reason of unemployment,
accident, disease, or old age. Uplift unionism varies
greatly in degree of inclusiveness, and in form of gov·
ernment. But the tendency seems to be toward the greatest practicable degree of mutuality and democracy. In
method, this type of unionism employs collective bargaining, but stresses mutual insurance, and drifts easily
into political action and the advocacy of coöperative enterprises, profit-sharing, and other idealistic plans for
social regeneration. The nearest approach in practice to
uplift unionism is perhaps to be found in the program
of the Knights of Labor, though that organization has
varied in many respects from the strict type.[9]

As a third distinct functional type, we have what most

[9] It has been strongly urged by a friendly critic, who is most
intimately acquainted with the organized labor movement in the
United States, that business and uplift unionism are not in reality distinct and independent types, but rather two varieties of
one type more comprehensive than either. The argument put
forward is that no business union can be found which has not
also the uplift in mind, and an idealistic viewpoint. It is suggested that this inclusive type might be called *bargaining unionism* or *constructive business unionism*.

appropriately may be called *revolutionary unionism.*
Revolutionary unionism, as the term implies, is extremely
radical both in viewpoint and in action. It is distinctly
class-conscious rather than trade-conscious. That is to
say, it asserts the complete harmony of interests of all
wageworkers as against the representatives of the employing class, and seeks to unite the former, skilled and
unskilled together, into one homogeneous fighting organization. It repudiates, or tends to repudiate, the existing
institutional order and especially individual ownership
of productive means, and the wage system. It looks
upon the prevailing modes of right and rights, moral and
legal, as, in general, fabrications of the employing class,
designed to secure the subjection and to further the exploitation of the workers. In government it aspires to
be democratic, striving to make literal application of the
phrase *vox populi, vox Dei.* In method, it looks askance
at collective bargaining and mutual insurance as making
for conservatism and hampering the free and united action of the workers.

Of this revolutionary type of unionism there are apparently two distinct varieties. The first finds its ultimate ideal in the socialistic state and its ultimate means
in invoking class political action. For the present it does
not entirely repudiate collective bargaining or the binding force of contract, but it regards these as temporary
expedients. It would not now amalgamate unionist and
socialist organizations, but would have them practically
identical in membership and entirely harmonious in action. In short, it looks upon unionism and socialism as
the two wings of the working class movement. The second variety of revolutionary unionism repudiates altogether socialism, political action, collective bargaining,

and contract. Socialism is to it but another form of oppression, political action a practical delusion, collective bargaining and contract schemes of the oppressor for preventing the united and immediate action of the workers. It looks forward to a society based upon free industrial association, and finds its legitimate means in agitation, rather than in methods which look to immediate betterment. Direct action and sabotage are its accredited weapons, and violence its habitual resort. These varieties of the revolutionary type may be termed respectively *socialistic* and *quasi anarchistic unionism*.[10] The former is perhaps most clearly represented in the United States by the Western Federation of Miners,[11] the latter by the Industrial Workers of the World.[12]

Finally, in the union complex, it seems possible to distinguish a mode of action sufficiently definite in its char-

[10] By many it would seem more appropriate to designate the second variety as *syndicalist unionism*. The name quasi anarchistic has been chosen, however, because there appears to be as yet little real syndicalism in the United States, and, further, because quasi anarchistic is the more inclusive term. It leaves open the opportunity for further subclassification should the conditions warrant.

[11] The present methods of this organization, now known as the International Union of Mine, Mill and Smelter Workers, are, in general, those of business unionism. [EDS.]

[12] In strict justice it must be stated that there are two general organizations in this country claiming to be known as the Industrial Workers of the World. The first, the parent body, has its headquarters in Chicago; the second, an offshoot, is officially located in Detroit. The latter is a representative of the first revolutionary variant. That is, it advocates political action and supports one of the Socialist parties. In ordinary usage, the term I. W. W. applies to the Chicago organization, and when unmodified is to be so understood in these pages.

acter and genesis to warrant the designation, *predatory unionism*. This type, if it be truly such, cannot be set apart on the basis of any ultimate social ideals or theory. It may be essentially conservative or radical, trade-conscious or class-conscious. It appears to aim solely at immediate ends and its methods are wholly pragmatic. In short, its distinguishing characteristic is the ruthless pursuit of the thing in hand by whatever means seem most appropriate at the time, regardless of ethical and legal codes or effect upon those outside its own membership. It may employ business, friendly, or revolutionary methods. Generally, its operations are secret, and apparently it sticks at nothing.

Of this assumed union type also there appear to be two varieties. The first may be termed *hold-up unionism*. This variety is usually to be found in large industrial centers, masquerading as business unionism. In outward appearance it is conservative; it professes a belief in harmony of interests between employer and employee; it claims to respect the force of contract; it operates openly through collective bargaining, and professes regard for law and order. In reality it has no abiding principles, and no real concern for the rights or welfare of outsiders. Prevailingly it is exclusive and monopolistic. Generally it is boss-ridden and corrupt, the membership for the most part being content to follow blindly the instructions of the leaders so long as they "deliver the goods." Frequently it enters with the employers of the group into a double-sided monopoly intended to eliminate both capitalistic and labor competition, and to squeeze the consuming public. With the favored employers, it bargains not only for the sale of its labor, but for the destruction of the business of rival employers and the exclusion of rival workmen from the craft or industry. On the whole its methods are a mixture of open bargaining coupled with secret bribery and violence. This variety of unionism has been exemplified most frequently among the building trades organizations under the leadership of men like the late notorious "Skinney" Madden.

The second variety of predatory labor organization may be called, for want of a better name, *guerilla unionism*. This variety resembles the first in the absence of fixed principles and in the ruthless pursuit of immediate ends by means of secret and violent methods. It is to be distinguished from hold-up unionism, however, by the fact that it operates always directly against its employers, never in combination with them, and that it cannot be bought off. It is secret, violent, and ruthless, seemingly because it despairs of attaining what it considers to be legitimate ends by business, uplift, or revolutionary methods. This union variant has been illustrated recently in the campaign of destruction carried on by the Bridge and Structural Iron Workers.[13]

[13] It has been suggested that there is still another functional union type which might be called *dependent unionism*. It is well known that there are unions whose existence is dependent wholly or in large part upon other unions or upon the employers. Some unions, for example, could not exist except for their labels, which secure a special market among other unionists or union sympathizers for the goods which they turn out. Such unions are sometimes demanded or initiated by the employers, who see in the label a good commercial asset. Again, there are unions instigated and practically dominated by employers, organized and conducted on especially conservative lines with the purpose of combating or displacing independent unionism. We may then, perhaps, be justified in recognizing here a fifth functional type with two subordinate varieties.

The writer is aware that, apparently, strong objections may be urged against the assumption that these diverse expressions of union viewpoint and action represent true functional types.[14] It has been admitted that probably the ideals and modes of action of no particular union organization correspond exactly to any one of these so-called types. It is a fact, moreover, that the programs of most unions are undergoing a pretty constant process of change and sometimes shift rapidly. It is true further that the membership of any union may include representatives of all kinds of unionism—business, uplift, revolutionary, and predatory. It might then be argued that what have here been called types are mere individual attitudes, or, at most, aspects or tendencies of one and the same union species. It will be the purpose of succeeding chapters, therefore, to test the reality of these assumed types and varieties, and to interpret them causally by means of a brief study of the genesis and development of organized labor in the United States. Incidentally this study should reveal also the general laws of union development.

[14] The writer is also fully alive to the fact that no first attempt at functional analysis of unionism can be regarded as final, and will welcome any and all criticism and coöperation that may lead to greater accuracy in this respect.

CHAPTER III

THE ESSENCE OF UNIONISM AND THE INTERPRE-
TATION OF UNION TYPES

In the preceding chapter, on the general character and types of trade unionism, two leading propositions were advanced as working hypotheses for the interpretation of the facts: first, that unionism is not a unified, consistent entity; secondly, that what is called unionism is in reality the manifold expression of a series of distinct and essentially contradictory types and varieties. Such types and varieties were distinguished tentatively with respect to both structure and function, and the leading representatives in each division were briefly characterized as they appear to exist in the United States today. Thus, structurally, the union complex was analyzed into six main forms of organization, each represented by a series of territorial and sometimes industrial units; viz., the *craft union,* the *trades union,* the *compound craft union,* the *quasi industrial union,* the *industrial union,* and the *labor union.* Functionally, the attempt was made to distinguish four main types and four subordinate varieties; viz., *business unionism, uplift unionism, revolutionary unionism,* and *predatory unionism* as types; [1] *socialistic* and *quasi anarchistic unionism* as varieties of the revolution-

[1] A possible fifth type was also suggested, viz., *dependent unionism.*

ary type, *hold-up* and *guerrilla unionism* as variants of the predatory type.

This discussion of the general character and types of unionism was professedly tentative and suggestive. At its close the writer admitted that apparently strong objections might be urged against the hypotheses advanced. Therefore, in view of their supreme importance in connection with the whole interpretation of unionism, our judgments of it, and any practical proposals with regard to it, the promise was made to subject their validity at once to the inductive or historical test. Specifically stated, this requires us, if our hypotheses are to be maintained, to prove by reference to undisputed facts, past and present, that these union types do exist as described, and that their nature and relationships are such as to allow of no escape from the conclusion that unionism is essentially a series of independent group manifestations which from the practical standpoint cannot be interpreted, evaluated, and judged as a simple consistent whole, or as a succession of more or less accidental and temporary variations from a single normal type.

At first blush the process of proof here required appears to be very simple. It would seem necessary merely to furnish undisputed evidence of the existence, past and present, of unions or union groups possessing the characteristics of these assumed types. A moment's thought, however, makes it clear that something other than this is required to prove that unionism is in reality nonunitary in character. For it is evident that the mere successive existence of such variations in the past might in itself indicate only adaptations of one and the same unionism to a changing environment, while their present existence alone might be evidence either of survivals of past adaptations destined shortly to disappear or of merely temporary aberrations from the normal. In either case, if nothing more were adduced it would be possible still to regard unionism as a single definite entity, since successive adaptations of a species to alterations in environment do not necessarily destroy its identity, nor do concurrent variations, unless these become permanently established as conflicting or rival forms.

What, then, are the real tests or criteria of distinct union types, and what is the process of proof necessary to establish their existence? It is evident that to answer this question with assurance, and therefore to remove all doubt in regard to the mode of procedure here demanded, a more thorough understanding is required of the nature and interdependence of these union variants which we have described. This involves a positive interpretation of unionism in terms of its general functional and structural character and relationships. Let us then attempt to indicate clearly the essential quality and conditions of existence of this combination of function and structure called unionism.

Students in general have approached unionism on the structural side, and have treated it as though the union were essentially an organic unit with certain functional attributes; and hitherto we have spoken of the functional and structural forms as though they were independent and coördinate expressions of unionism. Both of these attitudes are untenable. From the standpoint of motives and ends, as well as from that of its character and significance as a social problem, the real unionism—its primary and essential expression—is functional. The structural form is altogether secondary and dependent. This will

be made evident by a brief analysis of the motives which
actuate prospective unionists and the manner and purposes for which the union is brought into being.

What concerns men primarily in their social relationships as ends to be striven for is not forms of organizations but standards of living—using this phrase to cover
not merely the narrow economic aspect of life but social
standards generally, including moral and judicial as well
as material conditions, rights, and privileges. As social
beings we are all concerned primarily with the problem
of living as presented by these conditions and standards;
and our attention is focused on the solution of this problem in terms of our particular needs and the peculiar circumstances which we have to face and overcome. In
our efforts to comprehend and solve this problem each of
us develops more or less completely and systematically an
interpretation of life—an explanation of things as they
are in terms of the conditions and relationships of which
we are conscious and the forces which determine these.
And along with this interpretation there tends to grow
up in the mind of each some plan or scheme for the modification or complete alteration of the situation in the
furtherance of his special ideals or interests.

The wageworker is no exception in respect to all this.
His hopes and fears center primarily about such matters
as employment, wages and hours, conditions of work,
modes of remuneration—in short, the most vital concerns which immediately touch his present and future
well-being—and the economic, ethical, and juridical conditions, standards, and forces that practically determine
these matters; and his mind focuses on the problem of
living as presented in these terms. In his attempt to
comprehend and solve this problem he also develops some

sort of social viewpoint—an interpretation of the social situation as viewed from the standpoint of his peculiar experiences and needs—and a set of beliefs concerning what should and can be done to better the situation, especially as it bears upon the conditions of living which he faces.[2]

The scope and character of this viewpoint and the mode of its development in the mind of the worker vary with the individual. If he is by nature and training thoughtful and independent, he may work out his own conclusions, subject of course to the unconscious influence of the general body of opinion about him, and his interpretation and solution may cover the widest range, including not only the immediate economic conditions and relationships which confront him, but the ethical and legal foundations upon which these rest. One indeed fre-

---

[2] The statement in the text does not of course attempt to carry the analysis back to its ultimate basis. To quote a comment by Professor George H. Mead: "This process is fundamentally a process of the coming to a new self-consciousness on the part of the laborer in the changing industrial conditions in which he finds himself. It is a great mistake to identify this fundamental impulse with the occasions which give it expression. The individual laborer can become conscious of himself only in so far as he realizes himself in the common attitude of the group over against the employing class or another group of workers, and the whole history of the development of society has shown that this negative attitude must precede any consciousness of common interests which bind this group to others in society. The trade union is then one step in the process of socializing the laborers brought about under the modern process of industry, and goes through the same stages through which the community itself has passed in advancing from hostile groups into a conscious organization of diverse but interacting elements of society."

quently encounters workmen who have thus possessed
themselves of a complete and often esoteric social philosophy.

If, on the other hand, the individual worker is intellectually untrained and sluggish, his view is likely to be
relatively narrow, concerned mainly with his own immediate conditions and relationships, and taken over
bodily from the current opinion of his associates.   In
such cases he is likely to reflect merely the opinions of
some stronger or more expansive personality who has
constituted himself a leader.   But whatever its range or
quality, and however it may have been acquired, each
worker possesses and is guided by some sort of social
philosophy rooted in his peculiar temperament and in his
immediate experiences and relationships.

It is evident that under these circumstances workers
similarly situated economically and socially, closely associated and not too divergent in temperament and training, will tend to develop a common interpretation of the
social situation and a common solution of the problem
of living.   This may come about gradually and spontaneously, or it may be the apparently sudden outcome of
some crisis in the lives of the men concerned.   It may,
for example, result immediately from some alteration for
the worse in the conditions of living, or an interference
with what are considered established rights and modes of
action, of which cases in point would be wholesale dis-
charges from employment or the discharge of favorite
individuals, a lowering of the wage rate, the requirement
of more onerous or more dangerous conditions of work,
a sudden rise in the prices of necessities, some police
action or legal decision which touches the workers on the
raw with respect to modes of action or their assumed dig

nity and rights as men.   Or this crystallization of sentiment may come about as the result of the appearance from
without or the rise from within the group of a purposeful agitator and leader—a man whose personality or
position commands attention, who is capable of putting
into general form the discontents of the individuals and
offering a positive solution of their difficulties.   But
whatever the immediate cause, the result is the same.   A
social group is thus constituted, marked off by a more
or less unified and well-developed but effective viewpoint
or group psychology.

As soon as this state of affairs has been reached group
action is a natural consequence.   Those whose interpretations of the situation and solutions of the problem are
sufficiently alike to make coöperation apparently possible,
spontaneously or under purposeful leadership band themselves together for common effort and mutual assistance.
They come together thus, not primarily to establish and
vindicate a form of organization—the organization is
merely means to end—but to establish and maintain certain conditions of living—to put through a remedial program based on their common interpretation of the social
situation viewed from the standpoint of their immediate
conditions and needs.

Thus the union comes into existence.[3]   It goes back in

---

[3] Unionism then is not a thing which exists only among wageworkers.   In its broadest sense it may be as pervasive as social
grouping.   It may exist wherever in society there is a group of
men with consciousness of common needs and interests apart
from the rest of society.   What distinguishes *trade unionism*
from other forms is that it expresses the viewpoint and interpretation of groups of wageworkers.   As a matter of fact we
have no lack of unions of employers, unions of merchants,
unions of farmers, and unions of professional men.   The cu-

its genesis ultimately to the common needs and problems of the wageworkers; it arises immediately out of the consciousness of the common or group character of those needs and problems; it exists for common action looking to the betterment of the living conditions; it appears primarily as a group interpretation of the social situation in which the workers find themselves, and a remedial program in the form of aims, policies, and methods; the organization and the specific form or structure which it takes are merely the instruments which the group adopts for propagating its viewpoint and putting its program into effect. In short, looking at it from the standpoint of motives and ends, as well as from that of its character as a social problem, the heart and core of the thing—its essential aspect or expression—is functional. Its structural or organic expression is secondary and dependent.[4]

rious thing is that men who themselves are members of one sort of union, in so many cases cannot be made to believe that unions of another sort are anything but unnatural and vicious products.

[4] In practice and specifically, the genesis of unions is, of course, a matter of much variation, and the actual order of events is not always as stated in the text. Spasmodic action often precedes organization, and organization frequently antedates any general or rationalized formulation of viewpoint, interpretation, and program. Frequently blind and spasmodic revolt against some particular grievance or condition is the first objective step in the formation of a union. This revolt may be brought about by the personal influence of one or a few men, and the crowd may act more as the result of imitation or emotion than from clear consciousness of a common viewpoint and problem; after which a paid organizer appears and attempts to teach the workers or a select number the union viewpoint and program, and to effect a permanent organization. But even in such cases some

If, then, functional and structural types of trade unionism exist, we have here the most definite indications of
what must be their nature and relationships.   Assuming
their existence, the functional type is simply a specific
case of group psychology.   It is a social interpretation
and remedial program held by a group of wageworkers.
Obviously there may be as many of these functional
types as there are groups of workers with vitally different
social viewpoints and plans of action.   The structural
type, on the other hand, is simply one of the organic
methods by means of which the functional types seek to
maintain discipline among their members and to put into
effect their programs of action.   Evidently there may be
as many structural types as there are distinct organic
modes of combination effective for these purposes.   The

consciousness of common needs and problems has preceded action and organization, and unless the conditions are present for
the development of a common viewpoint, interpretation, and
program, and, further, unless the organization is adapted to
make these effective, it will not work.   Unless these elements
are present some organization may indeed be created, but it will
soon disintegrate.   This accounts, indeed, for the great proportion of unions that prove altogether ephemeral.   They are based
on the temporary existence of special and exceptional circumstances, or are the work of one or two men whose special influence has for the time created the semblance of a group psychology among a body of men incapable of continuous common
thought and action.   Under these circumstances, as soon as the
special exigency is past, or the special leadership withdrawn, the
group is bound to break up.   In other words, the native consciousness in the group membership of actually existing common
needs and problems is primal.   Without it and without adaptation to it no organization can long exist and function.   In the
most vital sense, then, the statement in the text represents the
true genesis of the union and the true relation of its functional
and structural expressions.

functional type *is* unionism of a certain species. The structural type is one organic form in which it may clothe itself. In other words, the structural type is related to the functional type somewhat as government is related to the nation. It is altogether a subordinate and dependent manifestation.

But do such types exist? So far as concerns structural types, this has been generally conceded. What can we say, then, in regard to the functional aspect of the case? Let us carry the analysis a step farther. It is evident that, once the viewpoint stated above is comprehended and accepted, we should look for distinct and conflicting varieties of unionism, functionally speaking. We should expect these to appear wherever and whenever there exist groups of workers with well-defined and conflicting social viewpoints. Moreover, we should expect to find them existing not only in succession but concurrently, and not only in different industries but among the workers in the same industry and even in the same craft. For as soon as we concede that the union is in essence an expression of group psychology we realize that it will get its specific character not merely from environmental conditions but from these in conjunction with the temperamental characteristics of the workers concerned, and that consequently union variants are likely to appear with a variation in either of these factors. In short, we should expect to find concurrent functional variation and conflict to be among the chief features of contemporary unionism in a country like our own, with its diversity of environmental conditions and its richness of racial and temperamental contrasts.

And the facts amply confirm the deduction: not only does the student of American unionism encounter differ-

ent union groups in different industries with widely varying viewpoints and interpretations, but different unions
with varying aims, policies, and methods contending for
the domination of the same industry. And nothing is
more characteristic of the situation than the descent of
this form of conflict into the particular union where rival
groups or factions struggle for the control of the organization in the interests of conflicting interpretations
and programs. The bitterness of these contests and their
continuance over long periods and under different sets
of leaders leave no doubt that they spring, in part at
least, from the existence of irreconcilable viewpoints.[5]

[5] As illustrations of the statement in the text the following
specific cases of union conflict based mainly on differences of
viewpoint and program may be cited: In the eighties and early
nineties the American Federation of Labor, claiming to represent in general what we have called business unionism, was engaged in a struggle for supremacy with the Knights of Labor,
the assumed proponent of idealistic uplift unionism, and since
1905 the American Federation has had to encounter the bitter
opposition of the quasi anarchistic Industrial Workers of the
World. During the most of this time the control of the Federation has been more or less seriously threatened by the socialistic unionists working within the organization. The I. W. W.
has been in a chronic state of internal conflict since its establishment in 1905. In 1908 it split into two irreconcilable factions resulting in the formation of a socialistic I. W. W. (the
Detroit I. W. W.) which has since maintained a separate existence. At the present moment the older organization is in most
serious straits due to internal dissensions. Serious contests over
general policy are not infrequent in state and city central units
of the American Federation of Labor. A notable example is
the case of the Chicago Federation of Labor, the control of
which some years since was threatened by the violent efforts
and the drastic measures of a predatory group ruled by "Skinny"
Madden, and which has been almost constantly harassed by the

Conflicting functional variants then certainly do exist in the union complex. But are these variants union types in the sense that they preclude the assumption of a single consistent unionism at bottom? This is the question for practical proof. In order to clear the ground for direct consideration of this question, one more point in the general interpretation of unionism demands consideration.

If the validity of the preceding analysis be conceded, it is evident that the orthodox causal and historical interpretation of unionism must be abandoned or thoroughly revised. It has been the habit of students to look upon trade unionism as fundamentally an economic manifestation and to interpret it almost exclusively, or at least primarily, in terms of industrial or economic factors. Thus one school would explain unionism in terms of the development of the process of production in its narrow sense, making of it a succession of organic adaptations to the conditions and needs of the workers produced immediately by the successive types or units of capitalistic enterprise, e.g., the small craft unit, the industrial unit, and the enlarged industrial unit or trust.

efforts of the socialistic unionists to force upon it their viewpoint and policies. Contests within national and local unions between rival factions representing conflicting union varieties find well-known recent examples in the cases of the United Mine Workers, the Electrical Workers, the Association of Machinists, the Painters, Decorators, and Paperhangers, the Bakery and Confectionery Workers, the Carpenters and Joiners—to name only a few of many. Contests between national unions for control of the trade or industry find current examples in the struggle between the Brotherhood of Railroad Trainmen and the Switchmen's Union of North America, and between the two unions in the boot and shoemaking industry.

Unionism thus appears ultimately as the organic corollary of the form of the tool or machine. Another school insists that unionism is to be explained primarily in terms of the development of markets and the character and scope of market competition, endeavoring to show that the different forms of unionism correspond naturally to the conditions existing in conjunction with the customs market, the retail competitive market, and the wholesale market. Here transportation is perhaps the most potent underlying determinant. It is not denied that other factors have a formative influence, especially, for example, the presence or absence of free land, the political ideals and situation, and the state of public education. But these factors are looked upon as modifiers. Environment is practically the sole, and economic environment the chief, formative force, and unionism is again regarded as a series of successive adaptations of one and the same thing to the changing environmental conditions.

These attempts at explanation simply or mainly in industrial or economic terms result largely from the habit of regarding unionism primarily as an organic phenomenon and thus centering the attention on structural forms and changes, and are the chief cause for failure to recognize the possible nonunitary character of unionism. For as soon as we discard the older mode of approach and look at unionism as primarily functional in character, the appearance of orderly succession vanishes, and the simple modes of interpretation described above are seen to be altogether inadequate to account for the facts. We have then to explain chiefly the existence of contradictory group interpretations and programs which succeed each other apparently in no order accountable for by changes in the economic situation, and which appear, as we have pointed out, not only consecutively in conjunction with different systems of production and marketing, but concurrently, and not merely in the same general industrial and social *milieu,* but among workers in the same trade and even in the same union.

Evidently functional variations thus existing and persisting cannot be explained in economic or even in environmental terms alone. They can be accounted for only on the supposition that primary forces besides the industrial and environmental are vitally responsible for their genesis and being. In short, an interpretation of unionism, not in monistic, but in dualistic or pluralistic terms is required.

What then conceivably are these relatively permanent, non-industrial factors which enter into the determination of the primary or functional character of unionism? Since these diverse viewpoints and interpretations which make up unionism are obviously specific cases of group or social psychology, we have merely to inquire what are the determining factors of the psychology of social groups. This query the social psychologist stands ready to answer with considerable assurance. He assures us that one of these factors is environment—not economic environment merely, but political, social, and traditional as well, in the sense of the whole body of transmitted sentiments, ideas, and precepts—moral, religious, and customary. But he assures us also that over against environment as thus broadly interpreted is another factor, perhaps equally potent and certainly more permanent. This is the subjective factor. It includes temperament and aptitudes, both personal and racial, which show themselves as between different races and individuals in relatively permanent and conflicting feelings, ideals, and attitudes. It is these temperamental differences plus environmental influences that at any moment cause individuals to differ in respect to what is good and bad, right and wrong, just and unjust; which mold and color their social interpretations, and thus, through the primal forces of association, bring about psychological groups with diverse and conflicting viewpoints and programs of action.[6] We may then reasonably conclude that the existence of concurrent and conflicting functional variants is to be explained as the outcome of different combinations of all these relatively permanent forces that affect the psychology of group membership, both environmental and subjective or temperamental, and since the functional aspect of unionism is its primary and essential expression it also is to be explained causally and historically in the same terms.[7]

With this general interpretation of unionism in hand we are now in a position to comprehend the nature of the problem involved in the assumption that unionism is at bottom nonunitary, and to state clearly and specifically the character and methods of proof which are required to validate this assumption. The problem is one which evidently concerns primarily the existence, and character of functional union types. We shall therefore consider

[6] See C. H. Cooley, *Social Organization;* W. G. Sumner, *Folkways;* W. I. Thomas, "Race Psychology," *American Journal of Sociology,* XVII, 725-775; G. Tarde, *The Laws of Imitation.*

[7] This insistence on a dualistic interpretation of unionism is not necessarily out of harmony with a belief in philosophical monism or even with adherence to the "economic interpretation of history." It implies nothing in regard to the ultimate determinants of racial and temperamental differences. It takes them simply as fixed data for the present and recent situation.

this aspect of the matter first, postponing for the present the discussion of structural types and their relation to the main issue.

We have seen that functional union variants do exist. What then must be proved with respect to them in order to establish the main contention? It would follow from all that has been said that the real tests of the validity of these variants as types are *concurrent existence as rival forms* of unionism and *relative permanence or stability* as such. Only in so far as they stand these tests can we be sure that they are more than successive adaptations of one and the same unionism to changing environment, or more than temporary and accidental variations from a single union norm; and only in so far can we assert that unionism is not after all an essentially consistent though developing whole.

But the question at once arises: Just what is implied specifically in the terms "rival forms or expressions" and "relative permanence or stability"? In order to constitute a type must there be a perfectly defined and completely isolated union variant, exactly objictified in a formal organization which has existed from the initial genesis of unionism, or will less rigid requirements suffice?

Certainly it must be shown that these functional variants exist at the same time among the wageworkers as consciously formulated and essentially conflicting social interpretations with special regard to the needs and problems of the workers and the best methods of arriving at their solution; and that these conflicting interpretations, once established, persist and, so far as we can see, do not tend to revert or to develop into some one of the interpretations or into a single common interpretation.

On the other hand, at least three apparent qualifications

of these conditions are possible without destroying the practical reality and significance of distinct functional types. In the first place, no specific degree of scope and generality with respect to the group interpretation and program is essential. These may be exceedingly narrow, concerned merely with the immediate economic conditions, relationships, and standards of living of the workers involved; that is, they may comprehend simply a set of more or less coördinated assumptions in regard to the rights of the men with respect to wages, hours, and conditions of employment, the mode of determining these, and the methods to be used in securing reasonable terms with the employer and enforcing them. Or the group interpretation may constitute a complete, definite, and rationalized social philosophy, and the program may cover the whole field of economic, political, ethical, juridical, and social conditions and relationships of the workers. The only essential point is that the viewpoint and program, whatever their scope and character, shall command the adherence of the membership of the group so as to constitute an effective motive and guide to group action. If this condition is met the type exists. The interpretation may be what it will; the question is: Does it work as a unifying and dynamic group force?

It is equally true, secondly and thirdly, that these functional types can exist, and can in so far show the essential diversity and manifold character of unionism independent of any structural qualifications whatever and apart from the existence of actual union programs conforming exactly to them. For the functional type, it must not be forgotten, is a group viewpoint or interpretation and, provided it exists, persists, and its adherents strive to secure for it practical effectiveness and the structural means appropriate thereto, it is a union type, regardless of the structural form through which or with which it may be obliged to work, and regardless of the ability of its advocates to secure its exclusive objectification in the programs of any particular organizations.[8] It is not necessary, even, that different functional types should always find expression in different and conflicting union organizations. On the contrary, it is possible, and indeed it often happens, that the conflict between the functional types goes on within one and the same union organization, taking the form of a struggle for control between two or more factions holding to vitally different social viewpoints and interpretations. As a matter of fact this internal conflict is a characteristic feature of unions, and at any moment there is almost always some factional compromise and some practical admixture of functional type programs. Official union programs, therefore, rarely exist perfectly true to type. This is one reason why the multiple-type character of unionism has been generally overlooked. But this admixture in practice no more negates the fact and significance of union types than does the practical absence of pure democracy, unmixed oligarchy, or absolute despotism negate the varied type and character of government, nor does the fact that most capitalistic incomes are mixed negate or

[8] A good illustration of this statement is furnished by the American Syndicalist League. No one prepared to admit the existence of functional types at all would deny a place among them to revolutionary syndicalism. Yet it is not the primary aim of the Syndicalist League to form separate union organizations with correct syndicalist programs, but gradually to transform American unionism by the process of spiritual penetration. It advises all syndicalists to join the unions of their trade and to agitate within the organization.

destroy the significance of the truth that social income, aside from that which goes to wages, is divided into the essentially diverse income types—profits, interest, and rent—and that actual distribution is to be so far interpreted in terms of these types and their fundamental determinants.[9]

If there is any doubt in regard to the aptness of these analogies, let us put the case in the worst possible light for our contention, and then deal with it on its own merits. We have from the first insisted that unionism is what it is, and must be interpreted as we find it. But if there is no exact correlation between functional and structural types, and if actual union programs rarely occur type pure, how then can these functional types be the effective guides to union action or true clues to the interpretation of actual unionism? The answer is to be

[9] Neither is the existence and significance of union types negated by the fact that in times of serious crises unionists and unions of one type are likely to rally temporarily to the support of those of another, nor by the further fact that within unions bodies of men are found who act now with one and now with another faction. The first case finds its analogy in war between nations, when for the time being partisans of all types of government unite against foreign aggression. The second case illustrates the force of personality and imitation in the determination of social grouping. In the unions there are a few men of strong personality and decided opinions. There are more of an imitative disposition who get their opinions from others. The former in their positive interpretations and programs represent and maintain the distinct and conflicting union types. The latter are followers who sometimes shift in their allegiance from leader to leader and thus from type to type, with changes in associations and conditions. This fact does not negate the existence of the types, but throws light rather on the conditions which determine the outcome of contests between factions representing types.

found in the pragmatic and dynamic character of unionism. It is not a made-to-order and finished product, but
is in a constant state of flux and development. For the
most part it changes, not by the process of creations
de novo, but by the slow transformation of existing programs and structure. Unionism as it is, then, is not a set
of fixed forms and programs, but is a developing process,
and it is just this process of change and transition that
the student must chiefly consider if he is to understand
and interpret the phenomenon.

But what is the real nature of this process of change?
No one who has made a careful study of unionism can
doubt that it is a matter of practical adaptation to the
existing relative strength or of continuous readjustment
to the shifting of balance of power between contending
groups and factions. New conditions arise, creating new
problems which must be faced and solved. Each group
has its solution based on its own general viewpoint and
interpretation. The actual resultant in terms of the
union program and structure will reflect the relative
power of the groups. Or new members are admitted,
and, the personnel having changed, a new balance of
power between factions is established. Soon this new
balance will be reflected in the official policies, methods,
attitudes, and perhaps structural features, of the union.
Thus, while the types persist, the actual union program
and methods change and develop. It is then evidently in
terms of the interpretations and programs of these conflicting groups, i.e., in terms of the types and their causes,
that we are to find the clues to the interpretation of
unionism as it actually exists and is becoming.

And just because unionists are in the main pragmatic
in their outlook we should not expect, except rarely, to

find actual union programs and union structures existing type pure. Nor should we ordinarily expect any definite correlation in practice between functional and structural types. Doubtless such a correlation naturally exists to a considerable extent, certain structural arrangements being naturally adapted to the carrying out of certain group programs. But ordinarily while there is hope of a gradual transformation toward the desired type its adherents will remain in the union. It is only when one faction gives up hope of working its will from within that it will withdraw and set up a new organization, and it is only, therefore, under such circumstances that we ordinarily find an exact correspondence between the actual union programs and structures and the pure types. We may safely conclude, then, that the absence of exact correlation between structural and functional types in practice, and between the latter and actual union programs, does not militate against the reality of distinct and persisting functional types and their practical significance.

Turning now to the matter of structural types, it is evident that the problem before us assumes a very different and much less important aspect. Distinct structural types do exist, as is generally admitted, but neither are they always rival forms nor is there always absence among them of developmental mutability. It does seem to be rather characteristic of the existence of these types that their several advocates should be in actual conflict in the endeavor to displace one by another; but, on the other hand, they are often found in quite harmonious and supplemental relationship in the same organic group, each appearing to meet a different practical need. A well-recognized case in point is the existence and relationship within the general organization of the American

Federation of Labor of craft and trades unions. Nor do these distinct structural types always appear to be quite independent in their genesis. This happens in some cases, but there seem to be clear cases of developmental transition. Thus the compound craft union is sometimes a transformation of the craft union by the simple process of combination, and the industrial union seems often to be the outcome of a simple enlargement of the elements in the compound craft union.

If, then, structural types stood in the same relationship to our problem as functional types, and if, therefore, in order to establish the manifold character of unionism it were necessary to apply the same criteria to them with the same degree of stringency, there is no doubt that the case could not be maintained. Here we doubtless find the chief explanation for the fact that students have yielded so long and so generally to the popular assumption that unionism is at bottom one and the same thing, that union variants are but adaptations of a single norm to changing environment, or at most temporary and accidental aberrations from it.[10] This is the conviction with which the student of unionism would naturally, and indeed almost inevitably, be impressed if he entered upon the study primarily from the structural standpoint, and placed his emphasis upon structural forms and relationships. He would then see unionism beginning in the local craft organization as a response to the conditions created by the primitive type of capitalistic enterprise or to its corresponding market structure, and developing by a gradual transformation through larger

[10] The populaı assumption seems to be in itself partly a matter of blind partisanship, partly a matter of tactical advantage, and partly a belief in things hoped for.

units to more complex structural arrangements to meet
conditions imposed primarily by economic evolution.
And so long as he looked at the union primarily as a
structural entity, and thought of aims, policies, and activities as functions or means of the organic thing, he could
adopt no other than the unitary or normalistic assumption.

If, however, the primary and essential union expression is functional, and if it is further true that functional
variations may exist regardless of any structural qualifications whatever—the same functional variant making
use of different structural forms without losing its identity or permanency, and, contrariwise, distinct and contradictory functional variants working through the same
structural arrangements—it is evident that this appearance of things would be far from conclusive of the real
character of unionism. Doubtless entire absence of distinct structural types would render impossible positive
proof of the nonunitary character of unionism, but it is
evident that the tests which need be applied to prove their
existence in harmony with this hypothesis are not the
same as in the case of the functional types. Absolute
rivalry is not essential. It is sufficient if the modes of
organization be vitally different in principle. In short,
the tests of distinct structural types demanded by our
hypothesis seem to be merely the contemporary and historical presence in the union complex of distinct and
alternative forms of organization.

To recapitulate, then, briefly in regard to the nature of
the problem involved in the assumption that unionism is
nonunitary in character: It has been seen that this assumption is one which rests almost exclusively on the
existence and persistence of functional union types.

In order to prove the truth of the assumption beyond reasonable doubt, it must be shown that these functional types exist concurrently as conflicting or rival social interpretations and remedial programs, held and advocated by different groups of wageworkers; it must be shown that, once established, these rival viewpoints persist and exhibit no tendency as such to revert to a single or common viewpoint; but it is not necessary that they should be shown to attain any specific degree of scope or generality beyond what is necessary to command group adherence and effectively to guide group action, that they should be necessarily associated with any particular organic forms or structural types, that each should find practical expression exclusively in a different organization, or, finally, that the program of any particular organization or group of organizations should at any moment conform exactly to any one of them. In the matter of structure it is necessary to show merely the existence of distinct and alternative forms of organization.

Such being the problem, what is the process of proof required? Evidently we have here a matter which must be dealt with historically. We must first determine which of these distinct union variants have had more than an ephemeral existence. So far as structural forms are concerned, this should be sufficient. In regard to those functional variants that have persisted, it must be proved that they have had their genesis in different combinations of relatively permanent factors both environmental and temperamental.

To be exhaustive, the proof doubtless should be both positive and negative. Negatively it should be established that where no concurrent and conflicting functional variants exist the environment of the workers entering into combination is essentially uniform and that the workers themselves, racially, temperamentally, and traditionally, are essentially homogeneous. Positively it should be proved that existing and historically concurrent conflicting variants owe their origin and persistence to vitally diverse combinations of environmental and subjective factors operating in connection with the groups concerned.

Perfectly complete and satisfactory proof of our fundamental hypothesis respecting the general character of unionism and union types in the United States would then demand the most searching study of our union history with special reference to the economic, political, traditional, and temperamental factors involved. It is not possible to secure complete proof in this wise, owing to the paucity of well-authenticated historical material. We shall, however, attempt to assemble enough evidence of this character for the practical testing of our thesis and for significant generalizations in regard to the general character of union development in the United States.

CHAPTER IV

A BRIEF HISTORICAL REVIEW[1]

Unionism first appeared in this country about the close of the eighteenth and the beginning of the nineteenth centuries,[2] in the form of local craft unions, mainly among the printers, cordwainers, bakers, shipwrights and carpenters. These unions did not appear earlier in this country because not until about this time was there any well-defined separation of the employing and laboring functions, and therefore, only then were there the beginnings of distinct groups of employers and

[1] The historical study of unionism is valuable just in proportion as it gives insight into the real character and causes of unionism. The facts as facts mean nothing, and the knowing of them means nothing except as they help toward knowing what unionism is and why it is. Throughout the discussion, therefore, this should be kept constantly in mind. As a general hint in this connection, we should consider carefully the question: Is there any such thing as unionism, i. e., unionism as a whole, unionism as such? On the answer to this question will depend not only the nature of one's generalizations but one's whole attitude toward union phenomena and the union problem. (See Notes on Method, p. 376.)

[2] There had been labor organizations in America before this, as far back as the seventeenth century. These organizations, however, were not trade unions, but craft guilds of workmen who combined in themselves the functions of laborer, master and merchant. They were organized to license, or otherwise limit the number of legal craftsmen, to regulate the quality of work, and to maintain customary prices.

wa₤ ₤ earners.   Nor did they appear as the result of any
theory of unionism or of any social theory.   Indeed, the
prevalent political and social theory of the time—the
eighteenth century theory of natural order and natural
law—which held the notions of individual equality,
harmony of interest, and free competition for absolute
truths, was directly opposed to labor combination.   The
prime cause of the appearance of these unions seems to
have been that as soon as a distinct differentiation between employers and workers began to appear, the employers took advantage of the breaking down of the old
customary and legal trade and labor regulations, especially of apprenticeship regulations, to utilize the competition of "illegal" men in attempts to lower wages and
increase the hours of labor.   In short, at the earliest appearance of the employing group and relatively free competition, there began a struggle between the employers and
the wageworkers which forced the latter to combine.

The functions of these unions were not definitely
formulated in advance, but grew naturally out of the
conditions and problems which they had to face.   Since
the efforts of the employers were directed to lowering
wages and increasing hours, the workers attempted the
regulation of these through a union or a combined group.
Since the employers were successful, however, because
of the breakdown of apprenticeship and the influx of
"illegal" men, the unions attempted the defense of apprenticeship and the exclusion of those who had not
passed through it, i.e., the closed shop.   They attempted
to enforce their demand by strikes.   Moreover, since the
employers proceeded against them for conspiring, and
since under the competitive régime they were thrown
upon their own resources, they were obliged to add to·

their functions legal defense and mutual insurance, sick and funeral.

Why did the first unions take the craft form, the local organization of a particular craft? It was because of the nature of the principal problem which confronted the workers, the nature of the functions they were therefore called on to perform, and the form of the business unit and extent of the market. That is, the problem was to prevent the employers from lowering wages and increasing hours by taking advantage of the labor competition of "illegal" men. Thus the principal function of the union was to guard the competitive area. This area, on account of the trade character of the business unit and the local character of competition, was the craft in the local community. Hence the union was a local craft union.

Here appears what may be taken as a hypothetical general principle of unionism, if there is such a thing. The union organization tends to parallel the capitalistic or employers' organization. It attempts to cover the industrial field within which there is labor competition with respect to work, wages, and conditions of employment. If this principle be true, it will explain many of the most significant things about unionism. Let us follow this as one clue and attempt to unravel the history of unionism in this country.

First, by way of hypothesis then, in testing results, consider to what extent, if at all, this principle really explains the history of unionism and what other working factors must be brought in for this. If this principle were true would unionism probably be a relatively fixed or highly protean or changing thing? How would it be likely to develop to meet the situation, where, apprenticeship being broken down, the competitive area of workers or the workers' market becomes intertrade, i.e., where competition of workers in several skilled trades in a given locality exists? Trades unions and city centrals would develop. Suppose that transportation improves so that this competitive market of skilled workers becomes intercity or national? What then? National trades unions would arise. Suppose that a craft or several crafts should succeed in building up apprenticeship again or enforcing a closed shop, but transportation has developed so that the craft members compete directly, not only locally but generally throughout the nation? National craft or trade unions would spring up. Now suppose that, as the result of the introduction of machinery in production, the task becomes similar in different skilled crafts and that unskilled workers can compete with skilled craftsmen? Labor unions, first local and then national, would come into existence. Finally, suppose that the capitalistic or employing unit enlarges to cover and control the whole industry? Then would come into being the industrial union.

Now, did the actual development of unionism follow the line laid down hypothetically? To test this we must consider the periods of the history of unionism in the United States and examine each. The basis for periodization is the development of predominant types. The response of unions both structurally and functionally, especially to economic influences, will be somewhat delayed on the principle of retardation.

1. Beginnings in the local craft union, 1798-1827.

The economic causes at work were the differentiation of the employing and working functions, a small business unit,

and local markets. The causes of the first appearance of
trade or labor unions were the development of a master-
workman-retailer and especially of the jobber and merchant
middleman, a development made possible by the introduction
of machinery, accumulation of capital, increase of population, and improvement of transportation with consequent
widening of market—dividing the ranks of the craftsmen
into two classes, masters and journeymen, i.e., establishing
the wages system. Then came labor unions. They were
organized because of the coming of capitalistic conditions,
an employing class, general market, labor competition, strategic advantage of the masters with a tendency to lower
wages, to bring in inferior workmen,[3] the lengthening of
hours, and also because the association of a large number
of journeymen workers in each craft made organization
natural and possible.

The first local craft unions to arise were the Philadelphia Carpenters, 1791, the Philadelphia Federal Society
of Journeymen Cordwainers, 1794, the Typographical Society of New York, 1794, the Baltimore Tailors, 1795, and
the Baltimore Typographical Society, 1803. There were no
national organizations, though local unions of the same craft
occasionally corresponded on matters of common interest.
Industry had not yet been organized beyond the craft, a
building was put up by an employing mason, employing
carpenter, etc. Markets were not yet national, for transportation would not admit of wide markets, and intercity
competition was little felt. The main problems which these
early unions had to face were: The securing of better

---

[3] Under the domestic and handicraft systems the interest or
duty of employers is to teach beginners the whole trade. Under
the new system there is no such interest or duty. The purpose
is simply to get the work done cheaply. So boys are hired and
kept at one task, thus nibbling off the skilled work of journeymen and creating two opposed classes of workers.

wages, hours and conditions of work, in the face of local competition of inferior and "illegal" workmen, and prosecution for conspiracy, and the care of unfortunate members. The main resultant functions of these first unions were accordingly: Mutual insurance, sick and funeral benefits, collective bargaining, regulation of apprenticeship, regulation of wages, hours and conditions of work, exclusion of "illegal" men, defense against prosecution (conspiracy cases) and strikes.

II. Predominance of trades unions, 1827-1837.[4]

City associations of craft unions and the beginnings of national trade unions appear. The causes are economic and social. The economic cause is the broadening of markets and competitive areas; the social cause is manhood suffrage, which stimulates to the correction of social and political evils, mainly inflated money and the high cost of living, educational and assumed political inequalities. This period may be divided into three phases.

First phase, 1827. The Philadelphia Mechanics' Union of Trade Associations, 1827-1832, as a type, developed into the Workingmen's Party of Philadelphia. It stood for

[4] The first unions are confined to one particular group of wageworkers. Within this group conditions such as we have assumed would produce only one functional type of union—the business union. The structure is determined by this viewpoint and program and takes the craft form. After an expansion, there is a dying out into mutual insurance groups. Then the unionism which revives in the thirties as contrasted with the old unionism supplies the historical test of functional types. Was it the renewal and adaptation of the old unionism in a new and distinct functional type? Was it made up of the same men or same class of workers? Did the business union movement run parallel to it? If so, were the two movements actual rivals? Is the new movement hitched genetically on to the old? What

shorter hours, free schools, the abolition of imprisonment for debt, the reform of the militia system, mechanics' lien law, equal taxation, cheapened legal procedure, no religious legislation, direct election of public officials, and opposition to banks and other monopolies.

Second phase, 1832-1837. There are national trades unions and local trades unions. This was a period of reaction against political methods. But the political issues of the previous period were continued. Demands were made in regard to hours, wages, money, public employment, factory legislation, competition of women and prison labor, freedom of public lands, and coöperation.

Third phase, 1835-1837. At least five national trade unions were organized; cordwainers, comb makers, carpenters, hand-loom weavers, and printers. The causes may be found in the increased competition in the craft, broadening with transportation and markets. The period ends with the crisis of 1837, and an interregnum follows.

III. Predominance of utopian, socialistic and social uplift unionism, 1844-1853.

The Workingmen's Protective Union was organized in 1847, the New England Workingmen's Association, and the Land Reform Movement in 1844-1845. Industrial Councils and Working Class Congresses were held.

Their aims were the establishment of coöperation, communities, land reform, and the ten-hour day. Great waves of utopianism swept over the country, resulting in Brook Farm, etc. There was a general disposition to try communistic and coöperative schemes, all of which resulted in practical failure. A general humanitarian and democratic agitation resulted in attempts to form parties. The ten-

were the racial, temperamental, and class contrasts between the membership of the two movements?

hour movement was started but was unsuccessful. The woman and child labor and free land agitation was partly successful. The free school movement succeeded. Numerous political reforms furthered democracy. After 1852, the slavery agitation absorbed attention and the panic of 1857 killed the movement.

IV. Reorganization of local unions and beginnings of national trade unions, 1853-1860.

The causes were increase in cost of living and the national markets, bringing about national competition which led skilled craftsmen in a few trades to seek to cover the competitive area.

V. The revival of trades unions, 1860-1866.

The beginning of the new movement is due largely to the high cost of living resulting from currency inflation. Machinery was breaking down trade exclusiveness, markets were becoming national, and the business unit was enlarging. Thirty city trade assemblies sprang up before 1865. Objects were boycotts and aid to strikes. In 1864 the first National Industrial Assembly of North America dealt with primary boycotts, strikes, the truck system, coöperation, prison labor, competition, and woman's work.

VI. Attempted amalgamation of national craft unions, 1866-1874.

The causes were those given under V above, the high cost of living, and the increase of competition due to the return of soldiers and to immigration. Two phases characterized this period. The first was that of the National Labor Union, organized in 1866 at Baltimore. It was a federation formed by trade unionists but all labor organizations were represented. A general union did not appeal, however, to a majority. They were craft unions, but with political functions largely. In 1866 the federation

[handwritten note at top: trade union very weak in U.S.A. 1820–1850 due to lack of industry & after 1860 renewed large scale immigration.]

stood for the eight-hour day, coöperation, publicity, tenement house reform, and public lands only for settlers. It recommended trade organization and the association of those workers who had no trade with labor unions, the rigid enforcement of the apprenticeship system, workingmen's lyceums and reading rooms. It opposed strikes except as a last resort and was in favor of arbitration. In 1867 it dealt with the money question, and opposed the national banking system. It now also stood for an optional form of organization, aid to women workers, coöperative stores and workshops, and mechanics' institutes. It was opposed to marketed convict-labor goods. In 1869 began its decline and in 1872 it died. The second phase was that of the Industrial Brotherhood. A call was issued in 1872 by the national trade unions and the first convention was held in 1873. A preamble or declaration of principles was adopted, which was later taken over by the Knights of Labor, except that the Industrial Brotherhood called for monthly payment of wages by corporations, public markets, cheap transportation, apprenticeship laws and the exclusion of the Chinese. It contemplated organization by trade. Its failure, says Mr. Powderly, was due to the dislike of trade unionists for the idea of unity with men outside their own trade, and in particular with common laborers. There was a labor reform party from 1869 to 1872.

The general tendencies which characterized the development of American unionism after the Civil War were the beginnings of working class consciousness, socialist effort to control the unions, increased political and militant activity, and universal centralized organization.

VII. Predominance of the universal labor union, the Knights of Labor, 1879-1890.

Craft exclusiveness was being broken down by machinery and trusts, and employers' associations were being formed, and the competition of the unskilled was being felt. The aims of the Knights were idealistic, humanitarian, and political.

VIII. Predominance of federation of national craft unions, 1890 to the present. The American Federation of Labor, and National Employers' Associations.

IX. Beginnings of industrial unionism.

Industrial plants, employers' associations and real class consciousness developing.

To summarize briefly the character and causes of the development of unionism in the United States, we may say that its genesis was in economic and political causes, in the separation of functions and the rise of classes, and the breakdown of customary and legal rules. The situation created a need for combination of the workers to protest against the reduction of wages, etc. These and the character of the employing unit and market determined the form, the local craft union, and its functional type, business unionism. The widening of the market and increased competition demanded enlargement of the union unit; manhood suffrage turned attention to legislation and political means. Hence we find trades unions, local and national, with a legislative program added to the economic, and a tendency to political party activity. The failure of political methods caused a reaction to economic means as the best instrument under the circumstances. There are national trade unions which are examples of business unionism. The hard times wipe out the movement. The utopian and philosophical spirit and theories create political and uplift unionism again. The drawing off of idealistic elements with the Civil War causes a renewal of national trade unions and business unionism. A struggle between business and idealistic, political, uplift unionism results in the triumph of business unionism, the American Federation of Labor, the national craft federation. An enlargement of the business unit in industry and theorizing result in the industrial union, which is revolutionary. The failure of craft unionism added to the experience of business unionism turns business-craft unionism into predatory unionism.

Craft unions tend to be businesslike, selfish, nonidealistic, nonpolitical, nondemocratic; trades unions tend to be group-conscious and political; labor unions tend to be idealistic, moralistic, theoretical, political, but nondemocratic; industrial unions tend to be class-conscious, socialistic, and theoretical. But while there is some sort of correlation here between structural and functional types, would it be possible to explain the functional type on the basis of the single principle involved? Does not causation seem to run from function to structure, more than the other way? Conditions and problems produce aims, attitudes, and theories; these produce policies and demands and methods. In the actual history of unionism do we not find structural and functional types correlated in different ways? For example, at one period all the unions of different structural types seem to be closely alike functionally.

The structural and functional types sometimes stand in coöperative and interpenetrating relationship, sometimes in a state of rivalry; sometimes they are rival or alternating modes of organization and action, springing up independently. Sometimes one is the product of the other. And in other cases there are purely distinct types representing different conceptions or interre-

lations of a situation or a different situation. We start
with the business type. Where this fails the tendency is
to degenerate into friendly societies. We have then business unionism as a minor aspect, uplift as the major
aspect. Finally, business unionism goes on, uplift unionism is a settled thing, and the revolutionary type begins to come to the front. The history of unionism thus
shows two opposite tendencies, toward the harmoniza-
tion and unification of structural types, and the fanning
out, separation, and distinction of functional types.

At the present time the Knights of Labor number less
than ten thousand. Of what significance are they to this
study and why should we consider them? In the effort
to solve the trade union problem of control we must know
what type of organization can and what type cannot be
maintained under present day conditions. The Knights
of Labor had elements of temporary success but on the
whole it was found unfit. It is essential to know why.

The general governing body of the Knights of Labor
is the General Assembly. This is a delegate body from
organizations directly subordinate. Its base is a local
assembly. Some locals are attached directly to the general assembly but most of them are organized into district and state assemblies. The district assembly is made
up of delegates from five or more locals. It may be
subordinate to a state assembly, to a national trade assembly or to the general assembly. The membership
basis may be craft or mixed. The state assembly has
jurisdiction over all the territory not organized into
mixed district assemblies. The national trade assembly
has jurisdiction over local trade assemblies.

The centralization of the Knights of Labor is perhaps

best shown by the fact that all the organizations have their character and rules defined by and are governed by one constitution. To understand completely the structure and function of the Knights of Labor it is necessary to read but one constitution. To understand fully the functions and structure of the American Federation of Labor, over a hundred constitutions must be read. The Knights of Labor is a sovereignty, the American Federation of Labor is a federation of sovereignties. The centralization is also shown in the regulations in regard to strikes. Local assemblies choose executive boards to which are referred any grievances between employer and employed; should they fail to adjust the matter reference is made to the national or district executive boards; should these fail, it is referred then to the general executive board. No strikes are permitted to be declared or entered upon without sanction of the national, district, or general executive board. Finally, centralization is also shown in the matter of discipline.

The essential functions of the organization are revealed by the following quotation:

The Knights of Labor Assembly is not a mere trade union and beneficial society. . . . It aims to assist members to better their condition morally, socially and financially. . . . Among the higher duties that should be taught in every local assembly are man's inalienable inheritance of and right to share, for use, the soil; that the right to life carries with it the right to the means of living and all statutes that obstruct or deny these rights are wrong, unjust and must give way. Every member who has the right to vote is a part of the government . . . and has a duty to perform. . . . In short, any action that will advance the cause of humanity, lighten the burden of toil or elevate the moral or social condition of mankind . . . is the proper scope and field of operation of a local assembly. (Constitution [1908], pp. 40-41.)

The Knights of Labor is not a revolutionary organization. It does not reject and seek to overthrow the present social and industrial order, although the constitution says that its purpose is to secure to the workers the full enjoyment of the wealth they create . . . to enable them to share in the gains and honors of advancing civilization (Constitution, p. 3, II) ; and that strikes at best afford only temporary relief and members should be educated to depend upon thorough organization and political action and through these the abolition of the present system. (Constitution, p. 40.)   Its program rather is progressive, with some revolutionary items. It includes direct legislation, the initiative, referendum, the imperative mandate and proportional representation; labor bureaus, to promote the educational, moral and financial knowledge of the laboring masses; a demand for occupancy and use as the sole title to land, the unearned increment to go to society; dealing in options to be made a felony; abrogation of unequal laws, of delays, discriminations, and unjust technicalities; health and safety laws in industry; accident insurance; the incorporation of labor organizations; weekly payments in money; mechanics' lien law; abolition of the contract system on public works; opposition to strikes and boycotts; support of laws compelling arbitration; prohibition of child labor under fifteen years; compulsory education and free textbooks; coöperation "such as will tend to supersede the wage system"; graduated income

tax; direct issue of legal tender; no private banking corporations, nor interest-bearing government bills of credit;
postal saving banks; government ownership of the tele-
graph, telephone and railroads; prohibition of convict
labor; and prohibition of hired out and contract immigration.

The Knights of Labor is not a class organization. In
it are crystallized sentiments and measures for the benefit of the whole people. (Constitution, preamble.) It
calls upon all those who believe in the greatest good
for the greatest number (*Ibid*), and it approves any
action that would advance the cause of humanity, lighten
the burden of toil, or elevate the moral and social condition of mankind (Constitution, p. 41). It demands
the abrogation of all laws which do not bear equally
upon capitalists and laborers (Constitution, preamble,
p. 4) in order that the bond of sympathy between them
(employers and employees) may be strengthened (Constitution, p. 5). It deprecates attacks upon the constituted authorities such as the judiciary. At least three-
fourths of the general assembly must be farmers or
wageworkers. (Constitution, p. 43.) The purpose of
its organization is the organizing, educating and directing of the powers of the industrial masses (Constitution, preamble, p. 3) while it gathers into one fold all
branches of honorable toil (Constitution, p. 40). It de-
clares that the alarming development and aggressiveness
of the power of money and corporations under the present industrial and political systems . . . lead to hopeless degradation. (Constitution, premable, p. 3.)

Mr. Powderly attributes the enormous growth of the
Order between the latter part of 1885 and the early part
of 1886 to two circumstances, for which the Order it-

self is not responsible. One was the movement for the establishment of the eight-hour day, the other was the spread of an extravagant idea of the strength of the Order. The public believed that a strike had been ordered by the Knights to take place May 1, 1886, for the purpose of shortening the hours of labor. Because of this belief an exaggerated popular opinion of the power of the Knights spread. Hundreds of thousands who hoped to get profit from it, without any desire to give as well as to get, joined the Order. Its membership was reported to be 104,335 in 1885, and jumped to 702,-924 in 1886. Mr. Powderly claims, however, that the actual number was not over 90,000 in 1885 and 600,000 in 1886. The membership reported in 1888 was 259,-518.[5]

The fundamental underlying causes of the failure of the Knights of Labor consist in the fact that it was contrary to the reality created by modern industrial forces. Machinery was forcing a materialistic contest. This contest is not between the "money power" and the people, but between the employers and the workers. Any attempt to hide this under the cloak of a concept of "society as a whole" is bound to fail. Likewise, attempts to bridge it over by coöperation and idealism must fail. The contest is opposed to industrial peace and good-fellowship ideas; the age of utopianism is past, and the idealistic attitude is not fitted to cope with the workers' problem. Hence the Knights succumbed in the contest with the American Federation of Labor, which stood more nearly for the ideals and demands of the workers.

The Knights of Labor proceeded upon two false assumptions, and as a consequence attempted to do two

[5] Report of the Industrial Commission (1901), vol. XVII, p. 8.

impossible things. First, it assumed no fundamental disharmony of viewpoint and interest between wage-workers and employers as such. It therefore tried to unite workers and the middle class against the "money power." Secondly, it assumed that the viewpoint and interest of all wageworkers are identical. It therefore tried to unite the workers of all degrees of skill and of all crafts and industries into one organization and under one central authority which should direct the actions of each group in the interests of all.

The first assumption was false and the effort to organize and act upon it a failure, for reasons we have already discussed. Under the capitalistic wage system, the product of industry is divided into two parts, each part going to a distinct class, the one, exclusive owners of the material means of production, the other, the exclusive owners of labor. The immediate interests of the two classes must thus center in the division of the product and be opposed, and it is the immediate interests of men, especially of the workers, who must depend upon immediate incomes in order to live, that determine the possibilities of organic union and coöperation among them. Hence, these two classes are bound to be opposed unless they can get together to "do" some one else.

Under the system of machine industry, the division of function throws the workers and employers into such diverse material and social environments that inevitably diverse viewpoints develop and create a belief in diversity of interest even when this diversity does not exist—a belief that must exist as long as machine industry with its functional and environmental corollaries exists. The Knights of Labor was thus built upon a permanently false foundation, and its failure goes far to show that the union problem cannot be solved by any attempt to bring together into one organization the employing and working elements. Successful unionism must be an organization of wageworkers, and unionism as a social problem must be accepted as an organization of wageworkers seeking their own interests as such.

The second assumption, that the viewpoint and interest of all workers are identical, was equally false for the time, and apparently for the present and the discernible future. So long as there exist among the wageworkers practically what the economists call noncompetitive groups, that is, so long as there exist distinct crafts in industry whose members do not compete, and so long as machinery has not broken down the practically noncompetitive barriers between skilled and unskilled workers, no general organic union of all the workers, each acting in the interest of all, can be secured. Under these circumstances each craft and group of workers must have its own conditions and problems to face and to solve. No one else can understand its peculiar conditions and problems well enough to formulate rules applicable to its ends. Its problems can be solved only by rules applying particularly to its conditions, without reference to any more general situation. Each craft and industry, then, can best serve its own economic ends by acting alone, unhampered by outside restrictions, and regardless of outside interests and purposes. Under these circumstances, again, the immediate economic interests of the different groups are not identical or harmonious. It is not true, as the Knights of Labor supposed, that an injury to one is an injury to all. This is perfectly evident if we take a practical common sense view of the matter. Let us take the case of wages. Just so far as general competition exists, the interests of one craft may be definitely opposed to the interests of others. When one stands to gain, the others may stand to lose, and vice versa. This is equally true between craft and craft, and between skilled and unskilled workers. To show this, take the case of craft A which is struggling for an increase of wages. If it succeeds, the increase of wages may be an increased cost of production of the goods, and may be an increase of the price of the goods. This would be a lowering of the real wages of other crafts whose members consume the goods.[6] Every increase of the wages of skilled workers under these circumstances is a lowering of the standard of living of the unskilled, and vice versa. Looking at it in another way, one of the means of securing a rise of wages in a single craft is through a limitation of numbers. What does this mean? It means turning men into other crafts or into the unskilled mass to increase the numbers and the competition of workers with the result of lowering wages there. In a very real way then, the workers are themselves divided into numerous groups with opposed economic interests.

It is only on the one hand, as the employing unit enlarges and employers unite so that a single craft finds itself face to face with a superior force, capable of playing off craft against craft, that the craft unions are brought to see their common economic interests and the necessity of common organization and common action.

---

[6] Only as we look at the matter statically need the effect of one group's advance on other groups be considered. If we view the matter dynamically, labor's demands will force employers to make improvements, increase efficiency in spite of labor's hampering influence, and thus secure more for all.

It is only, on the other hand, as machinery gradually breaks up industry into little tasks that can be performed by unskilled workers, thus destroying the apprenticeship system, and so letting in the competition of the unskilled on the skilled, that the real interests of the two groups seem to be common. These are the economic reasons for the development of industrial unionism, and the growth of working-class solidarity. The skilled workers in general have no love for the unskilled, the successful for the unsuccessful. There is every economic reason why they should not have. They worry about the unskilled when they are in danger of losing their advantages and places, due to the unstinted competition of the unskilled, and they then develop a "labor as a whole" attitude. So long as the craft organization can keep up a successful fight of its own it is not going to forego its advantages for outside labor, and, equally, the crafts cannot be made to combine together, except as loose federations mainly for legislative activity and mutual aid. Immediate economic interests, wages, hours, and conditions of employment are still the predominant matters in the minds of the rank and file of the workers, rather than general political and social interests. In these matters group consciousness of the workers is still in the craft stage rather than in the class stage. Differences in craft interest still mean more than unity of class interest. Conditions, needs and problems of workers are different in different industries and different places, and hard and fast attitudes, policies, and methods applicable to all are bound to fail. Therefore, members of the different crafts could not be forged by the Knights of Labor into effective weapons of attack and defense. Members of each craft tended to cling together to get what they needed without regard for, or even at the expense of, other crafts. They were jealous of other crafts and of the unskilled. Furthermore, common rules necessary for the prevention of undercutting were not possible for a group of crafts.

At the time of the Knights of Labor, economic factors tending to emphasize the common economic interests of all the workers had only just begun to develop. Even yet they are not powerful enough to offset the real differences of interest. The Knights of Labor, then, was inevitably doomed to failure, regardless of its political policies and its disastrous strikes. It was far ahead of its time, altogether utopian. Its main result was to produce a strong reaction to the craft union ideal and basis. It proved that unionism cannot succeed unless it keeps close, in the character of its organization and policy, to the economic realities, and that successful unionism above all must be opportunistic, that unionism is bound to develop according to the real conditions and needs of the workers, and that so long as the economic conditions create among the workers group interests and group antagonisms, unionism is bound to be, in the main, a selfish, craft entity.

Unionism arose in America when conditions first appeared of such a nature as to induce the formation of wageworkers' group psychologies, interpretations and programs. This has been true throughout the history of unionism in the United States. In so far as unionism has always been in the main the wageworkers' interpretations and programs under the system of capitalistic production, with the definite separation of employer and employee, these groups and group psychologies are found

in opposition to the employer. "Hold-up" unionism and
dependent unionism, both parasitic and "yellow," are the
exceptions. The aims, policies, and methods of trade
unions are the result of the peculiar problems which the
unionists have to face and of the conditions accompany-
ing these problems. The character of the aims, policies
and methods determines the structure or organic character of the union. In other words, problems and conditions determine function, function determines structure. Unionism develops by the trial method—is a process of adaptation to a developing environment. Present unionism is an outcome of a process of trial and
elimination. The union organic structure shows a tendency to parallel the capitalistic, a union unit to meet
each capitalistic unit. Union history shows a constant
struggle between the forces of centralization and decentralization, autocracy and democracy, social idealism and
enlightened self-interest, narrow trade autonomy and
industrialism, economic and political method. The failures of unionism in the past have been largely the result
of centralization, democracy, social idealism, industrialism, and political method. Unionism today, notwithstanding, seems to show a constant tendency toward
higher integration, centralization, autocracy, social idealism, industrialism and political method. What then is
unionism?

BIBLIOGRAPHY

ADAMS AND SUMNER. *Labor Problems* (1908), pp. 215-
228.
BARNETT, GEO. E. "The Printers," *American Economic
Association Quarterly*, Third Series, vol. X, No. 3
(1909).
BLISS, W. D. P. *Encyclopedia of Social Reform.*

BOGART, E. L. *The Economic History of the United States* (1913).

BURKE, W. M. *The History and Functions of Central Labor Unions,* chap. I. Studies in History, Economics and Public Law, edited by the Faculty of Political Science of Columbia University, vol. XII, No. 1 (1899).

CARLTON, F. T. *The History and Problems of Organized Labor* (1911), chaps. II, III, IV, V.

——. "The Workingmen's Party of New York City" *Political Science Quarterly,* 22:401 (1907).

COMMONS, JOHN R. "Labor Organization and Labor Politics" (1827-1837), *Quarterly Journal of Economics,* 21:323 (1906-1907).

——. "American Shoe Makers" (1648-1895), *Quarterly Journal of Economics,* 24:39 (1909-1910).

DEIBLER, F. S. "The Amalgamated Wood Workers' International Union of America" (1912), *Bulletin of the University of Wisconsin,* No. 511, Economic and Political Science Series, vol. VII, No. 3.

Documentary History of American Industrial Society, vols. III to X.

ELY, RICHARD T. *The Labor Movement in America* (1905), chap. III.

HERRON, BELVA M. "The Progress of Labor Organization among Women," *Bulletin of the University of Illinois* (1905).

HILLQUIT, MORRIS. *History of Socialism in the United States* (1903).

——. *Recent Progress of the Socialist and Labor Movements in the United States* (1907).

KIRK, WILLIAM. *National Labor Federations in the United States,* Johns Hopkins University Studies in Historical and Political Science, Series XXIV, No. 9-10 (1906).

MCNEILL, GEO. E. (Ed.). *The Labor Movement* (1887), chap. IV, pp. 67-123.

A BRIEF HISTORICAL REVIEW 101

MITCHELL, JOHN. *Organized Labor* (1903), chaps. III, IV, VII, VIII, IX.

POPE, JESSE E. *The Clothing Industry in New York,* University of Missouri Studies, Social Science Series, vol. I (1905).

POWDERLY, T. V. *Thirty Years of Labor* (1899).

Report of the United States Industrial Commission, vol. XVII, pt. II (1901).

SWINTON, JOHN. *Striking for Life* (1894).

WOOLLEN, EVANS. "Labor Troubles Between 1834 and 1837," *Yale Review,* I :87 (1892-1893).

WRIGHT, CARROLL D. *Industrial Evolution of the United States* (1907), chaps. XVIII, XIX, XX.

The Knights of Labor

Constitution.
Addresses of General Master Workman.
Official Journal.
Preamble and Declaration of Principles.
Requisites of Knighthood.
Charges.
Instructions to Organizers.

ADAMS AND SUMNER. *Labor Problems,* pp. 219-221, 225-228.

BLISS, W. D. P. *Encyclopedia of Social Reform,* "Knights of Labor."

CARLTON, F. T. *The History and Problems of Organized Labor,* pp. 71-74.

CASSON, HERBERT NEWTON. *Organized Self-Help* (1901).

Documentary History of American Industrial Society, vol. X, pp. 19-35.

HILLQUIT, MORRIS. *History of Socialism in the United States,* pp. 289-294.

HOLLANDER AND BARNETT. *Studies in American Trade Unionism* (1912), chap. XII (Wm. Kirk), pp. 353-380.

Levasseur, E.   *The American Workman* (1900), pp. 196-203.

Martin, C. R.   *Official Historical Handbook of the Knights of Labor.*

McNeill, Geo. E. (Ed.).   *The Labor Movement,* chap. XV, pp. 397-428; chap. XIX, pp. 483-496.

Wright, Carroll D.   *The Industrial Evolution of the United States,* pp. 246-252.

——.   "The Knights of Labor," *Quarterly Journal of Economics,* 1 :137 (1887).

CHAPTER V

PRESENT UNION GROUPS

With the passing of the Knights of Labor as the central figure in the American labor world, we touch the borders of the contemporary situation. As we shall be treating it in some detail in this chapter, we need, in continuation of our history of development, only such bare outline as will make the broad features of the present situation clear.

Contemporaneously with the idealistic labor union movement of the Knights of Labor, there was a developing, vigorous, and independent trade union movement, represented by national trade unions, each with subordinate locals. These trade unions tended toward general aggregation also. But, as pure trade unionism is in general practical, businesslike, selfish, and nonidealistic, each trade union had its own special interests and purposes, not always in harmony with and not rarely antagonistic to the purposes and interests of other trade unions. Trade unionism showed itself, therefore, incompatible with strong, universal, centralized organization. It tended toward loose federation. A contest for supremacy between the form of organization represented by the Knights of Labor and that represented by the Federation, compatible with trade union organization, was inevitable. This contest became a reality in 1881, when the Federation of Organized Trades and Labor

Unions of the United States and Canada was formed, committed to the principles of trade autonomy, and industrial, as opposed to political and socialistic, ideals and activity. In 1886 the convention of this organization amalgamated with the convention of the independent trade unions to form the American Federation of Labor, which, strengthening gradually, has ever since occupied the central position in the American organized labor world.

In the success of the American Federation of Labor and the failure of the Knights of Labor have triumphed the principles of weak federative organization versus strong centralized organization, autonomous trade unionism versus labor unionism and industrial unionism, selfish trade interests versus altruistic labor brotherhood, and hard-headed business unionism versus idealistic radicalism. Yet it is to be noted that within the American Federation of Labor there have been developing steadily the principles of industrialism and idealistic radicalism, as evidenced by: (1) the admission of industrial unions, such as the International Union of the United Brewery Workmen and the United Mine Workers of America; (2) the creation of subfederative units, the departments; (3) the development of a broad social program; (4) reëntrance into politics; and (5) the growth of a considerable socialistic membership. Indeed, the American Federation of Labor, in taking the place of the Knights of Labor, has occupied a sort of middle ground between the adherents of the extreme trade union and the extreme industrial and labor union principles. It has satisfied neither. In fact, the last generation of the labor movement has been characterized by a three-fold development. On one side of the American Federation of Labor there has gone on a steady development of the independent, national trade union movement; on the other, a fitful and as yet unsuccessful movement toward a universal, centralized union of labor organizations to take the place of the moribund Knights of Labor,[1] and, finally, an independent trade union movement represented by a fluctuating body of some twenty national unions,[2] with perhaps a membership of 500,000, or about one-fourth of the American Federation of Labor.

In a descriptive account of American unionism, the Railway Brotherhoods deserve separate consideration, because railway unionism has been the stronghold of the idea and practice of independent, unaffiliated trade or craft unionism, and pure trade unionism has among these unions had its greatest success and clearest exemplification. Here we can see most clearly what *trade*

---

[1] The fitful movement toward centralized industrial organization, idealistic and radical in temperament, has not been kept alive by the Knights of Labor, which has dragged out to a useless old age. The torch was first carried forward by railroad workers. In 1893 the American Railway Union was organized and aimed to be the universal, centralized, industrial organization of railway workers. In 1894 it called a strike in sympathy with the Pullman workers, with Debs leading. This wrecked the union, although in 1895 it still claimed a membership of 150,000. (Bliss, *Encyclopedia of Social Reform.*) The movement was then carried on for a time by the Western Federation of Miners (recently renamed the International Union of Mine, Mill and Smelter Workers), an industrial organization of miners, mainly metal workers in the Rocky Mountains, organized about 1893 and with a strength of perhaps 40,000. The Western Labor Union was formed about 1898. Shortly after came the American Labor Union, which claimed at one time 135,000 members. The Industrial Workers of the World was organized in 1905.

[2] For a partial list of these unions see Reports of the New York Department of Labor, published annually since 1901.

unionism means in spirit and results. By this it is not meant that industrial unionism has not appeared in the railway field, nor that the railway unions have all remained aloof from the general labor federations, nor that they have consistently spurned federative relations with one another. On the contrary, several unions in the railway field are now affiliated with the American Federation of Labor, and the past shows notable attempts at industrial railway organization, such as Debs' American Railway Union of 1893-1894, and such attempts at federation as the United Order of Railway Employees in 1899, the Federation of American Railway Employees of 1898 and 1900, and the Cedar Rapids Agreement. But, in spite of all this, the group has deserved the characterization given above, for, in the main, the oldest, strongest, most successful of the railway unions, those commonly spoken of as the Brotherhoods, have maintained and still maintain their strict trade character and independence and their trade union ideals and methods. As representing the unalloyed trade union type, a brief general account of them in contrast with the American Federation of Labor is most enlightening to anyone who is trying to discover just what unionism is and signifies in contemporary society.

There are perhaps a score of unions whose work is exclusively or mainly concerned with railroading. In common usage, however, the term "railway unions" ordinarily covers only those engaged in moving freight and passengers or maintaining the roadway for this movement. Using the term thus, the principal unions of this group are the Grand International Brotherhood of Locomotive Engineers, the Order of Railway Conductors, the Brotherhood of Locomotive Firemen, the Brotherhood of Railway Trainmen, the Order of Railway Telegraphers, the Brotherhood of Railway Carmen, the Brotherhood of Railway Trackmen, the Switchmen's Union of North America, and the Brotherhood of Railway Bridgemen. As the term Railway Brotherhoods is ordinarily used, however, it refers especially to the engineers, conductors, firemen and trainmen. Sometimes the telegraphers are included, but rarely the carmen, maintenance of way employees, or bridgemen. What is said further in this connection is to be taken as referring to the Brotherhoods in the narrower sense of the term.

The organization of the Engineers is typical of the characteristic features of the Brotherhoods. The units of the international are the Grand International Division, which includes a bargaining and an insurance organization, and subordinate units—the Executive Committee, Merged General Standing Committee of Adjustment, Standing General Committee of Adjustment, Standing Local Committee of Adjustment, Subdivision or Lodge, and Legislative Board. Supreme authority rests with the Grand International Division, "which shall have exclusive jurisdiction over all subjects pertaining to the Brotherhood, and its enactments and decisions upon all questions are the supreme law of the Brotherhood, and all Divisions and members of the Order shall render true obedience thereto." [3] "It shall also have full power to order the expulsion of any member of any Division and in the event of such Division failing to comply with such order, the Grand Chief Engineer shall recall its charter." [4] Delegates to the Grand International Division

[3] Constitution of the Brotherhood of Locomotive Engineers (1912), p. 5, § 3.
[4] Ibid., p. 6, § 3.

shall continue as such until their successors are elected and shall be subject to the call of the Grand Chief Engineer to assemble at any time during their term of office." [5] The regular meetings of the Grand International Division are triennial. The Grand Chief Engineer "shall decide all controversies which may be appealed from the Divisions . . . and such decisions shall be final and conclusive until the . . . triennial meeting.[6] . . . Factional disputes or individual injustices are settled by the Grand Chief Engineer. His decision is final until the next Grand International Division convention.[7] Any subdivision willfully violating any rule or regulation of the Grand International Division of the Brotherhood of Locomotive Engineers may have its charter suspended by the Grand Chief Engineer until the next meeting of the Grand International Division.[8] The Grand Chief Engineer shall have full power to inflict such suspension on his judgment of violation.[9]

The standing General Committee of Adjustments exists on railway systems where two or more divisions are organized; the local Committee of Adjustments where there is only one. Members of the committee are elected triennially, one representative with one vote for each division.[10] General Committees of Adjustments may be merged on any system of roads into a Merged General Committee of Adjustments on two-thirds vote of mem-

[5] Constitution of the Brotherhood of Locomotive Engineers (1912), p. 13, § 23; p. 25, § 3.

[6] Ibid., p. 7, § 8.

[7] Ibid., p. 50, §§ 86, 87.

[8] Ibid., p. 43, § 66.

[9] Ibid., p. 77, § 38.

[10] Ibid., p. 63, §§ 1, 2.

bers affected.[11]   Where there are two or more roads or systems an Executive Committee of two members for each road is elected by the General Committees of Adjustments from their members.[12]   The Executive Committee's duty is to adjust all matters referred to it with the officers of the road or syndicate after the Grand Chief Engineer has exhausted all means.[13]

The mode of adjustment is as follows: (1) the grievance goes to the local or merged committee of adjustments which, with the local officials of the road or system, exhausts all efforts at settlement.[14] (2) The chairman of the general committee of adjustment may then be called upon to act with the local.[15] (3) The general committee of adjustments may next take it up and after exhausting every means for settlement with officials of the road may call on the grand chief engineer who must drop everything else and try all honorable means to settle the dispute.[16] Or (4) the executive committee may act, and failing to come to agreement with the officials of the system, may call on the grand chief engineer.[17] Action by the grand chief engineer stands as law until repealed by the committee or a two-thirds vote of the membership involved or by the grand international division.

Divisions in each state or territory by two-thirds vote may form a legislative board to convene at the capitol. This board shall have power to take action on all busi-

[11] *Ibid.*, p. 65, § 4.
[12] *Ibid.*, p. 66, § 6.
[13] *Ibid.*, p. 67, § 7.
[14] *Ibid.*, p. 70, § 13.
[15] *Ibid.*, p. 70, § 14.
[16] *Ibid.*, p. 71, § 16.
[17] *Ibid.*, p. 67, § 7.

ness of a political nature wherein the interests of the Brotherhood of Locomotive Engineers are involved.[18] Such legislative boards may elect representatives to act with representatives of other organizations in forming joint legislative boards with the purpose of securing legislation in the interest of labor.[19] The Locomotive Engineers' Mutual Life and Accident Insurance Association is a separate organization of elected delegates.

The functional type of the Brotherhood [20] is indicated by the following: "The interests of the employer and employee being coördinate, the aim of the organization will be coöperation and the cultivation of amicable relations with the employer and to submit questions of difference to arbitration when an agreement cannot otherwise.be reached, and to guarantee the fulfillment of every contract made in its name by the use of every power vested in it. . . . The purpose of this organization shall be to combine the interests of Locomotive Engineers, elevate their social, moral and intellectual standing; to guard their financial interests, and promote their general welfare." [21]

The Brotherhoods rest on the trade or craft basis, but structurally they tend to be more complicated than the ordinary union. Their discipline is stricter and their government more centralized. In general, it may be said of them that their membership is made up of relatively

[18] Constitution of the Brotherhood of Locomotive Engineers (1912), p. 84, § 1.

[19] *Ibid.*, p. 85, § 7.

[20] Compare with the Bridge and Structural Iron Workers and the I. W. W. Can these three be lumped together? Can there be unionism as such, considering these differences?

[21] Preamble of the Constitution of the Brotherhood of Locomotive Engineers.

skilled, specialized, and highly paid workers; that they are highly exclusive; that they are highly conservative in their attitude and method; that they refuse to join with other unions in coercing employers; that they stand for business methods, that is, collective bargaining with most elaborate machinery, trade agreements mutually helpful to employers and employees, sacredness of contract, and no strikes if it is possible to avoid them; that they have strong treasuries which make them powerful in dealing with employers; that they stand for a relatively high development of union insurance. As applied to the craft group but not to the class, their ideals are largely those of the Knights of Labor. Within the craft group they are highly altruistic and idealistic. In short, they exhibit no consciousness of a working class and working-class interest. They are middle-class in their viewpoint, exclusive, conservative, businesslike and self-reliant. They thus represent the essential characteristics of trade unionism as against industrial and labor unionism.

There can be little doubt that the Railroad Brotherhoods have succeeded in large measure. The causes of their success are: (1) the confining of the scope of the organization and activities of economic interest to the craft, where conditions, needs, and problems are common to all and common rules are possible; avoiding disruptive social, political, and religious considerations; (2) having as the basis of their membership a picked class of workers unusually intelligent and skilled; (3) the stressing of organization, and being able to organize the craft so thoroughly that there is no need to bother about undercutting or the establishment of the closed shop, in order that their rules may be standardized for the entire group; (4) having the membership under thorough control by highly centralized authority and by stressing insurance; (5) being moderate, conservative in their attitude and demands, businesslike in their action (respect for contract), backing all this up with a reserve fund that allows them to wait; and (6) being in an especially strong strategic position where they can paralyze the whole industrial process if their demands are not conceded.

Granting then the extreme success of the Brotherhoods, and admitting that they have practically solved the union problem in their field, can we assume that this type of union would work over the whole field of industry and solve the whole union problem? Does it furnish a way of getting the benefits of unionism for the workers most in need of them, and of doing away with the economic and social evils of unionism, in matters of efficiency, unhampered industrial development, universal opportunities to the workers, social order, and industrial peace?

The essential structural character of the American Federation of Labor is that of a loose federation of national and international unions, which under stress of circumstances has developed a great variety of structural units and relationships; in fact, everything found in the history of American unionism. It was organized on the principle of craft autonomy [22] with loose federation for the administration of intercraft union affairs, in the belief that the ends or functions of unionism could

[22] Constitution of the American Federation of Labor, art. II, § 2.

best be furthered by having a union for each craft [23] acting independently in its relations with employers, but cooperating with other craft unions in matters of more general concern. As I have said, the tendency has been to develop away from the strictly craft character of unions. Several industrial unions are now members. There has also been a tendency for the development of federative forms and activities. The primitive structure consisted of locals, internationals, and the Federation. The two other lines of development are (1) the allied trade union federation (i.e., the departments and subordinate councils) concerned with working conditions mainly; and (2) trades unions and trades union federations (i.e., the territorial units, city centrals and state federations) largely political and uplift in their activities. As at present constituted, the American Federation of Labor consists of the general organization and, roughly speaking, seven general types of subordinate organization, namely, the national or international, the local, the district council, the local council, the city central, the state federation, and the department.

The national or international union is a trade or industrial organization bringing under one jurisdiction the local unions connected with one craft or industry in the United States and Canada and, in some cases, in Mexico; e.g., the International Union of United Brewery Workmen and the Glass Bottle Blowers' Association of the United States and Canada. In the American Federation system the national or international is as yet the really strong and authoritative body. It is in no sense a federation of locals but on the contrary creates its local bodies. It exercises a really effective control over

[23] *Ibid.*, art. IX, § 2.

them through the influence of officers and organizers,
charter revocation and financial assistance, and, on the
other hand, it is practically independent of higher federal authority. The American Federation of Labor, so
far as its relation to the national and international is
concerned, is still what it was in its inception—a federation of independent unions. Each national union is
free to withdraw from the Federation, and it possesses
all the machinery for an independent existence. In
spite of the centralizing tendencies that have been going
on in the Federation, the autonomy of trade unions is
carefully safeguarded and every move in the direction
of centralization is made with the reservation that the
independence of the national union is in no way infringed
upon.

In general, the organic structure of the internationals
varies considerably. The simplest form is the national
or international craft or trade union with subordinate
locals. There is a tendency to develop, between the
local and the national,[24] local, district and state councils,
which are combinations of locals, and state legislative
boards, and executive committees. The industrial nationals, such as the United Mine Workers, tend to be
more complex. Subordinate to the national union is the
district council, an interstate body corresponding to the
competitive field, composed of representatives of the
locals of the district. It is responsible to the national
and concerns itself mainly with trade agreements and
working conditions. The subdistrict council is composed of delegates from the locals and is responsible to
the district council. The railway unions also tend to
develop a complicated system of legislative boards and

[24] *Cf.* the Carpenters and Joiners.

committees standing between the national or international union and the locals or lodges and divisions. These boards and committees are sometimes territorial in their organization and supervision. More generally, however, they are coterminous with railway systems and divisions. A clue to their character is found in the attempt to have a union body governing the affairs of men working under similar conditions and with common interests to protect, where common rules as to wages and conditions of employment can be enforced. Here the union organization is coterminous with each competitive area. That is to say, whenever there is a capitalistic organization or unit, there is the attempt to parallel it with a labor organization or unit, the significance of which will appear in the study of collective bargaining. This means that the union organization is constantly developing to fit needs. The tendency would be, when trusts enter the field, to parallel the complicated trust organization with union organization—the trial method again.

The general functions of the national or international union are varied. Through its officers, organizers and charters, it creates locals and intermediate subordinate organizations. Through charters and constitutional provisions it determines membership, and membership conditions and privileges; the functional character of locals; their officers and duties; discipline of members and general conduct of the affairs of the local. Through the constitution it determines the general economic policy and methods of the local—formulates the general working rules; sanctions or rejects local demands upon employers; determines the rule for negotiating agreements and for the calling and conduct of strikes. Through the constitution and officers it controls and administers the general finances and insurance funds of the union. It publishes the trade organ and is the general source of the trade propaganda material and publicity. In short, it is the economic unit of unionism *par excellence*. It must be borne in mind that in all this each national is practically a law to itself and great variation occurs.

The local union might be called the organic cell of unionism as represented by the American Federation of Labor. It is to be noted, though, that it no longer represents the genetic and vital force of unionism. As the organic basis of unionism, there are three general types of the local. First, there is the trade local composed of men all of the same trade or craft. It is the organic basis of trade or craft unionism. It is usually a small body—seven being most generally fixed as a minimum membership—but it may include all the men of a prosperous craft in a large city, when its membership may run into the hundreds or even thousands. Such are the Cigarmakers of Chicago and Typographical Union, No. 16, of Chicago. The majority of the locals in the American Federation of Labor are of this type. It appears in the Federation in two distinct organic relationships to the whole. In most cases it is the local representative of a national or international union. When no national or international of the trade exists, however, it is the policy of the American Federation of Labor to organize trade locals and affiliate them directly with itself. For example, in Chicago are the egg inspectors', hair spinners', flat janitors', and suspender workers' unions. Such unions are the federal trade locals. They are the nursery for national unions. When there is a sufficient number of them in any trade throughout the country, it is the policy of the Federation to issue a charter for an

international of the trade to which all these will hence-
forth be responsible.   Secondly, there is the industrial
local, the organic basis of industrial unionism.   This
local includes all the local workers in the crafts of a
given industry, as, for example, all the workers in a given
locality engaged in the brewery industry, including not
only the men engaged in the technical process of beer
brewing, but the engineers, firemen, teamsters, etc., employed in and about a brewery.   This type of local unit
is naturally larger than the trade or craft local, depend-
ing on the number, size, and pay roll of the particular
local firm in the industry.

The antagonistic character of these two types of locals
can readily be seen.   Where they exist side by side in
the same town they are bound to run afoul of each
other, for the industrial union claims the membership
and authority over some of the men in several definite
and organized crafts and also jurisdiction over some of
the work done by several different organized crafts.
This not only weakens the craft unions numerically and
financially, but it lessens the demand for their members,
the amount of work they can control, and their financial
strength, and prevents a great show of force and united
action on the part of all the members of a craft in time
of struggle with the employers.   The craft unions, therefore, have resolutely fought the industrial union in the
American Federation of Labor, but in the long run to
no purpose.   The American Federation of Labor has
threatened, suspended, expelled, but in the end has found
it necessary to compromise with the industrial principle.
As a contest between business group unionism and the
broader class principle, it is of significance in the interpretation of unionism.   The industrial unions in the

American Federation of Labor are in the minority, but
the tendency seems toward this basis of organization,
not so much perhaps through abandonment of the trade
or craft as the lowest organic local basis as through the
tendency of the craft units to amalgamate for certain
purposes into what are practically industrial local units,
like the councils in the building trades.

Thirdly, there is the labor local. This is an indiscriminate union of men of all trades and industries in a
given locality. It is the typical organic basis of the
Knights of Labor. A little consideration will show that
such a union is bound in general to be ineffective. The
men of different trades will inevitably differ on matters
of ideals and practical policy. A consistent policy vigor-
ously supported is, therefore, almost impossible to get
and to maintain. Hence, very largely, the impractical
idealism and practical failure of the Knights of Labor.
Such unions tend to degenerate into debating societies.
So much was this the case under the old régime that
many local unions now have rules definitely forbidding
the discussion in meetings of certain topics, such as
politics or religion. The labor local is tolerated in the
American Federation of Labor only where no other
kind of organization is possible. In small places, where
there are not enough workmen in crafts to organize on
the craft basis, labor locals are formed and attached
directly to the American Federation of Labor as "federal labor unions." It is the policy, however, to organize craft unions in such places as rapidly as a sufficient
nucleus is available.

These, the trade or craft, industrial and labor, are
the distinct general types of the local. There are, however, possible variations from these. In transportation

where the industry cannot be said to have a local habitation, the tendency is to make the smallest union unit coterminous with the smallest division of the transportation system. These "locals" are usually called lodges.[25] In some trades the local is not the smallest unit of trade organization, though it is the smallest unit specifically legislated for. Genetically, the union was a shop club; that is to say, a meeting of the workers in a shop or factory to consider the wages and conditions of employment in the particular shop, and in some unions shop clubs are still a recognized part of the union machinery. In the printers' trade it is known as the chapel.

Functionally, the local is the financial wellspring of unionism. It is practically the working tool of the national or international in matters of local import, mainly economic and social in character, excepting publicity and education for which the national takes care. It sees to it that the national union rules in regard to wages, hours and conditions of employment are observed; under constitutional regulations it grants working cards and regulates apprenticeship, and it may call and conduct local strikes; its officers and committees see as far as possible that the members are kept employed; in certain cases it negotiates agreements with employers; it sees that union label goods are patronized and unfair houses discouraged, that the union spirit is kept alive through the display of buttons and insignia.[26] Its officers are

[25] The Machinists' Union and some other organizations call their local unions "lodges."

[26] See Constitution, Chicago Photo Engravers, No. 5, art. II; Book of Laws of International Typographical Union, pp. 48, 51, 55, 79; Constitution of Machinists, pp. 26, 27, 30, 35, 36, 38, 39, 40, 41.

supposed to exert an educative and salutary influence over its members.

The local, looked at as the fundamental and essential trade union unit, is the spontaneous outcome of the problems that face the rank and file of the workers and the conditions under which they work. Historically it is thus the source of ideals and policies and of authority, that is, genetically and theoretically speaking, unionism is a spontaneous and democratic creation. Practically, at the present time, this is not altogether true. While, historically speaking, the local is the parent body and the union fabric or organization is the result of integration, currently the growth of unionism is for the most part just the other way—from above downward. The internationals, in general, and the American Federation of Labor have each their paid organizers whose business is to go about the country among unorganized workers, preach to them the advantages of unionism, get them to apply for a charter, organize them and teach them to run their union local. The local thus organized is a product of the international or national, chartered by it, largely directed by it, bound to obey it in matters of policy and method or suffer revocation of charter, loss of counsel and financial support in time of trouble—all of which ordinarily means speedy dissolution. In spite of this systematic development of unionism, there is still a good deal of spontaneous genesis. Strikes among the unorganized furnish a prime occasion for this formation. When strikes occur and a temporary organization has been spontaneously effected, organizers, local or general, hasten to the place and endeavor to make the organization effective and permanent. Nevertheless, a very large proportion of unions thus generated and affiliated die when the immediate occasion has passed. Men have not yet acquired the spirit of prolonged self-sacrifice and coöperation, and effective local leaders are not always found.

Locally and economically, organization on distinct craft or trade lines is found by experience to have two great defects or weaknesses. First, the separate craft unions of a single industry or of closely allied industries come constantly into conflict over jurisdiction and membership. The result is jurisdictional disputes in which one union may tie up the whole job, throwing out of employment all others, with injustice to employers and in some cases the playing off of union against union by employers. Second, the separate craft union, dealing separately with the employer of all, is relatively weak. The consequence is the tendency of local craft unions in the same or allied industries to form organizations to govern interrelations and deal for all with employers. These are the local or district councils such as are found in the building, printing, and metal trades. Such councils are delegate bodies from the locals, the delegates being ordinarily local officers. Their functions are to determine local jurisdiction and to discipline local unions for violations; to act for the locals in making local agreements as to wages and conditions of work with employers; to act together in disciplining employers by strike or otherwise; to assist employers in securing and maintaining monopoly of the field.

Effective machinery for the purpose of the building trades' council exists in the board of business agents, who keep watch for each other of violations of union rules, formulate and present demands, etc.

Such local councils have tended to amalgamate into

state and national councils to deal with the interests of
allied trades country-wide. There is a distinct need for
them, since employers thus organize, and if unionism is
to maintain its power and to combat employers successfully, organization must meet organization. For this reason and the even more important purpose of prevention
and settlement of jurisdictional disputes, the American
Federation of Labor entered upon the logical and systematic organization of federal units of allied trades—the
Departments [27]—thus taking a tentative step toward industrial organization. The Departments chartered by
the Federation of Labor are federations of allied nationals and internationals and serve as a sort of clearing
house for difficulties arising between them. Membership
in the department is shifting and overlapping—that is to
say, a national union may be affiliated with more than
one department, as in the case of the machinists, boiler
makers, etc., who are affiliated with the Metal Trades
Department, and also with the Railroad Employees' Department. The plan of organization varies; each Department, however, organizes federated trades locals.
The annual conventions of the Departments are bodies
of delegates from the internationals.

The Building Trades Department [28] includes nationals
or internationals of the asbestos workers, bridge and
structural iron workers, carpenters,[29] cement workers,[30]

[27] Constitution, American Federation of Labor, art. XV; and
Report of Proceedings, 30th Annual Convention, American
Federation of Labor, pp. 54, 57.

[28] Constitution, Building Trades Department, pp. 3, 4, 9-10,
12-13, 20.

[29] Report of the Proceedings, American Federation of Labor
(1915), pp. 122, 125, 167.

[30] *Ibid.*, p. 166.

electrical workers, elevator constructors, steam engineers, granite cutters, hodcarriers, lathers, machinists, marble workers, sheet metal workers, metal workers, painters, decorators and paper hangers, plasterers, plumbers, roofers, stone cutters, etc. From nationals and internationals one delegate for each 4,000 members is sent to the convention.

The Department's functions are in the main the formation of local organizations; the conferring of such power and authority upon the locals as may advance the interest and welfare of the building industry; the adjustment of trade disputes and the creation of harmonious feeling between employers and employees; and securing recognition of trade jurisdiction. The Department aims to guarantee to the various branches of the building industry control of such work as rightfully belongs to them and to which they are justly entitled. The structure of the Department includes the nationals, local trades councils, and state trades councils organized in states where three or more locals exist.

The Railway Employees Department includes the nationals or internationals of the blacksmiths, railway clerks, switchmen, maintenance of way employees, steamfitters, railway telegraphers, boilermakers, iron shipbuilders and helpers, freight handlers, etc. "The object of this department shall be to enhance the welfare of the railroad employees, to aid in more closely organizing all such employees, to encourage such organizations to affiliate with the American Federation of Labor, to further the interests of employees by legislation and to take such action as may be mutually agreed upon to protect the interests of all concerned, and to recognize the jus-

tice and necessity of well-defined jurisdiction. It shall
be the aim to use its good offices in assisting affiliated
national and international organizations in adjusting any
dispute arising over a question of jurisdiction." The department issues charters to system federations, responsible to the Department, composed of one delegate from
each trade or calling in the system affiliated with the
American Federation of Labor. Each system federation may organize at each division point on the system
local boards, responsible to the system federation, composed of one member for each organization at that
point.[31] "Each organization shall be entitled to one delegate from each system federation" to represent it in the
convention.[32]

The Metal Trades Department membership includes
the nationals or internationals of the sheet metal workers, blacksmiths, boilermakers, iron ship builders, electrical workers, steam engineers, foundry workers, machinists, molders, metal polishers, pattern makers, stove
molders, etc. The nationals or internationals are entitled to one delegate for each 4,000 members in the Department convention. Each local council is also entitled
to one. The functions of the Department are the formation of local councils and the conferring of such power
upon them as will advance the interests and welfare of
the industry; the adjustment of trade disputes, the establishment of more harmonious relations with employers
and the adjustment of jurisdictional disputes.

The Mining Department includes the United Mine

[31] Department Leaflet, D. W. Roderick, Secretary-Treasurer.
[32] Constitution, Railway Employees Department, American
Federation of Labor (1912), § 5.

Workers, the Western Federation of Miners,[33] the Amalgamated Association of Iron, Steel and Tin Workers, the International Association of Machinists and the International Brotherhood of Steam Shovel and Dredgemen. The delegates to the annual convention are the delegates representing their respective organizations in the American Federation of Labor convention. Each delegate has one vote, but a majority vote of each delegation is required to carry any proposition. The object of the department is the greater unity of all its workers and the furtherance of the principle that "an injury to one is the concern of all." [34]

The Union Label Trades Department includes all national and international unions using labels, cards, or buttons upon the product. Its functions are to promote the demand for label products and union labor; to investigate, devise and recommend the advertisement of label products; to educate unions and the public upon the economic, social and moral uplift furthered by the trade union movement; to further the general welfare of affiliated organizations and to aid in the work of organization. It organizes local departments.

In spite of all its selfishness of purpose and narrow exclusiveness, trade or craft unionism inevitably develops a very broadening spirit of mutuality among the workers. The unionists come to feel their economic oneness and interdependence as a class. With the dawning of this consciousness of class character and class interest comes the knowledge that there are many things which

[33] The Western Federation of Miners is now known as the "International Union of Mine, Mill and Smelter Workers."

[34] Constitution of the Mining Department, §§ 2, 4.

the workers as a whole need that cannot be attained by union for dealing merely with the employer. Common needs which can be satisfied only through universal union for social and political and economic betterment are recognized. The recognition of these needs has bred in the American Federation of Labor general federative units of a functional character. These are, leaving aside the Federation itself, the city central and the state federation.[35] The functions of these organizations are mainly political, legislative and social—active political effort, securing laws in favor of the workers, furthering the use of the label, carrying out the boycott, mediation between unions and between unions and employers, carrying aid and sympathy, organizing and working for social uplift.

The city central labor union is a body composed of delegates, one for each hundred members, from the locals of the American Federation of Labor in a given city.[36]

[35] *See* Report of the Proceedings of the Thirty-fifth Annual Convention of the American Federation of Labor (1915), pp. 61-62.

[36] *See* chap. 11, p 39, note 4.

Some idea of the multiplicity of interests of a city central may be gained from the following topics which among other things obtruded themselves into the discussion at one of the ordinary meetings of the Chicago Federation of Labor: the function and control of public opinion; the character of financiers; the inequality of justice as between employers and workers (this apropos of the indictment of about forty labor leaders for extortion, wrecking of property and slugging); enforcement of employment of union men; fire protection—the two-platoon system; policy of national preparedness; public ownership of utilities; protection against abuses by public

The state federation is an organization of the American Federation of Labor union bodies or units of a given state. It is made up of delegates from locals, city centrals and various councils. The constitution of the Illinois State Federation reads: "The object of this federation shall be the securing of legislation in the interests of organized labor, to promote the use of the union label and the purchase of union label goods, to make more effective legally declared boycotts and, in general, to promote the work of labor organizations."[37] It investigates strikes and lockouts and gives information about them and issues

utility corporations; the economic and social desirability of blocking the proposed sale of the Automatic Telephone Company to the Bell Company; unemployment; vice; corruption of city politics; use of charitable contributions by corporations to prevent opposition to jobbery by women's organizations; government subsidized military training in schools; public licenses for operators of moving picture machines; enforcement of purchase of union-made goods; the right of labor organizations; the recall of state officials; the duty of making charitable contributions at home instead of for the war sufferers in Europe; financial assistance to workers in various sections of the country; government ownership of mines in Arizona; the initiative and referendum; vested rights; the case of Scott Nearing and the pernicious economic influence of universities; the Chicago school situation; the desirability of a city ordinance to allow anyone arrested for petty crimes to be released on his own recognizance until the day of trial; inequality of law in this connection, i.e., the poor man goes to jail; the municipal court act; the political power of unionism; picketing—the unfairness of the law; boycotts and unfair lists; legal theory—human versus property rights—the concept of labor as a commodity, contempt of court; the antitrust laws and their interpretation; methods of securing local, state, and national labor legislation.

[37] Constitution of Illinois State Federation of Labor, art. 2.

appeals.[38] Every organization of one hundred or less shall be entitled to one delegate and one additional for every one hundred members or major fraction thereof. All central bodies may send five.[39]

Crowning and uniting this complexity of organic units, industrial and territorial, is the American Federation of Labor itself, the universal industrial and territorial unit. Its founders declared themselves "in favor of the formation of a thorough federation, embracing every trade and labor organization in America, organized under the trade union system." [40] Its organic character in this narrower sense of the word is quite simple. It consists of a delegate legislative body—the convention—which meets annually for a two weeks' session, and the officers of this body, who hold over between conventions, and who in their several capacities, organized as an executive committee or cabinet, carry on the executive and legislative work of the Federation. In addition, the convention usually appoints a number of special committees, which act between sessions in the capacity of commissioners of inquiry and as judicial bodies

Sovereignty in the American Federation of Labor resides finally in the convention, to which national unions, city centrals, state federations, federal labor unions and local federal unions send delegates as follows: From national and international unions for less than 4,000 members, 1 delegate; 4,000 or more, 2 delegates; 8,000 or more, 3 delegates; 16,000 or more, 4 delegates; 32,000 or more, 5 delegates, and so on; from central bodies,

[38] Constitution of Illinois State Federation of Labor, art. 2, p. 11.   [39] Ibid., p. 3.
[40] Preamble of the Constitution of the American Federation of Labor.

state federations, federal labor unions and local unions having no national or international union, one delegate.[41] In addition, the following fraternal bodies are now represented: The British Trades Union Congress, The Canadian Trades and Labor Congress, The Woman's International Union Label League, the National Woman's Trade Union League of America, the Federal Council of the Churches of Christ in America and the Farmers' National Congress. All are entitled to one delegate with the exception of the British Trades Union Congress and the Federal Council of the Churches of Christ, which send two.[42]

The number of delegates sent by the national and international unions ranges from one to eight. The number of delegates actually sent by these organizations is not in strict proportion to the membership, but legally each delegation is entitled to cast a number of votes in this proportion. The United Mine Workers, sending 8 delegates in 1915, were entitled to 3,116 votes; the United Brotherhood of Carpenters and Joiners, sending 7, to 1,956; the Brotherhood of Painters, Decorators and Paperhangers, sending 6, to 753 votes; each delegate voting his proportional number. This gives the control of the convention and its policies absolutely into the hands of the nationals and internationals and to the few big organizations, at that, no federal body having more than one vote. On practically all ordinary questions, however, voting is by a show of hands—a compromise which satisfies the smaller and federal organizations, as

[41] Constitution of the American Federation of Labor, art. IV, § 1.

[42] Report of the Proceedings of the Thirty-fifth Annual Convention of the American Federation of Labor, p. xv.

This simplified schematic representation of the organization of the American Federation of Labor is artificially
abstract to make it possible to grasp the main outlines of
the scheme. There are many relations not clearly shown
even by the constitutions, and many variations as between
national or international unions because of growth by the
trial method, all impossible to indicate here. There are,
however, to be found on the chart:

    1. The fundamental structure of craft local, national and
Federation. Superimposed on this is (1), a trades union,
and (2), an allied trade development.

    2. Local industrial unions united into national industrial
unions.

    3. The territorial units—city federations united into
state federations.

    4. Locals directly affiliated with the Federation not suf-
ficient in number to form nationals.

    5. Federal locals, i.e., labor unions in small places where
there are too few workers to form craft locals.

Locals of the following unions are represented thus:

X   United Association of Plumbers and Steamfitters of
      the United States and Canada.

O   United Brotherhood of Carpenters and Joiners of
      America.

▢   International Hodcarriers, Building **and Common**
      Laborers' Union of America.

▯   International Brotherhood of Blacksmiths.

⊖   International Typographical Union.

⊟   Switchmen's Union of North America.

▽   Suspender Workers' Local Trade Union.

⌂   United Mine Workers of America.

△   Federal Labor Union.

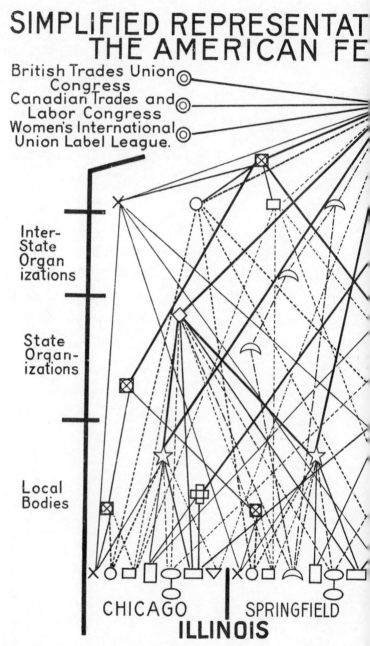

SIMPLIFIED REPRESENTAT
THE AMERICAN FE

British Trades Union
Congress
Canadian Trades and
Labor Congress
Women's International
Union Label League.

Inter-
State
Organ
izations

State
Organ-
izations

Local
Bodies

CHICAGO   SPRINGFIELD

ILLINOIS

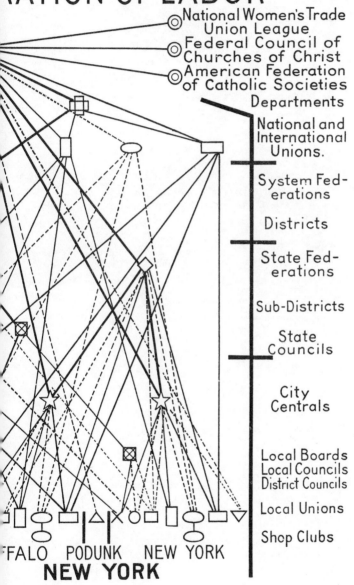

National Women's Trade
Union League

Federal Council of
Churches of Christ

American Federation
of Catholic Societies

Departments

National and
International
Unions.

System Fed-
erations

Districts

State Fed-
erations

Sub-Districts

State
Councils

City
Centrals

Local Boards
Local Councils
District Councils

Local Unions

Shop Clubs

FALO   PODUNK   NEW YORK

NEW YORK

the equal vote of states in the Senate satisfies the smaller
states of the Union. The Convention is, in the main, a
body of officers of the unions and subordinate federations—a body, in other words, of professional unionists.
Its composition, at least as to leaders, does not vary
much from year to year.

The objects of the general federal unit are: organization and federation; settlement of jurisdictional disputes; maintenance of peace and harmony among the
unions; enforcement of unitary organization; maintenance of craft autonomy; encouragement of the labor
press and the union label; securing labor's rights by
legislative and political action; education and publicity,
and giving financial and moral assistance in strikes. The
president, eight vice-presidents, a treasurer and a secretary constitute the executive council. This council,
which is practically continuous, is the really powerful
initiatory and authoritative body of the Federation.
Its duties are to watch and initiate legislation, organize
unions, report boycotts for indorsement, unify organizations, send out speakers, help settle jurisdictional disputes, assist federal unions, and grant and revoke charters when ordered by the convention.[43]

The actual strength of the American Federation of
Labor stated in terms of its units and individual membership is about as follows:[44] national and international
unions, 111; local unions, 21,711; local trade and federal
labor unions, 705; city central bodies, 717; state federa-

[43] Constitution of the American Federation of Labor, art.
IX, §§ 1-10.
[44] Report of the Proceedings of the Annual Convention of
the American Federation of Labor for 1916, p. 47.

tions, 45; departments, 5; local department councils, 417; total membership for 1916, 2,072,702.

The American Federation of Labor has both succeeded and failed. The causes of its success may be explained largely by its supremely adaptable and catholic character, made possible by its nontheoretical, opportunistic, trial method and ideals, and its loose organization. It is thus sufficiently broad and elastic to have a place within itself for every form and type of organization—structurally and functionally—that has arisen and proved itself effective in the history of American unionism. It has found a place and function within itself for the trade union, the trades union (city central and state federation), the labor union, the industrial union, and the various transitional forms; for business unionism, uplift unionism, radical or revolutionary unionism and predatory unionism. It is loosely enough organized to allow of every variation of centralization and discipline which the particular needs and conditions warrant. For example, there is centralization and strong discipline of national unions where conditions demand them and decentralization and weak discipline of federal forms where needs and jealousies exist. It is theoretically and organically elastic enough to allow scope to the principle of change and growth, and thus to the adoption and creation of new forms and the assumption of new functions as developing conditions demand them, such as system federations, departments, and its political program. It thus reflects in a remarkable way the changing conditions, needs, problems, and methods of the workers within the field of its operation. Within this field it reflects pretty accurately—subject of course to the law of retardation —the character of capitalistic organization, that is, the

degree of craft-wise and industrial-wise business organization and the idealism and materialism, the radicalism
and conservatism, the mutuality and selfishness, of the
workers. In short, it pretty accurately reflects within
the field of its operation the degree of unity, and of
community of spirit, the extent of common problems,
ideals and conditions of the workers. It has always
made everything else secondary to the supreme need of
the workers in terms of immediate results, or, as Mr.
Gompers says, "more, more, more, now," in the form
of higher wages, shorter hours, better working conditions here and now. In other words, its prime aim is
"to deliver the goods." And finally, it has had extraordinary fortune in the continuity and character of its
leadership. Mr. Gompers has been at the helm since
1886, except for one year, 1894; it has had, therefore, a
continuous policy and has been delivered from the struggle for leadership. In short, the American Federation
of Labor is an organization structurally and functionally of such a character that, while guaranteeing to each
craft autonomy in trade affairs, it can unite them on
economic grounds, smooth out their differences, and
gradually *educate* them to closer relationship.

But *has* the American Federation of Labor succeeded?
(1) Though it claims to represent the working class and
aims at universal organization, yet in more than thirty
years it has succeeded in organizing less than ten
per cent of the workers. (2) It lacks the adherence of
some of the strongest and most successful unions, such
as the Railway Brotherhoods. (3) It has found itself
unable to make headway or maintain its position in great
trust-controlled industries. (4) It has proved unequal to
its adversary in its struggle against strong employers'

associations. (5) It has failed generally to organize and help the unskilled workers. (6) It has not been able to prevent altogether predatory combinations between employers and unions to the detriment of other organized workers. (7) It has failed thus far to solve the problem of jurisdictional disputes involving destruction alike of the welfare of the workers, the employers, and the public. (8) It has failed to secure unanimity and general support of its broad welfare policies, for example, the use of union labeled goods. (9) It seems impotent against scientific management and advanced management with its progressive specialization and destruction of the very essence of the craft foundation of unionism.

After having considered the general character of the American Federation of Labor and reviewed its successes and failures, can we say that it presents the key to the solution of the union problem? Does it furnish a means of getting the benefits of unionism for the workers most in need of them, and of solving the problems of efficiency, unhampered industrial development, universal opportunity to the workers, social order and industrial peace? In so far as it has failed in this connection, what are the prime causes of its failure? There appear to be two which stand out clearly: First, under the present system of capitalistic enterprise based on machine industry, no common standards of right, rights, and justice exist which can be appealed to for securing working class betterment. Therefore, the general betterment of the workers' condition through unionism requires a general organization of the workers superior in power to the employers. Second, no working class power superior to the employers can be developed in pursuit of the ideal of immediate results secured by bargaining, because under the capitalistic system immediate betterment can be secured by the workers through bargaining only by control and manipulation of the labor supply. This means that the pursuit of the ideal must immediately develop the selfish and monopolistic group feeling. This effectually bars out the attainment of working class solidarity and power, for it causes the stronger unions to hold aloof, pits the organized against the unorganized, and causes a constant desertion of the brains of the movement to the employers. In short, if the failure of the American Federation of Labor could be simmered down to a single phrase, it would be "lack of practical idealism." It is another question whether this idealism —the unselfish class spirit—can be developed under present conditions where the mass of the workers are barred out from taking a broad and long-time view of life's affairs by the cold fact that, as things are, their immediate conditions of life do depend upon the labor supply and they can have absolutely no guarantee of the future.

BIBLIOGRAPHY

Constitution, Statutes and Agreements: Brotherhood of Locomotive Engineers, the Brotherhood of Locomotive Firemen and Enginemen, the Order of Railway Conductors, and the Brotherhood of Railway Trainmen.

Journals: Locomotive Engineers' Journal, Locomotive Firemen and Enginemen's Magazine, The Railway Conductor, and the Railway Trainman.

BLISS. *Encyclopedia of Social Reform,* "Railway Brotherhoods."

Bulletin of the U. S. Bureau of Labor, No. 98 (1912):
"Mediation and Arbitration of Railway Labor Disputes
in the United States," by C. P. Neill, pp. 1-63.

CEASE, D. L. "Organization of Railway Employees," *Outlook,* 86:503 (1907).

CUNNINGHAM, E. J. "Two Views of the Railroad Question: Brotherhoods and Efficiency," *Atlantic Monthly,*
104:289-302 (1909).

FRICK, F. L. *The Life of Railway Men.*

HOLLANDER AND BARNETT, *Studies in American Trade
Unionism,* chap. XI, "The Beneficiary Features of the
Railway Unions," (J. B. Kennedy).

McNEILL, GEO. E. *The Labor Movement,* chap. XII,
"The Rise of Railroad Organization," (P. M. Arthur).

*Report of the Board of Arbitration—in re—*Eastern Railroads and the Locomotive Engineers, 1912.

Report of the U. S. Industrial Commission, vol. XVII, pp.
821-838, 847, 852-857 (1901).

Constitutions: The American Federation of Labor, Departments, State Federations of Labor, City Centrals, National and International unions, Local and District councils, etc., National Woman's Trade Union League,
Woman's International Union Label League and Trades
Union Auxiliary, Etc.

Convention Proceedings: Reports of Proceedings of Annual Conventions of the American Federation of Labor,
Departments, Nationals and Internationals, State Federations, and affiliated bodies.

Journals: The American Federationist, Weekly News Letter, the journals of the Nationals and Internationals.

Official Directories.

General Propaganda Leaflets:
The A. F. of L., A Few of Its Declarations.
The A. F. of L., Aims and Objects.

The A. F. of L. Endeavors to Unite All Classes of Wage-workers.

The American Labor Movement, Its Make-up, Achievements and Aspirations. Gompers, Samuel.

The Eight-hour Workday. Gompers, Samuel.

The Economic and Social Importance of the Eight-hour Movement. Gunton, Geo., Eight-hour Series, No. 2.

The Eight-hour Primer, The Fact, Theory and the Argument. McNeill, Geo. E., Eight-hour Series, No. 1 (1899).

Hail to Labor.

Has the Nonunionist a Right to Work How, When, and Where He Pleases? Foster, Frank K. (1904).

History and Philosophy of the Eight-hour Movement. Danryid, Lemuel, Eight-hour Series, No. 3.

How to Form a Trade Union or Federal Labor Union.

Industrial Unionism in Its Relation to Trade Unionism, Rochester Convention (1912).

Legal Rights of Workingmen, Argument Before the Judiciary Committee of the House of Representatives, 59th Cong. (1906). Spelling, Thos. C.

Men of Labor, Lovers of Human Liberty.

Open Shop Editorials. Gompers, Samuel.

Organized Labor, Its Struggles, Its Enemies, and Its Fool Friends.

Philosophy of Trade Unionism. Lum, Dyer D. (1892).

The Safety of the Future Lies in Organized Labor. Lloyd, Henry D. (1893).

St. Louis Exposition, Exhibit of the American Federation of Labor (1904).

Some Reasons for Chinese Exclusion.

Textbook of Labor's Political Demands. The Executive Council of the A. F. of L. (1906).

The Union Label, Its History and Aims, Prize Essays.

Wageworkers of America Unite. The Executive Council and Gompers, Samuel.

Why Central Labor Unions Should Be a Part of the A. F. of L.

Why We Unite.

ADAMS AND SUMNER. *Labor Problems*, pp. 219-223.

ALDRICH, MORTON A. "The American Federation of Labor," *American Economic Association, Economic Studies*, vol. 3, pp. 213-266 (1898).

BLISS. *Encyclopedia of Social Reform*, "The American Federation of Labor."

BURKE, W. M. *The History and Functions of Central Labor Unions.*

CARLTON, F. T. *The History and Problems of Organized Labor*, pp. 74-82.

"Gompers, the Man Between the Two Millstones," *Current Literature*, 48:33 (1910).

HOLLANDER AND BARNETT. *Studies in American Trade Unionism*, chap. XII. The Knights of Labor and the American Federation of Labor, Wm. Kirk.

KIRK, WM. *National Labor Federations in the United States.*

MITCHELL, JOHN. *Organized Labor*, chap. X, "The Constitution of the American Trade Union," and XLVI, "Labor Federation in the United States."

WOLMAN, LEO. "Extent of Labor Organization in the United States," *Quarterly Journal of Economics*, XXX, p. 486 (1916).

WEYL, W. E. "Samuel Gompers, Representative of American Labor," *Review of Reviews*, 31:44-47 (1905).

CHAPTER VI

THE INDUSTRIAL WORKERS OF THE WORLD AND
REVOLUTIONARY UNIONISM

The American public has been frightened by the impressionist school of reporters and magazine writers into vital misconception and tremendous overestimate of the power and significance of the Industrial Workers of the World. This is the one outstanding fact revealed by the eighth annual convention of that organization held in Chicago late in September, 1913.

The first significant fact revealed by this convention, and by the whole history of the I. W. W. as well, is that this body, which claims as its mission the organization of the whole working class for the overthrow of capitalism, is pathetically weak in effective membership and has failed utterly in its efforts to attach to itself permanently a considerable body of men representative of any section of American workers.

In spite of eight years of organizing effort and unparalleled advertisement, the official roll of the convention indicated that its present paid-up membership[1] entitled to representation does not much exceed 14,000 men, while the actual constitutional representation on the convention floor was probably less than half that number. Nor was there anything to make it appear that this was regarded by the leaders or members as an exceptional or disappointing showing. The fact is, impossible as it

[1] November, 1913.

may seem to those who have read the recent outpouring
of alarmist literature on the subject, that this number
probably comes near to representing the maximum, permanent, dues-paying membership at any time connected
with the organization. For notwithstanding extravagant
statements made in the past and a present claim of an
enrollment approximating 100,000,[2] it is admitted by the
highest official of the Industrial Workers that up to the
time of the Lawrence strike the membership never
reached 10,000, the highest yearly average being but
6,000; and the convention debates indicated clearly that
the great bulk of those enrolled during that strike and
in the succeeding period of unusual agitation and activity have retained no lasting connection with the organization. It was shown that the effective force of the
union at Lawrence is already spent.[3] The representa-

[2] The actual membership of the I. W. W. is unknown even
to the officials. The records of the general office show an
average paid-up membership for the year of 14,310. It is estimated that local and national bodies have an additional dues-
paying membership of 25,000 on which no per capita tax has
been paid to the general organization, and that there is, besides, a nominal non-dues-paying enrollment of from 50,000 to
60,000. The truth seems to be that 100,000 or more men *have
had* I. W. W. dues cards in their possession during the past
five years. How much of this outlying membership fringe
is now bona fide it is impossible to estimate. Some part of it
represents members out of work or on strike and therefore
temporarily unable to pay dues. Even this portion, however, is
organically ineffective and is constantly dropping out. We
seem justified, therefore, in taking the actual paid-up membership as the nearest approximation to the permanent effective
strength of the organization.

[3] The membership now claimed at Lawrence is 700. After
the strike it was said to be 14,000.

tives of the whole textile industry, indeed, cast but 31 votes in the convention, developing the fact that the total paid-up membership in this line of work probably does not now exceed 1,600,[4] and a communication was received from one of the local unions still remaining at Lawrence complaining of the methods of the organization and threatening adhesion to the American Federation of Labor. At Akron, again, where during the rubber strike early this year apparently more than 6,000 were added to the roll, the convention vote cast indicated a present membership of 150 or thereabouts, and statements on the floor revealed the fact that most of those who joined at the time of the strike did not retain official connection with the union long enough to pay the second assessment of dues.[5]

Evidence to the same general effect might be multiplied almost indefinitely. Everywhere the history of the organization has shown this same inability to maintain a stable and growing membership. There are without doubt reasons for this fact apart from the special character and methods of the I. W. W., but these are beside the point. The point is that by reason of lack of sufficient membership this body is and seems destined to be utterly inadequate to the tasks which it has set itself to accomplish. It aims to educate and organize the working class and claims to have discovered the effective ideals and organic basis to this end, but during eight years of strenuous effort it has succeeded in reaching and hold-

[4] By constitutional provision one vote is allowed in the convention for every 50 members or major fraction thereof.

[5] At the time of the strike the local purchased 11,000 dues stamps from the general office. A membership of 2,000 is claimed at present.

ing less than one in 2,000 of the workers of this country alone. Its first great organic tasks, if it is to attain this end, are the displacement of the American Federation of Labor, the railway brotherhoods, and the Socialist party, but it has not been able to organize effectively for these purposes a body of men equal to one per cent of the membership of the American Federation alone, or to one-sixtieth of those who act with the Socialist party; it proposes a united and successful direct industrial assault upon capitalism, but it has not thus far drawn to itself on this basis a permanent enrollment equal in number to the employees of many a single capitalist enterprise. Plainly no further proof is needed that those who are attached to the present order have nothing now to fear from I. W. W.-ism judged from the standpoint of mere numbers and power of appeal to the great body of the working class.

But numerical weakness is not after all the chief handicap of the I. W. W. in its struggle for positive achievement. This convention secondly brought into clearest relief the fact that this feeble body is in a state of organic chaos as the result of apparently irreconcilable internal conflict, and the history of the organization makes it appear that this state of affairs is chronic and inevitable. The conflict, the keynote of I. W. W. history, was waged in the present convention under the guise of centralization versus decentralization. It is at present, objectively, a contest virtually between the East and the West. The so-called decentralizers, mainly westerners, sought in the convention by every conceivable means to cut down the power and authority of the central governing body. This central authority already had been reduced almost to a shadow. As the result of previous

phases of the contest the office of general president had
been abolished; the executive board had been placed under control of the general referendum which could be
initiated at any time and on all subjects by ten local
unions in three different industries, while its efficiency
had been minimized by inadequate financial support; and
the locals had become to all intents and purposes autonomous bodies.   But all this has brought no permanent
satisfaction to the decentralizing faction.   Its ultimate
ideal apparently is, and has been from the beginning, not
"one big union" but a loosely federated body of completely autonomous units, each free to act in time and in
manner as its fancy dictates, subject to no central or
constitutional guidance or restraint—in short, a body
of local units with purely voluntary relationships governed in time, character, and extent of coöperation by
sentiment only.

Actuated by this ideal, the decentralizers conducted in
the recent convention a twelve days' assault upon what
remained of central power.   They attempted to abolish
the general executive board; to paralyze the general organization by minimizing its financial support; to abolish
the convention and provide for legislation by means of
the general referendum only; to place the official organizers under the direct control of the rank and file; to reduce the general officers to the position of mere clerks,
functioning only as corresponding intermediaries between
the local organizations; and by other means to give to
each of these local bodies complete autonomy in matters
of organization, policy, action, and financial control.   It
matters little that at this particular convention the centralizing faction, mainly by virtue of superior parlia-
mentary tactics, succeeded in staving off the attacks of

its opponents and in saving, at least until the matter goes
to referendum, the present form of the organization.
The significant facts are that the same factional strife
has existed from the moment when the I. W. W. was
launched; and that it apparently is bound to exist as long
as the organization lasts; that the decentralizing forces,
though often defeated formally, have in practice succeeded and seem bound to continue to succeed in working their will inside the organization, with the inevitable
result of disintegration and organic chaos.   Evidence
of this is everywhere apparent.   During the past year
ninety-nine locals, ignored and uncared for, went out of
existence entirely; in New York the relatively strong
local assembly is working at cross-purposes with the central organization and successfully defying its power; in
the West, locals are being formed and managed on extra-
constitutional lines; throughout this part of the country
members are being expelled by one local and straight-
way admitted by another; so diverse are the local ideals
and so uncertain the means of intercommunication that
in practice it has been found generally impossible to get
ten locals into the requisite harmony to initiate a referendum; sabotage is being openly practiced by the local
membership against the organization itself and has recently resulted in the suspension of one of its two official
organs, the *Industrial Worker;* in fact, it is freely admitted and apparently is looked upon with satisfaction
by the decentralizing faction, that there are at present
fifty-seven varieties of Industrial Workers of the World.

The net result is that the I. W. W., instead of being
the grim, brooding power which it is pictured in popular
imagination, is a body utterly incapable of strong, efficient, united action and the attainment of results of a

permanent character; a body capable of local and spasmodic effort only. True, it has a constitution which provides in a most logical manner for the welding of the workers into a great, effective, organic body. But this constitution is a mere mechanical structure in the interstices of which organic accretions have here and there settled. The little organic bodies are sovereign, each of their members is a sovereign, and to both member and organic unit the constitution is a thing subject to their will. The fact is that the I. W. W. is not an organization but a loosely bound group of uncontrolled fighters. It is a symptom if you will, and in that alone, if anywhere, lies its present social significance. But decentralized as it is to the extent of organic dissipation, atomistic and rent by bitter factional strife, it has no present power of general persistent or constructive action.

The I. W. W., however, is not only weak in membership and organic unity; it possesses, further, no financial resources even in a slight degree adequate to advance and maintain its proposed organization of the working class or to carry forward any consistent assault on capitalism; and, moreover, it has shown itself incapable of controlling for its main purposes even the financial resources which it does possess. Advocates of the movement, it is true, minimize the importance of mere money in the kind of warfare which they propose to conduct. This is supposed to be one of the pregnant ideas of the direct actionists. They do not propose, it is said, like the Socialists, to support a horde of parasitic labor politicians, nor, like the trade unions, to out-wait the capitalist. They will force the capitalists to abdicate by the simple process of making it unprofitable for them to conduct industry. And this can be done practically without funds—where it will suffice—simply by keeping the worker's hands in his pockets; where this will not produce the desired result, by striking on the job. I do not purpose in this connection to enter into any discussion of the theory of direct action. All that I wish to do is to point out the fact that much of the present weakness of the I. W. W. is due to financial want and a constitutional inability to control the actual financial resources at hand. Time after time the I. W. W. has been obliged to let slip favorable opportunities for organization and has lost local bodies because it could not furnish the carfare and meal tickets necessary to send the gospel to the workers groping in darkness. Time after time it has seen promising demonstrations collapse and the workers drift away from the point of contest and from its control because it could not finance organizers and supply food and lodging to tide over the period of temporary hardship. The whole experience of the organization has, in fact, proved that, short of a condition of general and desperate distress, progressive and permanent working-class organization requires ready and continuous financial support. And here lies the most vital error in the practical theory and calculations of the I. W. W. The American workmen as a body are not, and are not likely to be, in a condition of general and desperate distress. It is, therefore, to the unskilled and casual laborers alone that the I. W. W. can bring home its appeal and to these only that it can look for the funds to put through its organizing projects. It is this chronic financial distress that more than anything else has caused the dissipation of its membership after each of its brilliant but spasmodic efforts.

LITTLE
POVERTY?

The case is made more hopeless by the inability of the organization to control the little financial power it can command. This lack of financial control is another outcome of the decentralizing mania which grips the membership. The average local has not developed the ability to conserve its own resources. Rather than support the central authority and submit to its financial management, the local suffers its funds to be dissipated by incompetent members or stolen by dishonest officials. Nothing was more striking in the recent convention than the stories of local financial losses. "All down through the line," said one delegate, "we have had experience with secretaries who absconded with funds." "No less than three have done the same thing [in our local]," was the testimony of another. This has happened three times to one local in one year according to a third statement. Indeed, so loose is the local financial control and the general interrelationship of organic units, especially in the western country, that there appears to exist a body of circulating professional agitators who make it their business to go from locality to locality for the sole purpose of getting themselves elected to the treasurer's office and absconding with the funds. The local unions do not seem to be in sufficiently close touch to ferret out the malefactors and check the practice, nor will they heed the warnings of the general office. Indeed, in some locals the feeling seems to prevail that the local secretary is entitled to what he can make away with. Such are the financial conditions in the organization which claims to have the only means of opposing to the capitalist class a solid and effective organization of the workers, and asserts that it is training the workers for the task of reorganizing and managing the industries of the country.

From what has already been said it might readily be inferred that the I. W. W. would be incapable of successful general assault on the present social and industrial organization or of any effective reconstructive effort, even though it should succeed in greatly enlarging its membership, reconciling its factions, and overcoming its financial difficulties. Such a conclusion in fact seems amply warranted. It rests on a threefold basis of fact: First, the membership of the I. W. W. is and is bound to be of such a character that united, sustained, constructive action is practically impossible for it without a consistent body of ideals and a relatively permanent leadership of the highest organizing and directive quality.

As already intimated, the I. W. W. must depend for the bulk of its membership on the least capable, least developed, lowest trained, and poorest paid of American workmen. To these may be added an element made up of irresponsible atomists who are so constituted that to them all authority is an ever-present challenge. No American workman of constructive mind will permanently affiliate himself with a revolutionary industrial organization which abhors half-measures and political action, so long as he can see ahead the hope of immediate betterment through the gradual development and enforcement of an improved system of working rules and conditions. This does not mean that the I. W. W. is composed of the so-called "bum" element, as is so often asserted. Far from it. But it does mean that it is the desperate elements of the working class, the men who have not developed and cannot develop, under the existing system, organic discipline and constructive ability, to whom the I. W. W. appeals—in the East the "Hunkies" and underpaid mill hands, for the most part unas-

similated Europeans; in the West the "blanket stiffs,"
the "timber wolves," "the dock wallopers," and the pa-
drone-recruited construction gangs; and everywhere the
man who because of temperament or oppression has become a self-directing enemy of whatever stands for authority or things as they are.   One had but to observe
the recent convention to recognize these types and these
characteristics as predominant even in this picked assembly.   Undernourishment and underdevelopment were
prominent physical characteristics of the group.   The
broad-headed, square-jawed, forceful, and constructive
type, so marked in trade-union assemblies, was conspicu-
ous by its absence.   By many of those present organic
strength and action were evidently regarded as correla-
tives of oppression.   To some these ideas seemed so foreign that the general character of the organization appeared to be unknown to them.   The rule of the majority, except in so far as it applied to the local group,
was repudiated many times during the course of the
debates.   Add to all this the presence in the assembly of
members of secret committees whose actions are beyond
even the knowledge and control of the local groups—
and we have a fair conception of the difficulty here presented of united and controlled action.   Obviously only a
body of leaders strong in intelligence and personality,
bound to a consistent body of ideals, harmonious in action, and long in the saddle, could hope to weld such
elements into an effective, organic whole.

But, secondly, the I. W. W. has failed to develop and
sustain such a stable body of leaders and shows no capacity to do so.   Of the original group of men who organized and outlined the policies of this new venture in
unionism, only one was seated in the convention and

only one or two besides are prominently connected with the organization at present. Moyer, Debs, Mother Jones, Pinkerton, and others, signers of the original manifesto, effective leaders of the past, many of them yet effective leaders in other labor organizations, have all disappeared from the councils of the I. W. W.—nagged out, kicked out, or driven out by despair or disgust. This result has been in part the inevitable outcome of the hatred of authority which expresses itself in the decentralizing movement. Partly, as will be shown later, it is the outcome of an incongruity and shifting of ideals within the organization; but, to no small extent, it is the product of a strong force of romantic idealism which, strange as it may seem, exists in the minds and hearts of the downtrodden constituency of the I. W. W. In spite of the fact that these men will have none of the regularly constituted authority when it makes for strength, they are hero-worshipers and are easily led for the moment by the "heroes of labor." These heroes are the momentary leaders of strikes and of battles with the police and militia, those especially who have gone on trial and suffered imprisonment for violence or the disturbance of the public peace. They are, in general, men who themselves have not involuntarily suffered at the hands of society but have provoked its vengeance. They are largely well nourished, quick, and intelligent, but, with exceptions, they are men who have deliberately discarded all constructive ideals, deliberately thrown off social restraint, and, in the spirit of the medieval knight or the revolutionist of the well-to-do classes in Russia, have constituted themselves the personal avengers of the wrongs of the working class. Such men grip the imagination of the rank and file and make of what would otherwise be an ultra-democratic organization, relatively unfitted for constructive effort, a positively destructive force in spirit and action. They are the inventors of new forms of sabotage, the guerilla leaders, the members of "secret committees," the *provocateurs* in the free-speech fights; the men who create the sentiment that the only existing standard of right is might, that opposition to authority is a virtue, that imprisonment is an honor. It is these labor heroes, rising from time to time before the admiring vision of the undisciplined membership of the I. W. W., who have displaced the men already in power and, to a large extent, have made impossible the development of a stable body of leaders capable of welding the membership by patient effort into an organic whole.

Underneath all this, however, making consistent action and therefore permanent development impossible for the I. W. W., there exists and has existed, thirdly, a fundamental conflict of ideals. Much has been made of the sabotage and other modes of direct action current among the members of the I. W. W. Because of the prevalence of these methods, the conclusion has been accepted uncritically that I. W. W.-ism is another name for syndicalism. This, however, is but a half-truth and even as such it needs qualification. The truth is that the I. W. W. is a compound entity whose elements are not entirely harmonious. It was launched in 1905 as a protest against craft unionism and the conservative attitude and policies of the American Federation of Labor. It was originally composed prevailingly of a body of men socialistically inclined who believed that betterment of the condition of the workers as a whole and permanently could be attained only by organizing all of them by in-

dustries into one big union with the ultimate object of
the overthrow of the capitalist system. In order to attain this end they outlined an organization which should
bring the skilled and unskilled workers into one structural body with highly centralized authority, so that the
whole power of the organization—especially its financial
power—could be quickly concentrated at any one point
where contest existed between the employers and the
workmen, and which should coöperate with the Socialist
party on the political field. The slogans of the organization were: "Labor produces all wealth"; "might makes
right"; "an injury to one an injury to all"; "no contracts
and no compromise"; "industrial organization"; "one big
union"; "workers of the world, unite." The I. W. W.
showed at this time no essential characteristics of what
has since become familiar as revolutionary syndicalism.

No sooner, however, had the organization been
launched than a conflict of ideals appeared. The first
year saw a fatal blow struck at the idea of one big union
with strong, centralized authority—in a disruption which
resulted in the abolition of the office of general president
of the organization. In 1908 a second split occurred
which banished the Socialistic element from power. Political action was stricken from the preamble to the constitution and direct action as a revolutionary slogan arose
alongside the notion of one big, centralized, industrial
union. From this time forward the internal history of
the I. W. W. has been a history of the conflict of these two ideals—the one, industrial unionism, standing for permanent organization of the workers and immediate benefits, requiring a strong central
authority well financed; the other, revolutionary syndicalism, standing for uncontrolled agitation and guerilla

warfare, whose adherents chafe against central authority and its financial support.

Out of this conflict of ideals the contest between centralization and decentralization arose. The decentralizers, mainly westerners, imbued with the revolutionary ideal because they were for the most part casual workers with no big industries to organize, whose main recourse was to stir up trouble, argued that since this was the purpose of the organization all central authority was to be reckoned as irksome restraint. The local membership could best judge when the time had come to act. A central treasury was not needed since one or a few individuals acting on their own responsibility could wreck machinery, destroy materials, and precipitate a contest with political authority. Therefore they raised the banner of decentralization and direct revolution. Thus was syndicalism born and nourished in the I. W. W. But it was mainly an instinctive syndicalism, a blind, destructive force, lacking in general the vision and well-rounded doctrine of the European syndicalists. Even yet it is safe to say that few among the rank and file who call themselves syndicalists could state the theory of the European movement. Meanwhile in the East the relatively permanent character of the unskilled workers, and the necessity of wrenching from great industrial organizations immediate and permanent gains, still emphasized the need of regularity, authority, and permanent power —in short, industrial unionism in its original connotation. Hence syndicalism and industrial unionism have remained as conflicting ideals within the organization, preventing the development of that leadership which alone can give to the I. W. W. consistent action, permanent growth, and effective power. So long as the conflict holds, the organization must remain weak, spasmodic in action, and destructive in results.

But it is doubtful if the final triumph of either of these ideals would suffice to make of the I. W. W. a real power in this country. In this connection two points need emphasis: first, in so far as the I. W. W. aspires to represent syndicalism pure and simple the conditions are not here for its growth. Syndicalism as it has developed in this country is a doctrine of despair. However much its proponents may attempt to stress its ultimate ideal—the rebuilding of industrial society—it is essentially a destructive philosophy. As stated above, it will not be adopted, except temporarily and under special stress, by any body of workmen who see hope ahead in gradual betterment through constructive industrial and political action. Such a body is the organizing element of the American working class as evidenced by the two and one-half million trade unionists, and the growth of the Socialist party since it has taken an opportunist position.

Secondly, in so far as the I. W. W. aspires to represent the movement toward industrial unionism, the field of action is already occupied. The American Federation of Labor through its local councils, its central organizations, its system federations, its departments, and its amalgamated craft unions, is creating the machinery for the practical expression of the industrial union ideal as rapidly as the circumstances of the worker's life and needs allow of its development. The process is perhaps slow but it is sure and effective. It is proceeding by the trial-and-error method which alone has proved adequate to the permanent advancement of the interests of the workers. And when it is considered further that within the American Federation one industrial union alone outnumbers in membership the whole effective force of the I. W. W. in the proportion of twenty to one, the prospect that the latter will be able to oust its rival from the field becomes too small for consideration.

The fact is that the I. W. W. faces a perpetual dilemma. The bulk of the American workmen want more here and now for themselves and their immediate associates and care little for the remote future or the revolutionary ideal. These will have none of the I. W. W. The others have not, and under the existing conditions cannot develop the capacity for sustained organic effort. Whichever way the organization turns, then, it seems doomed to failure.

Viewing the situation in any reasonable light, therefore, we find it difficult to escape the conclusion that the Industrial Workers of the World as a positive social factor is more an object of pathetic interest than of fear. It has succeeded in impressing itself upon the popular imagination as a mysterious, incalculable force likely to appear and work destruction at any time and place. It has terrified the public because its small body of irresponsible and foot-loose agitators scent trouble from afar and flock to the point where social rupture seems to be for the moment imminent. They are like Morgan's raiders. By rapidity of movement and sheer audacity they have created the impression of a great organized force. But in reality they are incapable of anything but spasmodic and disconnected action. As a means for calling attention to the fact that machinery is breaking down the distinction between skilled and unskilled labor and is thus rendering craft organization ineffective; as an instrument for rousing the public to a consciousness of the suffering and needs of the unskilled and transient workers and of the existence here of a compelling social problem; as a spur to the activity of the more conservative and exclusive labor organizations, the I. W. W. may have a useful social function. As a directly effective social force, however, it has no considerable significance.

The conclusion, so far as it concerns the problem of syndicalism in the United States, would seem to be obvious. But I am well aware that those who feel a vital, constitutional need for visualizing and magnifying such a problem will not abandon their beliefs merely on this showing of evidence. They will doubtless point to the undeniable growth of industrial unionism within the American Federation of Labor, and to the many sporadic outbreaks of violent and predatory action with which the history of our labor movement has been checkered, as indicating the development of syndicalism in spirit and action within the American labor movement quite apart from any formal organization or teaching—a great ground swell, they will say, carrying the whole movement onward toward the syndicalist bourne. But let us see whether these are really syndicalistic manifestations. I doubt it, and for these two reasons:

First, I venture to affirm that there is no more necessary connection between industrial unionism and syndicalism than between capitalism and monarchy. Industrial unionism on the face of it is merely an attempt to parallel capitalist organization. It is perfectly compatible with collective bargaining and with what we might call business unionism, as is illustrated by the case of the United Mine Workers. It is the ideal type of unionism advocated by the socialists. On the other hand, it may grow up along with nonsocialist political action, as in the American Federation of Labor, where a strong tendency toward industrial organization has gone hand in hand with a robust development of legislative and political activity. Evidently, then, it indicates a hopeless confusion of ideas to identify syndicalism with industrial unionism, and it is a misuse of reason to predicate the one as necessarily the result of the other.

How then about union violence and predation? Do they show any necessary affinity between unionism and syndicalism? In order to answer this question correctly let us look for a moment at the most usual occasion for deliberate violence and predation on the part of old-line unionists. It is a fact that almost any body of union men, whatever their principles and ordinary methods, and for that matter almost any body of workers, will tend to resort to violence and perhaps predation if they are face to face with systematic and long-continued aggression, or are brought up against a blank wall of resistance to demands for the absolute essentials of a safe and decent existence, *provided there is no relief in sight through law or public opinion.* But the same is true of any body of men with red blood in their veins or of women, for that matter. Shall we then dissipate our concept of syndicalism by making it cover the action of the Boston Tea Party, the Ku-Klux Klan, the Mexican revolutionists and the militant suffragettes? Surely we must not confuse spasmodic outbreaks against specific oppression with direct action as the corollary of a fixed and general aversion to peaceful opportunist effort and political action. Only, then, when union violence and predation have been the outgrowth of a permanent aversion of this kind, or when such aversion has grown up with the violence and has become a fixed creed of a union can we rightfully speak of them as syndicalistic in character.

But shall we nowhere find this permanent attitude outside of the Industrial Workers of the World? The American Railway Union was not adverse to political action; the Western Federation of Miners has again joined forces with the American Federation of Labor; the Bridge and Structural Iron Workers show no signs apparently of going over to the syndicalist camp.

Must we not then conclude that, in drawing the Industrial Workers of the World into the picture in its proper character and proportion, we have pretty thoroughly disposed of syndicalism as a serious American problem?

So far so good; but have we any assurance that we shall not soon have to face a serious syndicalist problem in America? To satisfy ourselves on this point we should have to discuss our third question, namely: What are the causes of syndicalism, and what are the prospects of its future development? I shall not attempt to discuss this question fully, but shall be content to make one or two suggestive statements indicating why syndicalism has not developed and is not likely to develop on American soil, and the conditions which would be necessary for its development here.

Successful trade unionism as it exists in America today is not a made-to-order affair; it is not imitative of anything to be found abroad, nor is it the objectification of any general social theory. It is a means, slowly forged by experience, of meeting the immediate needs, and of solving the immediate problems of the American workers. It has been developed by the trial-and-error method; it is experimental, opportunistic, and pragmatic. And, if you will look back over the last century and a quarter you will find that this is the only kind of labor organization that has survived and worked in this country. Even socialism, before it could make any successful appeal to American workmen, had to cut loose from the ultra-revolutionists, thrust its theories into the background, and develop a program for meeting immediate needs and problems.

The immediate reason for all this lies in the character of the organizing element of American workmen. The great mass of organized American workmen are not conscious revolutionists, but optimistic opportunists. They want more here and now. Their attention is fixed on meeting immediate needs and solving immediate problems. They see hope ahead in a gradual improvement of existing conditions. They have little capacity for or patience with speculative theorizing. They are unwilling to leave the path which has been marked out by experience with its slow but sure advance, to plunge into theoretically assumed short cuts charted only by the imagination. This is the general attitude of that portion of the American working class which has alone proved itself capable of sustained organic effort.

This attitude is the outcome partly of the racial character of American workmen, and partly of American economic and social conditions. The hard-headed, tradition-bound, empirical element predominates in our labor movement just as it does in our business affairs, in law and politics and in our social ideals and affairs generally, and this characteristic, perhaps racial, has been reënforced by the fact that the economic and social conditions have for generations been such that the workers *could* see hope ahead in gradual betterment through constructive industrial and political action. The labor movement thus given character has assimilated and Americanized foreign accretions, just as in general we have assimilated and Americanized the immigrant, socially and politically.

It is true in the one case as in the other that assimilation and transmutation have not been complete, but if our labor history has proved anything, as indicated especially by the career of the Industrial Workers of the World, it is that those elements which have not been assimilated are incapable of consistent, and effective organic union and action, and that the spasmodic organic efforts of such a body as the Industrial Workers of the World fail to check the growth and do not essentially modify the ideals and methods of the American and Americanized labor movement.

On account of all this there is no syndicalist problem of consequence in this country. We shall have none of consequence, I believe, unless and until the great organic American labor movement finds its way barred to empirical advance. It is now feeling its way toward the organizing of the unskilled, and will doubtless organize them as fast as the psychology of the situation will permit; it is advancing experimentally toward the industrial form of organization, as anyone must concede who is at all familiar with the organic history and the declarations of the American Federation of Labor; it is at the same time forging ahead on the line of political action as fast as tradition will safely allow; it is gradually overcoming the employers' claims of autocratic rights, and establishing the principles and working rules of industrial democracy. Whenever it comes face to face with a blank wall of resistance in law and administration, whenever it encounters trusts and employers' associations bent upon its extermination, it is apt to adopt secret, violent, and predatory methods.   But when the temporary occasion is past it quickly returns to its ordinary ideals and tactics. And if I read the character and spirit of the American labor movement aright, it would take a deal of useless battering against an impenetrable wall of legal and industrial resistance to create in the American labor movement the general psychology compatible with a real and robust development of syndicalism.

The Industrial Workers of the World is one aspect of revolutionary unionism.   To understand it, therefore, we must have some understanding of the larger thing of which it is a part.   In the popular conception of things revolutionary unionism is generally distinguished by violence and sabotage.   The tendency, however, to make violence the hall-mark of revolutionary unionism is a great mistake.   The bulk of revolutionary unionists embraces the most peaceful citizens we have, and on principle.   Most violence in labor troubles is committed by conservative unionists or by the unorganized.[6]   In Chicago violence has become inseparably associated in the public mind with organizations in the building trades.   "Slugging" raids and shooting affairs have come to be taken as a matter of course and excite little interest.   A few years ago these union tactics attained their highest development under the leadership of "Skinny" Madden, then in control of the central building trades organization.   But Madden and his men were not looking to any overthrow of existing conditions.   His were the methods of predatory hold-up union-

[6] That is to say, the violence which is due to the labor unions.

ism. Nor was the recent dynamiting campaign of the
Bridge and Structural Iron Workers the product of revolutionary unionism. Here, rather, was a case of a conservative union fighting with its back to the wall against
a campaign of annihilation by an employers' combination. In the last ditch, it turned, not to revolution, but
to guerilla warfare and *guerilla* unionism. And this also
to a large degree characterizes the recent violent acts of
the miners in Colorado. In short, violence in labor
troubles is a unique characteristic of no kind of unionism, but is a general and apparently inevitable incident
of the rise of the working class to consciousness and
power in capitalistic society.

Secondly, revolutionary unionism is not to be marked
off from other kinds of unionism by its employment of
sabotage as an offensive and defensive weapon. It is
true that sabotage is a weapon whose use is highly characteristic of revolutionary unionism, but the notion that
its use is confined to revolutionary unionists fades out
the moment its true character and varied forms are
known.[7] It is moreover distinctly repudiated by many

[7] Sabotage is an elusive phenomenon and is difficult of accurate definition. Briefly described it is called "striking on
the job." J. A. Estey, in his "Revolutionary Unionism," does
well when he says: "In Syndicalist practice it [sabotage] is a
comprehensive term, covering every process by which the
laborer, while remaining at work, tries to damage the interests of his employer, whether by simple malingering, or
by bad quality of work, or by doing actual damage to tools
and machinery" (p. 96). This definition puts admirably the
essential, underlying characteristics of sabotage, but in practice
it ranges even beyond such limits. There are almost an
indefinite number of ways of "putting the boots to the employer" which have come properly to be included under the
general designation, and some of them have been employed by

revolutionary unionists, is not confined to revolutionary
unions, and, it might be added, is not confined to the
workers alone.[8]   It is clear then that revolutionary
unionism cannot, by this practice, be marked off and made
a definite and clearly recognizable thing.

What, then, is revolutionary unionism, and how are
we to distinguish and recognize it? Revolutionary unionism is in essence a spiritual something, a group viewpoint,
a theory and interpretation of society and social relationships held by groups of militant wageworkers, and an
attempt to realize this theory and interpretation by means
of a program of action. A distinct organization committed to this program and viewpoint is a thing always
striven for, but is not an essential feature nor at present
a general characteristic of revolutionary unionism in the
United States.   That is to say, while there are distinct
revolutionary organizations in this country, such as the
Industrial Workers of the World, and lately the Syndicalist League, most revolutionary unionists· are' found

conservative unionists time out of mind. *Ca' Canny* or soldiering is one of them, which was a practice long before revolutionary unionism was known to the mass of the workers. In
essence it is practiced by every union that sets a limitation
on output. Living strictly up to impossible safety rules enacted
by the employers for their own protection is another method.
Wasting materials, turning out goods of inferior quality or
damaging them in the process, misdirecting shipments, telling
the truth about the quality of products, changing price cards,
sanding the bearings, salting the soup and the sheets, "throwing the monkey wrench into the machinery"—all are methods
of practicing sabotage that have become familiar.

[8] As the unionists point out, essentially the same thing is
practiced by employers and dealers who adulterate goods, make
shoddy, conceal defects of products, and sell goods for what
they are not.

within conservative trade unions, with no separate organic expression of their own. To distinguish revolutionary unionism, therefore, and to get an accurate understanding of the matter in hand we must distinguish its varieties before going further. The first, *socialistic* unionism, is represented organically by the Detroit Industrial Workers of the World and by a small number of national unions in the American Federation of Labor. The larger number of socialist unionists, however, have no separate union organization. They are to be found in the supposedly conservative business and uplift unions of the American Federation of Labor and the Railway Brotherhoods. The mine workers, the painters, the bakers, for example, are largely socialist unionists. The second variety of revolutionary unionism found in this country is *anarchistic,* or more accurately, *quasi anarchistic.* It is best represented by the Chicago Industrial Workers of the World. But, again, there are quasi anarchistic unionists scattered through the conservative and socialistic unions.

Revolutionary unionism, in both its forms, starts with the assumption that society is divided into two warring classes, between which there are no common interests and no possibility of compromise. The workers produce all wealth; the employers systematically rob them. The workers cannot secure and enjoy what they produce until they rule society.[9] In this fight, the revolutionary union-

[9] *See* Constitution, Industrial Workers of the World, Preamble §§ 1, 2; also Industrial Unionism vs. Anarchy and Reform, p. 4, Detroit Industrial Workers of the World. But see also Declaration of Principles of Bakery and Confectionery Workers, a compound craft union in the American Federation of Labor.

ists refuse to recognize the validity of the standards of right and justice, the laws and the rules of the game current in society. There is no such thing as society as a whole. Established notions of right, established rights and the institutions in their support are the devices of the employing class designed to keep labor down and exploit the workers. Therefore, the workers are not bound by these things. For the workers—just as well as for the employers—whatever is for their interests as a class, whatever furthers their ends, is *right*. In short, in the last analysis, there is no standard of right and rights but might. This doctrine is held without reserve by quasi anarchistic unionists. It justifies to them violence, destruction of property and even killing. It would be unfair, however, to say this of the socialistic unionists. While they declare that actual rights are based on might, they refuse to admit that might *ought* to make right, and, therefore, stop short of justifying violence and killing.

It is the primary aim of all revolutionary unionists to overthrow the existing institutional order; to do away with individual ownership of the means of production and the profit system; to put social and industrial control into the hands of the workers. To accomplish this, they propose to unite the workers not by crafts, as is the case generally of conservative unionism, but by industries, and, finally, into one great working class organization, so that in a fight workers cannot be used against workers, but the whole power of the class can be brought to bear against the employers at any point. But beyond this, the socialist unionists and the quasi anarchistic unionists differ vitally and widely. They differ as to ultimate aims, as to program, and as to methods.

The socialist unionists look forward to a state of society which, except for common ownership and control of industry and strong centralized government in the hands of the working class, does not differ essentially from our own. They would in general attain this end by peaceful means, both industrial and political. Industrially, they would organize the workers into larger and larger units, and by the usual trade union methods secure for them better and better conditions and a greater and greater voice and place in the control and management of industry. Politically, they would unite the same workers into a great party designed to educate them and others in civil affairs, to push for legislation in the social and industrial interests of the workers, and ultimately to secure control of the legislative, administrative, and judicial powers of the government. Ultimately, the industrial employer would be eliminated by the working class state.

The quasi anarchistic unionists have a different ultimate aim. They look forward to the *complete* abolition of the state and of existing governmental machinery. They visualize, not a political, but an industrial society, where the *unions* would be the government. All political action is abhorrent to them, partly because the state is outside their scheme of things and political action is a recognition of a compromise with it, but largely because they believe that experience has proved it to be not only useless as a working-class weapon but positively harmful to working-class interests. They have noted that political associations and political gains make the workers soft, conservative, and nonrevolutionary.

Revolution degenerates into mere reform, and political preferment makes traitors of working-class leaders. The middle-class tendencies of the Socialist Parties in Germany, France and the United States, and the action of such men as Briand and John Burns have brought them to this view. Direct action, therefore, has become their slogan, that is, the making and enforcing of demands upon the enemy directly by the workers, through demonstrations, strikes, sabotage and violence. At this point, however, the quasi anarchistic revolutionary unionists themselves split into two camps, centralizers and decentralizers.

The centralizers believe that the actual building up of the industrial organization will train and educate the workers in the conduct, not only of industry, but of all social affairs, so that when the organization has become universalized it can perform all the necessary functions of social control now exercised by the state in its legislative, executive and judicial capacities. This universal organization of the workers will then displace the state, government and politics in the present sense; private ownership, privilege and exploitation will be forever abolished. The one big union will have become the state, the government, the supreme organic and functional expression of society; its rules and decisions will be the law.

The decentralizers look forward to what they call a free industrial society. Each local group of workers is to be a law to itself. They are to organize as they please. The present industrial and social arrangements are to be overthrown simply by making it unprofitable for the employing class to own and operate industries. Future society is to consist of independent groups of workers freely exchanging their products. The proper proportions of investment and production, the ratio of exchange of goods, etc., will automatically be determined, just as they are under competitive industry, only then the competition will be between groups of workers, instead of between individuals. Universal knowledge and a superior morality, which will spring up as soon as capitalist society is abolished, will take the place of our present complicated system of social control and do away with the necessity of government in the present sense.

Beyond this, the characteristic theories, policies and methods of the two varieties of quasi anarchistic unionists, in general, agree. The central purpose of all their efforts, as we have seen, is the overthrow of the capitalist system, and the establishment of working-class social control. But this cannot be accomplished by a gradual process of immediate gains in the form of better wages, shorter hours, better working conditions, etc. The end is retarded rather than advanced by such immediate concessions and advantages because these tend to make the workers conservative, satisfied with the present system, and those who gain most become selfish and detached in interest from the whole working class. The main immediate object of all their efforts is not material results, but agitation, education, a rousing of the workers and employers to mutual hatred and bitterness. Hence they count everything in the way of a fight, whether won or lost, as a gain. To them, no strike can be lost, since the very failure, in the common way of looking at it, is the surest way to secure the psychological results they are after. Therefore, they are always alert to take every opportunity for fighting, whatever the odds against them. Their motto is anything to stir up trouble between the workers and the ruling class. A contest with the police over free speech or with the church is as good an opportunity as a strike. And they count all things as good that may irritate the employers or authorities to action against them. Trouble is what they thrive on.

The revolution, then, must be the work of the unskilled—the true proletariat. They must be roused and united and educated—the whole object of the agitation is this. But is this possible when we consider the character and conditions of these unskilled workers? The great mass of them are untrained, unintelligent, cowed, subservient, satisfied with things as they are because they know nothing better. Get them together and there is no unanimity of ideas; poll them and the sodden majority would overwhelmingly outvote the alert, revolutionary minority. How, then, can the unskilled proletariat create the revolution? The quasi anarchistic unionists answer with what is perhaps their most distinctive and pregnant idea, *the theory of the militant minority*. They are no levelers; they do not propose to poll the proletariat; they do not really believe in democracy. Throughout the history of the world, they will tell you, everything has been achieved, every advance has been pushed through, by the intelligent minority. Every revolution has thus been accomplished. The mass of men in all grades of society are unintelligent, but they are imitators. Given a sufficiently intelligent and active minority which understands this and does not allow itself to be swamped by democratic ideals and arrangements, and the mass can be roused to action and be made to work its will. The quasi anarchistic unionists are the

intelligent minority of the workers. The proletariat is
their instrument. Their task is to tune it up to the
revolutionary pitch, and use it as a revolutionary force.
But how? Obviously the way is to stimulate a constant
and ever-growing fight between the proletariat and their
enemies. This can be done partly by general agitation, but the fight must be conducted also on the industrial field. And how best conduct this industrial
fight?

Here the quasi anarchistic unionists are moved partly
by theory and partly by the necessities of the situation.
On the basis of theory alone, the thing is not to work primarily for material gains. Such gains, we have seen, put
the instrument out of tune, relax the strings. Hence
the old-fashioned strike is not appropriate. And, beyond
this, necessity makes it an impossible weapon. The old-
fashioned strike is essentially a trial of financial strength
between the employers and the workers. Its success also
requires sustained coöperative effort on the part of the
mass. But the proletariat has no financial strength and
cannot be held to its task for long periods. The ordinary strike then is out of the question as a revolutionary
weapon. If it succeeds it weakens the revolutionary
spirit of the workers; if it fails it strengthens the employers. A weapon, then, must be devised which shall
keep alive the revolutionary spirit, be inexpensive to the
workers, require no sustained coöperation, and weaken
the employers. Here, finally, we reach the *raison d'être*
of the great industrial weapons of the quasi anarchistic
unionists—the intermittent strike and sabotage. They
keep the workers and employers constantly embroiled in
a way to arouse mutual bitterness and hatred. They
are inexpensive to the workers; the intermittent strike

does not demand continuous coöperation over long periods, while sabotage need not require coöperation at all; it can be carried on by the individual alone. They hit the employer at his most vulnerable point by making it unprofitable for him to operate. Hence the great industrial slogan is, "Strike on the job." But all these methods we have mentioned are not the ultimate means of the quasi anarchistic unionists. They are but the *means to the means* for the final end. Agitation of all sorts, the intermittent strike, sabotage and violence,[10] have the primary purpose of developing solidarity among the proletariat which will make possible ultimately the general strike that shall finally overthrow capitalism, and of educating the workers to a capacity for the conduct of social affairs.

There is no way of arriving at even a moderately accurate estimate of the strength of revolutionary unionism in America. As has been seen, most socialist unionists are scattered through nonrevolutionary organizations. This is true to a lesser extent of quasi anarchistic unionists. Unions keep no records of character of membership. They would not give it out if they did, and the records would not be worth anything if given out. The national officers of the socialist party refuse to estimate. In the 1912 convention of the American Federation of Labor, the socialist candidate for president polled 5,073 out of a total of 17,047 votes cast. Estimating the American Federation of Labor membership at 2,000,000, the socialistic membership, if this vote

---

[10] But note that this is said only of the quasi anarchistic, revolutionary unionists. The socialistic revolutionary unionists, who are by far the majority in this country, altogether repudiate violence, sabotage, etc.

were indicative, would number 846,000, or forty-two per
cent.

But a vote of unions one way or another is no indication of the strength of internal factions. The socialist
party vote is somewhere near thirty per cent as large as
the estimated number of trade unionists, but it is to a
considerable extent a nonunionist vote. The best we can
say is that socialist unionists are a fairly large and apparently growing minority. The quasi anarchistic unionists are probably mostly in separate organizations, but no
accurate figures can be obtained of these. The Industrial
Workers of the World claim to have issued cards to
something over 200,000 since its establishment. The
Syndicalist League is only a handful, if it exists. It is
possible that all revolutionary unionists combined in this
country number perhaps one-third of the organized workers, or in the neighborhood of 800,000. Lacking statistics of its growth, the only way we can discuss the
prospects of revolutionary unionism is in the terms of
its causes and the character of its adherents.

In attempting to account for revolutionary unionism,
stress has ordinarily been laid almost entirely on industrial conditions and forces. It has been pointed out that,
with the development of modern industry under the
stimulus of machinery and the machine process, the relationships between employers and workers are becoming remote and impersonal, and each class is coming to
be subjected to a different environment and is thus developing different sets of ideals and interests. To those
who accept this theory, class conflict and the growth of
class conflict alike are inevitable. Revolutionary unionism is one aspect of this conflict based on industrial conditions. It is bound to exist and bound to develop

rapidly in this country now that our free land is exhausted, and that in other respects the opportunities for escape from the working class are being cut off.   There is a strong element of truth in this explanation and prediction, especially as applied to socialistic unionism.   On the other hand, economic conditions alone cannot account for revolutionary unionism.   This is evidenced by the fact that in the same trades and industries, and notably in the same uniòns, we find both conservative business and revolutionary unionists.   I am inclined to think that revolutionary unionism, especially as regards the quasi anarchistic variety, is largely a matter of individual and racial temperament.

To judge of the outlook for revolutionary unionism in this country, we must consider both our temperamental and environmental situation and tendencies.   A large proportion of our organized workers are probably temperamentally conservative and would never become revolutionary unionists no matter what the industrial development.   A growing portion of the workers—largely as the result of our recent immigration—are temperamentally radical.   In so far as they become unionists at all they are bound to be revolutionaries.   Between these extremes are the floaters, the negative mass, perhaps the largest proportion of the workers.   They will be swayed by their associates and by industrial and political conditions.   As skilled workers they are likely to be conservative; as unskilled, revolutionary.   In times of prosperity they will become satisfied and temperate; in times of stress, radical.   Political disability and casual work, such as the migratory worker suffers, will draw them into the revolutionary camp.   Reforms—workmen's compensation, health and safety legislation, old-age pensions—

will tend to make them supporters of the existing system. Militant action by employers' associations and
trusts, and unfavorable legislative action and court decisions will make militants of them. Speaking, then, of
revolutionary unionism as a whole, and not of syndicalism or the Industrial Workers of the World, we shall
see more rather than less of it. It is bound to develop
with unregulated immigration and the lack of a comprehensive and thoroughgoing program of reform. It
is one of the big problems of our time.

BIBLIOGRAPHY

Constitutions: American Labor Union, Industrial Workers
of the World, and the Socialist Labor Party.
Convention Proceedings: Proceedings of the Conventions
of the Industrial Workers of the World; Report of the
General Sec'y.-Treas. to the Second Convention.
Journals and *Newspapers:* The International Socialist Re-
view, Industrial Worker, Solidarity, Voice of the Peo-
ple, and newspapers in Hungarian, Italian, Spanish, Jew-
ish, Finnish, Portuguese, Russian, Swedish, Slavonian,
Polish, Etc.
Manifesto of the Industrial Workers of the World
(1905).
Propaganda Pamphlets:
Analysis of the Preamble of the I. W. W.
Anarchist Morality.
Appeal to Wageworkers.
The Burning Question of Trades-unionism.
The Class Union for All Workers.
Class Unionism. Debs, Eugene V.
Craft Unionism. Debs, Eugene V.
The Eight-hour Work Day.
Eleven Blind Leaders.

Ettor-Giovanitti Speeches.
Farm Workers and Industrial Unionism.
Flashes of the Amsterdam Congress.
Getting Recognition.
The General Strike.
How to Overcome the High Cost of Living.
Industrial Unionism. Debs, Eugene V.
Industrial Unionism. St. John, Vincent.
Industrial Unionism—I. W. W.
Industrial Unionism—The Road to Freedom.
Industrial Unionism versus Anarchy and Reform.
Industrial Union Methods.
The I. W. W. Woehlke.
The I. W. W.—Its History, Structure and Methods. St. John, Vincent.
Is the I. W. W. Antipolitical?
Judicial Murder.
One Big Union.
On the Firing Line.
Packing House Workers.
Patriotism and the Worker.
Political Parties and I. W. W.
Preamble of the I. W. W. De Leon, Daniel.
Proletarian and Petit-Bourgeois.
Reform or Revolution.
The Revolutionary I. W. W. Perry, G. H.
Revolutionary Unionism. Debs, Eugene V.
Sabotage. Flynn, E. G.
Social Democracy.
The Socialist Labor Party and the War.
Song Books.
Story of a New Labor Union.
Trades-unionism in the United States.
Two Kinds of Unionism.
The Two I. W. W.'s.
Union Scabs and Others.

War and the Workers.
What Every Policeman Ought to Know.
What Means This Strike? De Leon, Daniel.
Why Save Men's Souls?
Why Strikes are Lost.
Working-class Revolution.

BOYLE, J. "Syndicalism, The Latest Manifestation of Labor's Unrest," *Forum,* 48:223-233 (1912).

BRISSENDEN, PAUL F. The Launching of the I. W. W., *University of Calif. Pub. in Economics,* vol. 4, No. 1.

BROOKS, JOHN GRAHAM. *American Syndicalism, The I. W. W.* (1913).

DELAND, L. F. "The Lawrence Strike," *Atlantic Monthly,* 109: 694-705 (1912).

DIMNET, E. "Syndicalism and Its Philosophy," *Atlantic Monthly,* 111: 17-30 (1913).

ESTEY, JAMES A. *Revolutionary Syndicalism* (1913).

GOMPERS, SAMUEL. "Industrial Unionism," *American Federationist,* (May, 1912).

——. "Syndicalism, Partyism and Unionism," *American Federationist.* (May, 1912).

KIRK. *National Labor Federations in the United States,* Part I, "The American Labor Union," and Part III, "Industrial Unions."

LEVINE, LOUIS. *The Labor Movement in France* (1912), chap. V, "The Doctrine of Revolutionary Syndicalism."

——. "Direct Action: The Philosophy of the Labor Struggles of Today," *Forum,* 47:577-88 (1912).

WALLING, W. E. "Industrialism or Revolutionary Unionism," *The New Review* (Jan. 11, 1913).

CHAPTER VII

THE LEADERS AND THE RANK AND FILE

While unionism in its ultimate effect on industrial organization and conduct of industry is democratic, in the sense of its effort to take from the hands of employers autocratic feudalistic control and put a share of the control and conduct into the hands of the workers—tending to democratic industrial revolution—unionism in its own organization and conduct is hardly to be called democratic. At least this is true of the business union type and successful unionism. Power in both cases centers in the hands of officers and leaders. They determine immediate policies and tactics to a very large extent. And this seems to be the natural and necessary outcome of the situation. While unionism as a whole is the spontaneous outcome of the conditions, needs and problems of the workers, the rank and file in general are not in a condition to formulate methods for meeting needs or solving problems, and, apart from the direction of competent leaders, have not the intelligence to combat employers successfully. Therefore, unionism, as a fact, in its constructive aspects is taught to the rank and file by the leaders. Only when the union is weak and the leaders unsuccessful do the rank and file take control.

In general there are two classes among the rank and file. The bread and butter unionists are ordinary work-

177

(Economism)

ers chained to the wheel, the bench, or the counter, good men, but without leisure or education or experience for much thought or union action. They are apt to regard the union—when all is going well—as a matter of course, or an instrument for food and shelter. While meetings are held regularly and members are free to go and determine the conduct of affairs, as a matter of fact, in time of peace, they are lax about attendance. They are content to leave the running of affairs and the thinking to the officers. They are, by virtue of character and circumstance, pretty much clay, although at times very stubborn clay, in the hands of the officers in the ordinary administration of affairs. It really cannot be otherwise; the workers, untrained and exhausted by daily toil, cannot keep track of affairs. The officers are specialists—good talkers—and the rank and file must trust them. What they demand of leaders is that they "deliver the goods," in terms of high wages, short hours, and good conditions. So long as they do this they do not care to interfere. They are not surprised if occasionally a leader is crooked, or gets his "rake off." When he fails to "deliver the goods," they turn on him with every conceivable denunciation and rend him. Then indeed they are likely to run amuck, overbear the authority of the officers, and commit all sorts of acts in violation of constitutional authority. The second class are the radical unionists, always suspicious and at constant war with the officials.

(RADICALS)

There is a real contest between the leaders and the rank and file, especially in the case of business unionism. So long as the union is small and the officers work at the bench, there is no friction, but when the union grows and the officers give up work and become paid officials and de-

vote their whole time to official duties, then friction between the leaders and the rank and file almost inevitably
arises.   The farther up we go in officialdom the less sympathy and mutual understanding we find.   The leaders for
the most part reciprocate the feeling of the rank and file.
Their attitude is likely to be one of contempt mixed
with fear.   One trade union leader says that the rank
and file are ignorant, have to be wheedled, and, when that
fails, driven by physical force if necessary.   Even leaders who pride themselves on keeping close to the man at
the bench speak contemptuously of the crowd.   "The
successful leader," one of them says, "must be a leader
both intellectually and physically.   He must be able to
face a crowd that suspects him and be able to convince
either by argument or force.   He must be able to out-
force any opposition from the 'dee, dis, dat' rank and
file."

The causes of the contest between the leaders and the
rank and file are partly inherent in the situation.   The
rank and file are ignorant and impulsive; they do not
know anything about business and market conditions and
trade.   They think all business is making enormous profits, and that there is no limit to the amount they can
squeeze out for themselves if strong enough.   Sometimes they suffer until beyond endurance or are aroused
by leaders and then break out, wildly demanding the impossible.   Their environment tends to make them radical; they have nothing to lose—no responsibility.   All
the conditions, on the other hand, tend to make the leaders conservative.   Responsibility sobers them.   As soon
as they engage in negotiations they realize the power of
the employers, and the limitations in the ability of employers to meet demands.   Moreover, when the leaders

get away from the bench, their environment becomes
more of the character of the employer's than of the
worker's. They no longer deal with the physical, but
with the spiritual, in negotiations and in the handling of
men. Almost inevitably they develop something of the
employers' viewpoint and feeling, and thus become unable to see things from the workers' angle and to feel
with and for the workers as before. The worker is
something to be manipulated. But partly, also, the contest is due to the character of the men who get into
power in the unions. Very generally it is not the good
worker, but the big, jolly, hail fellows well met, natural
born politicians, possessed of considerable administrative ability, men with the latent instinct of the boss and
employer, men who love power for its own sake. Moreover, the leader who rises from the rank and file at once
encounters temptations hard to withstand. Many go
wrong because they cannot stand prosperity. The sudden release from the bench, from the machine process,
unsteadies them; they become dissipated and dishonest;
they may fall victims to the "mahogany table," and to
what is on it. There is, too, a constant drain of leaders
by corruption, and by politics. Here is a great weakness of unionism—it dies at the top.

How is it that the leaders get and retain their power?
In the first place, the rank and file have learned by experience that if they want "more now" they must submit to leadership. They have somewhat learned the
lesson of democracy and its inefficiency. As one union
leader put it, "The successful officer tends to stay in office indefinitely, and grows more competent and more
powerful with service. As a democracy no union would
last six minutes." Secondly, it is somewhat like shak-

ing a dish of beans, the largest come to the top. The natural leaders tend to get the offices; they are in general the husky, strong-armed fellows. One keen trade union observer says that the workers trust big men because they have come to think in physical terms, but they must have brains too. Either they are like the cunning politician or, lacking the latter's qualities, they have superior intelligence and moral courage. Thirdly, once well fixed in office, the leader has every advantage over the rank and file and can make them practically dependent upon him. The worker in a negotiation cannot present his case; he is no match for the employer; he is dependent absolutely upon the labor leader for this. Moreover, the longer the leader is in office, the more proficient he becomes in the performance of his peculiar and, to the worker, absolutely necessary functions. He becomes more and more the possessor of specialized knowledge and power. Sometimes, too, leadership is retained by force. Everything thus conspires to support the leaders against the rank and file, as long as conditions are good, as long as they can "deliver the goods." All this goes far to explain the indifference of the rank and file and the strong antisocial aims and actions of some unions. Here many forces tend to raise to leadership those of the unidealistic type who are forced to "make good," with conditions tending to make them take the easiest methods. These remarks bring out one of the hardest problems of unionism, that of democracy versus efficiency.[1]

[1] The use of the referendum in the American Federation of Labor has shown that there frequently result delay, factionalism, and indifference on the part of the rank and file; and it is exceedingly expensive. The English unions found

We are all familiar with the tales of the walking delegate, which picture him as an autocrat who goes about browbeating employers and ordering out cringing workmen at his own sweet will and for his own profit. Contradictory as are the statements of unionists and business men concerning the business agent or the walking delegate, the available evidence seems to indicate that there is much truth on both sides of the controversy. Ordinarily and normally the unionists are right in describing the walking delegate as merely a useful and harmless local executive officer. Under constitutional conditions, the creation, powers, and duties of the walking delegate may be summarized thus: He is simply a local officer elected by popular vote, for a term ranging from three months to a year, usually holding office for six months. He is the general executive officer of the local. His customary duties are to act as the representative of the union in dealing with the employer; as such to see that union rules are not violated by employers, to present grievances to the employer, and generally to act as go-between for men and masters; to maintain discipline and to look after the financial affairs and general interests of the union; to see that members attend the meetings, pay their dues, and keep in general the union rules; to find employment for union men; and to solicit

that they had no time or money for anything else when they used it. The causes for this situation seem to be that the rank and file do not understand intelligently important questions which come up; that they act as a result of emotion rather than judgment. Radical leaders can stir them up to act unwisely. As a matter of fact the rank and file are always in favor of economy, and the attempt to have pure democracy has often resulted in greater control by leaders than under representative government.

men to join the union. In performing these duties the walking delegate is constitutionally under the absolute control of the local or district council; all his powers are delegated to him by popular vote, and all his acts must be reported to the union for popular sanction. He is legally the general servant of the union, and legally can do no act for it on his own responsibility. The necessity or desirability of such a local union officer, especially in his capacity of go-between for men and masters, is apparent when we consider that working members of the union are fully occupied in their manual tasks and that no employee can go to his employer. This gives a clear and undoubtedly true idea of what the business agent normally is, by whom he is controlled, what he can do, and what he cannot do under constitutional circumstances. But evidence also shows that the walking delegate is likely to become an extra-constitutional boss. This is shown equally by positive testimony of what he sometimes becomes and what he has actually done.

Theoretically, then, the walking delegate is what the unionists picture him, a harmless and useful executive officer. Practically, he may become what the employer pictures him, a supreme and irresponsible ruler, and the irresponsible ruler is the result of a simple process of evolution from the useful servant. Is the result accident or does it represent an inherent tendency? It seems that under certain conditions it represents an inherent tendency, that it is the natural outcome of the peculiar duties of the walking delegate and the peculiar situation of the rank and file.

The peculiar duties of the walking delegate are such as to give him easy ascendency over the rank and file. He looks out for employment for them; his duties lead him over the whole local field of labor, he knows where jobs are and how to get them, he can keep a man at employment, or he can keep him from it; he looks after the finances of the union, he sees that the members pay their dues, or he can make it easy for them; he presents grievances to the employer and can argue the case, for he is not dependent on the "boss" and does not fear him; he can help one to agreeable conditions of work or he can leave him unassisted and unprotected. Clearly he is a man to keep on the right side of, and to keep "in" with. He is therefore bound to become powerful if he has ordinary judgment and finesse. To be sure, his term of power is brief and the union can turn him out if it wants to, constitutionally. Practically it cannot and will not, once he begins to consolidate his power. When the union thinks of choosing his successor, there is no one in the union who can do his work half so well as he. He is acquainted with the whole field of operations, and he has an accumulation of knowledge that the ordinary worker, held to his bench or to his machine for nine or ten hours a day, cannot have acquired. These ordinary workers naturally come more and more to rely on his judgment. Moreover, he has learned how to deal with men in general and how to deal with employers in particular; he has learned how to talk and to persuade. In short, he is related to the ordinary workers in the trade as the ward boss is to the average voter. He is a specialist in labor politics, with favors to give and to withhold.

He is in a position, then, naturally to become a local labor boss, if he so desires, unless he is checked by some outside authority. The local is, however, jealous of its autonomy. Its officers are its officers, and not the

officers of the national organization. To be sure, there
are elaborate regulations that define its relations to the
central body, but, after all, they represent loose federative bonds. The essential thing is that the walking delegate does not have to take his orders from or report to
the national officers. He is responsible not to his superior officers but to his inferiors—the rank and file who
elect him. This means that, if he is so disposed, he need
not be responsible to anyone. If he is a self-seeking
demagogue, he naturally evolves into the labor boss.
And the conditions are also favorable to bringing forward this kind of man. It is the man who does not love
his work, who is astute and smooth, who will naturally
work into this office in a group made up for the most
part of hard workers and slow thinkers. The making of
the demagogic tyrant who orders strikes against the interests of employers and men, then, is a simple and natural process. A good talker gets his friends to vote him
into office, he learns the "ropes," he gathers about him
a clique of radical henchmen, an inner ring; they vote
him unlimited power, there is no superior authority, he
cuts loose, and you have a little example of the old
Greek tyranny that rose on the ruins of the democracy.
The two parallel very well. Of course this evolution of
the business agent from the harmless to the harmful
type does not always, nor perhaps usually, take place.
The most we can say is that it is apt to take place and
we have tried to show the reasons.

   The ordinary conservative business unionist carries
about with him two very distinct and perhaps contradictory conceptions of unionism and attitudes toward society. When he is dealing with trade matters, he is ordinarily a bread and butter unionist, a fairly sober, mat-

ter of fact, unemotional, hard-headed fellow who accepts the present system on the whole but means to get the most he can out of it in the way of higher wages, shorter hours and better conditions. As such, his craft interest stands first; it is the welfare of his craft which he is looking out for. He is conscious of little or no class interest or feeling. But when a matter comes up which is free from particular craft interest and concerns what he conceives to be employing class oppression and interference with his rights and business, such as the use of the injunction, damage suits against unions, the use of strikebreakers, or the calling out of the police or militia to prevent picketing or violence, then this hardheaded, conservative, business-unionist is apt to be suddenly transformed into a wildly emotional fighter, full of class interest and class hatred. This lasts until either a bread and butter proposition comes up again or until someone calls his attention to the fact that he is socialistic, when he as quickly changes to the hard-headed business unionist again. This is characteristic of the leaders also. I have seen the transformation many times in labor meetings. It is most significant because it means that a general attempt to coerce unionism means turning it into a class-conscious revolutionary movement.

In the unions there have gone on constant struggles for control between the business union element and the socialist or revolutionary element. This contest used to be open; it is now more or less subtle, but it exists just the same. Generally, the good business craft unionist is intolerant of socialism. The reason he gives is that he wants something *now*, and this is not to be secured by academic discussions of a mythical coöperative commonwealth in the future. This is not, however, the whole reason. The socialists have from the beginning stood for industrial unionism, and they have made it their mission to preach this in season and out of season to the craft unionists. They have joined the unions, got themselves elected delegates to central bodies and conventions and have used the discussion of every union problem, every difference between unions, every union failure or disaster, to point out with contempt the weakness of craft organization and to preach industrial unionism and party socialism. This has made most craft unionists, however revolutionary at heart, violent haters of socialism in its objective party form. Recently, the cooler headed socialists have seen that the American Federation of Labor is normally tending toward industrialism and that it was their fiery efforts more than anything else that held things back. They have therefore become very quiet and conciliatory. But the socialists are there in the unions and the sentiment is growing fast even among business unionists.

CHAPTER VIII

EMPLOYERS' ASSOCIATIONS

The social problem of unionism cannot be understood through a study of unions alone. The unions are but one factor in a great struggle going on which involves the fundamental questions of social rights and social welfare. The other factor is the employer, especially employers organized into associations to resist the efforts of unionism. Over against the complex organizations of the workers are the equally complex and perhaps more extensive and more powerful organizations of employers. To grasp the problem fully, therefore, to get the other side and to comprehend the situation as a whole we need a knowledge of the employers' organizations created for dealing with, and especially of the militant associations organized for combating, unions—their structure, aims, principles, policies, demands, methods, and attitudes; and the conditions and events which grow out of the existence of these two great organic forces. The contest between unionism and employers' associations has been largely one concerned with the rights of employers and of workers as embodied in law. As a basis for understanding it, therefore, as well as the general social problem of unionism, we need to get some idea of the legal status of unionism and the legal strivings of both sets of organizations. This aspect of the subject will follow in a subsequent chapter.

Structurally and functionally the employers' associations offer a striking parallelism to the trade union organizations. In point of structure there is, paralleling the local craft or compound craft and national union of the workers, the local craft or compound craft and national employers' association. The Chicago Team Owners' Association and the National Stove Founders' Defense Association are illustrations. As a counterpart to similar trade unions, there are local, state and national federations of employers, as, for example, the Chicago Employers' Association, the Illinois Manufacturers' Association, and the National Association of Manufacturers. Where the unions have developed an industrial type of organization, the employers have their local, district or national industrial associations. The local Newspaper Publishers' Association, the Illinois Coal Operators, and the Interstate Coal Operators are in point. Finally, as a counter-organization to the general labor union, there are general alliances and citizens' associations.

Similarly, from the standpoint of function, business unionism is paralleled by a type of employers' association, represented by the Stove Founders' Defense Association above referred to, which aims at collective bargaining and the stability of conditions obtained through it. The National Civic Federation, although not strictly an employers' association but generally regarded as such, is a counterpart to uplift unionism. Militant employers' associations, extremely conservative and bitterly opposed to unionism, are the "revolutionary" type among employers. The Metal Trades' Association is one of this group. And, lastly, there are predatory employers' associations, as there are predatory unions to be found in the building trades.

Following upon the great anthracite coal strike of 1902, which suddenly brought out the power of unionism to paralyze social activity, and the fact that unionism had grown stronger than the employers, the latter awoke to the need of better defensive organization and a great growth of radical or militant employers' associations took place. The immediate aims and policies of the employers' associations were accordingly directed to securing mutual aid in the industrial field, rigid enforcement of laws on unions through the courts whenever possible, and new legislation curbing the unions. Injunctions were increasingly sought and suits instituted against union workmen. As a later phase, special employers' associations were formed, such as the Anti-Boycott League. The purpose of this organization was to get the courts to decide that, although unions were voluntary organizations, they could be sued for damages under the Sherman Anti-Trust law as combinations in restraint of trade. Success along this line was calculated to cripple business unionism, for business unionism succeeds in collective bargaining only because it can threaten to strike and it can strike successfully only when there is money laid up to support members on strike. It all goes back to financial resources in the end. Unions have understood all this and for this reason they have stood out against incorporation because they want to do things in their struggles which would subject them to suit and loss of strike funds if they were incorporated.

At the present time the methods of the employers' associations, more especially of the militant, may be summed up as follows:

1. Effective counter organization; employers parallel the union structure, trade against trade (local, district

and national), city against city, state against state, national against national, and federation against federation.

2. Uncompromising war on the closed shop by asserting the right to hire and fire, to pay what the individual can be made to work for, and therefore to destroy uniformity and control hours, speed, and the conditions of employment generally; by continuous propaganda, conventions, meetings, literature and personal solicitations, showing the tyranny of the unions under closed shop rule, and the loss and waste in the closed shop from inefficient workers forced by the union upon employers, from loafing on the job, restrictions on output, and on apprenticeship; showing that the union label is a detriment rather than an advantage to the employer using it; urging employers not to use goods bearing the union label, nor to patronize any concern which does; and opposing the union label on publications of any branch of government.

3. The expulsion of members who sign closed shop agreements, with forfeit of contributions to the reserve fund.

4. Giving financial aid to employers in trouble because of attempts to withstand closed shop demands or to establish the open shop, by inducing banks to refund interest on loans during strikes, and getting owners not to enforce penalties on failure to live up to building contracts. The National Metal Trades Association, for instance, advocates a plan for the coöperation of bankers' associations to extend aid on a wide scale.

5. Mutual aid in time of trial and trouble with unionism; taking orders of a struck shop and returning profit; furnishing men from shops of other members and of

outsiders; paying members out of the reserve fund for holding out against unions—a kind of strike benefit; and endeavoring to secure special patronage for employers in trouble from members and outsiders.

6. Refusal of aid to any enterprise operating under the closed shop.

7. Advertisements in some newspapers and the withdrawal of advertisements from others friendly to unionism.

8. Detachment of union leaders by promotion or bribery, honorary positions and social advancement, thus constantly depriving unions of the directive force of their strongest men.

9. Discrediting union leaders and unions by exploiting their mistakes in strikes, or mismanagement of funds; appealing to the public by the prosecution of leaders; exposing records of fearful examples as types, e.g., Parks, O'Shea, and Madden, and by inciting to violence.

10. Weeding out agitators and plain union men by blacklists, card catalogs, lists of employees, and by identification systems, for example, the Metal Trades' card catalog, and the Seaman's employment book. Employment agencies for employers' associations require lists of all former employees, examine their records and require certificates of membership.

11. Detaching workers from the union and the union's control by requiring an individual contract with penalties, i.e., the loss of unsettled wages called deposit in case of strike; by welfare plans, insurance and pensions to the workers which depend upon long, continuous service and are forfeited in case of strike; selling stock cheap, giving the feeling to the workers that they have a stake in the game, and also by bonus and pre-

mium systems; and by "going the unions one better," i.e.,
paying above the union scale, giving special advantage to
superior workers, requiring good working conditions by
the members of the association, establishing accident
prevention bureaus, safety inspection, and giving care
to the housing of employees.

12. Conducting trade schools and agitating for continuation schools and vocational training; conducting
trade schools themselves or helping to support them;
having cities conduct continuation schools as in Cincinnati and Hartford. The National Metal Trades' Association coöperates with the University of Cincinnati in
engineering courses there; providing "instructors" to
teach the unskilled as does the National Founders' Association; advocating trade schools supported at public expense generally, and separate vocational schools; attacking the present system of academic education; donating
sums to certain societies for promoting industrial education, e.g., the National Metal Trades Association has
donated money to the National Association for the Promotion of Industrial Education.

13. Securing foreknowledge of union plans by the
spy system, use of detective agencies, spies in the union,
the shadowing of leaders, gaining their confidence or
using the dictagraph.

14. Systematic organization and use of strike breakers and counter-sluggers.

15. Organization of counter-unions.

16. Use of the police and militia. The unions, not
having been able to enact the rules of the game into
law, cannot gain their ends by the assertion of their
rights. With the law on the side of property, indorsing
individual liberty, to gain their ends they resort to force.

17. Systematic appeal to the courts, the use of the injunction, systematic prosecution for violence, the employment of a large corps of legal talent, the bringing into play of law and order leagues, suits for damages in case of strikes, and systematic attacks on the constitutionality of labor laws.

18. Opposition to labor legislation by organizing lobbies to appear before both state and national bodies; by a system of calling upon members of the association to send in letters and telegrams in great numbers; by having employers who will be most affected but who have good labor conditions appear before legislative committees to oppose labor legislation; and by having advertisements in many newspapers denouncing labor bills and calling upon citizens to write to legislators not to support them.

19. Political agitation and action such as urging employers to neglect party lines and to vote for safe and sane men only; supporting antilabor statesmen and opposing labor politicians and demagogues, by sending funds, men, and literature into the districts of candidates; exposing the weaknesses of the labor vote and the failure of labor to defeat men the association supports; preventing the adoption of anti-injunction planks or other class legislation, or allowing only meaningless ones in party platforms; denouncing the initiative, referendum, and recall, especially the recall of judges and judicial decisions; and defending the courts and the constitution.

20. Appealing to the public by the use of the press, publishing bulletins, and condemning papers which are unfriendly; systematically attacking unions and exploiting their violence; preventing the publication of seditious

articles like those in the Los Angeles papers; giving statements to the press during strikes, pointing out that the strike is for recognition and for the closed shop and not for better wages and conditions; pointing out, in case the strike is merely a matter of wages, that the trade can stand no more but is now paying higher than elsewhere, also that should wages be advanced prices would be higher, and the consumer would have to pay more in the face of the increased cost of living, and exploiting the losses of the workers in strikes, thus showing the folly of strikes; sending out circulars to educators and clergy; sending publications to the workers; for example, the National Founders' Association and the National Metal Trades' Association send their review to molders and machinists free; attacking Socialism and socialists and lauding ministers, educators, judges, and economists who show the fallacies of unionism and set forth the eternal verities.

The underlying assumptions, theories, and attitudes of employers' associations, more particularly those of the militant type, are: that a natural harmony of interests prevails in society and therefore the unions are to be restrained when they use coercive methods; that the employers' interests are always identical with the interests of society and therefore unionism is to be condemned whenever it interferes with their interests; that the interests of the worker and employer are harmonious, and therefore when the unions oppose the employer they are misled by unscrupulous leaders and are to be condemned; that the employer gives work to the laborers and therefore they are ungrateful and immoral and to be condemned when they combine to oppose him; that the employer has an absolute right to manage his *own* business

to suit himself as against his workers, and therefore the
unions are to be condemned when they interfere in any
way with that right; that the business is his, an absolute
property right, and to compel him to bargain with the
men collectively, instead of as individuals, is to compel
him to deal with men not in his employ, with an irresponsible committee, and to assert a voice in the matters
of hiring and discharge, the conditions of employment,
and a right to the job and the trade; that the employer
has an absolute right to manage his own business as
against workers *not* in his employ and therefore outside
workers are to be condemned when they act in sympathy with his workers; that every worker has an absolute
right to work when, where, and for whom he pleases and
therefore the unions are to be condemned when they
restrict this right and freedom; that free competition
of the workers is always in the interest of society and
therefore that any interference by the unions in this is
to be condemned; that the greatest possible production
is always in the interest of society and therefore the
union is to be condemned whenever it interferes with
this; that the law, the courts, and the police represent
absolute and impartial rights and justice, and therefore
the unions are to be condemned whenever they violate
the law or oppose the police.

The fundamental questions of the source of social
rights and the meaning of social welfare lie at the core
of a critical consideration of the employers' associations,
their theories and viewpoint. What is going to be done
with this social philosophy of God-given, inalienable and
absolute rights? If this be rejected, what is to be substituted? Shall we say, general social welfare? What
is that? Take the case of the introduction of machinery.

Is it right and just to make the workers pay for social progress? Shall we say, the upholding of established rights—of whatever is law? Where did these rights and laws come from? Or shall we say, substitute that which is natural? But what is natural? Is competition natural? Consider the historical effects of free competition. Then what *shall* be the basis?

Is there any more basis for the employers' claim of rights and condemnation of attacks of unions upon them, than for the counterclaims of the unions? Is it true that employers give work to laborers any more than that laborers give profits to employers? That the employer has a right to compel men to bargain individually any more than laborers have a right to compel employers to bargain with men collectively? Is it true that employers or workingmen have nothing to arbitrate? Is the employer any more justified in refusing to deal with men not in his employ than a group of workmen would be when in conflict with their employer in opposing the assistance of outside employers? Has every man a right to work where and when and for whom he pleases, regardless of the effects on his fellow workers? Is he not interfering with their business?

If it is wrong for the workers who have no grievances against their particular employer to help other workers who have, then why is it not wrong for employers who have no grievances against their particular workmen to help other employers who have? If the workers injure an innocent employer, employers injure innocent workers. If workers mix in the business of other employers, the employers mix in the business of other workers. The only difference is in method. Each side uses the best ones at hand for its purposes. If we feel that there is a difference, that it is somehow morally worse for the workers to strike in aid of those with whom their employer has no concern, than for employers to aid other employers with whom they have no concern, it means that we have been consciously or unconsciously holding to assumptions underlying the militant employers' interpretation of unionism: which is to say that there is no natural or normal coöperative relationship between workers as such; harmony of interests is between employers and workers, and the normal relationship between workers is competitive; therefore the supreme duty of the workers is to their own employer; that every employer has a right to manage his own affairs, especially as to his relationships with his workers, without any outside interference.

But why should we not assume a harmony of interests between workers, that they owe a supreme duty to one another? Why is this not the normal? We admit it readily enough for the employer. We do not feel shocked when the association comes to the relief of a struck employer. Is there any more reason for assuming harmony of interest between individual employer and his worker plus harmony between employer and employer, than for assuming disharmony of interest between individual employer and workers plus harmony of interests between workers? And if every employer has a natural right to manage his own business, free from interference from outside workers, why has not every group of workers of an individual business the right to manage its own affairs without interference from outside employers?

If we cannot feel this, it is because we have been corrupted by assumptions of normal and natural rights.

We have come to assume with employers that whatever has been is normal and right, while whatever is becoming is abnormal and wrong: that is, because employers have been able to act so and so, therefore, it is natural, God-given, normal, right, but because workers are only just beginning to be able or are striving to be able to act so and so, therefore, it is unnatural, abnormal and wrong. This is at bottom the old error of the absolute. It means that evolution is a form of words, not a reality.

The absurdity becomes apparent the moment we realize the notion of evolution and examine the nature and source of social right. Social rights exist only as confirmed by society. Their historical basis is in the power of the individual or the class. On this basis unions have the right to interfere with the employers' business when they can. If we seek a rational basis it lies in expediency. Society can curtail it whenever it sees fit, and in allowing workers to do so and so, it gives a right. The employers' plea is therefore false and its high moral basis is gone.

The militant employers' point of view finds no sanction in modern social scientific thought or in the spirit of the age. It is a relic of the preëvolutionary age, of dead and gone absolutistic philosophy, government, and economics. The only basis of social rights acceptable to modern thinking is social welfare and social will. The employers' claim of rights finds no practical sanction in social welfare because it is usually impossible to determine what is social welfare. For society is so constituted that what is good for one group or class may be bad for another, and there is no standard for determining the relative social importance of different classes. But we do not know enough about the nature of so-

ciety and the laws of developmental ends to determine
what is ultimately for the best. We are thrown back,
therefore, for the sources and sanction of rights to the
social will. Society alone can give social rights; society
alone can take them away. What society allows are
rights. Practically, social rights are the rules of the
game of the dominant class, but social rights thus granted
have no necessary moral sanction. Every group or class
can have its rights in proportion to the power to enforce
its claim. Hence, this insistence upon "rights" by employers and unionists is pretty much in the air; it means
practically an attempt to "bluff" society into helping
each group to uphold what it wants for its own good.
The most we can say of the employers' claim of rights
is that, so far as we can see, there is no more basis in
morals or social welfare for it, than for the unionists'
counterclaim, but that many of these rights are based
on outworn philosophy and false assumption of fact.

In conclusion: (a) The only rational basis of rights
is social will. (b) Actual rights are pragmatic in the
sense that they are historical products which have
"worked" to the benefit of somebody. (c) But many of
these rights are group or class standards masquerading
as social standards. They have been foisted upon society by a group or class falsely identifying itself with
society. (d) And there is a law of retardation here in
that standards and rights are maintained by supersti-
tion, faith, custom, law, and force long after they have
ceased to give useful social service. (e) "Established
rights," therefore, do not represent anything sacred or
necessarily right or good. (f) In matters where group
environments are sharply opposed, it is impossible to get
a consensus of opinion and to set up, therefore, real

social rights. (g) Where group interests are opposed it is not possible to determine positively what is for the social good, and, therefore, to set up social standards of judgment. (h) In practice every man must decide for himself what seems to him conducive to social welfare and, therefore, good and right, and the best each can do is to act strongly in coöperation with those who see things as he does. (i) However, each must realize that his decision is the outcome of inherited tendencies, teaching and environment, a matter of feeling more than of sound judgment, and that, therefore, he has no right to be dogmatic. (j) But it will be generally true to say that things are not necessarily right because they are established in law or custom, since in the last analysis "rights" generally represent—at least in this field—group power.

The employers' association movement was in the beginning primarily defensive. Just as the unions arose earlier in defense of the economic status and the assumed rights of craftsmen when in the development of modern industry the individual employer became too strong for the individual worker, so the employers' associations arose later in defense of the economic status and assumed rights of the employer of labor when unionism had so developed that it was stronger than the individual employer. This occurred roughly between the time of the formation of the American Federation of Labor and the demonstration of its great strength about 1902.

The problem of the employers' association was, they supposed, a comparatively easy one. They need simply refuse to countenance or deal with trade union organizations. They soon found, however, that they had made a big mistake. Unionism would not down, it evidently had roots in the soil of reality and its overthrow was going to be costly. As a result, employers divided into two groups of associations, those who took the narrow, selfish, immediate economic point of view, and were willing to purchase peace and prosperity by a compromise with unionism, and taking it out of the consumers, that is, mediatory or conciliatory associations, and those who retained the original purpose, but saw that the fight must be long, intense, and broadly educational. They were the militant associations.

Most of the mediatory or conciliatory associations developed along narrow, economic lines mainly. They attempted to strengthen themselves defensively against the particular unions with which they had to deal, and to develop with the unions a strong position as against society—a double-sided monopoly. The militant associations buckled down to their task of weakening or eliminating the union organizations. But in the course of this they encountered influences which greatly modified their character and viewpoint. They found that if they were to combat the unions successfully their own members had to submit to control. Thus, although they were seeking individualistic ends, they had to curtail the liberty of their individual members, just as the individual worker, in the words of Mr. Frey, editor of the *Molder's Journal,* "to gain and maintain his freedom has to submit to group control—to develop the spirit of coöperation within the group." This was a tremendous blow at the old *laissez faire,* individualistic ideal which they were seeking to defend. A strong, centralized authority had to be set up over the individual. The employers had to be made one as the unions had made the

workers one. They found also that if they were to combat the unions successfully, they had to meet the unions
on every field, not alone on the economic. This forced
them to enter politics and to study every phase of economic and social welfare; to consider the evil effects of
existing conditions inside and outside the shop that developed unions and contributed to union strength, and
to devise remedies. This drove them into welfare work
of all sorts, the study of safety and sanitation, workmen's compensation, the unemployment problem, and
industrial education. The result was a strong tendency
to educate and socialize these individualists, to force them
to consider constructive measures, to broaden their social outlook, to modify their militancy. They began to
see that if they were to eliminate or weaken unionism
they must give the workers what the unions sought to
give them. They found, finally, that if they were to succeed they must develop all sorts of spiritual and federative relationships to offset the union form and strength.
Out of this has seemed to be growing a class consciousness.

The survey of the militant associations, then, seems
to indicate that the employers as a class must organize
society and ameliorate social conditions. Unions had a
reason for existence because of the employers' failure to
meet the needs of the situation. The negative appeal to
individualism, natural order, and natural rights, the wild
denunciation of the unions as unnatural and corrupt organizations, is giving place to talk of fair conditions,
education of both employers and workers, and constructive measures as the way out. Thus the militant associations tend to turn uplift. And with the development
of this spirit has come a new form of organization typi-

fied by the National Civic Federation to include employers, workers and the public with the purposes of investigation, the consideration and trial of coöperation, profit-
sharing, and general betterment schemes.

The methods by which the employers' associations and
trusts have beaten down the union strength are indicative not only of the character and possible outcome of
the struggle, but also throw light on the employers' attitude and have caused and perhaps justified many union
points of view and methods. It almost seems that the
employers' association is stronger potentially than any
union movement can be, that the unions, having organized the individual workers of the group against the individual employer, have done their utmost, so long as they
lack the solidarity for a class movement; and that they
can at present find no offset for the strength of the
employers' association movement. On the other hand
the employers' association movement in its fight on unionism is becoming modified so that it is not likely to
push its advantage to the utmost. It holds out promise
of a social betterment movement far removed from the
old classical, individualistic, *laissez faire* position.

We have found unionism invading the consciousness
of the individual. So far so good. But does it tend to
develop social consciousness and valid social standards?
One of the hopeful things about employers' associations
seems to be that they are doing this. The great need of
the present time is to develop social consciousness and
to discover social standards. It seems as if the history
of modern industrial society shows us a succession of
swings through what might be called a typical cycle of
development. These cycles are marked by three stages:
the individual consciousness of the seventeenth and

eighteenth centuries; the group consciousness of the nineteenth; and the social consciousness of the twentieth.   In
the first stage, individualism is rampant.   The individual seeks only or mainly his own well-being, unconscious of a larger whole.   The contest is between individual and individual.   Then, gradually, groups with
common interests develop.   The consciousness of the
individual is enlarged.   He sees his interests in the
interests of the group.   Group standards arise.   The individual is subjected to them.   Then comes contest between groups.   Finally social consciousness emerges.
The individual identifies his good with the good of the
whole; social standards and social control arise.   Social
well-being is consciously sought and to an extent attained.   But all the while, conditions, needs, relationships, problems, terms of welfare, are changing.   The
standards of social welfare set up gradually cease to fit
needs; the system of social control, becoming invalid,
hampers progress.   There is a revolt.   Old standards
and systems of control are broken down.   Individualism
is again idealized and becomes rampant.   Then the process of socialization begins again.

A period of individualistic revolt took place in the
seventeenth and eighteenth centuries and swept aside all
social control.   There developed a philosophy of natural
order, natural law and *laissez faire*.   Social welfare, it
was declared, came through industrial competition.   We
are now in the second stage, group consciousness, group
standards and group fighting.   We are struggling toward a third stage, the development of social consciousness and social standards.   From individual consciousness and interest we progress through group consciousness and interest to social consciousness and interest.

We are studying groups to try to understand the forces with which we have to deal in this struggle forward, to see if we can find clues to social standards valid for our developing situation and a basis for social control. Standards have broken down in the past because they were absolute. Our great task now is to try, this time, to get standards that may be elastic and develop with developing situations and needs. We must take into consideration evolution. This means not only a study of present conditions and social expectation, but a study of the genesis and process of social development, a view not only of the factors of the present but of the whole developing process.

BIBLIOGRAPHY

Constitutions: American Anti-Boycott Association, National Association of Manufacturers, National Metal Trades' Association, National Erectors' Association, National Founders' Association, The United Typothetæ, Illinois Manufacturers' Association, Employers' Associations of Chicago and of Dayton, Ohio, Building Contractors' Association of Chicago, Chicago Typothetæ, The Citizens' Industrial Association, Etc.

Convention Proceedings: National Association of Manufacturers, National Founders' Association, National Erectors' Association, Etc.

Journals:

American Industries.

Manufacturers' News Report (Illinois State Employers' Association).

The National Civic Federation Review.

The Review (National Metal Founders' and Metal Trades' Association).

The Square Deal.

Pamphlets:

The American Anti-Boycott Association:

Analysis of Labor Union, Injunctions, Contempt Sections of the Clayton Anti-Trust Bill. Davenport, Daniel.

Bulletins

The Closed Shop.

The Davenport Testimonial.

Labor, Law and Order. Merritt, W. G. (Reprint, The Unpopular Review, 1915).

Labor Legislation. Merritt, W. G. (1914).

Million Against One (Tyranny and Abuse of D. E. Loewe & Co.). Brock, H. I.

Recommendations Submitted to the U. S. Commission on Industrial Relations (1914).

Report of Legal Activities (1916).

Some Phases of the Federal Industrial Relations Commission Report (1915).

Statements of Mr. Davenport in the Senate and House Hearings (1912).

The Citizens' Industrial Association:

Bulletin No. 1 (1903), History—Organization.

Citizens' Industrial Association.

The Citizens' Industrial Association from the Standpoint of the Manufacturers. American Industries (Dec. 15, 1906). Van Cleave, J. W.

Platform and Principles.

Work Accomplished to Preserve Property Rights.

The National Association of Manufacturers:

Address, J. W. Bryce, Pres. of National Trades and Workers' Assn. (1912).

Industrial Betterment Activities of the N. A. M.

The National Civic Federation:

Survey of Social and Industrial Conditions.

Pamphlets—Cont.

The National Erectors' Association:
Booklet (Nov., 1907).
Circular Letters.
The National Founders' Association:
Apprenticeship in the Metal Industries. Alexander, M.
W. The Review.
The Labor Secretary and Labor Questions (1913).
A Policy of Lawlessness (1908).
The National Metal Trades Association:
Basic Principles of Industrial Organization. Kimball,
D. S.
Certificate of Recommendation.
Conference Boards and Their Value in Industrial Co
operation. Alexander, M. W.
The Employment Bureau.
Industrial Betterment Activities.
A Lesson in Industrial Economy.
N. M. T. A. Safety Bulletin.
A Plea for Profit-Sharing. Barnett, M.
A Proposed Bill to Regulate the Manufacture of Ex-
plosives.
Report of Apprenticeship Committee.
Report of Committee on Industrial Education.
Report of W. H. Doolittle, Safety Inspector, N. M. T.
A. (1914).
Safety Appliances.
State Employers' Associations:
Annual Meeting.
Associated Employers of Illinois—Bulletins.
The Minimum Wage—Its Fallacies.
Service Rendered to Members.
To the Manufacturers of Illinois.
The United Typothetæ:
Bulletin.

United Typothetæ of America, What It Is, and What It Stands For.

The Value of Organization.

What Is the United Typothetæ of America? Why It Was Organized.

Propaganda Leaflets:

Don't Weep at the Ice House. Post, C. W.

Free Riot Laws.

Let Organized Labor Purge Itself. American Industries (Feb., 1913), pp. 7-11.

Mob Spirit in Organized Labor. Parry, D. M.

Progress and Industrial Freedom. Post, C. W.

A Tale of Two Cities. Job, F. W., Sec. Employers' Assn. of Chicago (1904).

They're After You. Post, C. W.

The Union Label a Detriment to Business. Starrett, L. T.

Educational Literature (Published by the National Association of Manufacturers, 30 Church St., New York City).

Maintenance of a Lobby to Influence Legislation—Hearing Before a Sub-Committee of the Committee on the Judiciary, U. S. Sen., 63d Cong., 1st Session (1913).

Materials of the Buck's Stove and Range Case.

Mulhall Exposé of the National Association of Manufacturers.

The United States Commission on Industrial Relations:

Report on the Colorado Strike (1915). West, G. P.

Report on the National Erectors' Association and the International Association of Bridge and Structural Iron Workers (1915). Grant, Luke.

ADAMS AND SUMNER. *Labor Problems,* pp. 279-285.

BAKER, R. S. "Organized Capital Challenges Organized Labor," *McClures,* 23:279 (1904).

BAKER, R. S. "Capital and Labor Hunt Together," *Mc-Clures,* 21:451 (1903).

CARLTON. *History and Problems of Organized Labor,* pp. 85-93.

ELIOT, C. W. "Employers' Policies in the Industrial Strife," *Harper's Magazine,* 110:528-33 (1905).

HOLLANDER AND BARNETT. *Studies in American Trade Unionism,* chap. VII, "Employers Associations in the United States." (Hilbert, F. W.)

JUSTI, HERMAN. *The Organization of the Employing Class* (1901).

——. *Sundry Papers and Addresses on Labor Problems* (1906).

MARCOSSON, I. F. "Labor Met By Its Own Methods," *World's Work,* 7:4309 (1904).

MITCHELL. *Organized Labor,* chap. XXII, "Organized Labor and Organized Capital."

STECKER, MARGARET. "The National Founders' Association." *Quarterly Journal of Economics,* 25:352 (1916).

VAN CLEAVE, J. W. "The Work of Employers' Associations in the Settlement of Labor Disputes," *Annals of the American Academy,* 36:373-80 (1910).

WILLOUGHBY, W. F. Employers' Associations, *Quarterly Journal of Economics,* 20:110-50 (1905).

CHAPTER IX

THE LAW IN RELATION TO LABOR

The specific dangers which we encounter in taking up a study of the legal aspects of labor are clear. We may lose our way in the esoteric technicalities of the law and go wrong in the facts; we may go much more deeply or much less deeply into the subject than is warranted by our purpose, needs and circumstances; and we may be led into discussions off the main track and of no particular value to us here. Therefore, there is a special need to begin with a clear-headed attempt to determine just what is the purpose in the study and what ought to be the method. What is the special significance of the legal status of labor and the employers in this connection; what is its special bearing on our problem?

Among the main fundamental forces and conditions that determine what ought to and can be done in the solution of labor problems, we find that the present legal status determines most largely the actual conditions and problems of labor, and that most labor problems must be solved in terms of rights and law by invoking present and changing rights and law. What should be the purpose then in studying the rights and legal status of labor and the employers? It should be to find out what are in essentials the law's chief characteristics; whether as it stands it puts the employer and the workers on an equal footing, and gives equal opportunity to them in working

out their problems for themselves; whether as it stands
it gives opportunity for constructive social effort in this
connection, and whether it furnishes a sufficient basis
for a constructive social program for betterment. If
not, what ought to be done about it? How ought it to
be changed in its general fundamental characteristics and
in its general character? Can such changes be made,
and if so, how?

The law rests on two fundamental and contradictory
concepts of society, of social relationships and social
rights, of justice, welfare and control, the absolutistic
and the evolutionary concepts. The absolutistic concept
assumes a fixed social constitution, fixed social relationships and positive standards of right and justice, resting
upon a natural order in which exist the natural and inalienable rights of private property, individual liberty,
free contract and free competition. It assumes that social right, justice and welfare consist in preserving these
natural rights, since, when they are preserved, equality
of opportunity is secured for all individuals and social
harmony prevails; that, therefore, the law should aim
solely to secure and preserve these rights; and that this
is best done by giving power to the courts to test all
legislation on the basis of those fixed and fundamental
principles of natural right and to declare unconstitutional
and void any laws which appear to violate them. The
evolutionary concept assumes a developing social constitution and changing social relations and relative standards of right and justice, resting on a denial of any fixed
natural order or natural and inalienable rights in regard
to private property, liberty of the individual, freedom
of contract, and free competition. It, therefore, assumes
that social right, justice and welfare consist in changing

or adapting rights and law to meet the particular needs and circumstances of developing social conditions and relationships, and that this is best secured when the people are allowed through their legislators to make the laws with regard to present and developing needs, relationships and standards.

As yet the law as it stands, in its fundamental assumptions, in its method and in its specific character, especially as it concerns the relations between employers and workers, is predominantly representative of the first of these conflicting concepts. The second shows its influence mainly in laws where it can be made to appear that the persons primarily affected are not complete individuals, e.g., women, minors, children, dependents, defectives and delinquents; or where it can be made to appear that the public is more concerned than the employers and workers, e.g., in cases relating to public health and safety, sanitation, nuisances, housing, accident and death, industrial disease, and compensation for these things. So far, then, as the labor field is concerned, with the exception of laws relating to women's work, child labor, charities and corrections, sanitation and safety, workingmen's insurance, etc., where there is a struggle on between the two principles, with the latter rapidly gaining, the law in principle, method and specific character still reflects the absolutistic principle.[1]

[1] Lest some assume that I am dogmatic and partisan in this treatment, a word may be necessary. What are we studying this for? Mainly, because the law is the chief tool that we have to use in solving our labor problems. Therefore, if it is unfitted for this in spirit, character and method of procedure, then the *big labor problem* is how to change it. We must know *what* it is in these respects and *why* it is what it is. Why do I state its spirit, character and method of pro-

The characteristics of the law may be summarized as follows:

cedure in terms of the absolutistic concept which underlies it? Because that concept still dominates the spirit, character and method of procedure of the law, especially with regard to labor matters. Am I trying in this way to make capital for the evolutionary concept which is just beginning to affect the law? No. I don't know what the character and method of the law would be under the influence of this concept. I have not had a chance to see. It might conceivably be worse. I simply know that the law as it is is not in harmony with the spirit of the age. Am I partisan then in my analysis? No. I am simply stating the facts and trying to find out why they exist. Am I dogmatic about it? No, because as far as possible, as far as the facts exist, I am trying to set forth all viewpoints and all sides. If anyone concludes from this that one side or the other is right or wrong, that is his affair. The dogmatic man is one who presents one viewpoint only, and keeps hammering away on that, but does not present it *as* a viewpoint, because he never clearly formulates it and never intimates that there is any other. Lawyers and judges do not claim that the law assumes to represent absolute justice, but only that they are approaching or approximating justice, and hence the law is not based on the absolutistic theory. On the contrary, it is based on the evolutionary theory evolving toward justice. In a certain sense, it may be said that the lawyers and judges are evolutionary, but the legal attitude comes to an absolutistic position in the end. To make this clear, we have to distinguish between two kinds of evolution, modern scientific evolution, which is relativistic, and teleological evolution, which is as old as history and is but one variation of the eighteenth century idea, and at bottom thoroughly absolutistic. Modern, scientific evolution knows no beginning and no end; it postulates simply change. It knows no absolute or final right or justice, but only right and justice relative to particular conditions, circumstances and ends. What was right a hundred years ago may be wrong now and vice versa. **And this always has been and always will be so.** Everything

1. As such, the law is archaic and antiquated in viewpoint and method. It accepts a social theory conceived

always has been, is, and always will be in flux. There is no assignable beginning and no assignable end to the process in which a fixed constitution of things will exist, and therefore, fixed standards of right and justice. Teleological evolution, on the other hand, assumes a fixed, ideal constitution of things, in which absolute standards of right and justice do exist, from which we have departed and to which we are trying to get back or toward which we are headed, and which we are trying to reach. While it admits, then, that our present standards of right and justice are only relative, it considers the situation, in a way, temporary and abnormal. It has always in view that absolute ideal, that fixed constitution of things, from which we have departed and to which we are trying to get back, or to which we are headed and toward which we are striving. Its ideal, therefore, is an absolute situation in which absolute standards of right and justice hold, and in its actual rules it is always trying to approximate these absolute standards. Its search then is always for absolute standards of right and justice that will hold for all time, and, at bottom, it is not evolutionary and relativistic in the modern, scientific sense but thoroughly absolutistic.

Hence, its decisions are always based on an assumed fixed situation, with fixed relationships, and fixed standards of right and justice, existing either at the beginning or at the end of things, rather than on the actual relationships and relative standards of rights and justice at the present. Therefore, it can proceed only on the basis of precedents based on an assumed fixed past situation or an assumed future perfect state of things. In either case it is quite out of harmony with modern evolutionary relativistic thought, and finds great difficulty in adapting itself to the existing situation—in reflecting and meeting existing needs and conditions. It is but a variation of the absolutistic theory deriving its inspiration and method from the story of the Garden of Eden and the fall of man, or from the utopian ideal of a perfect state. In the one case it postulates the divine architect who in the beginning more than a century ago and almost universally rejected today. It therefore tends to assume that social ideals, conditions and relations that existed more than a century ago exist now. It tends to base its judgments of right, rights and relationships on the conditions and relations that existed more than a century ago. Its method of procedure is that of precedent, i.e., it proceeds on the basis of fixed, absolute rules of judgment, formulated in the past, instead of on the basis of changing and developing standards based on present and developing conditions and relationships, standards and ideals of justice and welfare. It thus tends to be a system based on logic rather than on life. If the specific decisions in regard to the relations between employers and the labor groups are examined, it will be seen that all through they tend to be logical deductions from the original premises. An injunction is a civil writ issued for the protection of property from damage, the remedy for which cannot be had by criminal procedure but by civil suit for damages. This is the legal theory. Therefore, logically, when a man violates an injunction he cannot logically ask for a jury trial. Therefore, logically, his punishment must be by act of court alone. Hence, though present conditions and justice demand a jury trial, the law is not able to grant it to him. Its logical principle will not allow this adaptation to present needs.

2. As such, our law is individualistic rather than socialized. It postulates the individual as the center of the universe and does not recognize fully the existence of social groups and group relationships. It therefore does not know how to deal with social groups and group re-

created all things well; in the other, the natural order which is the normal situation.

lationships except to deny their normal existence. It knows no society apart from an aggregation of individuals and no social welfare apart from individual welfare. It is concerned, therefore, primarily in upholding individual rights, or in acting as the arbitrator in contests between individuals over their rights. In short, it is thoroughly atomistic.

3. As such, our law tends to place private property rights above personal and social rights. It places private property very close to the center of its social philosophy and therefore tends everywhere to emphasize private property rights at the expense of all other rights of the individual, and to overlook the rights of society.

4. Hence, the law, being absolutistic, individualistic, and concerned with property rights, is stiff, inflexible, inelastic, and ill-adapted to meet the conditions of a changing socialized situation. Its decisions are based on a system of fixed assumptions and rules. These assumptions and rules do not reflect existing conditions, and the law does not know how to create new assumptions and rules, since from its standpoint no such new assumptions and rules can have any valid existence, and even if it should admit this, its eye being ever fixed on the past, it is not sufficiently acquainted with and cannot understand the existing developing situation. In the eye of the law, the relation between workers and employers is fundamentally what it was when the law's assumptions and rules were established. If the relation has changed it is abnormal and artificial. It is the duty of the law to restore the normal or natural relationship. Hence, the lawyers and the courts have not felt obliged to acquaint themselves thoroughly with the existing economic situation and relationship, or, if they have, they have found great

difficulty in understanding them and fully acknowledging them as they are.

5. The law is ultraconservative and acts too slowly to meet the needs of changing conditions—the law's delays.

6. Nevertheless, the law is uncertain. Examine carefully the law relating to the status of labor associations, i.e., relations between the employing and labor groups, and you will see that it is vague, shadowy and contradictory in many respects. This results from several causes: (a) from the conflict between the two contradictory concepts at work in determining the character of the law; now the one, now the other holds the advantage; (b) from the fact that the interpretation of the federal and state law is in the hands of different sets of judges; (c) from the fact that each court, federal or state, is a different source of interpretation; (d) from the fact that each court in each state is a distinct authority; (e) from the fact that each judge to an extent is a different source of interpretation; (f) from the fact that the judges themselves are more or less under the domination of the contradictory principles at the foundation of the law. Hence, by picking your judges and your court, you can get varying interpretations of the law as between the United States and the states, as between the states, as between the courts, and as between the judges. It is true that there is an attempt at coördination through a series of judicial hierarchies with a system of appeals. But at the outset no one knows what the law is or means, and to follow up the process to the highest court takes much time and money. Only the employer individually can afford to do this, and in the meantime the outcome

is uncertain. And even the highest court may reverse itself.

7. The law is undemocratic. The people may think they know what they want and what is for social welfare; the employers and workers may agree on an adjustment of their relationships and on the basis of their decisions, laws may be enacted, but until the court has spoken this may not be law. Whatever the excellence of the statute, or its fitness to meet the needs of the developing situation, if, in the eye of the law and the mind of the courts, it violates the fundamental and unchangeable assumptions and rules of justice conceived in the past and relating to a past situation, and if somehow or other by legal fiction it cannot be made to appear to be in harmony with these assumptions and rules, the courts can and will declare it no law.

This brings us to the question again: Does the law as it stands put the employing and the working group upon an equal footing, giving equal opportunity to the two groups in the working out of their own problems, relationships and welfare, and if not, why not? To answer this question, we need first to get some standard of judgment by considering the relative footing or bargaining power of the individual employer and the individual workman under modern economic conditions; next, to examine the law as it stands in the light of this standard of judgment; and finally, to look at it historically, to examine it as it has worked. Let us then, first, consider the relative footing or bargaining power of the employer and worker under modern economic conditions.

Leaving the law aside, and looking only at the modern economic situation, are the individual employer and the individual worker on an equal footing or bargaining power and if not, why not? First, we may say that this may have been true in the period of handicraft industry, before the development of machine industry and modern capitalism. It may have been true when hand tools were mainly used, when these hand tools represented the main item in industrial capital, industry being carried on mainly in the home, when the capital necessary for independent enterprise was very small, when each workman knew the whole process and could practice the whole trade, and when any workman, therefore, who was not satisfied to work for an employer could easily accumulate or acquire capital for an independent enterprise and have the knowledge to conduct it.

But it must be noted that since the handicraft period the essential conditions of industry have enormously changed. With the progressive invention of machinery the amount of capital necessary to run an economic enterprise has progressively increased, until now no workman can ordinarily acquire it. Instead of a few tools, a cottage, and a small fund to be invested in materials, costly machines are required which must be housed in costly factories and a great capital fund must be had for materials and other exigencies. The capital now required for a successful enterprise must ordinarily be reckoned not in hundreds of dollars but in tens and hundreds of thousands. Thus, the modern worker who is not satisfied has little chance to set up for himself.

Moreover, the workman no longer knows his trade as he did under the handicraft system. Modern capitalistic and machine industry has progressively specialized him, and with this specialization has progressively abolished the system of apprenticeship by which formerly he acquired knowledge of a whole trade or craft, till now the average workman knows only one or a few minute processes connected with any enterprise and has no means of broadening his knowledge. Therefore, the modern workman, even if he had the capital, would no longer be in a position to use it independently. Under these circumstances the modern worker, typically, is practically compelled to remain a workman and finds himself thus as an individual compelled to bargain with an employer who owns and controls large amounts of capital and machinery, and who is the employer of a large body of workmen. The question then is, leaving the law aside and considering only the economic situation: Is the individual workman under these modern conditions on an equal footing or on equal bargaining terms with the employer, and if not, why not? We can, perhaps, best get at this question by asking why they should be put on an equal footing. The law assumes it, therefore we ask it. Experience proves that when they are not, one side takes the grossest advantage of the other, and there is bound to be on the whole discord of interests, and mutual misunderstanding. It is the same everywhere in life.

Under existing conditions the bargaining strength of the individual employer is greater than that of the individual worker because (1) the employer has superior knowledge of market conditions, better bargaining skill, and waiting power; the workers are confined to the bench; they have no experience in buying and selling, or in market prices; no knowledge of price movements nor foresight as to them; (2) the lesser thing is at stake with the employer—profits as against life; (3) there is always an actual or a potential oversupply of labor; there is always unemployment—a general over-supply and, since trades are minutely specialized, the next lower worker is always in competition for the next higher job; (4) the weakest employers industrially and pecuniarily are the strongest wage bargainers—in distress they must take it out of the workers or go to the wall; (5) the competitive strength of the labor group under individual bargaining is equal only, or tends to be equal only, to the competitive strength of its weakest member; (6) the full bargaining strength of the employer usually is bound to be exerted against the worker, under competitive conditions, because of the pressure of the consuming public for cheap goods, and because the most unscrupulous employer sets the pace; under monopolistic conditions, impersonality produces the same results. Therefore, under modern conditions, the worker is not on an equal footing with the employer unless he is allowed to combine or act collectively without doubt or hampering.

With this economic situation in view let us now turn to the law and examine this question of equal footing. Has the law taken into account these facts and been so developed as tó redress the disadvantages of the worker? Or, does it still proceed as if the employers and workmen were essentially in the same relative economic situation as in the handicraft stage when the individual workman and the individual employer were apparently on an equal footing, and by so doing does it place the modern worker at a great disadvantage relative to the modern employer?

The first step toward a specific understanding of the present law regarding the rights or legal status of labor and the employer, with a view to testing it in the manner suggested above, is to get before us a general outline of the present situation. In general the following would appear to be a summary of its main features: [2]

1. In the typical cases, under the present economic or legal organization, the employer furnishes, owns and controls the material and pecuniary means of production—the capital, land, buildings, machinery, tools and the raw materials. Subject to general restrictions on illegal acts and to the police power of the state, he is a free agent in the disposition of the means of production. He cannot be compelled to put or to keep them in productive use; he is free to hire or to refuse to hire whomever it may please him as workmen, and to discharge workers at will subject to the terms of his contracts with them.[3]

2. The worker has no legal right to work, being wholly dependent upon his ability to find some employer who is able and willing to give him employment.

3. The individual laborer, subject to general restrictions on illegal acts, so long as he does not interfere with the rights and freedom of action of others, is a free agent with respect to the disposition of his labor power. He cannot legally be compelled to labor, and is free, subject to the above restrictions, to apply his labor

[2] Any attempt on the part of a layman to present the legal situation may be assumed offhand to be faulty. Students must, therefore, take what follows to be a tentative statement, and they should subject it as far as possible to legal criticism. Only a few typical cases are cited, and the student should consult Clark, *The Law of the Employment of Labor;* Cooke, *The Law of Combinations, Monopolies and Labor Unions;* and Commons and Andrews, *Principles of Labor Legislation.*

[3] To the following general statements there are certain specific modifications which it should be the purpose of our study to disclose and account for.

power where and on what terms it may please him, or as
circumstances may compel him; to work under what circumstances, for what wage he pleases and to quit at
will, subject to the terms of his contract.

4. The above statements are subject to exception under the state's right of eminent domain and its police
power. The state has the right to take and use property
for public purposes, to suppress seditious acts and to
abate nuisances; to enforce the maintenance of contracts; to regulate dangerous insanitary conditions, etc.
The state may also interfere in many ways where it can
be shown that the contracting parties are not full individuals, acting without coercion or restraint, and where
the laborers are women or minors.

5. The relations between the employer and the laborer
are, in general, those of free contracting parties. The
employer contracts to provide the laborer with a certain
kind of employment for a specified period at a specified
wage; the claim of the. worker is liquidated by the wage,
except in special cases, and under special conditions, coming under the employer's liability for accident and death.
The ownership and disposal of the product and the good-
will of the business rest entirely with the employer, subject to a lien of the worker in case of bankruptcy.

6. The employer and the individual workers are thus,
in the eye of the law, and by commonplace assumption,
on a plane of strict economic equality.

7. The wage contract, including hours and conditions
of employment, is generally assumed by the law to be between the individual employer and the individual workman. Originally, only individual bargaining was legal.
Any combination of employers or workers which inter-
fered with or modified such individual bargaining was

conspiracy in restraint of trade, and, as such, illegal and punishable. Latterly, combinations to affect the wage bargain in certain ways have been ruled lawful by the courts or authorized by statute.[4]

8. In general, there is no limit set by law upon the wage which any laborer may contract for and receive. The worker is free to force the wage as high, the employer to force it as low, as free individual bargaining will permit. This rule is sometimes subject to modification in the case of women and minors.

9. There is no limit set by law upon the hours per day or week for which the laborer may contract to work. The worker is free to force the hours to as small a number, the employer to force them to as great a number as free bargaining will permit. This rule is subject to exceptions: the government, national, state or municipal, may set limits for itself, as employer, by statute or ordinance and may limit in this respect contracting employers doing work for it. This rule has also been modified in certain specific industries and for certain classes of workers, but, as applied to adult male labor, holds generally.

10. The method of remuneration, the mode, time, and material character of wages payment, are, for the most part, matters of free contract, though statutory restrictions have, to a considerable extent, modified this rule.

11. The freedom of contract between the employer and the worker has been greatly restricted with reference to the welfare of the worker and society at large. The worker cannot contract with the employer for the doing of illegal acts, or be forced to perform such acts. By common law, the employer is bound to furnish rea-

[4] *See* cases cited below.

sonably safe conditions of work for his employees. A great mass of statutory law has been enacted, varying with the different states, designed to protect the health and secure the safety and comfort of the workers in factories, mines, workshops and other places of employment.

12. Under the common law, the employer is liable to the worker for injury and death caused by accident in the regular performance of his duties, but only where it can be shown that the employer has not exercised reasonable care, and he may set up the defenses of contributory negligence, the neglect or disobedience of a fellow servant, contracting out, and assumption of risk on the part of the worker. The actual liability of the employer, under the common law, is generally determined by suit and jury trial, but the judge determines all points of law.

Recently, many states have enacted statutes dealing with the subject of workingmen's compensation, which generally greatly restrict the employer's defenses and fix definite payments to be made for accident or death directly by the employer or through state insurance. These laws also are designed to secure greater safety for the workers.

13. Aside, however, from what is contained in the various employers' liability and workingmen's compensation acts, there is no legal provision for the worker in the case of sickness, superannuation or death.

14. As stated above, the laborer has no guaranteed right to work. No statutory provision is made in this country covering unemployment, except through the provisions of free state and city employment bureaus.

With respect to combined action on the part of laborers, the present situation is, in general, as follows:[5]

[5] Suppose that some workers in a craft organize into a local and then into a national union. In what relation to the law are the unionists or the union in each case, and how does the law affect the union in each case? Is it fair in each case as between the unions and employers?

(a) Their purpose is to better conditions of employment, hours, wages, etc.

(b) They attempt to force all the workers in the craft to join.

(c) They attempt to force their own recalcitrant members to live up to union rules by ostracism, expulsion and endeavoring to secure discharge.

(d) They demand that employers discharge those who do not live up to rules.

(e) They make demands upon a local employer for higher wages and union officers threaten him with a strike.

(f) Strike is called in one locality to enforce demands for recognition of the union and the closed shop.

(g) The union establishes pickets.

(h) Union pickets follow those who continue to work and try to persuade them to quit.

(i) Later they threaten them.

(j) Finally they "beat" one of them up.

(k) They try to prevent the employers from bringing in new workers and importing strike breakers.

(l) They hold street meetings and denounce the employer.

(m) They threaten to do damage to the property of the employer but do not.

(n) They do, however, affect his production, sales and profit.

(o) An injunction is issued forbidding them to congregate near his plant, but they still picket.

(p) Failing to move the employer, and because he is being supported by the members of the employers' association, they call out in strike the workers in other shops owned by these employers.

(q) They refuse to buy the products of the struck shop.

Combinations of workers in trade unions for the purpose
of affecting the wage rate and conditions of employment,
are, *as such,* lawful.   Unions in themselves are lawful
so long as they do no unlawful acts, i.e., the combination
for lawful purposes is not unlawful.   But no man can
lawfully surrender his rights, and the unions are lawful
only so long as they do not infringe on the rights of their
members, other laborers, employers, or society.   This implies that they do not interfere with the right of any
worker to refuse union membership, to violate union
rules, to work where, when, for whom, for what, and
under what conditions, if lawful, he pleases; or, with the
right of the employers to hire whom they will, refuse
to hire union men exclusively, discharge at will, trade
with whom they will; that they do not appear to the
courts to restrain trade in any way; that their *intent* is
not to do any of these things, and that they do not at-

(r) They refuse to trade with dealers who sell the products
of the struck shop.

(s) They call upon other unionists to refuse thus to trade
by publishing the names of employers and dealers unfair to
union labor.

(t) Finally, they win the strike and enter into a collective
agreement with the employer on the basis of recognition of the
union and the closed shop.

(u) The employer blacklists active members of the union.

(v) The employer refuses to live up to the terms of the
collective agreement and the union tries to force him to
arbitrate.

(w) They arbitrate, but the employer refuses to accept the
terms of the award.

(x) The union tries to enforce the collective agreement as
a contract at law.

(y) The employer tries to sue for damages received during
the strike, damage to business and to tangible property.

tempt to enforce any of these things by any act that may be interpreted by the courts as constituting intimidation, coercion, or violence or threats thereof. But unions, being restraining combinations, may, with the greatest facility, become in their actions combinations in illegal restraint of trade. As our law fundamentally was conceived for an individualistic society, in an era when the competitive ideal was uppermost, and among its main purposes are therefore the protection of freedom of individual contract, freedom of trade, free industrial action of individuals and property right, and as the aim of the unions is to protect their members against the effects of these things, and their main policies are directed against them, the legality of unions tends to mean little in fact. *As such,* they are legal, but as soon as they *function* they easily become lawless.[6]

The innocent and lawful act of combining for mutual benefit passes into conspiracy when threats or intimidation and violence are adopted as means of enforcing the demands of the associations on employers or third persons. Any conspiracy in restraint of trade is unlawful, under the common law, and sometimes by statute, and there seems to be no certain rule what the courts will hold to be conspiracy in restraint of trade. Many state statutes have been enacted tending to exempt unions from the application of the rule of combination in restraint of trade, and to exempt labor agreements from the category of conspiracies. Organized labor, for twenty-four years, after the enactment of the Sherman Antitrust Law, made strenuous efforts to secure the exemption of labor combinations from its application. On

[6] Mitchell et al. v. Hetchman Coal & Coke Co., 214 Fed. 685 (1914); Curran v. Galen, 183 N. Y. 207 (1905).

October 15, 1914, it succeeded in securing the enactment of the Clayton Law. Section 6 of this law reads:

That the labor of a human being is not a commodity or article of commerce. Nothing contained in the antitrust laws shall be construed to forbid the existence or operation of labor, agricultural, or horticultural organizations, instituted for the purpose of mutual help, and not having a capital stock, or conducted for profit, or to forbid or restrain individual members of such organizations from lawfully carrying out the legitimate objects thereof; nor shall such organizations, or members thereof, be construed to be illegal combinations or conspiracies in restraint of trade under the antitrust laws.

It is to be understood that both the Sherman and the Clayton Acts and the decisions of the courts with respect to the former hold only within Federal jurisdiction. They do not affect the action of state legislatures or state courts within the jurisdiction of the states. Moreover, the constitutionality of the Clayton Act has not yet been tested. A similar law in Massachusetts was declared unconstitutional by the state court in May, 1916.[7]

When incorporated, the unions are subject to general rules, applying to corporations, with statutory exceptions, often discriminating in favor of the unions. When unincorporated the unions, in the strict application of the common law, cannot sue or be sued, nor, if incapacity be pleaded, be enjoined, and no judgment will lie against them. Individual members are liable for contracts. But, in practice, of late, there seems to be a tendency for the courts to create the doctrine that the union can be sued,

[7] Bogui v. Perotti, 112 N. E. 853 (1916).

that judgments will lie against its property, first, and then against the property of its members. This tendency seems to rest upon a growing fiction that, though not an organization for holding property or doing business, the union is a partnership. Damage suits will lie against unions or union members for injurious interference with employment or business in connection with labor disputes.[8]

The union may call and conduct strikes legally, of course, even though such strikes interfere with the free conduct of the employer's business, and may cause the discharge and prevent the free employment of individual workers if the main purpose of the strike is the benefit of the members of the union. The strike is not lawful, however, if it has for its main purpose the injury of the employer or of other workers, or if it is conducted in an illegal manner, the court, of course, to determine upon these matters. But a strike to secure employment of none but members of the union is lawful if the motive is apparently the benefit of the membership and not an attack on others wantonly or maliciously to deprive them of employment. The assumption that workers would strike wantonly and maliciously to deprive others of employment shows how, by taking cognizance of motive, under the doctrine of conspiracy, the workers are at the mercy of the arbitrary discretion of the court. If the court does not understand the union viewpoint, such as the significance of the demand for recognition or for the standard rate, or for the control of the working personnel, it must judge motives by what it considers results, and thus may decide that no sufficient motive of self-benefit exists and so the strike must be for mali-

[8] Lawlor v. Loewe, 235 U. S. 522 (1915). Danbury hatters.

cious injury, when as a matter of fact, the strike is, in the view of the union, solely for the benefit of its membership.

Sympathetic strikes against employers where no direct grievance exists to force other employers to make concessions to workmen, such as a strike to prevent the use of materials produced by a struck firm, are illegal as interference with freedom of trade. The law limits the right of organized workers to use the strike solely as a means of influencing persons with whom the trade dispute actually exists, without involving disinterested parties, the court to decide. Thus the law, built on the individualistic basis, refuses to recognize that one group of workers in a union is vitally affected by or interested in the conditions of another group even in the same union, and in this it fails to recognize the interrelationship of the modern evolving industrial situation. It cannot do so, while it is based on the absolutistic assumptions of individual freedom and free competition. On the basis of these assumptions, it has little capacity for dealing with developed and developing machine industry.[9]

The striking workmen may peacefully persuade other workers to leave the employ of the master or not to engage to work for him, but may not make use of violence or of any force or intimidation. What constitutes violence, force or intimidation is determined first by the police, and finally by the courts. All destruction of the property or direct interference with the conduct of the business of the employer is forbidden. Where picketing is in aid of an unlawful strike, or is accompanied by violence or by such a display of force or numbers as to intimidate workmen or the public, or to obstruct the

[9] De Minico v. Craig, 207 Mass. 593 (1911).

highways, or approaches of business or employment, it is unlawful. If it appears that the purpose is to interfere with those passing into or out of the works, or those wishing to pass into the works, by other than persuasive means, it is illegal. If the design is to see who can be the subject of persuasive inducements, it is legal. Obtrusion upon others to impose upon them arguments or persuasion to which they are unwilling to listen is unlawful; since strike breakers, by the very nature of the case, must, or are determined, to seek employment, the courts may declare any effort to prevent them from doing so unlawful. In general, the courts have the power in such matters to hold the balance of power between the workers and the employers. They can make or mar any efforts of the organized workers to better their relations with unwilling employers. They hold the practical destinies of militant unionism in their hands. If, as judges, they are closely identified in viewpoint with the employers, they can destroy any practical equality of legal relationship between the two forces.[10]

The employer may hire strike breakers at will, and in case of fear of irreparable injury to property may secure an injunction from the court restraining the workers from interfering in any way with his business. An injunction is an order issuing from a court of equity for the purpose of preventing injury or of preserving the *status quo* until the final determination of rights. It is classed as an extraordinary remedy, usually for the protection of property or property rights and is to be resorted to only when the remedy at law is inadequate, as where the injury done or threatened is of such a nature that, when accomplished, the property cannot be re-

[10] Atchison, T. & S. F. Ry. v. Gee, 139 Fed. 582 (1905).

stored to its original condition or cannot be replaced by
means of compensation in money, or where full compensation for the entire wrong cannot be obtained without
resort to a number of suits.

In the practical application of the injunction, the
courts appear inclined to consider almost anything as a
property right and almost any act of strikers a possible
irreparable violation of property right. Thus, while injunctions will not issue to restrain libel or slander they
will restrain the use of unfair lists, boycott notices, and
the like, considered as intimidating or coercive. In practice, injunctions may issue to cover almost any human
act which the court may deem productive of irreparable
injury to property. For instance, in the Buck's Stove
and Range case, the injunction prohibited the officers of
the American Federation of Labor, officers and members of affiliated unions, agents, friends, sympathizers,
counsel, conspirators and co-conspirators from making
any reference whatever to the fact that the Buck's Company had ever been in any dispute with labor, or to the
fact that the Company had ever been regarded as unfair, had ever been on any unfair list, or on a "we don't
patronize" list of the American Federation of Labor or
of any other organization, and also prohibited any person from either directly or indirectly referring to any
such controversy by printed, written or spoken word.

Injunctions may be specific, i.e., directed against a
particular individual, or they may be blanket or "John
Doe" injunctions directed against any person or persons
whatever. Their violation is contempt of court. The
fact of violation is determined by the judge issuing the
injunction and the punishment is meted out by him.
There is no trial by jury. Injunctions cannot be made

permanent except after hearing the defendant. The injunction may paralyze the action of the union during the run of the preliminary or interlocutory decree even though this, on hearing, may be found to be altogether invalid. As the hearing may not take place for some weeks, the cause of the union may be absolutely lost meantime, for unionists stand in great fear of injunctions. Violation, even of the preliminary decree, which may be invalid, means contempt of court, and fine or imprisonment at the discretion of the judge issuing the injunction, with no right of trial by jury.[11] Unionists generally claim that injunctions should not issue in labor disputes, but that cases involving injuries to property during such disputes should take the regular course of adjudication afterward, and that contempt cases should also be settled by jury trial. The Federal law in relation to this matter of injunctions has been modified considerably in the direction of the union viewpoint by the Clayton Anti-Trust Act (§§ 20-25).

The legal status of the closed shop is somewhat ambiguous. The general rule seems to be that the closed shop will be considered legal, if the primary purpose is to benefit the members of the union rather than to injure nonmembers, if the agreement does not cover a field so broad that it practically makes membership in the union necessary for employment at the trade, or if the agreement is strictly voluntary and enforced by no coercion or intimidation. Otherwise the closed shop will be considered illegal. This means that the legality or illegality of the closed shop depends practically upon the viewpoint of the court, for usually courts can be found to hold against practically any closed shop agreement in

[11] *In re* Debs, 158 U. S. 564 (1895).

any of the above situations. We see here also how the legal status of the union may depend upon what the courts deem to be motive and effect, though practically the courts know little usually in regard to union purposes, i.e., why things really are done by the unions.[12]

Under the common law, the union label is not given the protection of the trade-mark. No injunction can restrain its unauthorized use. Quite commonly, however, it is protected by statute law.

Collective agreements are not unlawful when they do not violate the law through their terms. Injunctions may prevent union officers from counseling violation of agreements. But the law considers the real contract to be between the individuals concerned, hence, collective agreements do not prevent termination of individual contracts at will, on the ground that the contract did not call for the employment of particular individuals, but only of individuals of a certain class. Therefore, specific provisions of individual contracts, not in harmony with the collective agreement, cannot be prevented. The union itself, unincorporated, cannot be sued for a violation of the agreement.[13]

The combination of workmen may boycott their employer, that is, refuse to purchase his products, and unless their acts are construed by the courts as in restraint of trade, may persuade others to do so. But the secondary boycott, the boycott of the merchant who sells the goods of the employer, is unlawful.[14]

The blacklist is virtually legal where, as is usually the

[12] Curran v. Galen, 152 N. Y. (1897); Jacobs v. Cohen, 183 N. Y. 207 (1905).
[13] Hudson v. Cincinnati, etc., R. R. Co., 152 Ky. 711 (1913).
[14] Loewe v. Lawlor, 208 U. S. 274 (1908).

case, it amounts to mere exchange of information, leaving the employer free to act on his own judgment. This, in practice, takes the form of concerted information, or lists kept by associations of employers giving information in regard to workmen on the basis of which they are given or refused employment. The Metal Trades Association had some years ago a card catalogue of this kind which, it was claimed, contained 60,000 names. The object is sometimes secured by a white list, or by an employment or clearance card or book which must be presented to secure employment and surrendered while in employ. Statutes attempting to prevent employers from coercing men into withdrawing from unions by threatening them with discharge are held unconstitutional.[15]

A careful reading of the foregoing will show that the law, as interpreted by the courts, is in effect a series of logical deductions from a set of basic premises or principles. When it fails to satisfy the demands of justice it is not usually because the court is biased but because logical deductions from a set of fixed absolutistic principles cannot meet the needs of developing social ideals and relationships. In general, the courts through their unchallenged right to interpret the meaning and constitutionality of law which is based, as we have seen, first, on the assumption of a natural order and absolute natural rights, as expressed in the common law, which is itself a creation of the courts, and as confirmed by written constitutions, have much more actual power in determining the rights and legal status of labor and the employers than the legislatures and the people.

[15] Adair v. U. S., 208 U. S. 161 (1908); Coppage v. Kansas, 35 Super. Ct. 240 (1915).

The law, in so far as it assumes to represent the essence of positive justice but reflects the relations of handicraft industry, has no comprehension of modern industrial conditions, nor of their inevitable consequences, and no modes of dealing with them except by prohibition. It has no comprehension of a machinery for dealing out justice in a state of society changed and changing from that in which it was conceived. Being actually unable to outlaw combination, for industrial forces are more compelling than legal restraint, not being wholly uncognizant of the injustice worked by its arbitrary decrees, but unable to give up its preëvolutionary standpoint, it is obliged to seek actual justice by shuffling, halting, roundabout methods and disingenuous distinctions which vary with the intelligence and bias of the particular courts. As the law in spirit is individualistic, as it makes the freedom and sacredness of individual contract the touchstone of absolute justice, and as the unions are formed to escape the evils of individualism and individual competition and contract, and all the union acts in positive support of these purposes do involve coercion, the law cannot help being in spirit inimical to unionism. Unionism is in its very essence a lawless thing, in its very purpose and spirit a challenge to the law. Hence, even where the judges are understanding and intend to be sympathetic to unionism, if they are true to the law they must tend to be unfair to unionism.

The English and American law in its fundamental concepts of free contract, individual liberty, and property rights, was the crystallization of the social philosophy of the rising bourgeois or employing class, and still, in general, expresses the viewpoint of that class. Lawyers are trained in it and soaked with this philosophy.

Judges, therefore, inevitably tend to look at unions and labor controversies with the eye of the employer. And judges help make the law.

These are some of the reasons that account for the ambiguous and weak legal status of unionism and for the general attitude of the unionists toward the law.

With the purpose of determining whether the law as it stands puts the employing and working groups on an equal footing, giving equal opportunity to the two groups in working out their problems, relationships and welfare, and whether it furnishes an adequate basis for constructive social effort in the interest of labor and social welfare, we have examined its fundamental basis and general characteristics and the present legal status of employer and employee. It remains in this connection to inquire how the law has worked in the past with special reference to its effect upon labor and labor welfare. Here we are obliged to turn to England, since there we find the clearest record of the attempt to apply the fundamental viewpoint and assumptions underlying our law —the absolutistic viewpoint and the assumptions of natural right, individualism and free individual contract —and the clearest test of the results of the common law as administered by the courts on the basis of precedent.

This attempt was made in the latter part of the eighteenth and the early part of the nineteenth century. In the latter part of the eighteenth century England in her law accepted the absolutistic viewpoint and the theory of natural order and natural rights as we have attempted to state them, and the corollaries that the state has no right to interfere with individual freedom and free competition, its sole business being to guarantee these rights, and that when this is done, individual employers and individual workmen will be on a basis of competitive equality and the welfare of all will be subserved.

Hence, the England of this time practically adopted the rule of *laissez faire, laissez passer,* and proceeded to sweep away the restrictive legislation that had hampered the free activity and competition of individual employers and individual workmen. Combinations were forbidden by law and a fair field was guaranteed to all, subject to the interpretations of the courts based on the common law. The experiment began about the time when the industrial revolution in England was rapidly breaking up the old handicraft system of industry and developing in its place the modern system of machine industry and factory production, and paralleled this development. The results, it must be admitted, were affected by the Napoleonic wars, and especially by the sudden increase of the workers at the close of these wars. Nevertheless, the outcome gives us the best historical test that we have of the practical working of the dominant theory that underlies our law.

The results were not at all what the theory presumed or what the English anticipated. Instead of putting the employers and the workers on a plane of equality and subserving the best interests of all, the competitive strength and interest of the employer were found to be progressively advanced, while the competitive strength and welfare of the workers were relatively if not absolutely weakened. The result was an era of almost unbelievable suffering and degradation for the latter. In the midst of a period of great increase of wealth and "national prosperity," and with the courts carefully guarding the natural rights of all, as interpreted by the common law, all the modern labor conditions and problems from which we suffer and of which we complain arose and flourished like rank weeds; unemployment, child labor, women's work, long hours, low wages, insanitary and unsafe conditions of work, industrial disease, accident and death, lack of proper compensation for these, brutality in shop discipline, degraded home conditions and surroundings, poverty, misery and vice among the working people, all these came quickly to characterize the English situation. So that hardly had the *laissez faire* policy been launched before the British were again forced to allow labor combinations and to attempt again to build up a body of restrictive legislation in protection of the working people from the effects of free individual competition under these circumstances. The evils of the situation are proved and illustrated by contemporary writings and by the later work of investigators.

The question might be asked: Why or how did it come about that when social restraint was removed in England these results followed, contrary to theory? To account for the result, we must take into consideration that there was a conjunction of removal of social restraint with entirely new economic and social conditions to which old standards of thought and action did not apply. It takes time to build up a social and moral code applying to new conditions and problems. At a time when a new code had to be built up, England destroyed her old and left the immediate outcome to be determined by the unguarded struggle of man against man. Raw human nature had its innings. The successive steps by which this was accomplished in manufacture may be summarized as follows:

1. The new machinery which was the mechanical basis of the industrial revolution in manufacture, the

spinning jenny, the water frame, the mule, the power loom, the steam engine, was too expensive for the small independent worker, and thus he lost, very naturally, the ownership of the mechanical means of production—the tools.

2. The new machinery was too heavy to be installed in the house of the workman and the new power, steam, could not be economically applied to isolated machines; therefore the merchant gathered his machinery and his workers increasingly into factories or mills of his own, and thus the worker lost the ownership and control of the workshop. Thus deprived of his tools and his workshop, the worker ceased necessarily to be an independent producer; he could no longer purchase raw materials and contract to work it up into the finished product. Of necessity, therefore, he became a wageworker.

3. The new machinery altered the mode of production, splitting it up into many small processes which could be performed with little skill and training, and the doing of which led to no knowledge of the trade as a whole. Hence the worker lost his trade education, his skill and his control of the trade and trade conditions.

4. The new machinery had to be operated where power was to be had and power could be furnished economically only at certain times and when all the machines were running; hence the worker lost control of his hours of work. He had to go to the factory at a certain fixed time determined by the capitalist machine owner and remain at work while the power was supplied to the machinery.

5. The new power made possible control by the capitalist over the location of the factory. Before the advent of the steam engine such factories as there were

had to be scattered about wherever water power was to be secured. Now they could be brought together at the most advantageous points, considering sources of material, the labor supply, and the market. The factories were therefore concentrated and as a result there developed great manufacturing cities. The worker thus became a city dweller, and since he could not afford the ownership of city property, he thus lost the ownership or life-lease of his home and became the tenant at will of the employer or landlord.

6. The cutting up of the manufacturing process by the machinery into small and simple tasks, i.e., the minute division of labor, made possible the employment of weak and unskilled workers, and hence brought into competition with the old workmen not only unskilled men but women and children. These weak and unskilled workers therefore flocked to the new manufacturing centers or were brought or sent there and entered into competition with the former skilled workmen. The results were the lowering of the wage, and the throwing out of employment of the strong and skilled, because the unskilled women and children could be forced to work cheaper.

7. The manufacturing centers thus became frightfully congested. Old modes and regulations of life became inoperative. Housing and sanitary conditions were horrible, almost past belief. Morality degenerated to the lowest possible depths. Poverty, drunkenness and vice held undisputed sway.

Thus, within a generation, was the industrial worker of England, from an independent, skilled, tool-owning producer of goods for sale, or a worker in process of becoming such, a country or small town dweller, comfortably housed, fed and clothed, living a life governed

by definite customs, based on definite religious, ethical
and social concepts, protected by an intricate legal code,
reduced to an unskilled wageworker dependent upon a
master to whom he was merely a part in the process of
production, ill-paid, ill-housed, ill-clothed, ill-fed, deprived of the ordinary conditions and standards of life—
the basis of a new and distinct class in society. The process of transformation thus outlined applied in this form
only to the industrial and manufacturing trades, but the
industrial revolution in one form or another was general.
The transformation of mining industry went on hand in
hand with manufacture and sooner or later production
generally, except in agriculture, was transformed by machinery into capitalistic industry with its distinctly differentiated wage working class dependent upon the owners of the means and materials of production.

We have said that the law is based on the primary
assumption that there is a fixed natural social order in
which there exist certain immutable rights which persist under all circumstances, and that if the state will only
let things alone, simply guaranteeing these individual
rights through the courts, proceeding always on the basis
of precedent, equality of opportunity will exist for all
individuals and the well-being of all will prevail through
the general pursuit of self-interest. The question now is,
How did this come to be the theory of the law? What
forces and conditions produced it? Do these forces and
conditions exist now—so that we can hardly hope to
change the law fundamentally? Or have they generally
passed out, their places being taken by a new set tending to a new legal conception and mode of procedure,
more in harmony with existing needs, so that we need
not despair of the transformation of the law into a real

basis for constructive activity? We must answer these questions before we can know what can be done in this connection. Doubtless the lawyer has a definite answer to these questions, which is technically unassailable, but which, nevertheless, differs greatly from that given by the student of general social science. But however this may be, the answer given by the latter is somewhat as follows:

The fundamental assumptions and framework of our present law are an eighteenth century product. They developed partly as a reaction against a previous restrictive legal system which had outlived its workability and partly in response to a new social philosophy which attained definite form and acceptance during the eighteenth century. They were pragmatically true for the time of their development, i.e., they harmonized with the general thought of the period and they fitted the conditions and needs of the economic situation. Hardly had they been established, however, when the industrial revolution created a new economic situation which made them pragmatically false in their application, i.e., unjust and socially vicious. Somewhat later a new social philosophy developed with which they are entirely out of harmony. They persist, therefore, mainly by force of social tradition. The new economic condition and the new social philosophy are bound gradually to displace them and create a new legal basis and framework adapted to the new situation. To make the matter clear, we need to go back and trace the process somewhat in detail.

In the early modern era the chief need of western European society appeared to be not the greatest production of wealth but the establishment of stable political authority. When the ecclesiastical and feudal authority broke up, the old industrial standards and modes of social control gave way. Europe was split up into struggling and fighting local groups; social anarchy impended. The hope for a new and stable authority seemed to lie in the establishment of national states, and in subordinating everything else to the development of national power. This was sought largely through the regulation of industry. Suffice it to say that by the beginning of the eighteenth century there had been built up in each of the important countries in western Europe a vast, intricate system of restrictions on industry and trade called the Mercantile System, intended mainly to strengthen the nation as against its neighbors, and the central governing authority as against local authority. By the most minute and universal regulations each government sought to encourage manufactures, augment the population, and increase the quantity of money in the country, in order to attain industrial efficiency, and equip and maintain larger armies and navies. When this regulatory code was complete there was practically no free industrial enterprise or activity. The quantity of goods, the quality, the conditions and methods of production, the wages paid, the prices charged, were regulated by law. What could be produced, in some cases even what could be worn and eaten, was specified. Special privileges were conferred, special restrictions were imposed, and prohibitions enforced in a general effort to secure national power and what was deemed essential to it—the well-being of each individual and the prosperity of each essential industry in the state.

In short, under the Mercantile System, almost nothing industrially was left to individual initiative, or to the outcome of natural economic forces. Industry and the individual were wards of the state. Until the new national authorities had been firmly established in Europe this system appeared on the whole to work well and was generally supported, but by the beginning of the eighteenth century a great tide of reaction had risen against it. This reaction was the result partly of the positive economic evils which the system produced, partly of the chafing against the old and unfit restrictions of a new economic life which was developing, and partly of the advance of science. Out of all these things, as the spiritual background of the reaction against mercantilism and the guide to new action, arose a new social and economic philosophy. This new philosophy was based on the concepts of natural order and natural law. Science was demonstrating that the physical universe constituted an orderly and harmonious whole, expressive of the action of universal and immutable law. It dawned upon social and economic thinkers that this might be true also of society. The analogy was eagerly adopted and worked out. The resulting social philosophy was in briefest outline as follows: there is a fixed ideal natural social type or order of society governed by a code of natural law existing in human nature and antecedent to all human institutions. Left free to pursue his own interest, the individual as a rational being will obey this code. Obedience to this natural code results in entire harmony of interest and relations in society and in the highest social welfare of all. The evils of existing society are due to the interference with natural law and the perversion of the natural order by governmental restrictions. The remedy for these evils is the restoration of the natural order by the removal of restrictions, leaving the individual to follow his own interest in his own way. As

Adam Smith said in a famous passage in the "Wealth of Nations," book IV, chapter II, "He [the individual] generally neither intends to promote the public interest, nor knows how much he is promoting it. . . . He intends only his own security; and by directing that industry in such a manner that its produce may be of the greatest value, he intends only his own gain, and he is in this as in many other cases led by an invisible hand to promote an end which was no part of his intention."

The slogans of this new philosophy were natural rights, economic freedom, free competition, *laissez faire* and *laissez passer*. A curious and significant feature about this new thought, especially as it developed in England, was that its followers considered the fundamental institutions in their own country to be a part of the natural order. Thus the freedom that was demanded never contemplated the abolition of private property nor the violation of property rights. It was assumed that political equality and the abolition of restraints in free contract and free trade meant economic equality and complete economic freedom. All through the eighteenth century this philosophy gained ground and, as applied to economic affairs, largely through the interpretation of Adam Smith's "Wealth of Nations," it gained complete ascendancy toward the close of the century.

Under the influence of this philosophy the old legal regulations intended to protect the worker against oppressive working conditions and thus to secure for him work and a decent standard of living were swept aside. Combinations of the workers themselves in the interest of higher wages and better conditions were legally condemned as conspiracies in restraint of trade. Freedom of individual contract was made the keystone of public policy. The right of the individual employer to hire and discharge the individual worker at will, to pay the lowest wage that would secure workers, obliged to bargain individually and in competition with one another, to work them as long hours as he could force upon them as individual bargainers, to work them under as insanitary and dangerous conditions as he could impose, and the right of the individual laborer to work where, when, for whom, for what wages and hours and under what conditions he pleased, regardless of the effect upon himself and his fellow workers—these rights were made in England the foundation of the working-class legal status. While the industrial revolution was thus creating conditions capable of bringing all these evils upon the working class, the eighteenth century philosophy of *laissez faire* removed from the new industrial authority, the modern employer, the sense and duty of responsibility which rested on the old privileged orders.

The eighteenth century philosophy of Europe was taken over by America and crystallized in written constitutions. The Constitution of the United States is based definitely on the notions of natural order and natural rights. The natural rights which it especially guarantees are the right to property and the equal protection of the laws. The notion that government should keep hands off industrial affairs and relations, and that free contract is the touchstone of social and individual well-being, was adopted without question by the American courts. These rights of the individual employer and worker, intrenched by constitutional private property guarantees, thus became in America the basis of industrial law.

Now this social philosophy and its crystallization in

law were undoubtedly right and good relative to the conditions existing during the time of its development. It was a period of handicraft industry where capitalistic enterprise was slight, where the relations between master and man were, in general, close and sympathetic—master and apprentice were almost like the members of a family—where the dissatisfied workman could easily acquire the means of successful enterprise and set up for himself. Under such circumstances free competition did, to a very great extent, put employer and worker on an equal competitive basis, and free enterprise did mean in general the serving of the public good. But hardly had the *laissez faire* philosophy been established in practice when a new set of conditions arose which destroyed the equality of individual employer and worker and made it entirely unfit to meet the new conditions and needs. This was the industrial revolution whose effect on the relation of employers and workers we have already considered. And further, there soon arose a new social philosophy quite out of harmony with that which had given birth to the *laissez faire* theory and practice—the evolutionary concept of society.

The law then became out of harmony both with social theory and social needs and conditions. But such is the force of social habit and tradition that it is only now, after a century and more, that the fact is coming to be clearly apprehended. But just as the earlier restrictive system passed out as the result of the development of the natural rights philosophy and the rise of the industrial buyer class and free labor, so the *laissez faire* policy based on these things is bound to pass out as the result of the development of the evolutionary doctrine and modern capitalism, which contradicts the old assumptions.

The only question is, shall it pass quickly and give place to something based on knowledge and wise prevision, or shall we drift, the blind sport of circumstance, and perhaps get results from unintelligent democratic control that will be infinitely worse than what we now have?

I should like to ask regarding this characterization, therefore: is it true as far as it goes, is there not another side to the matter which should be stated? As things now are, should we be any better off if the law represented the evolutionary, progressive or democratic concept of society? How would the law proceed on the basis of that principle? What must we have before the law can safely be based and proceed on that principle? Undoubtedly there is danger of leaving the law completely in the hands of the democracy with the lack of any definite standards of justice or methods of procedure of an evolutionary character that might be substituted for those at present in use. What we need is machinery for securing reliable information in the field of labor problems, for creating standards, maxima and minima, rules of the game in this field that will reflect present conditions and will grow and change with developing conditions and relationships, and for educating an intelligent public in relation to these matters. All this seems necessary before we can hope for anything better from an evolutionary transformation and enlarged democratic control of the law. More especially we need: (1) To take out of the control of the common law, out of the field of contentious litigation, out of the hands of the court and out of the realm of court procedure much that concerns labor disputes and the administration of the law, where flexibility and judgment on a basis of existing conditions are especially needed and the present technical legal procedure is slow, inelastic, and obstructive;[16] (2) to adopt a method of securing up-to-date information; (3) to develop standards and rules of the game, *just* for the present, and flexible enough to meet changing conditions; and (4) to educate an intelligent public in regard to these matters, i.e., progressively to do away with the dangers of democracy.

BIBLIOGRAPHY

Annual Review of Labor Legislation, *American Labor Legislation Review.*

CLARK, LINDLEY D. *The Law of the Employment of Labor* (1911).

COMMONS AND ANDREWS. *Principles of Labor Legislation* (1916).

COOKE, F. H. *The Law of Combinations, Monopolies and Labor Unions,* 2d ed. (1909).

Decisions of Courts Affecting Labor, *U. S. Bureau of Labor Statistics, annual report.*

GROAT, G. G. *Attitude of American Courts in Labor Cases* (1911).

HAMILTON, W. H. *Current Economic Problems* (1915), pt. XII, "Social Reform and Legal Institutions," pp. 647-689.

LAIDLER, H. W. *Boycotts and the Labor Struggle* (1913).

POUND, ROSCOE. "Do We Need a Philosophy of Law?" *Columbia Law Review,* vol. 5, pp. 341-353 (1905).

STIMSON, F. J. *Handbook of the Labor Law of the United States* (1896).

COOKE-TAYLOR, RICHARD WHATELY. *The Modern Factory System* (1891).

[16] New York State Industrial Commission Bulletin, I, p. 9 (1915).

CUNNINGHAM, WILLIAM. *Growth of English Industry and Commerce in Modern Times*, vol. 3, *Laissez-Faire* (1903).

DOWNEY, E. H. *History of Work Accident Indemnity in Iowa* (1912), chaps. II, III, IV.

ENGELS, FREDERICK. *The Condition of the Working-Class in England in 1844* (1892).

GASKELL, P. *The Manufacturing Population of England* (1833).

GIBBINS, HENRY DE BELTGENS. *Industry in England* (1906), chaps. XX-XXV.

HAMILTON, W. H. *Current Economic Problems,* "The Industrial Revolution," pp. 36-70.

KYDD, SAMUEL (ALFRED, *pseud.*) *The History of the Factory Movement* (1857).

Report of the Minutes of Evidence taken before the Select Committee on the State of the Children employed in Manufactories of the United Kingdom, House of Commons (1816).

Report of Select Committee on Factory Children's Labor (known as "Sadler's Committee"), House of Commons (1831).

First Report of Commissioners on the Employment of Children in Factories, House of Commons (1834).

Reports from the Select Committee of the House of Lords on the Sweating System (1888).

TOYNBEE, ARNOLD. *The Industrial Revolution* (1890), chaps. VI, VII, VIII, IX.

CHAPTER X

COLLECTIVE BARGAINING AND THE TRADE UNION PROGRAM

By interpretation of the trade union program[1] is meant the explanation of the union aims, principles and theories in terms of the conditions which the workers have to face, the problems they have to solve, and the fundamental assumptions which they hold as a consequence. It is also the explanation of union policies, demands, methods and attitudes in terms of these aims, principles, theories and assumptions, and an attempted rough evaluation of the items of the union program in terms of social welfare.[2] In "Industrial Democracy"[3] we have found the only worth while systematic attempt at the general interpretation of unionism. To this store of fundamentals I propose to add a little through a brief consideration of collective bargaining and a statement of two or three significant bits of union reasoning which

[1] See Appendix II, p. 391.

[2] In proceeding to an interpretation of the trade union program the plan is to take up and show the character and derivation of the few fundamental economic policies, principles and theories of unionism that have not already been incidentally explained, and then to go through the specific items of the program and see how far they can be interpreted in terms of these. This at once shows how far trade unionism as such is economically and socially valid.

[3] Sidney and Beatrice Webb, *Industrial Democracy.*

have not been brought out in our study. At this point a word of caution against two things is needed; first, against expecting entire consistency between the different strands of union theory. Union theory is not a well knit and consistent whole—any more than is union action. As has been said many times, unionism is, above all, pragmatic and opportunistic; when a certain line of action seems to be demanded by the circumstances, unionists are inclined to seize upon the interpretation which seems to justify it, regardless of whether it is consistent with other general statements of their position. Secondly, the tendency which generally comes with the first part of the study to revert to a narrow economic conception of unionism as a device merely for raising wages and shortening hours must be avoided. It should be kept in mind always that unionism is much more than this, and that whatever the study seems to show as to its inability to raise wages and shorten hours generally, and its narrow group and antisocial character, it has vast influence outside this narrow field where its group interests and effects do not necessarily come into conflict with social interests generally. This outside field includes the education of its members, the reform of the law, protecting men and especially women workers from all sorts of indignities and arbitrary oppression from their superiors, establishing systematic constitutional government in industry in place of anarchic, or arbitrary absolutistic power, and thus creating among its own members a spirit of dignity and hopefulness and stimulating a spirit of striving among those outside its ranks. With these explanatory statements and cautions let us turn to the theory of collective bargaining.

There are four main strands to the theory of collective bargaining. The first is a theory of standardization. Wages and the conditions of employment are determined by the relative bargaining strength of the workers and employers of the industrial group. Under competitive conditions the bargaining strength of the employer is greater than that of the individual worker because (1) of the superior knowledge, bargaining skill and waiting power of the employer; (2) of the lesser thing at stake with the employer, profits as against life; (3) there is always an actual or potential oversupply of labor; (4) the weakest employers industrially and financially are the strongest labor bargainers; (5) the competitive strength of the labor group under individual bargaining is equal only (ultimately) or tends to be equal only to the competitive strength of its weakest member, as is illustrated by the case of ten places and eleven men; and (6) the full bargaining strength of the employer is bound to be exercised against the workers under competitive conditions because of the pressure of the consuming public for cheap goods transmitted through retailer and wholesaler; and because the most unscrupulous employer sets the pace, and under capitalistic monopoly conditions impersonality produces the same results. Therefore, individual or competitive bargaining on the part of the workers means progressive deterioration of wages and conditions of employment. The tendency is for wages and conditions to sink to the level which could be secured through the competitive strength of the weakest worker of the group. The only way to prevent this deterioration is to rule out all competition between the individual workers of the group, both in the making of the bargain with the employer, and in the subsequent interpretation of it and work under it.

This can be done only by the establishment and maintenance of two principles: the principle of uniformity in regard to all the conditions of work and pay where competition direct or indirect can take place between individual workers, and the principle of standardization, or restrictive regulation, by the group, of all changes in conditions of work and pay during the term of the wage contract. These principles can be established and maintained only through collective bargaining, and this is its principal function.

The second strand of the theory underlying collective bargaining is also a theory of standardization but of a slightly different nature, for it relates to definite, clearly cognizable standards of work and pay. It may be stated thus: The employer is constantly endeavoring to reintroduce individual bargaining and to force down the wage rate and increase the exertion and output for a given wage by indirect and specific encroachments on the existing status, for instance, by slight changes in method and process, by creating conditions which require slightly greater exertion or irregular home work and overtime; by division of processes and redistribution of work, by changes in tools, by changes in mode of payment, and by arbitrary fines and exactions. These changes for the most part have the effect of increasing work or reducing pay. In the absence of clearly defined standards they are easy to introduce and are often introduced so as to result in reductions without knowledge of this effect by the workers, and the individual worker alone is usually too weak, even if he does recognize their effect, to resist them. It is a method of forcing workers to compete against one another without their knowledge or consent. These encroachments mean, therefore, undercutting and a progressive reduction of wage rates and conditions of employment.

The only way to prevent this is to have all the incidents of work and pay most minutely and clearly specified and this specification rigorously maintained. This can be done only through collective bargaining. Many minute and harassing specifications are laid down, especially in regard to kinds of work that may be done by each worker, modes of doing the work, times and modes of payment, deductions and exactions, times of beginning and ending of work, machinery, materials, objectionable work, etc. Such restrictive regulations are reasonable if the employer is constantly trying to make encroachments. This he is doing, say the workers, for the employer's motive is profit, and these encroachments are in great part the little improvements in method and savings that, under fierce competition, mean the difference between reasonable profits or very low or no profits. He is forced to make them though he is naturally humane, but under competition the least humane rules, and, even under monopoly conditions, these are among the vaunted gains, or the savings, of competition.

The third strand of the theory of collective bargaining concerns its benefits to employers. Among the advantages to the employer arising out of unionism and the union shop, as claimed by the unionists, are these: (1) The unions claim to supply the employer with a sufficient amount of high-grade labor, intelligent, self-respecting, well trained and restrained. (2) The unions claim to exercise a disciplinary control over this labor, to see that the individuals give to the employer a fair day's work for a fair day's wage, to see that the workers as individuals or as a shop group do not violate their agreements with the employer, and to replace workers who cannot be depended upon in this way by those who can. (3) The unions claim to relieve the employer from the danger of sudden and ill-considered strikes to which the employer is apt to be subjected from unorganized and undisciplined workers.   (4) The unions claim that they protect the employer from waste of materials, misuse of tools and machinery, sabotage, and other individualistic and revolutionary methods of unorganized workers.   (5) The unions claim that agreement with them insures the employer the stability of industrial outlook which is essential to successful conduct of business.   They do this by entering into an agreement with the individual employer which guarantees that he shall have for a certain period an adequate labor supply, turning out a definite output, at a definite labor cost, and, where these agreements are made by the union with the employers covering the whole industry or the market area, that the employer is protected for the term of the agreement from the cutthroat competition of his rivals.   (6) The unions claim that their membership is capable of turning out a superior quality of product and that this lessens the necessary amount of expense of inspection; that their members effect savings of tools, materials and machinery, and prevent loss by minimizing the product that must be scrapped or reworked because of failure to come up to standard requirements, and that the union men require less supervision and instruction.   (7) The unions claim that their members are capable of performing many auxiliary operations which unskilled or specialist workmen cannot, as, for example, the adjusting of the machinery, the making of minor repairs, the laying out and setting up of work, the overcoming of special difficulties, etc., thus effecting further savings for the employer. (8) The unions claim that they put all the employers in the trade within the competing area on an equal competitive footing, that is, they rule out the special exigencies of the particular employers and they protect fair and honorable employers from the cutthroat competition of unfair employers; they even up the natural conditions, such as those of different mines and districts, which are given differentials in regard to wages, etc., that tend to put all into the market on a fairly equal footing.

The fourth strand concerns the double-sided monopoly possibilities and benefits of collective bargaining. Given a strong employers' association and a strong group of unions working together as, for instance, ordinarily in the building trades, collective bargaining may be a most effective means of creating monopoly conditions in the trade and reaping benefits in higher prices and profits on the one hand and higher wages on the other. Employers agree to the closed shop and the unions to harass rival employers.

Back of these strands that constitute the theory of collective bargaining are certain more basic theories that serve in part to interpret them. The first may be designated the standard of living theory and the second the group demand theory.

The standard of living theory runs as follows: Wages and conditions of employment are determined by the relative bargaining strength of the workers and employers of the industrial group. The bargaining strength of the workers is in direct proportion to the standard of living of the group and of the class. In bargaining for wages and conditions of employment the prevailing standard of living of the group tends to be taken as the standard of justice; therefore, a high standard in the group and class tends to strengthen the workers in their attempts to secure and maintain high wages and good conditions; hence high wages tend to breed high wages, and vice versa. In bargaining, the workers on a high standard of living are more capable of waiting, therefore their bargaining power is stronger; hence no wage reductions.

The standard of living of the group tends to be taken as the standard of justice in determining the wage rate. Therefore anything that indicates that the existing wage rate will yield more than the customary standard of living tends to decrease the bargaining strength of the workers and the wage rate and vice versa. Therefore the individual who works faster and turns out more product than the normal tends to lower the wage rate; hence the necessity of limitations on the day, rate of work, piece system, bonus system, etc.

We have seen that a large part of the trade union program is wholly or partially explained by the theory of uniformity or standardization. Another large part, especially limitation of output and limitation of numbers, is explained partly by what is called the fixed group demand theory. There is much scorn of unionists by economists and employers because of this lump of labor theory with its corollaries. This scorn is based on the classical supply and demand theory and its variants. Supply is demand. Increased efficiency in production means an increase of social dividend and increased shares, which in turn increase production and saving. Therefore, the workers cut off their own noses when they limit output or limit numbers. The classical position is undoubtedly valid when applied to society as a whole, if there is any such thing, and in the long run. But the trouble is that, so far as the workers are concerned, there is no society as a whole, and no long run, but immediate need and rival social groups.

The fixed group demand theory is as follows: The demand for the labor of the group is determined by the demand for the commodity output of the group. The community—wealth and distribution remaining the same—has a fairly fixed money demand for the commodities of a group. It will devote about a given proportion of its purchasing power to these commodities, that is, if the prices of the group commodity are higher, it will buy less units and vice versa, but expend about the same purchasing power. Therefore, the demand for the labor of the group, profits remaining the same, is practically fixed, and increasing the group commodity output means simply conferring a benefit on the members of other groups as consumers without gain to the group itself. Therefore, to increase the efficiency and the output of the group will not increase the group labor demand and group wages. Decreasing the efficiency and output of the group will not decrease the group labor demand and the group wage.

Increasing the number of workers tends to decrease their bargaining strength relatively and to lower the total wage and the wage rate. Increasing the efficiency and the output of the workers is equivalent to increasing the group labor supply, and so tends to lower the group wage and the wage rate. Decreasing the number of workers tends to increase their bargaining strength relatively and so to increase the group wage and the wage rate. Decreasing the efficiency and output of the workers tends to increase their bargaining strength relatively and so to increase the group wage and the wage rate. The introduction of labor saving devices is equivalent to increasing the labor supply and so lowering the wage rate. Limitation of output through shorter hours, etc., i.e., decreasing the supply of labor, increases bargaining strength and tends to increase the wage. Strikes and trade union insurance funds are means of temporarily withdrawing labor supply and so of increasing bargaining strength and increasing wages. In practice the group demand theory is simply the application by the unions of the principle of monopoly, admittedly valid. But this theory only in part explains union efforts to limit both individual and group efficiency and output and to limit numbers. These policies in part rest on other theories and considerations.[4]

Collective bargaining is a mode of fixing the terms of employment by means of bargaining between an organized body of employees and an employer, or association of employers, usually acting through duly authorized agents. But does collective bargaining have the effect of increasing or decreasing real bargaining in the determination of the terms of employment? The essential thing is that collective bargaining really puts the workers on a footing of equality with employers in regard to

[4] Cf. "The Trade Union Program," Appendix, p. 391, and note what policies and demands are intended to limit, or have the effect of limiting, output and so are to be at least partially explained by the group demand theory. A portion of the argument for restriction on output centers about the question—a central point in the opposition of the union against the employer—whether cheapness or men are more important, that is, to what extent it is justifiable to make society sacrifice greatest possible production in order that the worker may have a decent life.

terms of employment. It is a method of securing that equality which is presumed, under the free contract assumption of our law, to give to each party what he is entitled to and what is to the best interests of all. The essence of collective bargaining is a bargain between interested parties and not a decree from outside parties. But arbitration is often provided for in collective bargaining under certain contingencies and for certain purposes, especially when the parties cannot reach agreement, and in the interpretation of an agreement.

Conciliation is a term often applied to the act of collective bargaining, a term also often applied to the action of public boards which attempt to induce collective bargaining.

Mediation is intervention, usually uninvited, of some outside person or body with a view of getting conciliation or to force a settlement. Compulsory arbitration is extreme mediation. All these things are aids or supplements to collective bargaining where it breaks down. They represent the intervention of outside parties.

The trade agreement is an explicit statement of the terms of the collective bargain; it makes a formal compact. The essential parts of a trade agreement are: (1) A preamble, defining the parties to the agreement, its scope or field, its duration, and its general purpose. (2) A legislative code, giving the working rules, etc. The points covered by the legislative part of the agreement range from wages and hours to the most minute regulation of all the technical conditions or incidents of work and pay. (3) A judicial code defining the mode of interpretation. (4) An executive part, providing a mode of enforcement. Not all trade agreements have all these distinct and essential parts. They range from the rudimentary ones, including the preamble and legislative code, to those which are most formal and elaborate, containing all parts.

Types of agreement according to scope:
1. Local: shop, craft and industry.
2. Intermediate or district: craft, allied craft.
3. System and industry.
4. National: craft and industry.
Parties to the agreement:
1. Local: (a) single employer and shop; (b) local employers or employers' association and local craft union.
2. Intermediate: (a) local employers' association and local council of allied crafts; (b) system officers, allied crafts of system; (c) system officers and craft organization of system; (d) employers of district and district union organization.
3. National: (a) national employers' association and the national union, craft or industrial.
The scope is determined by:
1. The degree of uniformity of conditions.
2. The extent and character of the organization on both sides.
3. The area of competition.

Theoretically or ideally, corresponding to the three essential parts of the trade agreement, the legislative, the judicial and the executive, there are three distinct steps in the process of collective bargaining: (1) the creation of a trade agreement, (2) the interpretation of the agreement, and (3) the enforcement of the agreement. Each of these steps has its peculiar character and aim, and therefore each requires a special kind of intellectual and moral activity and machinery.

The creation of the agreement is a process of finding

and making specific applications, in the trade, of common standards of judgment as to right, rights and feasibility, or of compromising differences of opinion, interest and point of view on the part of the opposing parties concerned. It is, in essence, a legislative process. Its machinery should provide above all things for a contact of the parties most concerned, for the purpose of deliberation and discussion. To succeed in this process, there is required on both sides general and specific trade knowledge and the ordinary qualities of successful bargaining. In general, effective bargaining requires that the bargaining body should be small; that the negotiators should have full power, and that the personnel should be made up of veterans who possess (a) bargaining ability (shrewdness, knowledge of men, judgment, self-control, nerve, persistence, tact, unscrupulousness, etc.), (b) technical knowledge (more especially where piece rates are paid), ability to estimate effects of changes, new processes, machinery, etc., and (c) information as to the state of the trade.

The interpretation of the agreement, its application to actual cases which arise, the determination of the particular class to which a piece of work belongs and the rates and conditions which apply—such as a change in patterns, a variation in seams of coal, the introduction of new machinery—are, on the other hand, in general, matters of the application of law to fact. There are three classes of cases: (1) construction (interpretation) of rules; (2) questions of fact to which rules are to be applied; and (3) cases not provided for in the agreement.[5]

[5] For illustrations, see decisions of the Joint Board of Miners and Operators; rulings on railway agreements (printed along

This is a judicial process and as the facts to be determined and the rules applied are apt to be, as we have seen, very technical and complex, success in interpretation of an agreement requires chiefly expert technical knowledge. As the process is merely one of the application of fixed rules, the machinery need not, and, according to some authorities, should not provide for contact between interested parties and deliberation. It should be simple and its operation free from possible partisanship and bias, the work of a small body of experts. The ideal is some form of machinery that will be automatic, rapid, inexpensive, exact and matter-of-fact.

Finally, the enforcement of the agreement is a mere matter of authority, an executive process, and requires a series of executive or police working tools backed up by effective force.

In practice, especially in the United States as compared with England, these three essential parts of an agreement are not always or perhaps ordinarily distinctly recognized. Many of the agreements in fact consist merely of a statement of the agreement and a few specific working rules. Others, indeed, contain a multitude of working rules and provisions, and elaborate statements covering the settlement of disputes and the enforcement of the agreement, but the distinct character of the legislative and judicial functions is not very clearly appreciated. Consequently, distinct machinery is not always provided for the performance of these functions, and the machinery which is provided, especially for the

with such agreements); decisions of national arbitration boards of the International Typographical Union and the Newspaper Publishers' Association; decisions of Standing Committee of the Potters' Association and the Brotherhood of Operative Potters.

judicial function, is not generally appropriate. Like
everything else connected with American unionism the
methods and machinery of collective bargaining are in a
state of flux. They are being built up by the trial
method. There is immense variation, and to a large
extent they are in a rudimentary or crude state.

Let us examine a little more specifically the machinery
and methods in the creation of agreements. Here we
find, in the simplest situation in the case, that of a shop
agreement, what might be called a town meeting type.
The employer or foreman meets his workers and negotiations are direct, but this direct form of legislation is
impossible as soon as the agreement broadens out beyond the single shop. Then representative government,
at least on the side of the workers, becomes necessary
because the workers cannot stop work in order to negotiate; the body becomes unwieldy; agreement among the
workers becomes extremely difficult; and requisite skill
for bargaining is not possessed by many workers, especially by men confined in work to single processes and
uneducated, nor by employers specialized in large corporations. The negotiations then fall into the hands of
representatives, officers, committees, delegates, or boards
who may be given full power to negotiate and to determine, or who, more often, must report results back to
the body of workers for consideration and a referendum
vote.

On the side of the union, ordinary types of negotiating
bodies are:

(1) A temporary or special committee as in the buildings
trades unions, street railway employees, etc. The temporary committee is regularly composed of salaried (professional) union officers.

(2) A standing or permanent committee—as in the case of the railway unions, printing trades, and operative potters.

(3) A convention of delegates, as with the United Mine Workers of America, the Longshoremen, and the Amalgamated Iron, Steel and Tin Workers. (The convention of the last merely adopts a scale which is submitted to the several mills.)

On the side of the employer the negotiations are carried on by:

(1) His manager, etc., in effecting a shop agreement.

(2) Officers of the employing corporation, as in the case of a steam railway, street railway, Amalgamated Copper or the American Locomotive Company.

(3) Committees of employers' associations, i.e., salaried officers or important members, as with the Stove Founders' National Defense Association, Newspaper Publishers' Association, the United States Potters' Association, Lake Carriers' Association, Chicago Warehouse Men's Association, etc.

(4) A convention of employers (coal mine operators).

The existing agreement or working conditions, in the absence of agreement, is the basis of negotiations. The new agreement is reached by modifying the old. Demands on each side are formulated before actual negotiations begin, in meetings or conventions of employers and employees separately. The negotiators on each side are not absolutely bound by instructions but are left free to get as much as possible; and negotiation proceeds by a series of demands and offers, usually ending in a compromise.

It is plain, from what precedes, that a responsible union and, where more than one employer is a party to the bargaining, a responsible employers' organization or association, authorized to act for the individuals concerned and capable of enforcing the bargaining contract in all its incidents, are main conditions for successful collective bargaining. The necessity for this is evident, for neither side can afford to bargain where it cannot depend upon the enforcement of the contract; hence the necessity for the union to be strongly officered, and the impossibility of successful collective bargaining where membership is too radical and too socialistic to respect contracts. Indeed, enforcement of contract might be put down as the indispensable condition for collective bargaining. Where it fails, collective bargaining must fail.

Recognition of the union by the employers is obviously another essential condition of collective bargaining. There is no other medium through which the workers can be dealt with collectively. Before collective bargaining can begin the union must be actually or tacitly recognized. When the unions strike for recognition as they frequently do, recognition is not then, as usually supposed, an arbitrary demand but it is demanded in the interest of collective bargaining, and when the employer refuses to recognize the union he does so usually because he refuses to recognize collective bargaining as a mode of settling wage rates and working conditions, i.e., he refuses to admit that he has not a right to manage his business to suit himself, an admission which is involved in collective bargaining. Hence the frequent struggles over the demand for recognition.

As has been said, what is needed for the interpretation of agreements is machinery that will work automatically and rapidly, and be inexpensive, exact, and matter-of-fact, and these needs are best met by a small body of experts without interest in the outcome, and therefore without bias.   In practice, in the United States, this has not been generally followed.   The idea seems to have prevailed that the interpretation of agreements in the settlement of disputes is a matter of negotiation between interested parties, experts with presumably unbiased judgment being brought in only as a last resort.   The machinery generally provided is a series of tribunals with appeals from one to another.   The machinery differs with the union.

Important illustrations are:

1. In coal mining: (a) the primary tribunal to which is referred for adjustment a dispute between an individual workman and a mine foreman (or subordinate boss) is the pit committee and the mine foreman.   On their failure to agree, the dispute is taken to (b) the local officers and superintendent of the mine (or to the mine owner).   Upon their failure to agree, the dispute, if a question of discharge, is referred either to (c) an arbitrator whose decision is final, or, if any other dispute, to the president of the district of the United Mine Workers of America and the Commissioner of the operators.   Upon their failure to agree, the appeal lies with (d) the Joint Board, consisting of the executive board of the district of the United Mine Workers of America and the Executive Committee of the Operators' Association.   Their decision is final.

2. In the building trades: (a) an individual dispute is taken up by the steward or business agent with the foreman; (b) an appeal then may be made to the business agent and to the contractor; (c) when still unsettled, appeal is next made to the joint board of the union and the contractors' association; and (d) upon their failure to agree an umpire may be called in and the majority vote of the board with the umpire is final.

3. On railway lines: (a) an individual or general divi-

sion dispute is first considered by the division committee and appropriate division officer of the railway, who may be division superintendent, passenger agent, mechanical superintendent, master mechanic, superintendent of motor power, etc.; (b) upon failure of the division committee the dispute is taken up by the joint protective board or the general committee of the system (a chairman and from four to six members, the chairman of each division), appointed by the men, and appropriate officers of the railway system, such as general superintendent or general manager, and by that committee carried from successive officials of the railway hierarchy to the highest appropriate official for final adjustment.

4. In the printing trades the successive tribunals are: (a) chairman of the chapel and the foreman; (b) local joint board of the union and the employers' association; (c) local allied printing trades council and officers of publishers' association, and (d) national joint arbitration board.

It cannot be said that any generally accepted definite or adequate machinery has been developed in the United States for the enforcement of agreements. In some cases there is joint control. Joint boards[6] or standing committees are often empowered to fine, suspend, or expel individual employees, local unions or employers. But in the majority of cases, probably, enforcement depends merely on the inclination or authority possessed by each party to the agreement to discipline its own sub-

[6] Such boards are the Joint Board of Miners and Operators, the National Arbitration Board of Newspaper Publishers and the International Typographical Union, the Standing Committee of the Potters' Association and Operative Potters, and the Joint Arbitration Board of Carpenters' and Builders' Association and the District Council of Carpenters (Chicago).

ordinate bodies or individual members, or, in case of the employers, the legal power to discharge employees.

In general, this enforcement consists, on the side of the workers, in the power of the unions to discipline their members. The local officers have such authority; the international officers have authority to discipline individual members or locals; and district officers often have intermediate authority over locals and individual members. On the part of the employer, enforcement lies in his power to discharge individual employees or to discipline subordinate officers, foremen, superintendents, division officers, etc., and in the authority which employers' associations have to discipline employers.

Machinery for the enforcement of agreements on the part of the union is found in the steward, or the committee or other representative at the working place; and in inspection by the business agent or other executive officer. On the part of the employers the power rests with the foreman, superintendent or other representative at the working place; or through inspection by the executive officer of the association.

Penalties for violations are not usually provided for in the agreement or if so are not enforceable at law. For individual employees discipline may consist in discharge or lay-off by the employer, fine by the union, employer, or joint board, suspension from the union, or expulsion from the union. Local unions may suffer a fine by the district, or national, suspension or forfeiture of charter. The employer may be punished by a fine imposed by the union, or by the employers' association, or he may be suspended or expelled from the association.[7]

[7] The essence of the protocol consists of machinery for the settlement of difficulties as they arise, and so for building up a

Inviolability of contracts is preached and largely practiced by the Railway Brotherhoods, the United Mine Workers of America, the United Textile Workers of America, the Boot and Shoe Workers' Union, the National Brotherhood of Operative Potters, the Glass Bottle Blowers' Association, and the International Seamen's Union of America, etc. Cases are not infrequent among business unions where the keeping of contracts is enforced on a local.[8]

Agreement on general principles of right and justice is not the sticking point. Collective bargaining is rather a compromise. But we know that there are no standards which both sides recognize, and therefore the compromise is an unstable affair. Neither side is really satisfied. It is an inconclusive peace. Accordingly, the obligation of the contract tends to be taken lightly by both sides. This is one of the great weaknesses of collective bargaining, even as a settlement of group difficulties.

Collective bargaining and arbitration, however, are steps toward full labor control. They are an entering body of law for the shop. To make it work there is needed a new attitude on the part of the employer and a new type of union leader. The general type of the trade union leadership for it does not exist. Trade unionism, as we have seen it, would have to be greatly changed to make the protocol work. There is nothing about it that touches or tends to solve the intergroup problem—the broad social problem that we have visualized.

[8] Mr. Keefe of the Longshoremen, when a local union asked higher pay than the scale agreed upon, telegraphed the shipmaster to pay what was demanded. He then fined the local and suspended it until the fine was paid, and from the union funds repaid the excess to the shipmaster. The Locomotive Engineers have frequently expelled members for violating agreements. In fact, all the railway brotherhoods will furnish men in place of members who strike in violation of agreement.

wedge toward industrial democracy and abolition of the profits system. Recognition of the union is the first step, since individual bargaining gives the workers no voice. This, then, is the important thing—not the lack of a principle of justice. Collective bargaining is not an instrument of peace primarily. It is a step in the process of control. Indeed, the significant thing about unionism is the development of a process of control. This is the larger aspect of unionism and in this sense collective bargaining is a solution of the labor problem.

BIBLIOGRAPHY

Trade Agreements:
  Printing Trades, Building Trades, Coal Miners, Railroad Brotherhoods, etc.

Texts of Agreements:
  Bulletins of the U. S. Bureau of Labor, 44:132-135; 47:903-909; 48:1045-1063; 49:1312-1340; 50:132-147; 51:415-435; 52:638-650; 53:933-936; 55:1623-1635; 56:244-257.

Bulletin of the U. S. Bureau of Labor, No. 98 (1912):
  "Attitude of Employing Interests Toward Conciliation and Arbitration in Great Britain," by A. Maurice Low, pp. 161-178.
  "Attitude of Labor Toward Conciliation and Arbitration in Great Britain," by A. E. Holder, pp. 179-202.
  "The Canadian Industrial Disputes Investigation Act of 1907," pp. 64-81.
  "Conciliation and Arbitration in Great Britain," pp. 123-160.
  "Conciliation and Arbitration of Railway Labor Disputes in Great Britain," pp. 82-122.
  "Conciliation, Arbitration and Sanitation in the Cloak,

Suit and Skirt Industry in New York City," by C. H. Winslow, pp. 203-272.

"Mediation and Arbitration of Railway Labor Disputes in the United States," by C. F. Neill, pp. 1-63.

Bulletin of the U. S. Bureau of Labor, vol. XII, No. 62 (1906).

"Conciliation in the Stove Industry," by J. P. Frey and J. R. Commons.

Bulletin of the U. S. Bureau of Labor, vol. LX, No. 51 (1904).

"The Union Movement Among Coal Miners," by F. J. Warne.

Bulletin of the U. S. Department of Labor, No. 42 (1902): Report to the President of the Anthracite Strike Commission on the Coal Strike of 1902.

ASHLEY, W. J. *The Adjustment of Wages* (1903).

BARNETT, G. E. "National and District Systems of Collective Bargaining in the United States," *Quarterly Journal of Economics,* 26:425-443 (1912).

COMMONS, JOHN R. *Trade Unionism and Labor Problems* (1905), chap. I, "Trade Agreements."

COMMONS AND ANDREWS. *Principles of Labor Legislation* (1916), chap. III.

DONNELLY, S. B. "The Trade Agreement in the Building Trades," *Annals of the American Academy,* 27:510-516 (1906).

GILMAN, N. P. *Methods of Industrial Peace* (1904), chap. IV, "Collective Bargaining."

HOLLANDER AND BARNETT. *Studies in American Trade Unionism,* chap. VI. "Collective Bargaining in the Typographical Union," by G. E. Barnett; chap. VIII, "Trade-Union Agreements in the Iron Molders' Union," by F. W. Hilbert.

MITCHELL, JOHN. *Organized Labor,* chap. I, "The Philos-

ophy of Trade Unionism"; chap. XXXIX, "The Strike
versus the Trade Agreement."

PRICE, L. L. *Industrial Peace: Its Advantages, Methods
and Difficulties* (1887).

Report of the United States Industrial Commission (1901):
   Vol. VIII, pp. lxii-lxv, "Agreements Between Unions
   and Contractors and Violations of Them."
   Vol. XVII, pt. I, chap. 2, "Collective Bargaining, Con-
   ciliation and Arbitration."
   Vol. XVII, pt. III, chap. 1, "National and General Trade
   Systems in the United States."
   Vol. XVII, pt. III, chap. 2, "Local Collective Bargaining."
   Vol. XIX, pp. 833-862, "Collective Bargaining, Concilia-
   tion and Arbitration."

STEWART, E. "Trade Agreements," *Annals of the Amer.
Acad.*, 36:340-348 (1910).

SUFFERN, ARTHUR E. *Conciliation and Arbitration in the
Coal Industry of America* (1915).

TAYLOR, B. "The Labor Treaty in the British Shipbuild-
ing Industry," *The Engineers' Magazine*, 41:238-245
(1911).

WARNE, F. J. "The Trade Agreement in the Coal Industry," *Annals of the Amer. Acad.*, 36:340-348 (1910).

WEBB, SIDNEY AND BEATRICE. *Industrial Democracy*
(1902).
   Pt. II. chap. 2, "The Method of Collective Bargaining."
   Pt. II, chap. 5, "The Standard Rate."
   Pt. II, chap. 6, "The Normal Day."
   Pt. III, chap. 2, "The Higgling of the Market."
   Pt. III, chap. 3, § (b), "The Device of the Common
   Rule."

The Protocol

Annual Report of the Joint Board of Sanitary Control in
the Cloak, Suit and Skirt Industry of Greater New York.
Bulletin.

Bulletin of the U. S. Bureau of Labor, No. 145 (1914) :
"Conciliation, Arbitration and Sanitation in the Dress and Waist Industry of New York," by Chas. H. Winslow.

COHEN, J. H. *Law and Order in Industry* (1916).

Experience of Hart, Schaffner and Marx with Collective Bargaining.

HOWARD, E. D. "The Development of Government in Industry," *Illinois Law Review,* March, 1916.

MARCOSSON, I. F. "A Truce in the Trades," *Munsey's Mag.,* 49:517 (1913).

Protocol of Peace in the Dress and Waist Industry (1913).

Report of Board of Arbitration: Cloak and Suit Mfrs.' Assn., Northwest Cloak and Suit Mfrs.' Assn., and Ladies' International Garment Workers' Union.

CHAPTER XI

THE ECONOMIC PROGRAM OF TRADE UNIONISM

The union viewpoint and program is not solely economic. It is perhaps primarily so. But some of the union aims, principles and theories, and many of the union policies, demands, methods and attitudes are legal, political, ethical and broadly social. For this reason a study of the trade union program is difficult. The unions give no systematic statement of their aims, principles, policies, demands and methods. Not only do they not relate these things systematically—they do not even state them truly and clearly. The unionists do not usually independently understand the theory of their own demands or of their constructive program. They *feel*. But as always in working class movements the rationale of the demands and the movement has had to be worked out for them by middle class minds.[1] To a large extent aims, principles and policies must be inferred from demands and methods. What one must do is to study constitutions, working rules, rules for discipline, and above all agreements with employers which lay down the rules minutely covering incidents of work and pay, in order to discover demands and methods, and then with the help of declarations in constitutions and literature to try

[1] *See,* in confirmation, Webb, *History of Trade Unionism,* p. 229.

to build up policies, principles and aims—putting the whole thing finally into systematic shape.

The trade union program, or rather the trade union programs, for each trade union has a program of its own, is not the handful of unrelated economic demands and methods which it is usually conceived to be, but is a closely integrated social philosophy and plan of action. In the case of most union types, the program centers, indeed, about economic demands and methods, but it rests on the broad foundation of conceptions of right, of rights, and of general theory peculiar to the workers, and it fans out to include or reflect all the economic, ethical, juridical and social hopes and fears, aims, aspirations and attitudes of the group. It expresses the workers' social theory and the rules of the game to which they are committed, not only in industry but in social affairs generally. It is the organized workers' conceptual world.

The union program may be classified conveniently under six heads: (1) There are what may be called general or ultimate aims. (2) There are the union principles and theories. These principles and theories seem to be the natural and probably inevitable outcome of the peculiar conditions under which the laborers live and work, and the peculiar problems which they have to face and solve. They cannot be judged as right or wrong individually, or before the most careful study has been made of the conditions and circumstances which give rise to them. And they must be judged relatively to these conditions and circumstances. (3) There are the general policies. Here we have the general means by which the unionists, imbued with the principles and theories mentioned above, seek to control the concrete situation in the interest of their ultimate aims. (4) There are the demands. These represent the specific means by which the unionists try to put into effect their general policies. (5) There are the methods. These represent the specific modes which are employed to enforce the demands. (6) Finally, there are the attitudes. These concern mainly the broader economic and social ideas and ideals of the organized workers.

The program of each union type is an organic whole within which the specific items are closely related and mutually dependent. To understand fully the significance and causes of any one, the program must be comprehended as a whole. For example, suppose that it is a certain method which is in question. This is put in force in direct obedience to certain general union attitudes, and to enforce demands. One cannot understand the why of it, cannot interpret it fairly, until one understands the attitudes and demands which bring about its use. But the demands which lie back of the methods are made, not merely for their own sake, but to enforce certain general policies, and, therefore, to understand the why of the demands one must grasp the general policies which lie back of them. But we cannot stop there. Back of the general policies are the theories and principles, without a knowledge of which we are almost sure to go astray in any attempt to judge their significance. And, finally, the theories and principles have no sure significance apart from the general aims which they are intended to subserve.

No attempt will be made here to formulate separately the programs of the different types of unionism. Only a general compilation of the aims, principles and theories, general policies, demands, methods and attitudes of

unions of all types is submitted.[2] It, therefore, contains
many contradictory items and it reflects the diverse and
contradictory character of the different union types. It
exhibits the scope and character of union strivings and
furnishes a basis for discussion. As the types have to a
large extent different and sometimes contradictory aims,
principles, theories, policies, demands, methods and attitudes, the program as a whole is incapable of clear-cut
interpretation and causal explanation. What we need
now is to try to separate this general mixed program into
separate type programs, and attempt to get an interpretation and causal explanation of each one. What we
need is a study of each type separately to try to find out
what it stands for and the peculiar problems, conditions
and forces that have determined its program. We need,
for example, a special study of guerilla unionism as it
developed in the case of the Bridge and Structural Iron
Workers; of hold-up unionism as developed in the
Chicago building trades, etc. This will be a starting
point for further study of these groups, and a guide to
the study of other groups and to social action which we
may be called upon to take.

But while the trade union program as a whole and
as differentiated for each type of unionism is mixed and
incomplete, the economic program has for all unions a
single, definite, outstanding viewpoint. The economic
viewpoint of unionism is primarily a group viewpoint,
and its program a group program. The aim of the
union is primarily to benefit the group of workers concerned, rather than the workers as a whole or society
as a whole; its theories which attempt to explain the

[2] *See* Appendix II, Student's Report on **Trade Union Program.**

determination of wages, hours, conditions of employment, etc., are not general but primarily group theories.
They are attempts to explain how the wages, hours and
conditions of employment are determined for a group
of workers. The principles of action which it lays down
are primarily group principles and its economic policies,
demands and methods are primarily intended to protect
and benefit the group of workers concerned.

It is necessary to emphasize all this because most of
the fallacies which the economists claim to find in union
theories, principles, policies, demands and methods result
from the attempt to interpret these as applying to society
as a whole, whereas they are intended to apply only to a
particular group of workers. Much of the misunderstanding and controversy between scientific management
and unionism, for example, results from the fact that
scientific management argues in terms of the welfare of
the individual worker or of society as a whole, while
the unions argue primarily in terms of group welfare.
The economists declare rightly that unions by their methods cannot raise wages—meaning wages as a whole—
and assume wrongly that this indicates a fallacy in the
union theories and methods. The scientific managers
declare rightly that limitation of output must lower
wages—meaning wages as a whole—and assume
wrongly that this also indicates a fallacy in the union
policies and methods. They make both statements because they do not understand that the unions are not
primarily concerned with wages as a whole, but with
the wages and standards of living of particular groups.
To understand and to judge the union aims, theories
and program, then, we must always bear in mind that,
so far as they are economic, they are not general in

their scope but are applied primarily to the situation and welfare of the particular group of workers.

The principal economic aims of the union are to prevent the lowering and, if possible, to raise the wages of *all* the members of the group; to shorten the hours of work of the group; to increase the security and continuity of employment of the members of the groups and, if possible, *to secure steady and assured work for all in it;* to prevent the deterioration and, if possible, to better the general conditions of employment of all the members of the group—especially to better the conditions of safety and sanitation in the shop and to prevent arbitrary discipline, demotion and discharge of workers, and arbitrary fining and docking of wages.

The fundamental assumptions and theories upon which the unionists base their principles and program of action in support of these aims, we have already considered. In brief, they are these:

1. The interests of the employers and workers of the group are generally opposed; the employer is seeking the greatest possible output at the least possible cost; he is, therefore, constantly seeking to lower the wage rate, to lengthen the hours of work, to speed up the workers, to lower the wages by fining and docking, to weed out the least efficient workers, to maintain the poorest and least costly conditions of safety and sanitation compatible with the efficiency of the workers in the shop from day to day (regardless of the long-time effects upon the workers or their efficiency, since, if they are injured or made ill, there are plenty more outside to take their places); to lay off and discharge workers whenever it is temporarily economical; to degrade highly skilled and high-priced workers, or to displace these by

less skilled and lower-priced workers, and to lessen the number of workers employed to do a given amount of work wherever possible by the introduction of new machinery and new processes, etc. The union which represents the working group is seeking the continuous employment of all its members at the highest possible wage rates and under the best possible conditions as respects hours, security and continuity of work, safety, comfort and sanitation, etc. All the efforts of the employer just stated, in the interest of greatest possible output at least possible cost, are thus seen to be directly opposed to the interest and welfare of the working group.

2. The wage dividend of the group of workers is determined by bargaining between the employer and the workers over the division of the group product. The relative bargaining strength of the employer and the workers being determined, the workers stand frequently to lose in wage rates or in the amount of wages through increased effort and output of the group, since the increased output of the group means generally lower prices for the unit of the product, rarely or never an increase of the value of group products proportional to the increased effort and output and may mean simply increased effort and output for the same or even less value of product. Under these circumstances, increased effort and output of the group never mean a proportionate increase of wages for the group, but always a lowering of the wage rate, in the sense of the wages for a given amount of work and output, and they may mean more work for the same or even less pay. Thus the group which increases output generally benefits other groups at its own expense in wage rates or wages. Moreover, this increase of output of the group where the demand

for the goods is not extremely elastic, tends to weaken the bargaining strength of the workers and so still further to lower wage rates, since where it is the result of increased effort of the workers it means increased supply of labor without a correspondingly increased demand for it, and where it is the result of new machinery and new processes it means lessened demand for the labor without any lessened supply of it, speaking always in group terms. In the one case it especially exposes the workers to lower wage rates, in the other to unemployment.

3. The group dividend being determined, the wages and conditions of employment of the workers in the group depend upon the relative bargaining strength of the employers and the workers.

4. The bargaining strength of the employer is always greater than that of the individual worker, owing to circumstances which we have already discussed.

5. The full bargaining strength of the employer will always be exerted against the individual worker because of the opposition of interest and other circumstances already discussed.

6. Therefore, individual bargaining between the employer and the worker, that is, competition between the individual workers in the group for work and wages, will tend to result in lowering wages and conditions of employment and keeping them down to what can be demanded and secured by the weakest bargainers of the labor group.

7. This tendency applies not only to the case of the original bargain but tends to result whenever, after the workers of the group are employed, they allow the employer to pit them one against the other. This occurs whenever in the course of the work they enter into indi-

vidual bargaining, or whenever, as in the case already considered, individual workers of the group are forced or allow themselves to be tempted by bonuses or premiums to speed up, and thus to compete with one another.

The result of these assumptions, which are the workers' interpretation of group experience, is the positive economic program of unionism, the broad outline of which may be put into two propositions: (1) If the wages and conditions of the group are not to sink to what can be commanded by its weakest labor bargainer, they must make the strength of the weakest bargainer equal to the strength of the group. (2) If the wages of the group are to be kept from falling or to be increased, and the conditions of employment maintained or bettered, they must constantly attempt to increase the bargaining strength of the group as against the employers of the group and as against other groups.

How, then, can the unions carry this program into effect? First, how can they make the strength of the weakest bargainer of the group equal to the bargaining strength of the group? If we accept the position of the workers as so far tenable, it is evident that this can be done only by removing the possibility of all competition between the individual workers of the group. The general method devised by the unions for accomplishing this is to substitute collective bargaining for individual bargaining between the employers and the workers. This, however, tells us little. In order to understand what it means, we must ask, what are the principles which the unionists seek to establish by collective bargaining, and what are the policies, demands and methods which they find it necessary to adopt in order to maintain these principles?

The unionists say that it can be done only by the establishment and maintenance of two principles: (1) the principle of uniformity in regard to all conditions of work and pay where competition between the workers can take place; and (2) the principle of standardization or restriction on changes in the conditions of work and pay over considerable periods of time. That is, wherever the workers are doing the same kinds of work, the conditions governing their work and pay must be uniform for all, and wherever changes in the conditions might threaten conditions of uniformity of work and pay of all such workers, these changes must be made only on such terms as the union shall agree to. To get at the main union policies, then, we have only to ask, where might lack of uniformity in conditions of work and pay, or unrestricted changes in these, result in individual competition between the workers? And to get the rest of their program in this connection we have only to ask, what demands and methods are necessary to prevent competition and the violation of these principles, where all the assumptions of the unions are considered to hold?

It is evident, then, that competition can easily take place between worker and worker in regard to the wage rate. Therefore, in order to uphold the principle of uniformity, *a standard rate of wages* must be established for each subgroup of workers, at least as a minimum. Even with a standard wage rate, competition can take place with respect to the amount of work and output that shall be done. Hence, to uphold the principles in question, *a standard hour's or day's work* must be established for each subgroup—at least as a maximum—and all speeders must be eliminated. Competition can also take place in regard to the number of hours worked per day or week. Hence, if the principle is to be upheld, the necessity of *a standard day or week*. But it is evident that if these standards are established we have practically *a standard wage as a maximum*. It is evident, also, that nothing conduces so much to speeding by individuals and the violation of the standards previously mentioned as secret bonuses and premiums or any form of "efficiency payments." This is one reason why the unions look askance at piece work where they are not in a position to control its operation, and why they abhor premium and bonus systems of all kinds.

But competition or underbidding is possible not only in regard to wage rates, hours, and the exertion and output, but also in regard to the safety and sanitation of the shop, the comfort and convenience of working conditions, the men one is willing to work with, the times of beginning and ending work, the convenience of shifts, the time, place, mode and character of payment, the materials and tools used, and all the minor details and conditions of work and pay. Hence, to secure uniformity, the necessity from the union's standpoint of minute specification of standards in regard to all the incidents of work and pay, from which no deviation can be allowed. This explains the multitude of petty and harassing restrictions of which employers complain.

It is evident that these standards cannot persist if they are violated with impunity; yet successful enterprise demands some degree of flexibility. Hence a long list of irregularities and violations which the unions are forced to allow but which they seek to punish so that they may not become habitual and so break down the principle of uniformity. This is accomplished by charging enough extra so as not to allow of underbidding or of extra profit to the employer, such as extra pay (time and a half or rate and a half) for overtime, for doing extraordinary kinds of work, for work in irregular ways, at irregular times (Sundays and holidays) or under irregular circumstances.

It is evident that these standards cannot be maintained effectively so far as *all* the workers are concerned if the employer is allowed to adopt at will changes in methods and processes of work. Such changes make it possible for the employer to create new tasks and jobs for which no standards or uniformities have been established, to lop off parts of the work from the old standardized classes, along with laying off the workman himself, and' in both ways to create new classes of workers with new conditions of work and perhaps lower rates of pay. Hence, if the workers are to maintain their old standards of work and pay for *all* the members of the group, to prevent the degradation of skilled workers and the introduction into their midst of subgroups in which competition exists, they must prevent the introduction of such new conditions of work—the creation of new tasks and jobs and new classification of workers—except under their control and under conditions that will secure on the new jobs conditions of work and pay uniform with the old. Generally this means that they cannot allow these changes except when a new collective bargain is made, unless they can foresee and provide for them. They must restrict the change of conditions of work and pay over considerable periods of time if the principle of standardization or uniformity is to be upheld. This means that *they must carefully delimit the field of work of the group and keep it the same.* Hence, in part, the union tendency to resist new trades, new machinery, new methods and processes, and hence a part of their opposition to time study.

But under all these circumstances, with the constant menace of industrial change, the constant effort of the employer to induce individual workers to compete with their fellows for their own advantage by pressure, or by 'the holding out of immediate advantages in work and pay, competition cannot be kept out and these principles upheld unless there is a high degree of solidarity of the working group. The union must *control the working personnel* of the group, and all the members in the group must feel that their interests are common rather than individual and must be willing to sacrifice individual advantages to the common good. Hence, to maintain these principles, the union must determine who shall be members of the group and must be able especially to determine who shall come into the shop. *This is the real basis of the demand for the closed shop and the abhorrence of scab or nonunion workers.*

Furthermore, they must be able to exercise constant oversight in respect to the conditions of work and the workers in the shop. Hence one reason for the demand of union representatives on the job, stewards and business agents, and for the coming into the situation at any time of other union officials to pass upon conditions, to present complaints, to discipline workers, and to settle disputes. They have learned from experience that non-union men in the shop will not ordinarily live up to the rules of the union, and even union men who are dependent upon the employer dare not make full complaints and resist the demands of the employer. They require to be backed by the official representatives and to complain and negotiate through them.

But, further, the unionists have found that even in a closed shop where all the workers are unionists the solidarity of the group cannot be maintained where the workers are too highly specialized and lack a considerable degree of craft training. Under such circumstances it is easy for the employer to pit worker against worker, arouse jealousies, and induce individual competition. Hence, in part, the union *abhorrence of specialization* and their demand for the apprenticeship system.

So much for uniformity and standardization in order to make the strength of the weakest member of the group equal to the bargaining strength of the group as a whole. The methods by which they try to enforce these policies are in general *anything that works,* strikes, boycotts, legislation where necessary, violence, etc. It is to be noticed that these policies, while intended primarily to uphold the principles claimed, do generally result in the *restriction of output and industrial progress.* They are not so intended consciously but they do have these effects. All this also implies the necessity of a large control of all the conditions of industry, work and pay in the shop by the organized workers. This is what they call industrial democracy, displacing the complete authority of the employer in matters of hiring, discharge, discipline, promotion, demotion, and so on.

I pointed out that the broad outline of the program may be put into two propositions: (1) If the wages and conditions of the group are not to sink to what can be commanded by its weakest bargainer, the workers must make the strength of the weakest equal to the strength of the group. (2) If the wages of the group are not to fall and are to be increased and the conditions of employment bettered, the workers must constantly endeavor to increase the bargaining strength of the group as against the employers of the group and as against other groups. In general, the principles, policies and methods used to make the bargaining strength of the weakest equal to the bargaining strength of the group also have the effect of strengthening the bargaining power of the group as against the employer. In general, therefore, the program for the first purpose is also employed in the attempt to force the employers to advance wages and to improve conditions of employment, that is, to force a larger share of the output to be devoted to bettering wages and conditions.

These methods, however, so employed, are not so much in the interest of uniformity as in opposition to industrial changes which allow the substitution of less skilled for more skilled workers, of specialized workers for trained craftsmen, of machinery for hand labor, and, so, the elimination of workers in the group. It can readily be seen that, if these changes were allowed, wages and conditions of employment could hardly be advanced, and unemployment within the group, with greater competition and lower wages, might result even were the group dividend increased and the closed shop maintained, provided the union assumptions be maintained that wages and conditions are determined by bargaining under conditions which make the interests of the employer and the worker opposed. For these changes would constantly create what is virtually an increasing supply of labor in the group and would enable the employer more readily to substitute less skilled and low-priced labor for more skilled and high-priced labor.

The open shop would obviously aggravate these adverse conditions. Degradation of skilled workers, increased competition among the workers in the group, and greater uncertainty and discontinuity of employment inevitably result from unregulated changes in industrial conditions. The bargaining strength of the group against the employer cannot be increased or even maintained if they are allowed. In the attempt to increase this bargaining strength the union recognizes the advantage of a monopolistic control of the labor supply. Hence another reason for apprenticeship demands and the closed shop.

Moreover, the bargaining strength of the group is almost always bound to be weak compared with that of the employer. Inimical changes cannot be prevented, the closed shop cannot be maintained, advantage cannot be taken of favorable opportunities for advances, and losses in wages and conditions cannot be staved off under unfavorable conditions, granting the union assumptions, if the group is not *recognized* as the bargaining entity, and if it is not at least as acute a bargainer as the employer. This requires that the bargaining for the unions be carried on by skilled specialists—men who know all the conditions of the trade and the market. But the men in actual employ cannot have this knowledge and skill. Hence the union demand that the employer bargain with the group through *representatives* of the workers not in his employ. Thus we have representative bargaining. But the union still is not so strong a bargaining entity as the employer if it cannot enforce the terms of the bargain on the employer and its own members. Hence the necessity of a strong union with strong disciplinary powers, and hence, again, the necessity for group solidarity and the closed shop and apprenticeship.

The other part of the program which aims to strengthen the group against other groups is closely related to the group wage theory which we have discussed. Believing that wages and conditions of employment of the particular group depend on strengthening its economic position or bargaining power in the sale of its products as against other groups, the unionists naturally seek directly to limit the output of the group and directly to limit the labor supply of the group through apprenticeship regulations and the closed shop, on the basis of the same reasoning employed by capitalistic monopolies. From all this it can readily be seen why unionists object so strenuously to working with nonunionists or scabs, and to handling any work that has been done by scabs.

CHAPTER XII

SCIENTIFIC MANAGEMENT AND LABOR WELFARE

Scientific management, so-called, is one aspect of the general efficiency philosophy and movement which of late have gripped the imagination of the business world, and which may be said to constitute the latest phase of capitalistic industrial development.

The term "scientific management" is of quite recent origin. In its genesis, it had reference specifically to the "Taylor system," first developed and applied by Mr. Taylor, the well-known author of "Shop Management," and joint inventor of the Taylor-White process of the manufacture of high-speed tool steel.

By custom, the term scientific management has been gradually extended to include several modifications and imitations of the Taylor system and some systems for which independence of development is claimed. Thus, at the present time, it is generally applied in common usage indiscriminately to the systems of Mr. Taylor, Mr. H. L. Gantt and Mr. Harrington Emerson, and frequently to the principles and methods of several other "efficiency experts."

How extensively these systems are in actual operation, it is impossible to say. Both employers and systematizers seem loath to give information, except in cases of successful application. Probably there are not more than a couple of hundred shops, scattered through the various industries and in various sections of the country, which would be sponsored by the scientific management group, and relatively few of these would be regarded as valid examples of scientific management by the followers of Mr. Taylor. But the significance of the movement is not to be thus measured. The ideals, principles and methods of scientific management are permeating the whole business world, and the movement bids fair to affect in large measure industry and industrial relations generally. It touches, therefore, the welfare, not only of employers and workers, but of all individuals and groups in society, and warrants the keenest universal interest.

In its original conception the Taylor system of scientific management seems to have been literally a system of shop management concerned primarily with the problem of efficient manufacture or productive efficiency in the shop. The problem was to secure the most effective character and use of machinery, tools, and materials, the most effective material and organic arrangements in the shop, and the full coöperative activity of the workers. Mr. Taylor, in his paper, "A Piece-Rate System," presented to the American Society of Mechanical Engineers in 1895, confirmed this idea of the scope and character of the new system by contrasting the care with which managers often "go most minutely into every detail of the buying and selling and financiering, and arrange every element of these branches in the most systematic manner," [1] with the comparative lack of restrictions as to the principles and methods which the superintendent or foreman is to pursue, either in the management of his men or in the care of the company's plant, and by point-

[1] "A Piece-Rate System," § 3 f.

ing to the differential piece-rate system of payment as "the means which the writer [Mr. Taylor] has found to be by far the most effective in obtaining the maximum output of a shop, and which, so far as he can see, satisfies the legitimate requirements of the men and the management." [2]

As time passed, however, the character, scope, and significance of scientific management seem to have steadily enlarged in the minds of Mr. Taylor, his immediate followers, and his imitators, so that when the term "scientific management" was definitely adopted by adherents of Mr. Taylor as descriptive of his system, the intent, apparently, was to emphasize claims for it much broader and more fundamental than those originally made—claims which seem to warrant the following summarization:

1. Efficiency, not only in the mechanical aspects and as it depends on organic arrangements and human effort in the shop, but with respect to the functions of a going industrial establishment, is governed by fundamental natural laws, not made by man, and unalterable by man. And not only this, but the direct relation between productive effort and human welfare, as well as the distribution of the products of industry, is likewise governed by such natural and unalterable laws, i.e., the specific character and amount of work which any laborer can and ought to do, and the proportions of the product which ought to go to management and men and to each individual workman, are thus governed.

2. Scientific management has discovered the *means* by which the facts underlying these natural laws, which govern production in the larger sense—productive wel-

[2] "A Piece-Rate System," § 50.

fare and distribution—can be determined and established as objective, matter-of-fact data, quite apart and divorced from human judgment, opinion, or will; i.e., the means by which all productive arrangements and processes, and all the relations between managers or employers and workmen can be reduced to an exact scientific basis of objective fact and law—a means, in other words, in the application of which, human will, judgment, and cunning cannot enter so as to affect the result, and which, therefore, will necessarily reveal the truth in regard to the most efficient arrangement and method, the kind and amount of work which any man can and ought to do, and the share of the product which every factor and every individual ought justly to receive.

It is true that these sweeping claims have never been explicitly stated by authoritative members of the scientific management group in exactly this form, but they seem to be amply warranted by many spoken and published statements emanating from Mr. Taylor and those claiming to be his adherents.[3] Nor have the members of

[3] The following quotations are taken from the "Labor Claims of Scientific Management," authenticated by Mr. Frederick W. Taylor at the outset of the writer's investigation of scientific management and labor, made for the United States Commission on Industrial Relations. (*Scientific Management and Labor*, pp. 140-149. The italics are mine.)

"Scientific management is a system devised by industrial engineers for the purpose of subserving the common interests of employers, workmen, and society at large through . . . *the just and scientific distribution of the product.*"

"Scientific management is based upon the fundamental assumptions of harmony of interests between employers and workers. . . ."

"It substitutes exact knowledge for guesswork and seeks to

the scientific management cult pointed out fully the
means by which these claims are to be made good

establish *a code of natural laws* equally binding upon employers
and workmen."

"Scientific management thus seeks to substitute in the shop
discipline *natural law* in place of a code of discipline based upon
caprice and the arbitrary power of man."

"Every protest of every workman must be handled . . . and
the right or wrong of the complaint must be settled . . . *by the
great code of laws which has been developed* and which must
satisfy both sides."

"Scientific management guards the workers against overspeeding and exhaustion nervously and physically: (*a*) by substituting exact knowledge for guesswork in the setting of the
task; (*b*) by careful studies of fatigue and the setting of the
task on the basis of a large number of performances by men of
different capacities and with *due and scientific allowance* for the
human factor and legitimate delays."

"The speed of the men is determined by psychological and
physical tests and is always set with reference to long-time
results."

"Scientific management insures just treatment of individual
workers: (*a*) by substituting the *rule of law* for arbitrary decisions of foremen, employers, and unions; (*b*) by giving the
workers in the end equal voice with the employer. *Both can
refer only to the arbitrament of science and fact.*"

"Scientific management increases the skill, efficiency, and productivity of the workers: (*a*) by the *scientific selection of
workmen* so that each man is set to the highest task for which
his physical and intellectual capacity fits him."

"Scientific management . . . gives a voice to both parties,
and substitutes *joint obedience of employers and workers to fact
and law for* obedience to personal authority."

"Time and motion study is the *accurate scientific method* by
which the great mass of *laws* governing the best and easiest and
most productive movements of men are investigated. *These
laws constitute a great code which, for the first time in industry,
completely controls the acts of the management as well as those*

There is strong evidence, however, that both Mr. Taylor and many of his followers have believed that the prin-

of the workmen. . . . They substitute exact knowledge for prejudiced opinion and force in determining all the conditions of work and pay.

"They thus make possible . . . the adaptation of the task to the intellectual and physical capacity of the workers; the payment of the workers in *exact* proportion to their efficiency; the most efficient methods of performing the task . . . *exact cost* accounting . . . the elimination of ignorant and cutthroat competition."

"The modes of payment employed by scientific management insure pay according to efficiency . . . secure justice for each worker."

The following is taken from the record of an interview which the writer had with Mr. Taylor on November 11, 1914: "Taylor, in general, approved my statement of the labor claims of scientific management. He wants more emphasis placed upon the idea of government by law and democracy. He says that people, in general, have not a broad enough idea of scientific management. . . . Taylor emphasizes the notion that scientific management is working out laws in the place of opinion. These laws are not subject to collective bargaining, any more than the tensile strength of steel. . . . In going over my statement of the labor claims of scientific management, Taylor asked to have two changes made: under A-4, 'Scientific management seeks thus to substitute in the shop discipline . . . natural law in the place of . . .' he would add, 'No such democracy has ever existed in industry before. Every protest of every workman must be handled . . . by those on the management side, and the right and wrong of the complaint must be settled, not by the owner, the management, or the workman, but by the great code of laws which has been developed, and which must give satisfaction to both sides.'"

Under C-1-*a:* "Taylor objects to my consideration of time and motion study simply from the standpoint of efficiency and justice to the workers and the improvement of their conditions. He would say: Time and motion study is the accurate scientific cipal, if not the inclusive, means necessary to the discovery and establishment of the unalterable facts and laws of efficient production and just industrial relationships has been found in the special instrument which has particularly characterized all phases of scientific management, viz., *time and motion study.*

"Scientific management," declared Mr. Taylor, "attempts to substitute in the relations between employers and workers the government of fact and law for the rule of force and opinion. It substitutes exact knowledge for guesswork and seeks to establish a code of natural law equally binding upon employers and workmen." [4] In time and motion study it has discovered and developed an "accurate scientific method by which the great mass of laws governing the easiest and most productive movements of men are investigated. These laws constitute a great code which, for the first time in industry, completely controls the acts of the management as well as those of the workmen." [5]

Thus, time and motion study, according to Mr. Taylor,

method by which the great mass of laws governing the best and easiest and most productive movements of men are investigated. These laws constitute a great code which, for the first time in industry, completely controls the acts of the management as well as those of the workmen, etc.'

"Although I thought that I had taken particular pains in my statement of the labor claims of scientific management to bring out clearly and to emphasize the idea of the government of law in the place of force and opinion, as constituting the essentials of the scientific management spirit, Taylor continuously harped on this and upon my failure to grasp this idea, and, therefore, insisted that these changes should be made, in order to give proper emphasis to the idea."

[4] *Scientific Management and Labor,* p. 140.
[5] *Ibid.,* p. 147.

rules out, not only force and opinion from industrial affairs, but bargaining as well. There can be no legitimate bargaining, individual or collective, where the facts have been thus established. "As reasonably," said Mr. Taylor, "might we insist on bargaining about the time and place of the rising and setting of the sun." [6]

But, apparently, according to Mr. Taylor, time and motion study not only *makes possible* the ruling out of force and opinion from industrial affairs, a relatively just distribution of the product and the protection of the worker's welfare at all points, but, coupled with the fundamental natural laws which govern all industrial affairs and relations, it *actualizes* this possibility.

It *makes possible* the assignment of each worker to the task for which he is best fitted, and the safeguarding of him against over-fatigue and over-exhaustion; and because of this same harmony of interests it turns the possibility into reality.

It not only makes possible the removal of the higgling for advantage and the rough and arbitrary discipline of foremen and employers, but it actually eliminates these things.

"Scientific management," declared Mr. Taylor, "democratizes industry. It gives a voice to both parties, and substitutes the joint obedience of employers and workers to fact and law for obedience to personal authority." "No such democracy has ever existed in industry before. Every protest of every workman must be handled by those on the management side, and the right or wrong of the complaint must be settled, not by the opinion of the management or the workman, but by the great code of laws which has been developed, and which must sat

[6] *Ibid.*, p. 40.

isfy both sides." It gives "to the worker in the end equal voice with the employer. Both can refer only to the arbitrament of science and fact." [7]

All this and much more is the result of this instrument for the determination of the facts and laws of industry which scientific management claims to have discovered.

There can be little doubt, then, that Mr. Taylor looked upon scientific management as truly scientific in the sense that its productive and distributive policies and methods are based upon unalterable laws of nature and upon facts discoverable, but unalterable, by the management or workmen concerned. In this his followers appear to have been well in accord with him. Moreover, it is evident that time and motion study is the principal means upon which they rely for the discovery of this scientific foundation of scientific management. *Time and motion study, therefore, must be regarded as the chief cornerstone of scientific management, its main distinguishing feature, and the point of departure for any understanding and judgment of its claims, especially with reference to its scientific character and labor welfare.* Let us then examine the nature and uses and effect of this thing.

There seem to be at least two very diverse conceptions of time and motion study. The first is a very narrow one with respect both to its character and to its uses, held in its most typical form by labor generally, adherence to which, according to advocates of scientific management, leads to much misinterpretation of its real character and uses. The second is a far broader conception, not always recognized by scientific managers themselves, but clearly implicated in the later claims of Mr. Taylor, and in the statements and methods of the more advanced scientific

[7] *Scientific Management and Labor*, pp. 140-141, 145, 147.

managers, which has apparently developed along with the enlarged and enlarging view of the scope and character of scientific management previously noted.

In its narrower conception, and as understood by labor, generally, time and motion study is looked upon simply and solely as an instrument for task setting and efficiency rating, used thus, in the main, to determine how much can be done by a workman engaged in a given operation, within a given time, and, therefore, to set the maximum task accomplishable by him and the group of laborers to which he belongs. Labor thus pictures a cowering workman over whom stands a labor driver. In one hand he holds a split-second watch. In the other he has a sheet of paper on which are set down the elementary motions of which the job is made up, with spaces opposite each in which may be recorded the time taken by the workman to make each motion. The watch is started. The workman jumps to his task. The time taken for each motion involved in the doing of the job is recorded. The operation is then repeated enough times to satisfy the observer that he has discovered the shortest time required by the worker to make each motion. These shortest times are then summed up as the necessary time, and this, with some allowance for human necessities, breakdowns, and delays, is set as the task time.

This, I say, is labor's habitual conception of time and motion study. It is supposed to be employed only or mainly for the purpose of task setting, and it is assumed to be used to set the minimum time or the maximum task to which the laborers can be forced.

This view of time and motion study, however, accords ill with the later and enlarged conception held, apparently, by Mr. Taylor and by many, if not all, of the present members of the scientific management group. Judged by this standard, it is erroneous in two very essential respects.

In the first place, time and motion study, according to this later conception, when used for task-setting purposes, is not designed to discover and set the minimum time or the maximum task, but the scientific time or task, i.e., the reasonable or just task, considering the technical conditions, the character and training of the workmen, the element of fatigue, etc.

In the second place, time and motion study, in its larger conception, is not merely or perhaps mainly a method used for task setting and efficiency rating. On the contrary, in the light of the recent claims based upon its use, made by Mr. Taylor, and of the problems to the solution of which it is apparently being applied by progressive scientific managers, *time and motion study must be conceived as little less than a universal method of attempted accurate industrial analysis,* usable with or without the stop-watch, to discover, at almost every step of the productive and distributive process, not only the most effective material, organic, and human arrangements, adaptations, and combinations, but the reasonable demands which can be made upon the intelligence and energy of the management as well as the men, and the just apportionment of the product to all the factors and individuals concerned.

To show that this larger conception of time and motion study is not a mere deduction from the claims made by Mr. Taylor, we have only to consider the attitude of some of the advanced scientific managers in regard to its possible uses.

According to statements made by scientific managers,

this process of analysis or time and motion study, in the larger sense, should, where possible, begin with the determination of a site for manufacture. The really scientific manager, starting out *de novo,* will consider all available sites with reference to the time and motion expenditure, determined by actual experiment, necessary in securing an adequate supply of proper materials, in the going to and from the shop of the numbers of the different classes of workmen needed or likely to be needed in the shipment and marketing of the product, etc. Having in mind the character of the productive process, and the most efficient productive arrangements possible, he will then, with regard to the greatest possible saving of waste time and motion, work out, with the utmost care, and with reference to future expansion, the plans for the construction of his plant. This will involve a most careful study of all the general internal arrangements and processes, the most efficient methods of planning the work to be done and of routing it through the shop so that there may be no delay in transmitting orders, no waste carriage of materials and partly finished products, no lost time in the assembly room waiting for delayed parts. With the same ends in view, and in the same manner, he will also determine the most effective placement of machinery, the storage of tools and materials, and the location of the various elements of the office force.

The shop constructed and the machinery installed, he will apply time and motion study in an endless series of experimental tests to determine what possible improvements can be made in machinery and its operation, and in the tools, fixtures, materials, and specific processes of work. The best feed and speed for each machine, with reference to the different grades of materials, will then be established. The different jobs or processes will be analyzed and reanalyzed, and their elements experimentally combined and recombined, the tools and fixtures changed and rearranged, and all these variations timed and retimed in an effort to discover the most efficient productive combinations and methods.

This time and motion study analysis will extend, it is thus claimed, to every feature and all organic relationships of the mechanical process of production. But it will not stop there. It will be extended to cover the managerial functions and the office work. The duties of the managers, superintendents, and especially of the shop foremen will be analytically studied and reorganized. As a result, the work of the old managerial functionaries will be split up, and new departments with new department heads established. In place of the single old-line foreman, for example, charged with hiring, discipline, discharge, apportionment of work, the setting up of jobs, the determination of speed and feed of machinery, repair of machinery and belting, inspection of the product, etc., there will be a separate head charged with the selection, hiring, adaptation, and discharge of workmen, and a series of functional foremen, each responsible for a particular duty, e.g., a gang boss, a speed boss, a repair boss, an inspector of work, an instructor, a route clerk, a time and cost clerk, and a disciplinarian.[8] The methods of storage and delivery of tools and materials, the dispatching of orders from the office to the shop, the purchasing of materials, the marketing of products, and all the meth-

[8] It is not intended, of course, to imply that no other factors or considerations enter into the determination of such matters, aside from time and motion study.

ods of accounting will likewise be subjected to time and motion study, in this larger sense, with a view to discovering the most efficient means and methods. All this and much more is time and motion study in the larger conception of the term, which seems to be sanctioned by progressive scientific managers. And not until, through this broader time and motion study, a large degree of improvement and standardization of the general productive process has been well advanced, should the scientific manager, according to these experts, enter upon time and motion study in the narrower sense, i.e., putting the time-study men, with stop-watches, over the workmen engaged in a particular job for the express purpose of setting tasks and rates of wage payment.

Nor, under the direction of this really scientific manager, we are told, will this part of the time and motion study correspond to the conception of it held by labor. On the contrary, it will be done in the same spirit and with the same care that we have noted above. It will endeavor to discover by repeated analysis and experimental timing the best character, combination, and arrangement of tools, materials, machinery, and workmen, the most efficient and convenient lighting, heating, and seating arrangements for the workmen, the proper period for continuous operation by them, considering the element of fatigue, the rest periods needed, their most efficient character, combination, and sequence of motions, etc. Moreover, these particular job experiments will not be confined to one man, or to a few of those who are to accomplish the task. Many men will be timed with the idea of discovering, not the fastest speed of the fastest man, but the normal speed which the group can *continuously* maintain. If necessary, hundreds and perhaps thousands of time and motion studies will be made to determine this, before the task is set and the rate established. And whenever a new or better method or combination has been discovered by the time and motion analysis, which is supposed to continue even after the task is set, the whole process of careful and extended timing for task setting will be repeated, and new tasks and rates established reasonably conformable to the new conditions.

Finally, as an integral part of this broader time and motion study, all the results secured by it will be continuously and systematically filed as a permanent asset and guide to future action.

Thus conceived, time and motion study appears to be considered a method of analysis applicable to practically every feature of the productive and distributive process, considered apart from its purely financial aspects, a process of analysis applied continuously throughout the life of the establishment. And the scientific management based upon it is conceived to be a perpetual attempt to discover and put into operation the new and continuously developing technical, organic, and human arrangements, methods, and relationships constantly revealed by it to be more efficient and more equitable. That this broader conception of time and motion study as the essential basis of scientific managements exists, not as a mere dream, but as a practical ideal striven for with the confident hope of realization, the writer can attest from his experiences in the best class of scientific management shops.

So much for the conception of scientific management and of the essential means or methods upon which are based the claims put forward by Mr. Taylor and his adherents and imitators relative to its character and its

effect upon the welfare of labor.   Let us now consider
its possible and actual effects upon labor, granting the
reality of this broad conception of time and motion
study.

It is evident that the major claims of scientific management relative to labor are closely bound up with the
assumption that it is truly scientific in its dealings with
labor.   It is evident also that this assumption cannot be
evaluated and judged on the basis of the fundamental
postulates of scientific management, viz., that productive efficiency and just distribution of the product are
governed by natural laws, not made by man, and unalterable by man, and that a fundamental harmony of interests exists between employers and workmen.   These
assumptions might be true, and still scientific management would not be scientific in practice until it had discovered and based itself on the objective facts and laws
upon which these assumptions rest.   The practical question, then, whether scientific management is actually
scientific becomes, to all intents and purposes, the question whether it *has,* in fact, discovered a means by which
all productive arrangements and processes and all relations between employers and workers can be reduced to
a basis of exact objective fact and law, a means, in other
words, in the application of which human will, judgment,
and cunning cannot and will not enter so as to affect the
results, and which, therefore, will necessarily reveal the
truth in regard to the most effective productive arrangements and methods, the kind and amount of work which
any man can and ought to do, the share of the product
individuals ought justly to receive relatively to each other,
the savings effected, and prevailing wages.   Time and
motion study, as we have seen, is supposed to be the

most effective means to these ends. Let us then discuss it briefly from this standpoint.

In considering this question, we must carefully distinguish between two factors or elements which enter into the industrial process, the mechanical or material, and the human.

With respect to the first of these elements, the claim of scientific management seems to be fairly justified. Through time and motion study in its broader conception, it appears to be possible to discover and to establish in practice the objective facts and laws which underlie the most efficient mechanical arrangements, processes, and methods of production in the shop.

The moment, however, that the conception is broadened and the human factor enters into the situation, and the problem becomes one of setting each man to the work for which he is best fitted, determining how much work any man ought to do, the claims of scientific management with respect to time and motion study, and, therefore, with respect to the character and effects of scientific management, do not seem capable of practical realization.

Not only does it appear that the fundamental basis for these claims is lacking in the absence of discovered laws applying to such matters, but careful consideration shows that time and motion study, applied to the determination of the facts in this connection, is not capable of yielding objective results, uninfluenced or uninfluenceable by human will and judgment. On the contrary, the methods and results of time study used for task setting and rate making are, in fact, the special sport of individual judgment and opinion, subject to all the possibilities of diversity, inaccuracy, and injustice that arise from human ignorance and prejudice.

Fundamentally, the task set themselves by the scientific managers where the human element is concerned seems impossible of attainment, at least in the present or 'n the near future. Psychologists have, perhaps, developed a technique to determine which of two men is better able at a given time to perform a new task, but they have no technique as yet for determining which of two men would finally become the better worker at the task, or for determining in what task any man would reach his greatest development. Moreover, no definite laws have been discovered which, in the case of the individual worker, can be applied to solve the problems of fatigue and efficiency, much less any which reveal the long-time effects of any amount of work upon the worker.

The problem of relative productiveness and just distribution is still farther from scientific solution. It is possible, by time and motion study, to determine the relative productiveness of two workers engaged in the same task, provided all the conditions are identical, but it is not possible thus to determine the relative productiveness of two workers engaged in different lines of work involving different productive elements. Here qualitative factors enter into the problem. And this alone makes evident the impossibility of determining, by means of time and motion study, the relative productivity of the capital, the managerial factor, and the labor, which together turn out a given product; the impossibility, therefore, of determining, by time and motion study, the law or laws of the just distribution of the product among these factors. Here the qualitative element is supreme, and the problem has thus far baffled human ingenuity.

But even in the effort to disclose the simple objective

facts of human productiveness, uninfluenced by human will and judgment, and to use these facts as a basis for fair task setting, the method of time and motion study proves on careful analysis to be altogether inadequate. Such analysis shows that at a score of points in this process the judgment of the employer, the time-study man, or the workers may be and is exercised so as to produce variations that will affect and alter the task itself. In other words, the time-study process includes a score of factors variable with the judgment and will of those concerned, variation in any or all of which acts as a determinant of the factual results, thus belying the claim that time and motion study is a method by which the objective scientific facts concerning the amount of work or the extent of the task which any man or any group of men can and ought to perform may be scientifically demonstrated, if by this is meant that the results thus obtained are objective scientific data unaffected by human will and judgment.

Analysis shows that among the factors that may vary, subject to human will, and that thus do affect the results of time and motion study used for task setting, are:

1. The general attitude, ideals, and purposes of the management, and the consequent general instructions given to the time-study man.

2. The intelligence, training, and ideals of the time-study man.

3. The degree to which the job to be timed and all its appurtenances have been studied and standardized, looking to uniform conditions in its performance for all the workers.

4. The amount of change thus made from old methods and conditions of performance, e.g., the order of per-

formance, the motions eliminated, and the degree of habituation of the workers to the old and the new situation when the task is set.

5. The mode of selection of the workers to be timed, and their speed and skill relatively to the other members of the group.

6. The relative number of workers timed, and the number of readings considered sufficient to secure the results desired.

7. The atmospheric conditions, the time of day, the time of year, the mental and physical conditions of the workers when timed, and the judgment exercised in reducing these matters to the "normal."

8. The character and amount of special instruction and special training given the selected workers before timing them.

9. The instructions given to them by the time-study man as to the care, speed, etc., to be maintained during the timing process.

10. The attitude of the time-study man toward the workers being timed, and the secret motives and aims of the workers themselves.

11. The judgment of the time-study man as to the pace maintained under timing relatively to the "proper," "normal," or maximum speed which should be demanded.

12. The checks on the actual results used by the time-study man in this connection.

13. The method and mechanism used for observing and recording times, and the degree of accuracy with which actual results are caught and put down.

14. The judgment exercised by the time-study man in respect to the retention or elimination of possible inaccurate or "abnormally" high or low readings.

15. The method used in summing up the elementary readings to get the "necessary" elementary time.

16. The method employed in determining how much should be added to the "necessary time" as a human allowance.

17. The method of determining the "machine allowance."

That the factors thus enumerated are not constant in practice, and that the tasks thus set by time and motion study have no necessary scientific relation to what the members of a working group can or ought to accomplish, but are dependent chiefly upon the judgment of the time-study man, I can positively affirm as the result of many careful observations of time studies for task setting made in scientific management shops, and much analysis and discussion of results with scientific managers and time-study men. Especially is this true of the mode of selecting the workers to be timed, and their speed and skill relatively to the workers of a group, and of the methods of summing up the elementary readings to get the necessary elementary time. In these vital matters there are no generally observed rules, but each shop is likely to be a law unto itself. Nor does consistency prevail in the same shop, the result being that the task set may, and sometimes does, mean anything from the output of the "swift" to a "fat job" even for the plodder.

Such being the facts, however *scientific* scientific management may be in its technical and mechanical aspects, it is little less than absurd to speak of it as scientific outside of these spheres. It is not, and apparently cannot be, scientific in task setting. Indeed, under the general circumstances which prevail in industry, the very conception of a single task set for a whole group of workers or of an invariable task for an individual to be accomplished from hour to hour and day to day is unscientific, looked at from the standpoint of adapting the work to the individual capacities of the workers, or from that of strict justice. Nor, if our analysis has been correct, can scientific management be scientific in the matter of rate making, the distribution of the product, or, in fact, in any of its dealings with the human element. Its claims, therefore, relative to the discovery of objective scientific facts where working relations are concerned, which are not proper subjects for bargaining, and relative to the discovery and establishment of natural laws governing all the dealings of employers and workers, which cannot be violated or which insure justice in effort demanded and in wage payment, seem to have no legitimate foundation.

As the result of the lack of a scientific basis for scientific management and of anything in the system itself capable of preventing violation of its own standards, in matters which concern human conditions and relations, we find that in actual practice the relations of scientific management to the workers are, in the main, as elsewhere in industry, determined by the ideals and intelligence of the particular management, the exigencies of the particular shop, and the general industrial situation. No safe generalizations can, therefore, be made in regard to most of its dealings with the workers. Some of the managers are high-minded and intelligent, and their immediate relations to their workers are marked by liberality and fair dealing. Others are just ordinary, morally and intellectually, with the results that might thus be expected. It is not impossible to find men calling themselves scientific managers, and assuming to put into operation the Taylor, Gantt, or Emerson systems, whose sole or main intent seems to be to use scientific management methods to get as much as possible from, and to give as little as possible to, the workers. The movement is still in its infancy, and, in some respects, is, at best, still crude and inadequate in its dealings with the men. There is no doubt that adherence to Mr. Taylor's ideal of the strict maintenance of standard conditions of work and pay, as long as the efficiency conditions are not altered, marks a distinct advance in the interests of labor over the ideals which have been wont to govern the relations of employers to unorganized labor. On the other hand, it is an unfortunate fact that scientific management at the present time is desperately fake-ridden, and where the fakirs—experts or managers—are in the saddle, the results justify every charge that the workers hurl against the movement. Thus, in actual practice, scientific management varies from good, fair, and liberal through every gradation to bad and positively oppressive, in its methods and results, with respect to the selection and hiring of workmen, the adaptation, instruction, and training of workers, time study and task setting, rate making, modes of payment and maintenance of rates, protection of workers from overspeeding and exhaustion, opportunities offered for advancement and promotion, modes of discipline, methods of discharge, length of service, etc.

There are, however, at least three matters of vital general concern to the workers and society with respect to which safe generalizations with regard to scientific management seem to be possible.

First, scientific management has in it possibilities of enormous increase of productive efficiency. In time and motion study, broadly conceived, it has apparently discovered a means such as we have never before had for the systematic, continuous, and indefinite improvement of productive processes and methods. Moreover, if properly guarded and guided, this method may be used very effectively without entailing any evil results to the workers in the way of overspeeding and exhaustion. Scientific management, therefore, not only holds out possibilities of substantial benefits to labor, but it points the way toward raising the standard of living of all classes of labor and of society at large. No one who has grasped the import of the analysis which I have tried to give of time and motion study in its broader conception can, for a moment, doubt this statement.

Secondly, scientific management, as it actually exists, is, in spirit and results, undemocratic in so far as we associate industrial democracy with labor organization and collective bargaining. It generally tends to weaken the competitive power of the individual worker, thwarts the formation of shop groups, and weakens the solidarity of those which exist. It is generally lacking in the arrangements and machinery, which, considering the workers' experience and psychology, seem to be necessary for the actual voicing of their complaints, and for the consideration and adjustment of their grievances, except as individuals. Collective bargaining has ordinarily no place in the determination of matters considered by organized labor to be vital, and the attitude toward collective bargaining is usually tolerant only when it is not understood. Unionism, where it means a vigorous attempt to enforce the viewpoint and claims of the workers, is generally looked upon with abhorrence. A few of the adherents of scientific management are democratic in spirit and purpose. Some think themselves democratic, but analysis of their ideals and attitudes shows them to be in reality adherents of a benevolent industrial despotism. More are definitely committed to an autocratic attitude. But, whatever the spirit of the management, scientific management, *in practice,* by virtue of its most essential and characteristic feature, time and motion study, tends, apparently inevitably, to the elimination of what are considered by the organized workers as democratic arrangements and possibilities. The cogent reasons for this conclusion will appear immediately.

Finally, scientific management, *in its essential nature* and unsupplemented, seems to be a force tending to reduce the great body of workers to a little-skilled, practically interchangeable and unorganized mass, with all this implies with respect to possible insecurity and discontinuity of employment, wage leveling, and the mental and moral quality of the workers.[9]

Scientific management, at its best, furthers the modern tendency toward the specialization of the workers. Its most characteristic features—functional foremanship, time and motion study, task setting, and efficiency payments—all have this inherent effect.

Functional foremanship means that the worker is to have taken from him much that he formerly had to perform in connection with the particular task. It projects the managerial activity down into every phase of shopwork. As Mr. Taylor says, it effects a more equal division of the work between the management and the

[9] I cannot indicate this more clearly than by reproducing in condensed form the discussion of this subject embodied in the report on scientific management and labor made to the United States Commission of Industrial Relations.

men by taking from the latter much of the work which they were formerly obliged to perform. Under scientific management, as fully developed, the machine hand is intended to be, and is, in fact, a machine feeder and a machine feeder only, with the possibility of auxiliary operations clearly cut off; and what applies to the machine feeder applies with more or less thoroughness to machine and hand operatives generally.

But it is not merely in sweeping from the job its auxiliary operations that scientific management tends to specialize the work and the workers. Time and motion study, the chief cornerstone of all systems of scientific management, tends inherently to the narrowing of the job or task itself. The chief function of time and motion study, as we have seen, is the analysis of work, the reduction of operations to their elementary motions and units, and the recombination of these elements into operations more quickly and easily performed. Its preponderating tendency is to split up the work into smaller and simpler operations or tasks, and to further the invention of new machinery of a more automatic type, and of machinery for the performance of former hand operations.

With functional foremanship lopping off from the job the auxiliary operations, and time and motion study tending to the narrowing of the task itself, task setting and efficiency methods of payment come into play as forces tending to confine the worker to a single task or narrow range of operations. The worker is put upon the special task for which he seems best adapted, and he is stimulated by the methods of payment employed to make himself as proficient as possible at it. When he succeeds in this, to shift him to another task ordinarily involves an immediate and distinct loss to the employer and to the workman himself.

This inherent tendency to specialize is buttressed, broadened in its scope, and perpetuated by the progressive gathering up and systematizing, in the hands of the employers, of all the traditional craft knowledge in the possession of the workers. With this information in hand, and functional foremanship to direct its use, scientific management claims to have no need of craftsmen in the old sense of the term, and, therefore, no need for an apprenticeship system, except for the training of functional foremen. It therefore tends to neglect apprenticeship except for the training of the few.

But scientific management is not only inherently specializing, it also tends to break down existing standards and uniformities set up by the workmen, and to prevent the establishment of stable conditions of work and pay. *Time and motion study* means constant and endless change in the methods of operation. No sooner is a new and better method discovered and established, and the conditions of work and pay adapted to it, than an improvement is discovered, involving, perhaps, new machinery, new tools and materials, a new way of doing things, and a consequent alteration of the conditions of work and pay, with perhaps a complete reclassification of the workers. Change and more change is the special purpose and mission of this essential instrument and central feature of scientific management.

Certain conclusions inevitably follow. Scientific management, fully and properly applied, tends to the constant breakdown of the established crafts and craftsmanship, and the constant elimination of skill in the sense of narrowing craft knowledge and workmanship, except possibly for some members of the managerial staff and the lower orders of workmen.

Under these circumstances, the progressive degeneration of craftsmanship and the progressive degradation of skilled craftsmen, under scientific management, would seem inevitable, unless some means can be found for their preservation and development outside the shop.

What this means in increased competition of workman with workman can be imagined. Were the scientific management ideal, as at present formulated, fully realized, any man who walks the street might be a practical competitor for almost any workman's job. Such a situation would inevitably break down the basis of present-day unionism in its dominant form, and render collective bargaining, as now practiced, impossible in any effective sense in regard to the matters considered by the unions as most essential.

Granting the correctness of this interpretation, the more ultimate effects of scientific management, should it become universal, upon wages and employment are matters of pure speculation. It is apparent, however, that the highly trained workers cannot hope to maintain their wage advantage over the semi-skilled and less skilled workers. The tendency will be toward a realignment of wage rates. Whether this leveling will be up or down, it is impossible to say. At present, the writer believes that scientific management is making the relatively unskilled more efficient than ever before, and that they are generally receiving under it greater earnings than ever before. It is evident, however, that the native efficiency of the working class must suffer from the neglect of apprenticeship if no other means of industrial education is forthcoming.

If generally increased efficiency is the result of scientific management, unemployment would, in the end, seem to become less of a menace. But during the period of transition we should expect its increase. Moreover, the whole scheme of scientific management, especially the gathering up and systematizing of the knowledge, which was formerly the possession of the workers, tends enormously to add to the strength of capitalism. This fact, together with the greater ease of replacement, must make the security and continuity of employment inherently more uncertain.

Scientific management, then, like the progressive invention of machinery, seems to be a force urging us forward toward an era of specialized workmanship and generally semi-skilled or less skilled workmen. Here we glimpse the great problem with which its spread and development confront labor and society. What, then, is the solution of the problem thus presented?

I cannot believe that it lies in repressive measures. We surely cannot afford to give up the vast possibilities of increased productiveness which scientific management holds out. On the contrary, "our industries should adopt," and should be encouraged to adopt, "all methods which replace inaccuracy by accurate knowledge, and which systematically operate to improve productive methods and eliminate economic waste." The remedy, then, is not repression, but supplementation.

The need is a method by which the intellectual and moral content which the worker is losing through the destruction of his craft training and the loss of his craft knowledge can be restored to him. How can we secure this? It will not do, I take it, to demand this of scientific management. To attempt to limit specialization and restore the old apprenticeship system in the shop would mean to prevent to a large degree the productive effectiveness and the productive improvements which we cannot afford to forego. Moreover, to require that scientific managers themselves maintain training schools for all their workers, effective in a social sense, would severely penalize and handicap, if it did not eliminate, the system.

Nor do we wish the training of the workers to be centered in the hands and under the control solely of the employers. It seems that what we really need, as a supplement to scientific management—so that we may avail ourselves of its beneficial possibilities and eliminate or minimize its possible evil effects—is an adequate system of industrial education, socially launched and socially controlled—an integral part of our public school system. With such a system in vogue, we might hope, I believe, that what the workers lose intellectually and morally in the shop, under modern specialized workmanship, they would gain in the school, and that through this moral and intellectual gain they might become universally organizable and organized, and might develop policies and methods which, while not interfering with productive efficiency, would secure for them as a class improved conditions and a reasonable share in the increased social dividend which the development and spread of scientific management promise.

CHAPTER XIII

WHY ORGANIZED LABOR OPPOSES SCIENTIFIC MANAGEMENT

The various systems commonly included under the general term "scientific management" differ specifically in many respects, but they all have in common certain purposes and methods which constitute the basis of organized labor's opposition.

Theoretically, scientific management is an attempt through accurate industrial analysis to discover and put into operation the objective facts and laws which underlie true efficiency in production. In its broadest and best application it attempts through this process of analysis to determine the best location and structure of the shop for the particular manufacture designed; the most efficient processes and methods of production in general and in detail; the material, organic and human arrangements and relationships best suited to further the productive process; the most effective character, arrangement and uses of the machinery, tools and materials employed; the methods of selection and training of the workmen and managerial force most conducive to efficiency; the character and amount of work which can and ought to be performed by each member of the labor and managerial force; the payment to be accorded each individual in the interests of efficiency and justice; and in general it aims to discover all the material, organic and human qualities, arrangements and relationships which will result in greatest output and lowest cost.

The principal and distinctive device by which scientific management attempts thus to discover and put into operation the objective facts and laws of industrial efficiency is time and motion study.

It is the use of time and motion study, not only for task setting but for the improvement and standardization of all the mechanical and organic features and arrangements of the productive concern, that chiefly distinguishes scientific management from all previous systems of production. Through the use of time and motion study and the modes of payment which it has devised, it has been claimed that scientific management not only increases efficiency and lowers costs, but does larger and more difficult things. We are told that it substitutes in the shop the government of fact and law for the rule of force and opinion, i. e., substitutes the democracy of science for the autocratic rule of employers or workmen, and removes the rough, arbitrary and often unjust discipline of foremen and superintendents; assigns to each worker the task for which he is best fitted; trains the workers in the best and easiest methods of work; protects them from over-exertion and exhaustion; safeguards them against arbitrary discharge, and lengthens their term of service; raises wages; eliminates arbitrary rate-cutting, and affords increased opportunities for advancement and promotion; and, finally, renders unnecessary trade unionism and collective bargaining as a means of protection to the workmen.

Such in briefest outline is the essential character of scientific management and such are the essential claims made for it. Why then does organized labor stand in definite and uncompromising opposition to it?

There are more than a hundred specific reasons alleged by the representatives of organized labor to account for their determined opposition to scientific management, and, doubtless, there are many other points of opposition which are not openly proclaimed. In my study last year,[1] I attempted to gather up these scattered allegations and reduce them to some sort of system. Thus classified and generalized to the nth degree, they comprehend the following main points:

Scientific management, say the union representatives, is a device employed for the purpose of increasing production and profits, which concerns itself almost wholly with the problem of production, disregarding in general the vital problem of distribution. As such it is a reversion to industrial autocracy which forces the workers to depend upon the employers' conception of fairness and limits the democratic safeguards of the workers. It is unscientific and unfair in the setting of the task and in the fixing of wage rates; in spirit and essence it is a cunningly devised speeding-up and sweating system; it intensifies the modern tendency toward specialization of the work and the task; it condemns the worker to a monotonous routine and tends to deprive him of thought, initiative and joy in his work and to destroy his individuality and inventive genius; it lessens the continuity and certainty of employment, and leads to over-production and unemployment; it is incompatible with, and destructive of, collective bargaining and trade unionism.

Belief in these charges, in whole or in part, which I found on further investigation was general among or-

[1] *See* Hoxie, *Scientific Management and Labor* (1915).

ganized laborers, is sufficient to account superficially and immediately for the determined opposition of unions and union men to the introduction and operation of scientific management. Yet the statement of these objections does not furnish any very real or significant answer to the question, why organized labor opposes scientific management. It gives answer in terms of belief only. It gives no clue to the causes of this belief, and, therefore, none to the real nature of the opposition—to the forces which have created the opposition, and hence its strength and significance. In short, this statement of belief does not go to the root of the matter and enlighten us in regard to the fundamental question. In order to do this, we must dig below the surface and find the basic or ultimate reasons for these expressed beliefs.

During my work of investigation last year several suggestions were brought forward both by opponents and advocates of scientific management to account in general and causal terms for the attitude and belief of organized labor which I have tried to summarize above. It was suggested that the opposition was ascribable to various causes. (1) To general ignorance on the part of the union workers of the true nature, methods, and results of scientific management. (2) To general and fundamental distrust, which the workers have acquired from bitter experience, of anything new or different in industrial organization and methods. (3) To a propaganda of opposition among the rank and file of union men, conducted by the leaders, who fear that if a better understanding is allowed to grow up between the real workers and the employers, their prestige and emoluments will be decreased, and even perhaps their positions abolished and they be reduced again to the ranks. (4) To the crudities of scientific management, still in its beginnings, and to the many abuses of it in practice by charlatans and by ignorant and unscrupulous employers, who trade upon the name without understanding the intricate and delicate nature of the thing, the time and patience necessary for its development, or who deliberately violate its spirit and methods for labor driving purposes. (5) To present dominant ideals of trade unionism which are incompatible with those of scientific management as conceived by Mr. Taylor, a suggestion made by Mr. Taylor himself, who said: "Scientific management rests upon the fundamental assumption that a harmony of interests exists between employers and workmen. It is therefore organized for peace, while trade unionism is organized for war. . . . Scientific management rests upon the assumption that the welfare of all demands ever increased efficiency and output; trade unionism is committed to the limitation of output."

Doubtless each of these suggestions has some validity, but none of them nor all of them together seem sufficient to account for the general and determined opposition of the unions. Moreover, some of them, while perhaps not positive misstatements, are yet misleading in their implications. Let us then consider each of them briefly on its merits and through this try to arrive at the essential meaning of the union attitude toward scientific management.

(1) It is true that there has been and is now a great lack of adequate knowledge of the true nature, methods and results of scientific management as a whole on the part of the great mass of organized workers, both the leaders and the rank and file. But it is equally true that increase of knowledge, which is going forward steadily,

does not result in any abatement of union opposition. Here and there, individual members of unions or small groups of union workers who are brought into actual contact with efficiency methods in the shop do become reconciled to scientific management and are sometimes even enthusiastic advocates of it. But the significant thing to note here is that these same men generally cease to be "good unionists" in spirit, even if they do not drop their union affiliation altogether and become its opponents. The increased knowledge which leading unionists have recently gained of scientific management, in theory and in practice, has intensified rather than lessened their opposition and that of the union movement in general.

(2) There is no doubt that general and almost instinctive distrust of the new, strange and different has played a part in rousing union opposition and to a certain extent is effective in continuing it. It has been ground into the consciousness of laborers by long and bitter experience that industrial change through invention and the application of new machinery and processes, however beneficial it is to society as a whole and even to labor in the long run, usually results in taking toll immediately from the individual worker or the working group concerned. It leads to displacement or lessened security of employment, often in lower wage rates and long hours, through the increased competition of lower grades of workmen and the lower cost and prices of the products affected. The history of industrial development is full of incidents of this kind, and no better example can be found than the case of the English weavers and spinners which Mr. Taylor was so fond of citing. For more than a generation after the application of the

great inventions which revolutionized the cotton manufacturing industry in England, the competition of women and children operated to displace the men, to lower wages, and to lengthen hours, to such an extent that this industry as it then existed has become the classical example of modern labor oppression and degradation. The world, and even labor, ultimately gained; but meanwhile the workman concerned, the head of the family, sat at home, swept the house, cooked and darned, while his wife and children, down even to the age of five years, worked in the factory from four and five o'clock in the morning till seven and eight o'clock at night, under the most insanitary and unsafe conditions, often treated with unheard-of brutality, and for an aggregate wage that scarcely sufficed for the food, clothing and shelter necessary to keep body and soul together. And what was true of the English cotton industry has tended to be true in a lesser degree of industrial changes generally. The workmen immediately concerned have tended to be penalized that society might reap the advantages of industrial progress. What wonder then that they have come instinctively to dread change of any kind that immediately affects their work and to oppose such change unless it is accompanied by positive guarantees that they shall immediately share in the social gains, or, at least, suffer no loss of employment and no derogation of their standards of work and wages as the result of the improvements? And surely we can hardly expect the workman with a dependent family and no savings ahead to welcome innovations that threaten to render less valuable his acquired skill, to throw him even temporarily out of employment, or to transfer him to employment which commands a lower wage rate, simply because these changes will redound ultimately to the benefit of society, to labor as a whole, or even in the long run to his own advantage, when a month of unemployment, two weeks even, may bring him and his to the verge of want, while a few months or years of employment at a lower wage level may mean the wrecking of all his hopes for a home, for the education of his children, for provision against sickness and old age, or may mean even the break-up and scattering of his family.

(3) That trade union officers and leaders have of late carried on a persistent and ever increasing propaganda against scientific management cannot be gainsaid. Stray sentences from Mr. Taylor's works which could be interpreted as inimical to the workers and their welfare, and particular instances of abuses and perversions of scientific management, have been dramatically presented to the rank and file of unionism as indicative of the general character and results of the system, much in the same spirit as texts from the Bible were formerly used by the clergy to warn the unconverted of the dangers of hell fire. The motives which underlie this propagandistic work I need not attempt to interpret. Whatever the motive, the effect has undoubtedly been to rouse the latent distrust and quicken the opposition of the rank and file of organized laborers. But here again we find no force potent enough to account for the general opposition of the union laity; for it is a well established fact that the rank and file of unionism are quick to distrust their leaders when these leaders take a position which seems to run counter to their own preconceptions and beliefs drawn from immediate experience or tradition. Let the union leader endeavor to enforce on the rank and file something which is fundamentally opposed to

their standards and beliefs, and he soon finds that his leadership is of the quality represented by that of the man at the head of the charging crowd. If he is to lead he must run fast to keep them off his heels, and he must run where the mind of the crowd wills.

(4) The crudities of scientific management in practice, and its many abuses by charlatans or by ignorant and unscrupulous employers—conditions and abuses the prevalence of which the scientific management group would be the last to deny or to attempt to minimize— furnish the union propagandists with an inexhaustible arsenal of facts and inferences with which to illustrate their texts and reënforce the multitude of charges which they hurl against the new movement. But the very employment of these abuses to create opposition against scientific management *per se,* and the persistent refusal to attempt or even to admit any distinction between scientific management as exemplified in the better class of shops where its ideals and principles are being patiently worked out and its mushroom counterfeits where these ideals and methods are consciously perverted, point to grounds of opposition aside from and beyond its abuses, and grounds which evidently have not yet been disclosed.

(5) Finally, then, we come to Mr. Taylor's own explanation of union opposition in the incompatibility of the ideals of scientific management and unionism, in that the one is organized for peace and harmonious action between employers and workmen, the other for war; that the one demands an ever increased efficiency, while the other is committed to limitation of output.

Do we come here to the real and ultimate answer to the question, why does organized labor oppose scientific management? In a certain sense I believe that we do.

I believe that the persistent and growing opposition of unionism to scientific management does rest finally upon a fundamental opposition of the ideals essentially characteristic of the two things.   But I cannot subscribe to Mr. Taylor's analysis of this proposition—his explicit statement of the opposed ideals of scientific management and organized labor—because I believe that he has here misinterpreted the really fundamental ideals of trade unionism.   He has mistaken action for motive—the objective facts of union policy imposed by circumstances for the underlying purposes of unionism which have been forced to find expression in facts which belie their real nature.   In so doing, I believe that he committed an error similar to that of the unionists in judging the ideals of scientific management by its crudities and abuses.

In this connection it is misleading to speak of unionism as a whole.   In fact there is no such thing as unionism in the sense of a consistent organic or functional unity.   On the contrary, "there are in the United States today hundreds of union organizations each practically independent or sovereign, and each with its own and often peculiar structural arrangements, aims, policies, demands, methods, attitudes and internal regulations.   Nor is there any visible or tangible bond that unites all these organizations into a single whole, however tenuous. Groups there are, indeed, with overstructures and declared common aims and methods.   But group combats group with the bitterness that can arise only out of the widest diversity of ideals and methods."   In short, trade unionism is everywhere very much of an opportunistic phenomenon.   Unionists have been prone to act first and to formulate theories afterward; and they have habitually acted to meet the problems thrust upon them by immediate circumstances. Modes of action which have failed when measured by this standard have been rejected and other means sought. Methods that have worked have been preserved and extended, but always the standards of judgment have been most largely determined by the needs and experiences of the particular group concerned.

Under these circumstances, the generalization that we can most legitimately use is to speak of a dominant type of unionism, and we may perhaps say that this dominant type is represented functionally by the ideals and methods advocated by the leaders of the American Federation of Labor.

It is with respect to this dominant type of unionism that I believe Mr. Taylor has mistaken the objective facts of policy imposed by circumstances for underlying purposes. In the case of this dominant union type the reality seems to be this: it is not organized for war, though it *does* engage in warfare; it recognizes the crying need for increased efficiency and productiveness, though it *does,* as a matter of fact, under certain circumstances and for reasons which we shall see later, limit the output. In both cases it has been forced to modify its general ideals in practice by the conditions and circumstances which it has found itself obliged to face.

The truth is that the outlook and ideals of this dominant type of unionism are those very largely of a business organization. Its successful leaders are essentially business men and its unions are organized primarily to do business with employers—to bargain for the sale of the product which it controls. It has found, however, by long and general experience that if it is to do business with the average employer or with associations of employers it must be prepared to fight. But throughout its history this fighting has been predominantly conducted with the purpose of forcing employers to recognize it as a business or bargaining entity. Its position and experience have been very much like that of a new and rising business concern attempting to force its way into a field already occupied by old established organizations in control of the market. Like the new business concern, it has had to fight to obtain a foothold. But to argue from this that it is organized for war is a complete *non sequitur*.

A somewhat similar situation has existed in regard to the matter of output. Business unionism has recognized, in general, the evils of restriction and has been willing to allow and even to encourage the introduction of new machinery and improved processes and methods, and to sanction increased effort and productiveness on the part of its members up to reasonable physiological limits, provided it could be guaranteed that the improved methods and the increased exertion and output should not be made the means of lessening the share of the workers in the product or forcing upon them lower wage rates and inferior conditions of employment. But here again it has found the average employer or employers' association standing in the way. It has been taught by long and bitter experience that employers could and would make use of improvements and increased output by the workers not only to seize all of the gains but even to reduce the actual rates and returns to the workers.

The fact is that despite all theorizing to the contrary, the wages of workmen under the unscientific conditions that have prevailed in industry are not determined automatically by specific output or by supply and demand, but immediately by a process of bargaining. The two most important factors in determining the outcome of this bargaining process have been the customary normal or standard day's work and the customary standard of living of the workers concerned. These have been the practical standards of right, justice and expediency most generally considered. In bargaining between employer and workmen, as it has generally taken place in the past, if the employer could make it appear that, under the existing conditions, the workers were not producing up to the standard day's work, he had a strong case to show that wages ought to be lowered or that more work ought to be done for the same pay, which amounts virtually to lowering the wage. If, further, the employer could make it appear that, at the given wage rate, or on the basis of the standard day's work, the workers could secure a standard of living higher than that customary with them, he had a strong case to show that the wage rate ought to be lowered, or, at least, that it should not be increased. In a contest of this kind the employer has been fairly sure of the support of public opinion, arbitrators, the police and the courts.

Now the workers have been taught by long experience that the average employer is constantly seeking to take advantage of these facts to secure an increase of the output *and at the same time to lessen the share and the amount of the product going to the workers.* Thus, when new machinery and methods are introduced, he points to the fact that, at the old wage rates and under the old conditions of work, the laborers are able to secure earnings more than sufficient to maintain their customary standard of living, and makes this a basis for lowering of rates or at least for a refusal to increase wages and improve conditions of work. Where competition is keen, he has usually been able to carry this off by adding to the arguments stated above that profits have not risen or that they have positively declined as the result of the improved methods. Where competition has been absent, i. e., where a combination has controlled the goods market, the employer has usually been strong enough to carry his point regardless of facts and arguments. Thus, new machinery and methods have generally not improved the wages and conditions of the workers *immediately concerned* and, as a matter of fact, have not infrequently lowered them, especially where these improvements have created conditions of increased competition among the workers, as they very generally have done.

Turning now to the other aspect of the matter—increased effort and productiveness on the part of workmen where no improvement in methods has taken place —the experience of the workers has been that the old line employer has been constantly endeavoring to speed them up and overreach them by the creation of "swifts" and "bell-horses," through the introduction of "company men," by threatening and coercing individuals whose native resisting power was weak or whose circumstances were precarious. and by offering secret premiums or bonuses. When through these methods some man or group of men has been induced to speed up, their accomplishment has been taken as the standard for all to attain. Thus, in the case of day work, the accomplishment of the strongest and swiftest was the goal set up for all, if wages were not to be lowered, while in the case of piece work the rate of wages tended to be lowered by these exceptionally rapid workers, because at the given rate it could be shown that they could make more than was necessary to maintain their customary standard of living. Under these circumstances the workers found that increased efficiency and output by members of their immediate group tended to mean, not a corresponding increase of pay, but less wages for all, or more work for the same pay; and the only way they could see to prevent overspeeding and the lowering of rates was to set a limit on what any individual was allowed to do, in short, to limit individual and group output until the employer could be forced to guarantee increased wages for increased effort and output.

These are facts which, I believe, cannot be controverted. No one recognized this more clearly than Mr. Taylor himself, whose denunciation of the blindness and unfairness of the average employer on account of them has not been exceeded in strength and bitterness by the labor leaders, and who declared publicly that were he a worker up against such conditions he would feel as they have felt and do as they have done in the matter of limitation of output.

In view of the facts of the case, then, as truly stated by Mr. Taylor, the circumstance that they do make war and that they do limit output gives so far no positive grounds for Mr. Taylor's generalization that unionism is organized for war, that unionism is committed to limitation of output, that the present dominant ideals of unionism are incompatible with those of scientific management, and that it is from this source that the opposition of unionism comes.

But if these conclusions hold, why, then, you will at once ask, does not unionism make an exception in the case of scientific management, which is itself supposed to be engaged in a struggle to eliminate those very coercive and oppressive tactics of the old line employers that have forced unionism to limit output and engage in industrial warfare? Why, in the case of scientific management, which is supposed to be committed to the strict maintenance of rates, to the elimination of speeders and to the increase of earnings with improved methods and increased output by the workers, does it not cease its warfare and raise its embargo on increased output? Doubtless the various causes of union opposition which we have discussed are a partial explanation. Ignorance of the true nature, methods and results of scientific management, distrust of the new and the different acquired by bitter experience, the propagandist influence of leaders, the crudities and abuses of scientific management in practice—all undoubtedly tend to create and maintain union opposition.

But these things are not sufficient to account for it fully. The fact is, I believe, that behind and beneath all this there *is* an essential incompatibility between the basic ideals of scientific management and those of the dominant type of trade unionism. Not an incompatibility of the character Mr. Taylor believed to exist, but one still more fundamental. It is, I believe, this. *Scientific management can function successfully only on the basis of constant and indefinite change of industrial condition*—the constant adoption of new and better processes and methods of production and the unrestrained ability to adapt the mechanical, organic and human factors at its disposal to meet the demands of these new productive processes and methods. On the other hand, *trade unionism of the dominant type can function successfully only through the maintenance of a fixed industrial situation and conditions,* extending over a definite period of time, or through the definite predetermined regulation and adjustment of industrial change—the establishment of definite rules and restraints governing the adoption of new processes and methods of production and the resulting mechanical, organic and human adaptations which the employer shall be allowed to make. Scientific management is essentially dynamic in its conception and methods. To impose static conditions, or to restrain it from taking full and immediate advantage of dynamic possibilities, robs it at once of its special purpose and effectiveness. Trade unionism of the dominant type is effective only where it can secure the strict maintenance of the industrial *status quo,* or can make its influence count effectively in all matters affecting its membership during the term of a contract. The conditions necessary to the effectiveness of the one are, therefore, incompatible with the effectiveness of the other.

To show the truth of these statements we have only to examine briefly the character and results of the central methods or means through which these contrasted entities, scientific management and the dominant type of unionism, function.

As I have stated previously, the central and essential instrument or method of scientific management, the fundamental means through which it secures knowledge of the industrial situation and which guides it in action toward the attainment of its ends, is time and motion study, applied not alone to the setting of tasks and the making of rates, but to the discovery and inauguration of improvements in the material, organic and human conditions and arrangements of the productive process. Thus used, time and motion study means constant and endless change in the methods of operation. No sooner is a new and better method found and established than an improvement upon it is discovered, involving perhaps new machinery, new tools and materials, and a new way of doing things. Change, change and still more change is the special purpose and mission of this essential instrument and central feature of scientific management. In short, time and motion study in its broader conception appears to be a method of analysis applied to almost every feature of the productive concern and process. And it is something which is not done once and for all, but is applied continuously throughout the life of the establishment. The scientific management based upon it is a perpetual attempt to put into operation the new and constantly developing arrangements continuously revealed by it to be more efficient. Not the least of these are the discovery and adoption of new and more effective operations and tasks, the reclassification of the working force to meet the needs of these new conditions, the shifting of the individual worker from class to class and task to task in order to discover the work for which he is best adapted, the handling of the individual laborer's work and pay with reference to his particular quality and temperament so as to bring into play his best productive possibilities. To deprive scientific management of the immediate use of the results of time and motion study, especially to restrain it from taking advantage of the better classification of workers and the better adaptation of the particular worker to the particular task which time study reveals, would be to deprive it of its chief characteristic—its constant striving toward the end of maximum possible efficiency, the thing that essentially marks it off from ordinary systems of management and gives it productive superiority to them. In short, such deprivation would prevent it from functioning normally.

Turning now to unionism of the dominant type, we find that the great body of its essential policiés, demands and methods center about and are in the interest of one great principle—*the principle of uniformity,* as regards all the conditions of work and pay affecting the group of workers which it represents. The principle of uniformity, fully developed and applied, requires that all men doing the same work should be supplied with the same tools and conveniences, work normally the same length of time and at the same maximum speed, turn out the same maximum quantity and quality of goods, and receive the same rate of wages. It is in the interest of this principle of uniformity that the unionists demand the establishment of a standard rate of wages as a fixed minimum, a normal day or week as a maximum, a standard rate of work or a standard day's or week's work, which, in connection with a standard rate of wages, tends to make this standard rate a practical maximum. It is largely to penalize the violation of these standards, so that there may be no inducement to break down the principle of uniformity, that unions demand pay at an extra rate for overtime and for doing work in irregular ways or under irregular circumstances. It is to prevent the violation of these standards of work and pay, and so to protect the principle of uniformity, that they demand control over the working personnel through the closed shop, control over the output of the individual, the abandonment of bonuses and premium payments, and, finally, collective bargaining—a contract made with the whole group of workers, extending over a definite period and covering all the conditions of work and pay for all the men during the contract period.

The reasons for the insistence upon this principle of uniformity have been indicated earlier in this paper. It is not that the unions desire the limitation of output and are definitely committed to it, but that long experience with the average employer has ground into their souls the belief that employers as a class are constantly seeking to lower the wage rate, and at the same time to increase the speed and exertion of the workers of the group through driving or bribing individuals of the group to greater speed and longer hours; and then are setting up the work and pay of these men as evidence to prove that the others are soldiering on the job and must increase their exertions or suffer a reduction of wage rates or a lengthening of hours of work. The only effective way that the unions have found for preventing this underbidding on the part of individual workers and the consequences indicated, is to cut out all working competition between the members of the group, by insisting on the definite establishment of uniform standards to be observed by all and to cover all the conditions of work and pay—i. e., by the establishment and maintenance of the general principle of uniformity, applied to all the members of each particular working group.

And it is evident, say the unionists, that the principle of uniformity thus conceived cannot be established and maintained against the employer who wishes to violate it unless all the conditions and methods of work and pay are *fixed* for the term of a contract—that is, unless all change is either barred, or is predetermined and regulated through the establishment of definite rules and restraints governing the adoption of new processes and methods, and the resulting mechanical, organic and human adaptations and changes in payment which the em ployer shall be allowed to make during the contract period. Any change in machinery, processes, tools, materials, products, not predetermined or regulated, opens the way for new classifications of work and workers not covered by the contract and thus opens the way by which the employer may seek to overreach the men, to degrade workers, establish new and lower rates of pay and less advantageous conditions of work; in other words, to reintroduce competition of workman with workman and consequent underbidding among them, and thus demolish entirely the structure of uniformity which the unions have reared.

Nor is this all. Looking at the matter in the long run and assuming, as the unions habitually do, that the employer is on the outlook to profit at the expense of the workers, not even the predetermination and regulation of changes by means of periodical contracts between the employers and unions can save the principle of uniformity from ultimate destruction where time and motion study is tolerated. For time and motion study means a constant tendency toward the break-up of old established crafts and the substitution of specialist workmen for the all-round craftsmen. Further, through it there is a constant discovery, gathering up and classification by the management of the knowledge of the best ways of performing work, on the basis of which definite instruction cards can be issued. With these and the guidance of functional foremen, relatively unskilled workers can be taught in a short time to do efficiently a very great part of the work which only skilled craftsmen could be trusted with formerly. And still further, the possession of this definite information enables the employer to measure more accurately the work and capabilities of each man, and to determine more accurately what wage payments would induce each worker to do his best. Where time and motion study is allowed, then, even under regulation, the employer at the end of each contract period would be less and less dependent on the union and more and more inclined to substitute specialist workmen for craftsmen, and efficiency methods of payment for the uniform day wage. But it is a notorious fact that relatively unskilled specialist workmen do not make good unionists, and that efficiency methods of payment tend to center the attention and interest of each workman on his own affairs and thus to lessen the feeling of mutual interest and common dependence among the workers. Under these circumstances the union could not long maintain the conditions which it considers essential to industrial democracy in the shop and enforce the principle of uniformity against the will of the employer.

There appears to be no getting round the fact, therefore, that constant indefinite change of industrial conditions, such as is essential to the functioning of scientific management, is in clear contradiction to the principle of uniformity which is the central and fundamental principle of trade union policy and is absolutely essential, from the point of view of the dominant type of unionism, to its successful functioning. Instinctively, therefore, the dominant type of unionism fights against change and against time and motion study, the mother of change.

But, you will again say, granting the incompatibility of these fundamental principles, why does not unionism make an exception of scientific management and scientific management employers who are not trying to overreach the workers but on the contrary are definitely committed to maintenance of rates and to a leveling up of earnings with every increase of efficiency? The answer of the unionists is, that these may be the ideals of scientific management but they have not worked out in practice. Scientific management may maintain rates and level up the earnings of the workers at any given task; but what good does that do the skilled craftsmen, the bulk of the old line unionists, when, through the constant and unending change which scientific management is inaugurating, it destroys the very crafts to which the rates for which they stand apply, and forces them to join the crowd of specialized workmen whose earnings may be raised by scientific management but nevertheless will still be lower than the old craftsman's pay? In scientific management at its very best unionism of the dominant type sees its worst enemy, in that scientific management means the abolishment of the very craft conditions and the very psychology of industrial democracy upon which the unions have painfully erected their superstructure of uniformity, and upon whose continuation their identity and continued functioning depend.

Specialize the old line craftsman, destroy his craft, and however high your ideals and kindly your motives, you are destroying the foundations upon which the dominant type of unionism is reared. Every union leader feels this instinctively; every one who has come into contact with scientific management and who has an understanding of unionism knows that this is what it is doing. Here, I believe, we have the final answer to the question "why organized labor opposes scientific management." Scientific management, properly applied, normally functioning, should it become universal, would spell the doom of effective unionism as it exists today.

BIBLIOGRAPHY (*Chapters XI, XII, XIII*)

BRANDEIS, L. D. "Organized Labor and Efficiency," *Survey*, 26:148-151 (1911).

CARLTON, F. T. "Scientific Management and the Wage Earner," *Journal of Political Economy*, 39:834-845 (1912).

COMMONS, J. R. "Organized Labor's Attitude toward Industrial Efficiency," *American Economic Review*, 1:463-472 (1911).

——. "Restrictions by Trade Unions," *Outlook*, 84:470-476 (1906).

"Scientific Management and the Labor Unions," *World's Work*, 22:14311 (1911).

GANTT, H. L. Work, Wages and Profits (1913).

GILBRETH, F. B. Primer of Scientific Management (1912).

——. Motion Study (1911).

——. Psychology of Management (1914).

HOXIE, R. F. *Scientific Management and Labor* (1915).

"Organized Labor and Industrial Efficiency," *Review of Reviews*, 44:482 (1911).

Regulation and Restriction of Output, Special Report, *United States Bur. of Labor* (1904).

STRATTON, G. P. "Ca' Canny and Speeding Up," *Outlook*, 99:120-125 (1911).

Taylor and Other Systems of Shop Management, Hearings, H. Res. 90, Washington, Government Printing Office (1912).

TAYLOR, F. W. *Principles of Scientific Management* (1911).

WRIGHT, C. D. "Restriction of Output," *North American*, 183:120-125 (1906).

CHAPTER XIV

SOCIAL CONTROL

There are two current tests or modes of definition of classes—the objective or mechanical, and the subjective or psychological. From the objective or mechanical standpoint, classes are defined in terms of wealth or social position, occupation, character of income or market relationship, moral or intellectual character, etc. Thus we commonly speak of the rich, the middle class, and the poor, the leisure class and the producing class, the large capitalists or captains of industry, the small capitalists, the professional class, the salaried class, or the wage-working class. From the subjective or psychological standpoint, classes are defined in terms of viewpoint, i. e., in terms of motive, belief, attitude, interest, and sympathy. To illustrate the difference: from the objective or mechanical standpoint, all those who get their incomes from interest and profits belong to the employing class; those who get their income from wages constitute the working class; while those who get their income from neither or both these sources are sometimes called the middle class, sometimes the consuming class.

From the psychological standpoint, on the other hand, all those who see their interests alike, or whose motives, beliefs, social attitudes, sympathies and habits of thought are alike, constitute one class as against those of different or opposed interests, motives, beliefs, social attitudes,

sympathies and habits of thought, regardless of their
source of income. Thus, from the psychological standpoint, all those, whatever the source of their income, who
feel that their interests are identical with those of the
employers, whose motives, beliefs, habits of thought, social attitudes and sympathies are in harmony with the
mass of employers, belong to the employing class, while
those who feel that their interests are with the wageworkers, or whose motives, beliefs, habits of thought,
social attitudes and sympathies are in harmony with the
mass of the workers, belong to the laboring class.

But now there are those who say that this is a distinction without a difference; that at bottom these two standpoints are identical, since one's view of his own interests
or one's motives, beliefs, habits of thought, social attitudes and sympathies are determined by his economic interests or his objective environment. One who gets his
income from interest or profits, or who works as a
profit taker and lives among profit takers, will of necessity view his interests as in harmony with the employing
class, and will have the motives, beliefs, social attitudes
and sympathies of the mass of the employers, and those
who get their income as wageworkers will of necessity
be in harmony with the viewpoint of the mass of the
workers.

There are, however, two reasons for the failure of
coincidence of the objective or mechanical and the
psychological social groups. It is not a *part* of the environment of the individual, the economic part, that
makes him what he is spiritually, but the *total* social environment, his mode and conditions of getting a living
plus his social relations, his educational, moral and religious influences, his political environment, and so on.

Secondly, men are not wholly determined in their attitudes, habits of thought and sympathies, by the immediate environment, but also by personal and social heredity and tradition. They are bundles of inherited and traditional sentiments and impulses. Like father like son. Men carry with them into a new environment the traditions of the old.

There is, then, a real distinction between these standpoints or tests for judging of the existence or nonexistence of social classes, and it will make a difference which of these tests or standpoints we adopt, for the existence of classes is apparently much more easily proved from the objective or mechanical standpoint than from the subjective or psychological standpoint.

Which of these tests shall we then apply? The answer seems clear. The important test for us is the subjective or the psychological, because we are making a study of labor conditions and problems not merely to discover what conditions and problems exist, but primarily to determine what *can* and *ought* to be done to better conditions and to solve problems. While the determination that society is or is not composed of classes, looking at it from the objective or mechanical standpoint, might help us in determining what, in view of our individual standards, ought to be done, it would not help us at all in determining what can be done. To guide and help us here, we need to know whether society is a harmonious whole, viewed from the standpoint of motives and assumed interests, or whether from this standpoint it is composed of warring classes. In the latter case we need to know what causes these classes to exist, how they stand related to one another in interest and motive, and what their quality, organization and strength are. Only thus can we determine which of the things that ought to be are possible, and how to go about the task of making them so.

If, from this standpoint, we find that society is at bottom a harmonious whole, we can and in general ought to let things alone, assured that they will work out ultimately for the best interest of all, and that social tinkering will only delay the process. If, on the other hand, we find that society is composed of classes with opposed interests and opposed viewpoints, we can be assured, when we find apparent evils, that something ought to be done, and the character of the classes which we find, and their motives, solidarity, and strength will give us the clue to the remedy it is possible to apply, and how. If we want action, we can get it only through understanding *men*, not mechanical arrangements and relationships.

Social ethics is a matter neither altogether of the conflicting ideals of a mere aggregation of individuals nor of the ethical consensus of an undifferentiated social whole, but it is largely a net resultant at any time of the conflict and compromise growing out of the existence and struggle for recognition of social group standards. In other words, it is a recognition of the fact that society as it exists today is made up of a great series of functional social groups which, though perhaps holding in common a general fund of ethical concepts characteristic of the age, still has each its special ethical code peculiar in content or in the relative emphasis placed upon its elements, for which the group is struggling to secure universal acceptance. In so far as this is true, it is evident that ethical progress in a democratic society like ours depends upon our knowledge of these special ethical codes

and the conditions that create them, and of the effective
forces with which they are backed. If we are to guard
and guide the ethical standards of the nation we must
understand in what terms and for what ends appeal can
be made to its constituent elements—in short, we must
know the springs of action of the functional groups
which compose it.

Labor, using the term in the generally accepted sense
as including all those who work for hire, is not a true,
functional, social group possessing a single, distinctive
and consistent moral code, but is a group of groups representing, ethically speaking, common humanity in all
its heights and depths, manifold diversity and contradictoriness. In other words, those who work for hire constitute a single and distinctive social group only in a
mechanical or statistical sense of the term.

Functionally and ethically—that is, from the standpoint of aims, standards of right, rights and justice,
social policies, demands, methods and attitudes—this
mechanical or statistical group called labor is a great
complex of groups, diverse and often vitally opposed in
viewpoint. Its members are frequently component elements of functional social groups, made up not only of
those who work for hire, but of representatives of the
professions, the trades, the farmers, manufacturers, and
even of the so-called leisure class. The truth of this
statement is a matter of common observation once we
free ourselves from inborn preconceptions, indoctrinated
prejudices, traditions or theories, or the insulation of
social exclusiveness. That it is bound to be true in a
community democratic in character and made up of diverse racial and temperamental elements is evident from
a little analysis of functional social groups and of the

causes which create and maintain them. A functional social group may be defined as a body of individuals holding a common viewpoint in regard to one or a number of vital social matters and in this respect at variance with the viewpoints of other members of society. It is this common viewpoint and interest and the common purpose which results that make the group socially effective. It tends to act with respect to this common center of attention and toward all that most vitally relates to it as a unit with whatever strength of numbers, character, wealth, position and influence it may possess or can command, and thus to force society in this respect to adopt its standards and to modify social actions and institutions accordingly.

The common interest and viewpoint of a functional social group may be narrow and specific, its members united in sympathy or for common effort only on some one or a small number of social aims and purposes, with a correspondingly limited program of action. Or the members of a social group may have a common interest and hold to a common viewpoint with respect to a wide range of social matters, its outlook on life approximating a social philosophy and its program of action a comprehensive social policy. In a community relatively isolated from world contact and little affected by inventions, characterized therefore by status, the tendency is to the formation and relative permanency of these larger functional social groups. Society, then, tends to be divided into castes or classes, based on occupation, mutually exclusive in membership, each with a distinct social and ethical code and standards; but in a society like our own, democratically organized, characterized therefore by much and varied contact between the individuals of the different mechanical groups, exposed by intercourse to the ideas and ideals of every nation, changing in its composition by the influx of every race and order of men, applying new ideas and inventions to the rapid alteration of its methods of production, exchange and modes of communication, enlarging and shifting its wants, constantly developing new social problems and new social issues, there is little opportunity for the development of caste or class. Only those permanently isolated from the complex and shifting influences of a rapidly developing democratic society, by the leisure and exclusiveness conferred by the assured possession of wealth, or through hopeless submergence into the ranks of unskilled, uneducated and poverty-stricken labor, present the conditions favorable to the development of permanent functional groups, united by a common philosophy of life and a general program of action. Between these upper and nether strata the functional groups in modern, democratic, progressive society are for the most part of the relatively narrow and the specific sort whose members are united in viewpoint and action only on some one or a relatively small number of social aims and purposes.

The chief characteristic of such functional groups is that membership is not necessarily permanent and involves no necessary unity of viewpoint and action outside of and beyond its specific aims and purposes. The individuals who compose one group may at the same time be members of many other social groups, and in this manifold social grouping the individual may find himself now associated with and now opposed to his fellows of a particular group. Thus, of two members of a single business organization, for example, formed to secure efficiency of production or extension of the market, or for aggression or defense against organized labor, one may be a Christian, the other an atheist; one may be a subscriber to the doctrines, ethical and social, of the Catholic faith, the other an adherent of some Protestant church; one may be an ardent republican, the other an equally ardent democrat; one may stand for the enlargement of government functions, the other for the sacredness of natural individual rights; one may be an ardent supporter of social uplift, the other a firm believer in the "survival of the fittest"; one may be an advocate of the prohibition of the liquor traffic, the other, of "personal liberty"; in short, these two members of the employing group, united in a single organization, created for certain specific purposes, that is to say, in a specific functional group, may be found in opposing camps with respect to all other matters of ethical and social import, and each associated thus in turn with representatives of every so-called social class.

That this is bound to be true, not only of employers but of those who work for wages, becomes evident when we look to the causes which underlie and determine the formation of social groups. These groups are the outcome, in the first analysis, of the attractive force of like-mindedness and the repulsion of unlike-mindedness. Whatever operates to make individuals like-minded tends to draw them together into a group, narrow or comprehensive in its outlook according to the breadth of sympathy involved. Whatever emphasizes or creates difference of character, belief or interest tends to repel individuals and to force them into diverse and opposing groups. These groups, therefore, are the outcome of the attractive and repellent interaction of all the characteristics of individuals, relatively permanent and relatively

temporary and shifting, in all the infinity of their specific
manifestations and combinations, and ultimately of all
the forces, physical and social, which play upon, create
and change the character and immediate interest, attitudes, and beliefs of particular men.   They are the result thus, in part, of similarities and diversities of temperament and propensities, of interests permanent and
temporary, of race and physical characteristics, of sex,
and of environment.[1]   But the interest which prompts to
the formation and diversification of functional groups is
not economic interest alone.   The environment which
creates sympathy and antipathy is the whole social environment, including social traditions of every sort, the
educational influences and effects of the family, the
school, the church, the party, the infinite variety of social
organizations, the varied associations and contacts, formal and informal, involved in all the activities, the com-
ings and goings of life, as well as the diverse conditions,

---

[1] Unionism, using the term in its broadest sense, is the result of a universal social tendency—the tendency of men of
similar temperament and similar environment and interest to
get together for common action.   Unionism is, therefore, not
confined to wageworkers; it is one of the most fundamental and
pervasive of social phenomena, and is prevalent in every social
class.   But while unionism is generically the same in all classes,
there are in every class different and in many respects rival
and contradictory species and varieties of unionism.   This applies with special force to *trade unionism,* the unionism of the
wageworkers—where we have several rival forms of unionism
which represent the rival viewpoints and programs of different
working groups.   Trade unionism is distinguished from other
forms of unionism simply by the fact that it is the unionism of
the wageworkers, but it does not differ essentially in fundamental purpose and method from the unionism of other social
classes and groups.

standards of living, and relations involved in, and the outcome of, the industrial organization and activities of society. The purely economic activities, conditions and relations of the individual and the associations growing directly out of these do indeed play a prominent rôle in the formation of character and ideals, and in the determination of interest, and do thus determine to a very great extent the formation of social functional groups, but that they are predominant as against all other social forces, even with respect to the membership of the complex labor group, is a matter which admits at least of reasonable doubt. Not only do the individuals who compose this great labor group present all the characteristics, and not only are they played upon by all the formative forces which make for diversity of functional groups, but the groups to which they are found actually allied are extremely diverse, often in opposition, and often derive their membership partly or even largely from those who do not work for hire. The wageworking group includes every variety of temperament—the artistic, religious, constructive, destructive, conservative, radical, revolutionary.

Let us now take up the most important social theories and try to test them from the psychological standpoint. First, the classical economic and business man's theory.

The classical economic or business man's social theory postulates the rational individual as the unit of society. Each individual, according to this theory, is possessed of certain natural and inalienable rights. Fundamental among these natural and inalienable rights are private property, free competition and freedom of individual contract, noninterference with the natural law of supply and demand in the fixing of prices and wage rates, the right of the employer to manage his business to suit himself, and the right of the worker to work when, where and for whom he pleases.

It is considered to be the sole province of government and law to uphold these and correlative rights, thus allowing to the individual the greatest initiative and freedom in "life, liberty and the pursuit of happiness," so long as he does not interfere with the natural rights of others. But any combination of individuals which interferes with these natural rights, and especially with free contract and competition, is looked upon as artificial and against the laws of nature. Hence the doctrine of *laissez faire*.

When these rights are recognized and upheld, and the individual, so long as he does not violate the natural rights of others, is allowed to seek his own interest freely, equality of opportunity is realized, each individual naturally tends to subserve the interest of his fellows, harmony of interests prevails in society, and the social and economic position to which any individual may rise by the exercise of industry and thrift is limited only by his abilities. It is the disregard of these rights which produces the absence of natural social harmony and the appearance of classes and class conflict. Such classes and conflict are, however, unnatural, artificial, and, in the long run, cannot endure.

It will be seen that the fundamental assumptions underlying this theory are a natural social order, resting on unchanging natural law and natural rights, existing prior and superior to social organization and will, a fixed social constitution and relationships, sacredness of property, the rationality of human nature, and the competitive equality of individuals aside from personal differences

which tend initially to be slight. It is generally assumed
by those who hold to this doctrine that the common law
is the expression of immutable natural law, and that the
decisions of the courts are normally the expression of
natural justice. When the fundamental law and the
court decisions are allowed full force, the inalienable natural rights are preserved, the true interests of all the
individuals are subserved, and social harmony prevails.

While this classical economic and business man's social
theory is the most conservative and respectable thing in
the world, and held by the most conservative and respectable people, it is in very close harmony, in its fundamental character, with the theory of *anarchism.* The
reactionary conservatives and the philosophical anarchists build on the same foundation and are very closely
allied. Most of the postulates of the classical viewpoint
are anarchistic postulates: rationality, individual liberty,
natural law and natural·order (as opposed to social order
and law), natural and inalienable rights, likeness in human nature, *laissez faire,* and fundamental harmony of
interest. The main difference between the classical economic and business man's social theory and the anarchistic social theory is that the latter is more thorough. The
classical stops, in its *laissez faire* policy and in its demands for the freedom of the individual, before the
sacred institution of private property; here it has not the
courage of its logic. The anarchistic viewpoint carries
the thing through logically. Here is the main difference.
Drop the classical economist's and business man's awe of
private property, let it be the free sport of the rational
individual and your classical theory becomes practically
the anarchistic theory.

What of the validity or invalidity of the assumption of

human rationality? Two points need to be considered. First, are we not rational beings when we decide things and act for the best interests of others as well as when we decide and act purely with our own interests in view? The answer in the abstract is yes. But the answer from the standpoint of this classical theory and its conception of rationality is no. This theory distinctly assumes self-interest as the motive of rationality and rational action. Hear Adam Smith: "I have never known much good done by those who affected to trade for the public good. It is an affectation, indeed, not very common among merchants and very few words need be employed in dissuading them from it."[2]

Secondly, the perfectly rational man, preceding action, always weighs and balances utilities against disutilities, and always acts in the direction of the greatest net surplus of utility. This implies deliberate calculation before action, an entire absence of emotion, or else a complete disregard of emotion or feeling. If emotion is ever present in the rational human being it is never allowed to enter as a disturbing factor into his calculation or to influence his subsequent action. The rational man is never moved directly by fear, hate, anger, revenge, love of wife, home, country, love of approbation, desire for power or prestige. These things move him, if at all, only after being translated into terms of utilities and disutilities. He is never moved by any of these things to act impulsively or thoughtlessly. If you strike him, he always calculates the consequences before he strikes back.

This assumption of deliberate action also implies an entire absence of habit and habitual action. The rational

[2] Adam Smith, *Wealth of Nations*, Routledge & Sons (1892), bk. 4. chap. 2, p. 345.

man always weighs and balances before he buttons his
coat, or eats, or drinks, or smokes, or works, or plays.
It also denies the presence, as determinants of action, of
inherited tendencies and propensities, of individual preconceptions and prejudices, of passion of any sort.
Given a certain situation and two men similarly situated,
and, as rational beings, they will always act in the same
way. Is this true? Of course it rules out all instinctive
action or reaction. A fly hits a man in the eye. He
weighs and calculates utilities against disutilities before
he closes his eyelid.

Now, I do not intend to deny that men do weigh and
balance before acting, or to maintain that they are not
at all rational. What I mean to say is that they are not
altogether rational, that they are moved by love and hate,
fear and prejudices, habits and propensity, apart from
and often in opposition to the dictates of rationality.
And this is not only in line with common observation but
with modern psychology, which tells us that we are bundles of propensities, preconceptions, impulses, and habits
—some of them inherited from a remote past. We are
guided in our action both by feeling and habit, by intel-
lect, and perhaps more by the first than by the last. But
if it is denied that man is moved solely by rational self-
interest, this whole classical economic structure with its
assumption of harmony of interest in society topples
down. The direct bearing of all this on our immediate
problem is that we cannot get labor reforms through by
demonstrating their rationality. We shall have so to
move as to appeal to men's emotions and, in short, to
take into account their habits, thoughts, etc. This is
being practical, not academic.

Now this brings us to the second social theory, the

socialist. Let us take here a brief general view of the Communist Manifesto :[3] Society, since the dissolution of the primitive tribal community, has been composed of warring classes. The fundamental basis of these classes is opposition of economic interest, the outcome of private ownership. In the development of society these warring classes have been reduced practically to two, the bourgeoisie, owners of the means of production, profit takers, exploiters, and the proletariat, practically propertyless, wageworkers, and exploited. This situation cannot, however, last, for it produces a series of destructive contradictions: over-production with under-consumption, commercial crises; increased repulsiveness of work and decreased remuneration, increased plenty with progressive degeneration of the working class, cheapness with want; concentration of production and capital, with free competition. Or, as Engels states it, the situation is characterized by socialization of the means of production with individual appropriation; or socialized production and capitalistic appropriation; organization of production in the individual workshop with anarchy of production in society generally. Increase in numbers and organization of the working class is contradictory to the bourgeoisie rule. The inevitable outcome must be the destruction of the bourgeoisie, the triumph of the working class, the abolition of private property in the means of production and the final abolition of classes and class rule, when harmony of interests will prevail in the coöperative commonwealth.

Does this socialist theory rest on any of the fundamental assumptions of the classical economic theory?

[3] Karl Marx and Frederick Engels (1848), *The Manifesto of the Communist Party.*

On natural order and natural law? Yes, but it is a different order and law, not fixed, but developing and evolutionary. On natural rights? Yes, and the full product of toil, for example. Harmony of interest? Again yes, but it is an ultimate outcome. What assumptions of the classical economic viewpoint does this contradict? The rational individual as the unit of society? Not altogether, because each man is supposed to know his own interest. It contradicts the assumptions of human equality, of fixed social relationships, although ultimately not so, of sacredness of property and *laissez faire*. What other assumptions are there? Economic determinism. Man and social structures are molded entirely by the environment and by the *economic* environment and forces. Social evolution. Not the modern conception of evolution, of indefinite change, but of change according to a fixed program with a determinate end—God or Nature predetermining it—that is, teleological evolution. Inevitable determinism. No social effort can control or change the course of what is economically determined.[4]

The theory of Professor Veblen is generally fairly closely allied with that of the socialist. Like that, it sees society as made up of warring classes, mainly the employing and working class; like that, it is evolutionary —it sees these classes as the result of a process of evolution; like that, it lays immense stress upon the economic factor as a determinant of classes and class conflict. These classes are the product of modern machine indus-

---

[4] The Syndicalist theory is like the socialist, only different in its methods. It is opposed to political action and favors a physical revolution by the workers, and working class rule in society made up of self-contained industrial groups.

try, by it cut off from contact with one another, each with a separate molding environment and mental discipline.

This theory differs, however, from the socialistic theory in some very important respects. These classes exist apart and are at odds not so much because of a real fundamental opposition of interests, as because of an inability to see things alike, due to a difference in the economic functions and economic environment. This theory is evolutionary but evolutionary in a different way from the socialistic theory. There is constant change but in no assignable direction, and with no determination. There is not teleology in it. The difference in environment with its classes and class conflict is, therefore, likely to go on indefinitely—to be a permanent state of affairs. Another important implication is that there is no third or intermediary or mediating class possible; therefore, no compromise or higher social control. Veblen's theory postulates blind, opaque, physical force and causation as the chief social determinants. Man is not rational, there are no natural rights, no social norm, no natural harmony of interests, no final social time when harmony of interests will rule. Classes and class struggles are the inevitable social situation. There are no general social standards of right and wrong, good and bad, to which we can refer things for solution. All is in the grip of fate, of physical and economic causation. At present, then, we have two classes and the inevitable two-class struggle.

What is the matter with this theory? Does it work out in practice? Existing facts in this connection as to class solidarity confute it. Instead of one labor viewpoint we have business, uplift, revolutionary unionism and the Industrial Workers of the World. But is it true theoretically? It is in line with modern science as to nonteleological evolution. It is in line with modern psychology as to the nonrationality of man, who is a bundle of inheritances, propensities, prejudices and instincts. It is in line with modern sociology—no natural rights, no natural order, no natural law as distinct from social order and social law, nonharmony of interests, no absolute right and wrong. On the other hand, it places too much stress upon the economic environment as a formative force. Man is the outcome of his total social environment. The individual, according to Veblen, cannot react on this environment; he is not a center of force. But cannot we do something to change this environment by education, shop arrangements, etc.? Again, there are no such rigid economic environments and disciplines. There is much more social interaction than is supposed.

The progressive-uplift theory postulates a fundamental and ultimate harmony of interests in society. It recognizes the present existence of social classes and class conflict but regards these as the temporary outcome of lack of sufficient social interaction, knowledge and understanding. Science and democracy, however, are gradually overcoming these deficiencies. As science increases the knowledge of social facts, forces and relationships, as democracy, especially through universal education, develops, and particularly as the practices of industrial democracy, especially through collective bargaining, spread, there evolves a common social viewpoint, and a real social will of the people destined to do away with classes and class conflict, and to substitute in their place social justice and social harmony in the pursuit of general well-being.

According to this theory, present social conflict is due

mainly to the existence and mutual opposition of an employing and a working class. But already there is developing a strong third party—sometimes called "the people," sometimes "the consumers"—unbiased in its viewpoint, standing for social justice, and representing the true social will, a party already capable in ordinary cases of acting as mediator and arbiter between the warring classes. With the growth of knowledge of social affairs and the increase of social interaction fostered by democracy, this third party will gradually control the warring classes and ultimately absorb them. The social will will then be supreme, and social harmony will prevail. The attainment of this end involves a constant extension of social control in the form of legislation and public opinion in the support of the weaker warring class—the workers.

The progressive-uplift theory rests mainly on the following fundamental assumptions: (1) That man is not rational but is capable of a high degree of rationality. (2) That man is a product of his total social environment and inheritance. (3) That increased knowledge and increased association of individuals and classes will produce increased understanding, sympathy and harmony of viewpoint. (4) That a strong social group is capable of freeing itself from class interest and bias, of knowing what right, justice and welfare are for all in society, and of thus standing as an impartial arbiter between warring classes. (5) That social will is an expression of natural law. In the crasser statements of this theory social will is regarded as superior to natural law in social affairs.

Here various questions naturally arise. How do we know that there is a fundamental and ultimate harmony of interests in society—how prove it? What does the assumption go back to? What about the facts? Is it true in regard to some issues but not in regard to others? Even if we can get a third-party decision on each question, how are we going to know that it is right? Is lack of social interaction, i. e., lack of understanding, being unable to see the other person's point of view, the only basis of classes and class conflict? When there is a real fundamental difference of interest, can there be any real social will or any social justice, any social standards of right or wrong? Where would they come from, and what sanctions would they have? Is there any such class as consumers, the public, the people? Are not all consumers producers with producers' interests, allying them to one or the other group? Is not the interest of the public different, with different class inclinations on different subjects? Is the public always wiser than the class in the industry concerned as to what should be done? Has public control so far proved wise and efficient?

It is urged in criticism of this theory that there is a group of questions on which the interests of different social classes *are* opposed. But in respect to any specific issue, such as wages or hours in a particular industry, are the classes solidly lined up, and are those which are lined up usually a social majority?[5] Must we have agreement on standards of right and justice to get people to act together to better conditions, to get a real social will? Is there nothing for the public to do but helplessly to view the struggle between antisocial factions, or, at most, to play the subordinate and equivocally useful part of

[5] *See* C. H. Cooley, *Social Organization,* as to the multitude of overlapping groups different for each question.

"make-weight" between them? Must our final conclusion be thus negative and pessimistic? Personally I do not believe it. The apparent impossibility of a social will and a constructive social program comes from looking at the situation as a whole with a hidden assumption of class viewpoint unconnected with specific questions, and from assuming that standards of right and justice must be absolute. There *is* a door to constructive social opportunity and here, I believe, is the key with which it can be unlocked.

While in matters in which the interests of the warring classes are really opposed there appears to be no possibility of a third party altogether without any economic class interest and bias, or of setting up general and absolute or exact standards of social right or justice to which all or a majority can be depended upon to adhere, there *is* a possibility of discovering in connection with every such specific problem *minima* and *maxima* which represent a nearer approach than at present exists to social right and justice. These are the limits within which right and justice lie in the particular case, and to which it is often possible to get the adherence of the warring groups and almost always the adherence of those, whatever their general economic interest and bias, who are not directly concerned. Such, for example, are minimum wage rates, maximum hours, and maximum conditions of sanitation and safety in the different industries. On the basis of these specific minima and maxima, we can formulate a general constructive program of social betterment, and, I believe, develop a real third party in its support. It is true that between the limits thus set we shall apparently have to allow the warring groups to fight out the contest, but we can also establish maxima and minima in the form of socially tolerable rules of the game, in accordance with which the contest must be fought. The great thing is to get more social interactions. The solution, therefore lies logically outside the field of labor in education.[6]

It is possible that some might advocate doing nothing until we had a complete constructive program worked out and all of the machinery necessary for putting it into operation, for securing the facts, establishing maxima and minima of every kind in every occupation, establishing socially tolerable rules of the game in industrial contests, educating the public for perfect legislative action, and for fair adjudication, wise administration and enforcement of the law. This, however, would mean to leave everything for an indefinite period to be settled by raw partisan contests and the wiles of the politician, to be settled by the principle of might and cunning, with no approach, in the majority of cases, to justice and social welfare. Those who have had a vision of social justice and welfare should most decidedly get into the game and act up to their best lights on every occasion. That is the only way to keep things from going to rack and ruin while better standards and concepts are taking form. If action were never taken until all problems and all methods were perfectly worked out, there would be no progress at all. That is not the method of social progress. We progress socially mainly by the trial and error method; we learn by action that is partly right and partly wrong. But action should be foresighted and intelligent. We should not shut our eyes to the need of social standards, of a constructive program and of the machinery to

[6] In this connection read carefully the Commons' plan, Final Report, United States Commission on Industrial Relations, pp. 307-401.

put it into force. We should not despair and be content
simply to throw our might as partisans to one or the
other contending parties, blindly accepting all the errors.
Instead, while we are acting we should have always in
mind the larger and better thing, the long time outlook,
and try to make our experiences throw light upon it.   In
between periods of action there should be an effort to
advance in the formulation of standards and constructive action in the interest of all—to make action a school
for the development of social understanding and constructive ends.

The fault of reformers is not that they act, but that
they act blindly and act *only,* that they do not see the
whole of the social situation back of the particular incident, that they do not try to grasp this whole in the inter-
vals or try to formulate principles of action from it.
Being simply spasmodic and particularistic, regarding
each struggle as a case by itself, they do not make any
general advance.   The trouble with most people who
make proposals in the labor field is that they do not understand the broad features and forces with which they
have to deal.   They do not know, therefore, what ought
to be done, and if they find anything that apparently
ought to be done, they naïvely assume that because it
ought to be done, it *can* be done.   If men in society were
mere pawns to be moved about the board and if their only
good was their immediate material betterment and if reformers were omniscient and had the power of God, this
would be all right.   But none of these things are true.
Men have their own ideas as to what is good for them
and how to secure it.   And in a democracy you cannot
give men what is for their good except by their consent
and by moving them to go out and get it.   Trade union-

ism is a self-help institution. The trade unionist wants, not charity, not patronage, but justice. He prefers to get that by his own efforts. He does not want patronage, however good its objective results. He has no sympathy with the people or forces which would reach down to help him from above. To know what ought to be done for the workers, we must know the men themselves, their ideas, ideals, purposes and ways of looking at things; the relationships that actually exist among them and how they view these relationships and why.

The public should undoubtedly take a hand in such matters. This is an absolute necessity if these contests are ever to be settled in the interest of social welfare. Mere fighting between employers and workers will never attain this end. But the so-called public has no machinery of action, or constructive program, and no means of getting into the game before the struggle is on. It is practically inefficient, merely groping. After the struggle is on, it finds itself obliged simply to line up with one side as a partisan, usually for the workers. A strike starts as a little group contest, but the public, having no information or standards of judgment or means of independent action, must stay out or go in as partisan of one side or the other. Some do go in, enlarging the issues. That forces others in, and gradually many are forced in. The result is a gradual enlargement of the line-up, of broadening points of opposition; temporary class lines appear; a class struggle begins to emerge. All this is due to the lack of means of informing the public beforehand and settling the difficulty upon grounds of social welfare, or of enforcing the public will.

Our labor laws are built up haphazard, due to emotionalism after some disaster or revelation; they are a heterogeneous and frequently contradictory mass. Minutely specific and therefore inelastic and inadaptable, they are therefore often unenforceable, and often, if enforced, unjust to employers and harmful to the workers; they show no prevision, no program, no consistency in the same state or as between states.

The administration of the law is in the hands of different bureaus with ill-defined relationships, jealousies and cross-purposes. In Illinois there are the Industrial Board with powers undefined, a Board of Commissioners of Labor, the Department of Factory Inspection, an Employers' Liability Commission, a Bureau of Labor Statistics, a State Mining Board and Inspectors (five commissioners), a State Employment Office, and a Board of Arbitration. Political appointees hold offices; no confidence exists; there are lax administration, inefficient inspection, a lack of knowledge of facts, and appeals to courts because laws are unintelligent and unintelligently enforced.

In labor contests no foreknowledge exists; there is no machinery for getting it, no enlightened public opinion; there is arbitrary disregard of public rights (street car strikes), false claims and a helpless public. The workers want arbitration when weak but refuse it when strong. Arbitration is conducted on no principles; rather is it always a compromise against the employer. There are no real settlements.

We must have means for developing a body of exact and truthful information, developing common standards of right and justice (maxima and minima or rules of the game), developing a real public opinion back of them, developing a constructive social program, getting centralized, strong, able, elastic administration and enforcement of laws, with a view to the whole situation; getting and applying knowledge and standards to control, and in the settlement of contests, creating to this end social interactions. This understanding and knowledge can be secured only by the closest first-hand study in the field. It is all a matter of doing the work in a calm, orderly, large-minded and farsighted, constructive and scientific manner.

BIBLIOGRAPHY

Address of Theodore Roosevelt on the Principles and Policies of the Progressive Party, before the convention of the National Progressive Party (1912).
Bulletin of the Wisconsin Industrial Commission.
Bulletin of the New York Industrial Commission.
COOLEY, C. H. *Social Organization* (1909).
HOXIE, R. F. "The Trade Union Point of View," *Journal of Political Economy,* vol. XV, 345-363 (1907).
——"Is Class Conflict in America Growing and Is It Inevitable?" *American Journal of Sociology,* vol. XIII, 776-781 (1908).
LAUGHLIN, J. L. "Business and Democracy," *Atlantic Monthly,* 116:89 (1915).
MARX AND ENGELS. *The Communist Manifesto.*
The Progressive Party Platform (1912).
United States Commission on Industrial Relations, Final Report (1915), Report of Commissioners John R. Commons and Florence J. Harriman, pp. 307-404. Supplementary Statement of Chairman Frank P. Walsh, p. 297.
VEBLEN, THORSTEIN. *The Theory of Business Enterprise* (1904).

APPENDIX I

NOTES ON METHOD

HISTORICAL METHOD VS. HISTORICAL NARRATIVE

It is almost an axiom nowadays that "the present can be understood only with reference to the past." The general acceptance of this phrase is supposed to mark the triumph of the historical spirit and correlatively of the historical method. If this were true it would mean undoubtedly a great scientific advance. But to what extent is it true? Is there ground for the belief that the historical spirit and method, scientifically speaking, are comprehended by any large proportion of contemporary scholars and teachers? Are not the most evident results of the apparent dominance of the new ideal, at least in economics and closely allied disciplines, a great deal of misdirected and barren historical reading, and much indiscriminate indulgence in mere historical narrative?

As things go now, if a general theory of economics is to be exploited, it must be preceded by chapters on the development of English industry from the middle ages; if the discussion is one concerning capital and its uses, it must begin with an erudite consideration of the etymological development of terms; if a class is to be set to study contemporary municipal problems, it must first be made to drag slowly through the history of European municipalities; if a student undertakes to treat critically or constructively a bit of current theory he is likely to be regarded as unscientific and unscholarly if he fails first to read and summarize in a "historical part" all that has been written on the subject before. In fact, historical narrative, masquerading as historical method, has become a fad. The truly scientific historical method is exemplified only here and there in the work of a few thoughtful scholars and teachers, and counts for little because its real character and significance are rarely comprehended.

It is difficult to realize just what the authors and advocates of this sort of preliminary historical narrative and study expect it to accomplish. The well-meaning but vague phrases with which they introduce it certainly do not enlighten us. Apparently they think and act in obedience, more or less conscious, to the modern scientific imperative which demands that things, as they are found, be explained in terms of genesis and process. But, when one faces the question, how can these narratives contribute to any such explanation in any specific case? The historical narrative is "introductory"; it precedes the statement of any situation to be explained; its facts are neither selected nor arranged with reference to any specific problem. Apparently there is a vague idea that the "historical setting" is in some way endowed with the power both to evoke and to solve problems still unstated; and certainly no other supposition, in these days of multiplied interests, would justify the attempt to get at the meaning of any definite problem by first filling the mind with a mass of information, relevant and irrelevant, indistinguishably intermixed. The fact is that there is a vast difference between the historical method of science and this common, indiscriminate, historical narrative and study which is a travesty of it.

To understand the historical method and to make use of it in scientific work or in teaching we must first realize just what is the end of scientific investigation and how it is that an appeal to history can aid us in attaining this end. We are prone to think of scientific knowledge as an end in itself—to speak of the scientific spirit as simply a desire to know—to understand the existing situation—but is it not true that in reality all scientific investigation is undertaken in furtherance of some definite, vital, human interest? We wish to control the forces at hand so as better to realize some human purpose, therefore we seek to comprehend the existing situation from the standpoint of the purpose or interest in question. The scientific interest is therefore not merely academic but is in a sense practical—practical in the sense that it is an interest in understanding for the sake of the life of society or the individual. It follows that all scientific investigation is bound to be highly selective. We do not seek to understand the existing situation as a whole—that would be impossible—but we seek to understand the present in its relation to the interest at stake, the problem in hand. With this end in view we go as scientists to the past—to history—not to endeavor to "reconstruct the past," but for light on the practical problem before us. We go to the past in our scientific social studies because we recognize the fact that just as living individuals are not altogether what we see them to be in immediate thought and action, but are also bundles of suppressed and latent motives, propensities, and potentialities inherited, some of them, from a remote past, so social institutions are not merely what they can be shown to be by study of their present structure and functioning, but are also what they are actually or potentially in process of becoming as the result of the operation of forces past as well as present. Hence it is, in a sense, true, that the present can be understood only with reference to *its* past.

The elements of the historical method, as applied to social science, ought to follow as a series of simple corollaries from what has been said. The purpose of this method is evidently to further the solution of a definite problem through helping to explain a present situation—either the actual or some definite past institutional situation which is assumed for the purposes of study to be present. The problem presented is therefore specific, immediate, practical. The immediate historical question is: how did this situation come to be what it is? The data through which this question is to be answered are specific and selected; they are derived from its past as distinguished from the past of other institutions, or from the facts of general institutional history.

Clearly then the historical method in this connection presupposes a well-defined institutional situation—a descriptive account of what is or has been at some definite time—and the facts which it marshals out of the past in explanation of this situation are not general, but refer specifically *to* this situation; they aim to show definitely its genesis and the process through which it came to be what it is. In other words, the historical method of science, as applied to economics and kindred subjects, requires that the problem first be raised, that the situation as seen in the present first be stated, and that then, and not till then, solution of the question *why* be attempted by a careful study of the past out of which the situation given is supposed to have emerged.

With the simple exceptions of the character and source of its data, therefore, the historical method does not differ from the ordinary method of scientific investigation. The fact that we have to go to history for the data—to become in a sense historians—does not alter the scientific end and does not relieve us from the utmost exercise of our mental powers in hypothesis, analysis, discriminating selection, synthesis, and clear and logical statement. In other words, historical data are scientifically important only when they explain some matter of fact of vital interest to us. There is nothing sacerdotal about them. They have no importance merely because they refer to the past. Their importance is to be determined in any given case by exactly the same tests to which ordinary data are subjected.

To bring out more clearly the contrast between the historical method as thus characterized, and mere historical narrative misapplied, let us take an example or two. Suppose the matter under discussion to be the comprehension of the present capitalistic organization. The pseudo-historical schoolman starts out with a sketch of the industrial history of England and then, having done supposed homage to the scientific spirit of the age, he proceeds to a close taxonomic treatment of the present situation, interwoven with good old-fashioned explanation of it in terms of the mechanical equilibrium of present forces—human motives and physical forces. Just what has the historical introduction signified here? The true exemplar of the historical method, on the other hand, starts from an analysis and description of the capitalistic system as an actual complex institutional structure upheld, for the moment if you please, by the mechanical equilibrium of present forces. Looking thus at the thing as it now appears, he asks the question *why,* in his attempt to better understand the situation from the standpoint of his peculiar interest, and then proceeds to answer the query by specific historical investigation. The whole difference in this case between the two methods is that we have, on the one hand, the mechanical juxtaposition of historical narrative and analysis of present phenomena and, on the other hand, the scientific solution of a definitely stated problem by means of appropriately marshaled data.

Or suppose we are endeavoring to make an earnest study of the present trade-union movement. If we were to follow the example and spirit of those who preface economic texts with historical chapters, we should feel it necessary, before getting acquainted with the ideas and methods of Samuel Gompers, John Mitchell, and Cornelius P. Shea, to plod laboriously up through the history of labor conditions and organizations from the dawn of the era of free labor at least. Actuated by the historical spirit, we should first try to get at the present situation—the ideas, ideals, aims, and methods of the present unionists. Then we should call in the aid of past experience to help us determine the sources and the life history of these present notions and methods of labor, and, therefore, what as social and industrial institutions trade unions really are and are becoming, what their real relation is to the complex institutional situation of the present, and therefore, as a corollary, how they are to be looked upon and dealt with for the best interests of society.

It must be admitted of course that the present is no more capable of being completely realized than the past is of being completely reconstructed. Attempts both to realize and to reconstruct are bound to be selective. Unless the interest in the realization of the present is superior to the interest that prompts to the attempt to reconstruct the past there is no ground for preferring the one attempt over the other. But the "historical narrative" interest is mainly academic, while that interest in the realization of the present which makes use of the historical method in harmony with modern scientific insight, is, as we have pointed out, in a sense practical—practical in the sense that it is an interest in understanding for the sake of or in the interest of the life of the society or the individual. The historical spirit in harmony with the modern scientific spirit or attitude is simply the going to the past to gratify the same interest that prompts to the attempt to realize the present. The main trouble with those who indulge in historical narrative is that they seem to think that academic reconstruction of the past can contribute to the ends of the practical interest of the present. In this they are for the most part mistaken. From the standpoint of the practical interest involved the academic reconstruction is a hopeless tangle of relevancy and irrelevancy, altogether without definite teaching.

In conclusion it may not be out of place to note that while the prefacing of the discussion of economic principles and conditions by long-drawn-out historical narratives violates the most vital rules of pedagogy, the historical method lends itself admirably to pedagogical needs if rightly understood. It gives the student something definite, something with which he is ordinarily, through experience or reading, in some degree familiar; it rouses his interest by asking: what, in terms of some vital human interest, does this situation mean? And then it invites him to search for the answer to this question. This harmonious relationship between the scientific and the pedagogical method, however, should not too much prejudice the new race of university investigators who affect to deprecate the pedagogical point of view as unworthy the consideration of the scientist.

PROBLEM AND METHOD

The real problem method consists in taking some one vital social thing and in working it out as a problem, drawing into it and giving substance and practical application to the whole body of knowledge that you possess mechanically and absolutely. You thus locate and find use for what you have acquired without life connections elsewhere. Make all the work you are doing in the university and all your outside daily experience count. If you try thus to link this work up with daily life and not let it be merely an academic matter, you will be surprised where and how much suggestive material you will get. Everything that happens will contribute to throw some light on your problem. This is the direct corollary of pragmatism, its direct teaching and application.

All this means that no one should come into the course who is not vitally interested, who cannot see that the subject touches some life-purpose of his, and who is not prepared to work hard and at times to go far beyond the schedule of hours which university courses on the average presume to require. There are no carefully prepared lectures to ease over the places where materials are diffuse, ill-adapted and hard to get at. The whole thing is a problem to me as well as to you. We shall succeed, therefore, only if each one is vitally interested and contributes all that he can to the result.

In this course we have to formulate our own problems, determine our own method, plow our way through great masses of ill-adapted secondary materials for small significant results, and, for the most part, seek our materials in the raw. We shall have to attend union meetings; meet and study union officials; read and digest union constitutions and working rules, trade agreements, and convention reports; study union periodicals; follow in the newspaper union controversies; work up special topics; read court decisions; and, if strikes or lockouts occur in the city, get out and study them at first-hand, and watch the methods employed.

One of our first contacts with unionism will be attending a meeting of the Chicago Federation of Labor. This is a city central, one of the organic units of the American Federation of Labor. It is composed of delegates from local unions, mostly craft locals which are again members of national trade unions. Its members are officers of local unions or selected as representatives of them, and are not altogether typical of the rank and file. This will be an opportunity for you to determine what sort of people the unionists are. Note:

1. Their intelligence, force, sincerity, outlook on life and society, ideals, standards of morality, rights and justice.

2. Their viewpoint. Is it craft, class, social, or group? What kind of group concepts have they?

3. Are they conservative, radical, revolutionary, idealistic or materialistic, altruistic or selfish, highly emotional or rational?

4. Gather evidence of what they want and how they

propose to get it; their problems, aims, demands, methods and attitudes.

Note also:

   1. The nature of Unionism and general characteristics of the movement. Is it narrowly economic, or broadly political, ethical, social, etc.?

   2. What is its viewpoint and spirit? Narrow group, class or social? Evidence? Is it characterized by unity and solidarity or by narrow factionalism? Evidence? Is it altruistic or selfish, forceful or futile; characterized by intense prejudice and moved by emotionalism, or open-minded and rationalistic? Democratic or the reverse? Revolutionary or conservative? Two bases on which democratic or antidemocratic character must be judged?

   3. What are its educational and informational qualities? Compare the information of unionists and university students on current affairs. The meeting is the means of great dissemination of information, for the delegates carry back what they hear to 100,000 members.

   4. What functional types are represented?

   5. What *is* unionism anyhow?

These various meetings will help us gradually to build up our conception of what unionism is. Different students will get different evidence and also get the same evidence from different angles. By analyzing this evidence under the heads of the nature of the union group, the nature of the union personnel, and the nature of the union program, we shall get our *what* of unionism. Then it will be for us to attempt to interpret this, especially the program, which will give us our *why* of unionism. I think you will agree before we get through that this is the only way, but like all things worth while it is the hard way.

Meetings like this are valuable to put us in touch with the actual union movement. They give us a feeling of reality of the subject of study. The possibilities of these meetings are uncertain. There is likely to be little discussion, hence little chance to estimate or judge different types of men or conflicts of ideals and interests within the group. Possibly there may be a false appearance of unity and enthusiasm. However, there may be speeches voicing the concrete longings, troubles and strivings of unionists, and, therefore, putting us in touch with current things. Talk to the men and officers if the opportunity offers itself. Considerable time and experience are required to judge them, but get acquainted and begin to judge.

One most important thing in connection with the work we are trying to do which we have not emphasized thus far is that nothing worth while can come out of work of this character apart from the determination on the part of each one of you to put the very best of himself into it in the way of good, hard, persistent, consistent, independent thinking. This work will amount to nothing unless you make of this thing, unionism, a serious personal problem and determine to think yourself through to a series of vital conclusions. These facts which you get from the field work and the readings are absolutely worthless unless you get down seriously and dig the significance out of them. The facts as mere facts will not do you any good. They will soon be forgotten. It is what they mean in terms of the character of unionism and social welfare that is important. This meaning you cannot get by merely listening to what I say of them, or repeating them to me; nor if you regard the facts as intrinsic bits of information to be stored away, or the work as mere task work to be done well enough to satisfy me.

Only if you yourself get a clear understanding of their meaning by your own hard effort will they be of any lasting value to you. You must yourselves get at them and squeeze the last essence of significance out of them. And do not have it in mind that you must agree with me. I do not care what your conclusions are. What I want is evidence that you have put your soul into the work, that you have not been passive, that you have been intensely active, that these things have meant something serious to you, that you have brought all your faculties and all your experience to bear upon them in the effort to analyze, organize, and interpret them. If you have not the time to do all the reading and thinking I ask, do the thinking. In my opinion, an hour of good hard thinking is worth more than twenty hours of reading just to get over the ground. I would rather have a paper that showed one flash of real insight than the most elaborate and finished piece of copying or mere stringing together of information. The trained man, the educated man, is the one who has learned to grasp a problem in the complexity of facts, and see the relation of the facts to the problem, to separate the significant from the merely incidental, to probe for hidden meanings, to marshal evidence for a definite conclusion. He is the man who is going to do things in life. I want the work to be training to this end. I want you to throw yourselves into the work in this spirit. *Think* out the meaning of things. Never mind the outcome.

Research Methods

Success in research is preëminently an individual matter. No definite rule or method can be laid down that will insure success. Each person must work out his own peculiar method. Every different research problem requires a different method of attack and system of work. The reason for generally poor results of public research is that one stilted method is used. Research students work mechanically. The great essentials are personal qualities, the ability to formulate a problem, to grasp a situation as a whole, an analytic and synthetic ability, insight and suggestive alertness, selective ability or ability to distinguish between the significant and the insignificant, ability to weigh the evidence, to distinguish between the true and the false, a sense of proportion, infinite patience in the handling of detail, resourcefulness and flexibility in overcoming obstacles and creating means to ends, staying power, ability to draw together the scattered threads and to construct a clear-cut, pointed and logical outline or medium for presentation of results, ability to put results into good, crisp, forceful English, with plenty of lights and shadows and emphatic summaries.

Anyone who possesses these qualities actually or potentially will work out his peculiar and successful method of research. The most that anyone can do for such a person is to give him a few hints that may save him from getting into blind alleys and from wasting his time and energy. These hints concern mainly the choice of a subject, the preparation for investigation and note taking, the taking and filing of notes, the weighing of evidence, and the outlining of the thesis and the report.

A great proportion of failures in research results from the improper choice of a subject. The student takes a subject because the teacher sees something in it. This is all wrong. No one can do anything worth while with a subject unless he sees in it something definite, vivid, worth while, a vital problem, a vital thing to prove or disprove. He must have a warm, drawing feeling for the thing, must feel that there is something great in it. Without this the work will be pointless, the student will simply flounder. The teacher should not, therefore, choose for the student, but set the student first to make a choice, subject to the teacher's approval. The student should never take a subject in which he does not see a definite nut to crack. Therefore, a man should feel spontaneously attracted to the subject and consider it carefully for the vital object of interest. *This is the first essential step for successful research.*

Every piece of research, to be successful, requires that it have in view a definite problem for solution and a definite method of attack upon that problem. And every definite problem requires its peculiar method of attack or research

The determination of the definite problem and the definite method of attack must precede the actual systematic investigation of the facts and note taking, except notes on the nature of the problem, its essential aspects and ways of treating it. For not all facts are of the same importance or value. Many have no value at all for any particular end until the problem and method have been worked out pretty clearly. The student up to this time has no basis for the collection of facts, for distinguishing between what is important and unimportant. Note taking before this, therefore, will mean an immense waste of time and effort in accumulating unimportant information, and will often result in the student getting swamped in detail and utterly lost—never getting out. Therefore, the first thing to do after the choice of subject is settled is to go definitely and singly to work on the particular nature of the problem involved and the methods of research to solve it. This means, unless the student is already familiar with the field, two things: (1) Soaking in the general literature and the objective facts in the field; soaking full of the problem and thinking it out, not to a conclusion, but as a game to be played, with the sole object to find the nut to crack and the way to hold it and hit it, i.e., finding the definite problem and working out the definite method of attack. (2) Doing a ton of *thinking;* here is where the main part of your intellectual effort comes in, where you have to do your straining. If you get clearly oriented in these things the rest is comparatively easy; you will know what you are after, how to select, how to organize. It will be simply following out a plan. But while you are doing this soaking and thinking, you do not want to take notes except on a question of problem and method—no fact notes; you have not your basis for selection—and if you do you will waste an immense amount of time and effort.

When you have soaked and thought your way through to a definite understanding of your problem and method then make out your *outline for research*, your *questionnaire* or whatever you call it, to direct your specific investigation and to classify your notes. Then, not till then, are you ready for the actual systematic research and note taking or filing. This preliminary soaking has another vital purpose that will come out later.

All this soaking and thinking before the actual investigation is entered upon may seem at first sight something you have no time to do, but if rightly done it will save an immense amount of time and effort in the end. It not only guards against taking worthless notes, but guards against being swamped in undigested details at the end; insures that all through the work you know exactly where you are, and that everything you do is definitely pointed to a definite end. Your knowledge is systematized all the while, you are proceeding systematically toward definite conclusions, and when your research is over, you have simply to draw your threads together into an orderly whole, present the evidence in an orderly way, and draw your conclusions.

The prime object is to have each note so that one can refer to it instantly and can keep the whole situation fresh in mind. Mechanical matters generally mean: (1) a filing outline; (2) a filing case, guide cards; (3) small sheets to discourage too much volume—many notes are best simply as page references; (4) only one point on a sheet; (5) careful reference at bottom; (6) key at top; (7) kept filed as far as possible. The dangers are too much mechanism, dilettantism, and being swamped in complexity; the simplest form for the purpose is best.

Of course, all this will not get you anywhere if you do not know how to judge and weigh evidence. My experience is that almost all evidence is partisan. From fifty to ninety-five per cent of what you get as facts in books and in the field are attempts to mislead, or pure misinformation; in any case, false. Moreover, the facts are of great inequality in importance. Students thus must know, first, how to separate the false from the true, second, how to give facts relative importance. The only guide here is the knowledge one possesses, along with his experience in the judgment of men. You have almost got to know before you can successfully find out. Here again comes in the supreme value of preliminary soaking and thought. You must know enough about the whole situation and the men in it before you go in to gather facts so that you can exercise sound judgment, distinguish the important from the unimportant, and know which men are misleading. The best success then requires a background of broad general information, knowledge of men and motives, maturity and experience, and the soaking for the particular work.

The final step before writing up is the formulation of the outline of treatment. One should never try to write without a general outline, but there is danger in trying to outline minutely beforehand. Get the general sweep of the subject and outline ahead each day. Of course, I need not speak of proportion, emphasis and style.

APPENDIX II

STUDENTS' REPORT ON TRADE UNION PROGRAM

To get a concrete notion and tangible evidence of the trade union program or set of programs the classes read all the trade union literature available, with the idea of gathering up all the items and formulating them into something like a consistent whole. From the beginning of the course on trade unionism every member of the class turned in a written report of every labor meeting attended by the class, every talk on labor made to the class by an outsider, and every interview he held with a labor leader. In addition separate committees made special studies of the American Federation of Labor, the Railroad Brotherhoods, the Knights of Labor and the Industrial Workers of the World. All the papers were then reviewed by a committee whose duty was to cull out the aims, principles and theories, policies, etc., and to organize them into a systematic whole. This work was done by a number of classes, each using and building on the results of its predecessors.

The following is a preliminary report of the committee of the class on the Aims, Principles and Theories, Policies, Demands, Methods, and Attitudes of Trade Unionism.

I. AIMS

Expression of the self—personality, temperament, group philosophy.
Higher intelligence and capacity for enjoyment.

Looking to improved conditions—more now.

Improvement of working conditions, in the matter of:

Wages

Hours

Safety

Health

Security

Continuity

Exertion

Independence and personal dignity

Supervision and control.

Improvement of living conditions and standard of living:

More just distribution of wealth

Community of wealth and industry

Industrial democracy

Uplift of the working class

Uplift of the community as a whole

Obtaining rights as citizens

Extension of democracy

Self-help.

II. PRINCIPLES AND THEORIES

Essence of social maladjustment is the wage system.

Low wages cause of most human ills.

Unemployment is the result of social conditions.

Wealth is for the benefit of all, not for a special class.

Everyone has a right to what he physically produces.

Profits are robbery; whole returns of industry should go to labor, which alone creates.

Not opposed to past unjust accumulations but want better future adjustment.

Profits of capital belong to labor.

Common ownership of means of production by workers is inevitable and not far off.

Profits from improvements should go to labor.

Need for Unionism based on the present wage system.
To maintain wages all must unionize.
Belief in the wage fund theory (or lump of labor theory)
   causes opposition to:
     Industrial schools
     Immigration.
Disbelief in the wage fund theory:
   Immigration creates a demand equal to the productive
     power which it adds.
   Raising wages will simply increase the productive effi-
     ciency of employees.
Labor-Cost Theory—Labor alone the creator of wealth.
All workers are of the same benefit to society, whether
   skilled or unskilled, and all should therefore receive
   the same wages.
Higher wages do not raise the price of the product.
   Price depends ultimately on effective demand.
   Higher wages mean increased demand for goods.
Labor not a commodity: Unions not a monopoly.
Principles of standardization and uniformity.
Identity of interests of labor and capital.
Coöperation with employer whenever possible—the goal.
Certain classic "rights" of employers denied:
   Employer's right to run his business as he wishes.
   Employer's right to hire and discharge whomever and
     whenever he pleases.
Antagonism of labor and capital.
Competition causes perpetual and progressive increase of
   poverty.
Competition between man and man is healthy; between man
   and machine it is injurious to man.
Competition unrestricted makes unions necessary.
Fixed, absolute, unchanging system of things.
Society's obligation to the worker to help maintain his
   inalienable rights, including:
   Right to work—right to a job, a trade.

Right to organize.
Right to leisure.
Right to an education.
Right to free action vs. employer.
Good of all more important than good of a few.
Organization is essential to freedom from oppression.
Unionism does not take away the laborer's freedom.
Solidarity of the working *classes*.
Injury to one the concern of all.
Harmony of interests of all laborers.
No single trade organization capable of coping with employers as all combined are.
Interests of labor class are more fundamental than those of the craft group.
Cheap workingmen's hotels, minimum wage, etc., simply retard the one right way of bettering things—organization.
A working class organization should include farmers, business men, etc., all but large capitalists.
Only workingmen should be enrolled in labor organizations.
Interests of own group paramount—whether:
The trade or craft group, or
The industrial group, or
The federated trades group, or
Workers of the world.
Political action.
Might is right (when Unionists win).
Right and justice are the rules of the game of the ruling class.
Unions justified for the good they do, no matter how great the corresponding damage.
Ends justify the means.
Courts and law not so bad—only are under the influence of wealthy and powerful classes.

III. General Policies

As to Organization:

To organize to facilitate common action as an economic group.

To parallel the capitalistic group in the matter of organization.

To include all laborers.

Maintain mixed local assemblies to develop class consciousness.

Opportunistic organization to meet needs of all labor as may be necessary.

To organize the unskilled.

To organize the particularly skilled worker.

Limit the number of members by high dues and fees.

Limit the number of members to those who are most efficient.

To organize the workers in a craft to subserve craft interests.

To amalgamate craft organizations where jurisdictional conflicts and joint interests demand.

To organize the workers of allied trades to subserve kindred interests.

To organize the workers on the basis of industries.

To maintain a national and district organization to con trol labor conditions in all localities or localities having similar problems.

To maintain a single organization.

To maintain a highly centralized organization to further efficient functioning.

To maintain an autocratic organization (successful unions).

To maintain a national organization to protect crafts from rivals and seceders.

To retain sovereignty in local organization.

To maintain local independence.

To maintain a democratic form of organization—use of referendum, etc.

To maintain machinery for reducing internal friction.

To remain irresponsible, not incorporated.

To maintain a responsible organization.

To maintain legislative committees.

To maintain committees to further candidacies of **trade** unionists and sympathizers.

To affiliate with labor parties.

To affiliate opportunistically with major political parties.

To maintain an organization for mutual insurance.

No affiliation with welfare plans of other groups.

As to Activities:

To work with the present order.

To work against the present order.

To check the accumulation and power of wealth.

To adhere to the Common Rule—collective bargaining.

To control workers and conditions:

Machinery, tools, processes and improvements

All incidents and conditions of work and pay

Supply of labor

Output, product, materials

The closed shop.

To use only union made goods.

To act pragmatically and opportunistically, making use of:

Self-help only

Monopoly and strategic position

Strong treasury

Strikes

Boycott

Violence if necessary

Methods "within the law"

Mediation, arbitration and conciliation.

To cultivate business relations with the employer.

To develop a good reputation for business-like methods.

To comply strictly with all contract provisions.
To maintain efficiency and high moral character.
To encourage industrial education.
To develop and use public opinion.
To abolish the present wage system.
To establish industrial democracy.
To use direct action:
  Sabotage
  General Strike
  Violence.
No respect for contracts.
State socialism and any measure pointing that way.
To discountenance violence.
To exploit labor or social groups.
To use any method in a pinch.
To abstain from partisan political action.
To use the ballot independently.
To control administration of government for trade union
  purposes.
To use legal rights and processes.
To use a definite political program.
To use no political action.
To educate and uplift the union personnel.
To subordinate class, race and creed differences to economic unity.

IV. DEMANDS

From the Employer:
    Recognition of the union.
    Standard rate of wages.
    Higher wages.
    No reduction of wages.
    Extra pay for holidays and Sundays.
    Extra pay for overtime.
    Extra pay for extraordinary work.
    Extra pay for objectionable work.
    Extra pay for night work.

Extra pay for split shifts.
Pay for idle time on duty.
Pay for walking time.
Equal pay for men and women.
No bonus or premium system.
No profit sharing.
Abolition of sliding scale.
Definite place of payment.
Payment of special expenses when engaged in special work.
Abolition of truck system.
Abolition of payment by check.
Free tools and necessary work-clothing.
Free power.
Definite price for working materials furnished by worker.
Weekly payment.
The normal day.
The eight-hour day, with no wage reduction.
Definite noon and rest hours.
Definite beginning and ending hours.
Half holiday on Saturday.
One day's rest in seven.
Observance of Labor Day.
No overtime.
No split shifts.
Time work.
No piece work.
Abolition of "rushers" and "speeders."
Union shop.
Closed shop.
Preferential shop.
No use of nonunion materials or machinery.
Abolition of foot power.
No scientific management.
No changes in classification.

No unregulated change in:
  Character or quality of work
  Machinery or processes
  Grouping of workers.
Participation in the increased profit from new ma-
  chinery.
Limitation of machinery to be tended.
No subcontract.
No sweatshop work.
Protection against occupational diseases.
Sanitary shops, in respect to:
  Ventilation
  Lighting
  Humidity
  Heat
  Water supply
  Cloak rooms
  Rest rooms
  Toilet rooms.
Safety devices and appliances.
Efficient fire protection.
Abolition of company home.
Abolition of child labor and night labor.
Prohibition of certain work.
Recognition of jurisdictional claims.
Representation on the job.
Prohibition of casual work for regular workmen.
Regulation of:
  Hiring and discharging
  Fining and docking
  Promotion
  Mode of doing work
  Enforcement of agreements
  Settlement of disputes
  Tools and Machinery
  Materials

Processes

Apprentices

Number of helpers, boy laborers and women workers.

Legislative demands:

Restriction of immigration.

Abolition of Asiatic immigration.

Abolition of convict contract labor.

Abolition of all forms of involuntary servitude.

Prohibition of immigration of contract labor.

Abolition of sweatshop.

Abolition of child labor.

Abolition of truck payments.

Compulsory school attendance until sixteen years of age.

Minimum wage laws for women.

Restriction of women's work.

Eight-hour law for women.

One day's rest in seven.

Efficient factory inspection.

Prevention of stop-watch, high-speed schemes.

Employers' liability.

Workmen's compensation.

Old age pensions.

Abrogation of common-law defenses for employers.

Removal of unjust technicalities and law's delays.

Equality of capital and labor before the law.

Election of all judges.

Limitation of power of judges.

Regulation of contempt proceedings.

Abolition of use of injunction in labor disputes.

Prohibition of use of Sherman Anti-Trust Act in labor disputes.

Abolition of private detective agencies.

Prevention of the use of police and militia in labor disputes.

No nonresidents to act as deputy-sheriffs or police in labor disputes.

No compulsory arbitration or investigation.

Voluntary arbitration.

Conference with employers.

Initiative and referendum.

Imperative mandate and recall.

Public as against private welfare plans.

Public as against private industrial education.

Federal appropriations for trade schools.

Free and uniform textbooks.

Abolition of private employment bureaus.

Woman suffrage.

Free speech and freedom of the press.

Bureau of Labor Statistics.

Bureaus of labor safety.

Museum of safety.

Federal bureau of health.

Public baths.

Public playgrounds.

Workingmen's lyceums and libraries.

Municipal ownership.

Public ownership of railroads, telephones, telegraphs and natural monopolies.

Right of petition for government employees.

Citizenship for Porto Ricans.

Marine Laws.

Graduated income tax.

Inheritance tax.

Land held for speculative purposes to be taxed to its full value.

V. METHODS

Organization and use of organizers.

Collective bargaining.

Legislation.
Arbitration.
Increased membership.
High moral requirements for membership.
High apprenticeship requirements.
Limitation of number of apprentices.
Salaried officers.
Control of union by small group.
Prohibition of needless dual organization.
Coöperation with allied unions.
Fight competing unions.
Coöperation in demands.
Coterminous contracts for allied crafts.
War chest.
Strikes.
General strike.
Intermittent strike.
Sympathetic strike.
Boycott.
Picketing.
Violence.
Intimidation of employers.
Intimidation of scabs.
Sabotage.
Merciless punishment of those who fall out of line
    with machine in power.
Buttons and insignia.
"We don't patronize" and unfair lists.
Use of union label.
Strike defense fund.
Closed shop.
Union shop.
Preferential shop.
Political action—watch and publish records of leg-
    islators.
Publicity through:

Observance of Labor Day
Official publications
Lectures
Sending children away from strike districts
Opening reading rooms where their literature may
    be obtained.
Educational work through:
    Union trade schools
    University extension
    Night schools
    Vocational education
    Apprenticeship system and control of apprentices
    Emotional appeals to public
    Education of the public
    Inconvenience of the public
    Labor press.
Social Ostracism.
Special aid to employers.
Friendly conferences with employers.
Union employment agencies.
Discipline of members.
Discipline of employers.
Low initiation fees and dues.
High initiation fees and dues.
Clearance cards.
Increasing financial centralization.
Democratic procedure.
Mutual aid and insurance:
    Sick benefits
    Death benefits
    Tool insurance
    Old-age pensions
    Homes for aged
    Out of work benefits
    Strike benefits
    Victimization benefits.

Coöperative enterprises.
Lobbying and corrupt politics.
Injunctions and legal aid.
Commissions and investigating committees.
Grievance Boards.
Regular union meetings.
Moral suasion.
Control through superior competence and efficiency of union labor.

VI. ATTITUDES [1]

A. Questioning fundamental, accepted social standards.
"Moral and industrial worth, not wealth, the standard of human greatness."
Philosophical rights are incomprehensible.
"Property rights are not rights but privileges."
Loyalty to the group more fundamental than property rights.
Labor is right and just always. All opposed to labor is wrong and unjust.
"Physical power the motive force of everything; might is right."

B. Questioning the present organization of society.
1. Economic:
"The capitalist performs no useful work."
"The capitalist is on your back; he furnishes the mouth, you the hands; he consumes, you produce. That is why he runs largely to the stomach and you to hands."
"In capitalistic society the working man is not a man at all; he is bought in the open market the same as hair, hides, and other forms of merchandise."

[1] A large number of these are direct quotations from union leaders, meetings, or books. Others are a summary of attitudes as seen by members of the class.

"Increasing specialization of industry wrong, for the
benefit of the capitalists only."

"United States capitalism the rottenest in the world."

2. Political:

"The government does not represent the people faithfully."

"Majorities do not make governments: the financial
plutocrats of this country are a minority more
powerful than all its voters, because of their
economic power. They are its real voters."

"Labor has no protection—the weakest are devoured
by the strong. All wealth and all power center in
the hands of the few, and the many are their
victims."

"Labor has no reason to be patriotic; the capitalists
own the country."

"Courts and law are not so bad—only they are under
the influence of the capitalist class."

Justice and law are not the same for all.

"To hell with the courts" (hatred and suspicion of
them).

Capital punishment is brutal and ineffective in preventing crime.

3. Social (criticism of other social groups and movements):

"The Church and the State—the great pillars of the
capitalists and of capitalistic society."

"Religious publishing houses—the worst enemy to
organized labor."

"The ministers do not give a damn for labor."

"Militarism is the tool of the wealth interests."

"Immigration is more dangerous than an invading
army."

"Newspapers are at the beck and call of the capitalists. The public press—the tool of capital."

"Bankers, lawyers and gamblers are parasites on society."

Large fortunes are all wrong.

C. Labor Welfare:

"There is no silver lining to the clouds of darkness and despair settling down on the world of labor."

Nonunion labor is under-paid and over-worked.

"Workers are wage-slaves."

"Labor power is not a product; it is flesh and blood, brain and brawn; it is the human power to produce."

"Self-denial and saving are not virtues for the workers but should be condemned."

"The contented workman is a pitiable object. Think of a smile in chains!"

The employer's gift to charity or "welfare" is a confession of unearned interest or profits; increase the wage.

"There can be no peace so long as hunger and want are found among millions of working people."

"The labor movement is the hope of the world."

"Unionists are not theorists; unionism is an eminently practical thing."

The trade union comprises the most intelligent section of the working class.

"We have everything to gain and nothing but our chains to lose."

"We don't need capitalists as guardians of capital— we can do that ourselves."

"All that is not for labor is against it."

"Those who 'kick' without reason are better than those who do not 'kick' at all."

"No strike of wealth-producers, whatever the circumstances, is unjustified, is without motive cause, so long as such a strike is aimed at the citadels of the employing class and their outposts"

"Can't blame a man for not working if he can't get a decent living out of it."

Lists used by unions all right; those used against them all wrong.

"The workers are damn fools if they don't take what they want when they can't get it any other way."

"Public opinion of slight weight in aiding workers' struggles."

"What the hell do we care about facts? We will win if we have the power and not because of the facts."

"Grab the world."

D. The Laborer and the Employer:

"Not every employer is a horned monster."

Employers can meet with workers on a basis of justice to both.

"Contracts with the employer should be lived up to."

"Employers are hard-hearted; won't arbitrate. This proves that the employer is not as good as the unionist."

Employers are parasites.

Employers are always wrong.

"Contracts with the employers are not sacred."

No attempt to get the employer's point of view.

"Every welfare plan has a joker in it."

"No undue advantage can be taken of any of our employers, because they have no rights that the workers are bound to respect."

Strike is war, not a relation between employer and employees.

The employer is feared as well as hated.

Spirit of lockout is un-American.

E. The Laborer and his Fellow Laborer:

1. In the same group:

"Union workmen are the best men."

"Competition for others not for us. Rival organizations are futile and a detriment."

"The unionist is a traitor to unionism if he fails to stand in with fellow unionists in all policies."

"We have fought a good fight—therefore we deserve assistance."

Lack of sympathy—inability to coöperate—showing itself in jurisdictional disputes.

Unity on economic questions immediately affecting the group. Lack of it on broad social questions, even in the same group.

Conflict between materialistic majority—"bread and butter unionists," and the idealistic members.

Class loyalty and brotherhood, mainly one of catchwords; internal suspicion and desire on the part of each to gain his own ends.

2. In different, opposed, or competing groups:

Lack of broad class consciousness; instead there is small group consciousness. (How many unionists use only union-label goods?)

"Trade unionism—the bulwark of capitalism."

"The A. F. of L. is not a labor organization; it is simply a combination of job trusts."

"Trade unionism is helpless, impotent, worn-out, corrupt."

"When a man gets too wild for the A. F. of L. he goes to the I. W. W.; so the I. W. W. is a good thing."

"In case of foreigners of a low type organization is impossible; they are not intelligent enough to see the benefits of unionism, are afraid of losing their jobs; the general quality of such groups does not improve."

"Socialists—yellow dogs."

"A man is a scab when he gets in the way of your job, no matter how badly he needs the money."

"The scab is a traitor."

"Rival unionists are scabs. One set of union men was characterized by the leader of another union group whose jobs the former were taking when the latter were striking, as, 'The vilest creatures that disgrace the earth upon which they crawl.' "

3. The rank and file and the leaders:

"Union leaders are competent and are doing their best for us."

"Union leaders are czars, self-seeking, and dangerous."

The rank and file hesitated to pay a dollar to "them guys."

"You can't trust a business agent when he gets his feet under the mahogany table with the employers."

"When I pick up a capitalist newspaper and read a eulogy to some labor leader, I know that that leader has at least two afflictions: the one is mental weakness, and the other is moral cowardice—and the two go together."

"Men's unions have bosses; women's do not."

SUPPLEMENT

INTRODUCTORY NOTE

It is with great hesitation that one undertakes to make additions to *Trade Unionism in the United States*. An analysis such as Professor Hoxie made, not of ephemeral conditions but of underlying motives, problems, reactions, and attitudes of various labor groups, is as true to-day as it was when first given to his classes. Indeed, many of Professor Hoxie's terms have become current coinage among students of labor problems within and without the classroom.

Requests have come, however, from teachers who are using *Trade Unionism* as a text, for guidance in study and interpretation to their classes of incidents in the labor world that have arisen during the critical period of the War and its aftermath. The truest tribute to Professor Hoxie is this desire, voiced not only by users of his text in the classroom but by many who were closest to him, for his interpretation of significant events that have arisen since his death. Such an interpretation few, if any, in the country would feel qualified to make. Moreover, it is not the book's psychological analysis that lags behind the current history of the labor movement of the United States, but simply the delineation of the facts for whose understanding Professor Hoxie has already given us a clue.

However, since these facts are aften obscure, and since the merely mechanical task of keeping informed concerning the latest addition to the bibliography, to say nothing of the activities, of American trade unions is colossal, it has seemed to be a service toward better understanding of labor problems in this country to add a selected bibliography and brief outline of significant events that have occurred in the labor and industrial field during and since the War.

MOLLIE RAY CARROLL

RECENT TENDENCIES IN THE AMERICAN
LABOR MOVEMENT

THE WAR AND ITS EFFECT ON INDUSTRY AND LABOR

We are, perhaps, too close to events of the past eight years to be able to discern clearly essential elements in industrial development and in the labor movement during this time. It is, however, important, simply to record changes that have taken place since the beginning of the European war, since in this period complete transition from peace-time manufacture to organization for war production and back again to a peace program has been effected in practically all countries.

It is of value to study changes that have occurred in each transition and to attempt at least a tentative interpretation and appraisal.

The outstanding feature of the period under consideration has been rapid and extensive development of technology. Nations at war had to meet emergencies that meant victory or destruction. Success on the military front depended upon efficiency and speed in production. Nations mobilized their scientists and engineers to bring to bear on war production all that science and technology could offer. Tremendous effort was put forth to reorganize industry in a brief period of time. Policies and production organization began to follow or create a production technology rather than continue in the old easy-going trial and error method. Under war administration ordinary restraints were lifted and no experiments barred. Neither employer nor worker could openly oppose, pleading his rights as justification. Not only were science and technology injected into material and process aspects of production, but they became the shibboleth in human relations in industry as well.

A second significant feature of war-time production was the government practice which suspended anti-trust legislation. Economies were effected through combination or pooling trade information. The wastefulness of the competitive method could not be tolerated. Still another important influence was the cost-plus practice. Its effect was pernicious upon labor as well as upon management. It was extremely demoralizing; for not only did employers profiteer, but wage earners also encountered fewer difficulties in slowing down individual production. It was war; the government was to pay. Also, in the period of war production the government assumed either management or administration of some essential industries that had previously been under private direction. When the government took responsibility it established either in entirety or in some vital features the policy of collective bargaining. Under these circumstances organization of wage earners was desirable if not absolutely necessary. This made possible rapid increase in union membership.

American Labor Movement Tending to Parallel Industrial Organization

Following the tendency apparent in the labor movement of all lands, American labor just before and during the war increasingly developed larger and larger units for united action. It paralleled the trend of industrial organization, especially in those fields where trustification or continually closer coöperation among business executives was replacing older competitive methods. This tendency, which was well under way before the outbreak of the war, gained impetus through stoppage of immigration and the demand for increased production. Labor learned that absence of trade skill was no bar to unionization. Organization of so-called "common labor" and of those who worked in factories where specialization augmented the repetitive processes continued with increasing conviction and success. In this period the American Federation of Labor more than doubled its numbers. Almost all of this additional membership was added to trade organizations already in existence; though some new unions, such as those of oil workers, firefighters, teachers, certain federal employes and others in public service institutions, arose and developed rapidly. During the early part of this period there was a distinct tendency toward organization of government workers and of groups lying on the fringe between the trades and the professions. The strength of that movement later ebbed distinctly, reaction in organization of government employes developing after the strike of the Boston police.

Not only increase in numbers but actual change in emphasis in labor organizations indicated the trend toward paralleling industry. Principles of organization, which had been worked out for the skilled and semi-skilled, were applied to any group of workers who had economic interests in common. Structurally more and more industrial and quasi-industrial unions arose within as well as without the American Federation of Labor. Basic enterprises, such as coal, steel, railroading, building and clothing trades particularly showed a tendency to unite all workers engaged in the processes involved for the purpose of securing better terms, even as employers in these same processes tended to combine for purposes of mutual aid and better organization of the industry.

To the general public, this increasing trend toward industrial or quasi-industrial organization on the part of labor manifested itself most clearly in protracted strikes developing on a nation-wide or industry-wide scale. First came the concerted action of the four railroad brotherhoods in 1916, demanding the eight-hour day. Capacity for combination was illustrated by the steel strike of 1919, the printing strike of 1920, the railway and mine workers' dissatisfaction that caused disputes and stoppage of work in 1919 and again in 1922, the shortage of houses due, it is true, to buccaneer tactics of contractors and others concerned in the building industry, as well as to building strikes, and the textile workers' long strike in 1922. They evidenced a solidarity in industrial matters that was heartening or appalling, according to the convictions of the onlooker.

To those more versed in trade union organization, the increasing power of the railway, building trades', and metal trades' departments of the American Federation of Labor is an even greater indication of the tendency of unions to parallel the form of industrial organization. These departments are constantly increasing their scope of activity and the amount of actual work accomplished. For example, more and more, it is in their conventions rather than in those of the Federation, that jurisdictional problems are discussed. Especially has this been true since the adoption of the rule that departmental conventions be held before the annual conference of the Federation. The potentiality of these departments is tremendous.

The increasing activity of such large groups of workers as the Allied Printing Trades' Council illustrates another method by which labor in other trade organizations is able to deal with industrial situations. The steel and stockyards councils of 1919 show still another form. In the case of the latter the war administration afforded an opportunity for unionization. Workers in all parts of the industry were mobilized for common action and common production. After these councils were well established the various workers, according to their trades, were turned over to the appropriate trades unions. This development was characteristic of the American labor movement. It cared little for abstract theory but much for practical results. The groups were willing to coöperate upon what might be called a radical program and with certain individuals who had revolutionary contacts. As long as there was mutual confidence the plan succeeded. A few months later, when the same plan with practically the same leadership was tried in the steel industry, it failed because there was no longer mutual confidence.

In the clothing industry there has been an interesting tendency toward the amalgamation of craft groups into unions which then cover, in separate organizations, various sections of the field. These unions are comprised of workers in men's clothing, women's clothing and the making of cloth hats and caps, of furs, of neckwear, and of suspenders. There is considerable mutual interest and interaction between many of these groups in spite of the fact that some are within and some without the American Federation of Labor. The International Ladies' Garment Workers' Union is, of course, the largest of these groups within the Federation, as the Amalgamated Clothing Workers is the most powerful body without. Also outside of the American Federation of Labor are the Amalgamated Textile Workers, the Mule Spinners, and the United Shoe Workers.

From the standpoint of our interest in the tendency toward industrial or quasi-industrial organization, the divisions in the clothing field are of importance. The United Cloth Hat and Cap Makers and the Mule Spinners were suspended from the American Federation of Labor because they refused to obey the mandate to amalgamate with the United Hatters and the United Textile Workers respectively. These organizations, among the oldest of craft unions, refused because of historical traditions and for sentimental motives to follow the trend toward industrial organization. They represented a reaction against the tendency to develop larger and larger industrial units.[1] It would seem, therefore, that when craft unions have been well established the departmental form of

[1] The case of the Cap Makers is being adjusted by the American Federation of Labor, however.

organization rather than amalgamation may furnish practical
means of meeting industrial problems without antagonizing
strong forces making for craft organization.

The separation of the United Shoe Workers from the
American Federation of Labor dates back to the time of the
Knights of Labor and the conflict between the Knights and
the Federation over the open trade or the strictly craft union.
In the case of the Amalgamated Clothing Workers, secession
was caused by lack of agreement within the organization
which led the secessionists to turn their attention to the
unorganized districts in the clothing trade. They built up
constructive policies and methods in a new field instead of
contesting the old one with the union already established.
The Amalgamated Textile Workers were organized for
reasons somewhat similar to those causing the development
of the Amalgamated Clothing Workers.

Unions in the clothing trade are representative, therefore,
of tendencies toward decentralization which are at work to a
greater or less degree in all large labor organizations, tendencies which are, however, in the case of other groups,
counterbalanced by pressure of need for paralleling the form
of industrial organization.[2] In the clothing field sympathetic friendliness must take place of active alliance on
matters of general interest. Inasmuch, however, as industrial
organization in the clothing trades is still on a rather small
scale, this state of affairs has not been a serious handicap.
In fact, the International Ladies' Garment Workers' Union
and the Amalgamated Clothing Workers of America have
urged upon their employers the necessity of broader federation to deal, in trade agreements, with the union. It is

---

[2] It is possible, however, that centralization may be carried so far
that the union organization may become unwieldy or that it may
have power too great to use in industrial disputes, without paralyzing
an industry utterly essential to existence in our modern complex
society. Such a condition might render its threats futile. Then there
might well be tendencies again toward union decentralization along
craft or compound craft lines.

interesting, however, when we see the results to union organization in the other great industries, to speculate upon the possible strength of these individualistic tendencies among the groups of clothing workers should the executives in various branches of this hitherto highly individualistic industry decide to enter into one nation-wide organization.

The tendency of labor, paralleling industry, to develop larger and larger units, has had significant results. The great popularity of the American Federation of Labor during the war, when the President of the United States attended one of its annual conventions and when the advice of Mr. Gompers and other labor representatives was sought on every side, was due to the strategic position which that group had secured in the field of production. Even the more restricted place which it has occupied since the war [3] serves in a measure to show its strength and the fear in which it is held by its opponents.

The policies of the Federation have remained practically the same as outlined by Professor Hoxie. Essentially pragmatic, it has continued to embrace all structural union varieties known. Great latitude is allowed national and international unions within its membership. Many of them are contributing valuable experiments in the fields of production, industrial relations, producers' and consumers' coöperation, education, and research. The American Federation of Labor itself has kept, as its chief policy, the advancement of workers' interests through an aggressive economic program. Legislative or other methods are distinctly secondary and supplemental to steady combat for better wages and hours. Mr. Gompers and those about him have planted their feet firmly, resisting arguments and persuasions to change the policies of the Federation. They have had an instinctive rather than reasoned plan and have followed it. Herein lies

[3] The membership of the American Federation of Labor rose to 4,078,740 by 1920 and receded to 3,195,651 in 1923.

their genius. The future of the Federation is bound with securing leaders to take their places who will have as sound instincts as these pioneers have possessed concerning the program of the Federation for their day and as great tenacity of purpose.

The official limitation of the Federation's activities to more combatant methods, nevertheless, combined with its increased membership and power cause certain questions to arise upon whose answer depends the future of the organization. For example, limitation of membership is not a final solution of all union difficulties. Those outside the fold form actual or potential problems. On the other hand, the admission of great numbers, unused to subordinating their individual desires and impulses to the ruling of the group is dangerous to union solidarity. Coincident, therefore, with the gradual opening of the doors to women, negroes, immigrants, and the unskilled in general the Federation is laying increased emphasis upon restriction of immigration. Cutting down the immigrant labor supply might conceivably allow the American labor movement to absorb into its ranks most of the workers who are now in the country. Again, the policy of curtailment of production is becoming more serious with the enormous growth of labor organizations. A constructive policy of production is likely soon to be demanded and the future of American labor organizations may depend upon their answer. Mere efficiency in eliminating waste processes is no more the solution of this problem than is limitation of output. A constructive program must also cover steady utilization of labor and insurance against, if not elimination of, unemployment for all workers. Unions cannot hope otherwise adequately to protect their own members.

Aside from the American Federation of Labor which, because of its size, its influence and power, and its catholicity, really represents the American labor movement, we find also the Railway Brotherhoods, the Amalgamated Clothing

Workers of America and a few other unions in the clothing field, some other scattered groups, and the Industrial Workers of the World. The Railway Brotherhoods have maintained and, in fact, increased their strength and prestige in the period under discussion. Their policies, however, have remained substantially the same, with the exception of their promulgation of the Plumb Plan in 1919,[4] and their interest in coöperative production and banking.[5]

Since 1915, the Amalgamated Clothing Workers of America, unaffiliated with the American Federation of Labor, organized some two months after the outbreak of the European war, has risen to national prominence. It has experienced phenomenal growth to a membership of over 150,000. It has also acknowledged adherence to various constructive labor policies, already, for the most part, practiced by various unions within the American Federation of Labor but less known to the public. Other unions, on the whole, have not welcomed as cordially as have the Amalgamated Clothing Workers the interest and advice of intelligent and sympathetic people outside the labor movement. Like the American Federation of Labor, the Amalgamated Clothing Workers owes much to the continuous leadership, since its inception, of one man of great ability. Structurally the Amalgamated Clothing Workers [6] is a quasi-industrial union. Functionally it combines shrewd business ability with socialistic unionism and a high degree of practical idealism.

The Industrial Workers of the World, on the other hand, seems to have lost ground during the period under consideration. The imprisonment of many of its members during the war and numerous raids upon its offices during the anti-Bolshevik flurry after the armistice seriously crippled the

---

[4] See pp. 431, 434.   [5] See p. 434.
[6] For a discussion of the structural form of the Amalgamated Clothing Workers of America see "Proceedings of the Fourth Biennial Convention of the Amalgamated Clothing Workers of America," 1920, p. lxiv; also Budish, J., and Soule, G. M., "The New Unionism."

organization. The appeal of martyrdom temporarily caused an influx of members and gained for it the support of many who were not workers and who did not agree with the philosophy of revolutionary unionism. This increase, however, was ephemeral. The escape of its president, William D. Haywood, to Russia, when out on bond, did not increase its prestige. Moreover, the tendency of other labor organizations, paralleling industry, to admit more and more of the unskilled and to develop quasi-industrial forms has caused unions better fitted to survive because structurally more sound, to encroach upon the field of membership of the Industrial Workers of the World.

EMPLOYERS' ORGANIZATIONS, STRUCTURE AND FUNCTIONS

During the period under consideration in this study, employers' organizations, too, have enlarged their scope of activity, showing executives' growing appreciation of the rapid expansion of industry. Scientific management which made its first widespread appeal as a method of increasing output of labor by speeding up the worker after he had been subjected to job analyses and time studies, now interests business men as a method of effecting savings in production primarily through the development of management rather than through the exploitation of labor. Undoubtedly labor's opposition to the stop-watch and to so-called scientific modifications of the piece-rate has been at least partly responsible for the shift in emphasis. At any rate, plant location, construction of buildings with a view to most efficient routing of the product, production planning, stores handling, and cost accounting receive the major attention of the efficiency engineer. Still more recently economies possible through studies of waste, through stabilization and methods of eliminating the vicissitudes of business cycles are being appended to the score card which discloses management efficiency.

The recognized need for better technique in management and for application of scientific methods and principles to production problems has resulted in the development and maintenance of trade organizations. Well directed impetus has been given to this movement under the vitalized Department of Commerce, administered by a distinguished engineer. Valiant service has been rendered, too, by other engineers and by economists. The functions of such trade organizations are to develop criteria of production, to work out standard methods of record keeping and cost accounting, to maintain clearing houses of information available to members, to conduct research bureaus, and to make coöperative investigations into general or special problems concerning the industry.

This is the bright side of the picture. Progress is not uniform. One finds individual employers lagging behind. There remain also certain organized groups who still wish to base business administration upon policies of force. These latter are responsible for organized attacks against labor unions, characteristic of post-war reaction. Even these groups, though, find themselves compelled to use the new methods and language of industry. Some of them serve their clientele with research material. However, their reports are generally regarded as pretty heavily weighted in order to conform to certain standards and practices favored. On the whole, there seems to be increased emphasis upon industrial order, concentration on essentials, elimination of old, slip-shod unstandardized, individualistic procedure, and substitution of exploitation of the field of efficiency for militant tactics toward labor and cut-throat competitive methods toward fellow-producers.

THE BUSINESS EXECUTIVE AND LABOR

One of the important questions in a more scientific control of the problem of industry faced by the modern administrator concerns labor. The key to the activities of employers' associations in this field during the war may be found in the industrial executive's dawning realization of the evils of a high labor turnover, realization brought about by war-time shortage of man power and by cost accountants' analyses of the expense of training in new workers even for unskilled jobs. With efforts to decrease labor turnover has come the development of employment or personnel departments. A wide variety of activities has arisen as a result of this emphasis on personnel work in industry. It includes more careful attention to hiring, placing, training, transferring, promoting, and discharging workers; welfare, health and safety activities by and for employees; and interest in employees' participation in management, illustrated by installation of shop committees in many plants and in others, by consummation of trade agreements with unions. Much of this personnel work has involved merely addition of new forms and new officials and has resulted in accumulation of records, additional bookkeeping and increased overhead. However, those able to distinguish the genuine from the spurious have found personnel administration to be in part an engineering problem in which labor and production policies mesh in together.

Many employers who did not give unqualified consent to such methods of dealing with labor and some who even opposed in principle any form of collective bargaining nevertheless followed war-time methods. At times they grudgingly kept the letter if not the spirit of their agreements with their employees. When the armistice came, bringing with it slackening of the whole machinery of industry and consequent unemployment, many new devotees of personal work, of shop committees, and of trade agreements changed their policies. Progress had been too rapid to be wholly permanent. The reaction which was to be expected, did not, however, lose all that had been gained. The conduct of reactionaries was based primarily on divergence of opinion as to methods of securing the most efficient labor supply. Harsher tactics were in many instances employed. Men worked for longer hours at lower wages. Fear of losing the job often, alas, made labor more efficient in production than it had been during the war, though at times this increase in efficiency may have been more apparent than real.[7] Anti-union agitation became frequent. The so-called "American plan" of running a non-union shop was much discussed. Personnel activities were greatly curtailed. Shop committees, particularly in certain non-union plants, that had not already been abandoned because of their inherent defects, voiced more than ever employers' wishes. Their members feared to lose their jobs. On the other hand, while some personnel departments and shop committees died out or ceased to exert any active influence in the industry, others that weathered the period of reaction gained valuable insight into labor problems through experience with both labor shortage and unemployment.

Coöperation or Conflict Between Worker and Employer

From this brief survey of the activities of unions and of employers' associations it will be seen that the concentration of industry into larger and larger units has enormously enhanced possibilities either for friendly relationship or for competition and conflict between labor and capital. It is not strange, therefore, that two fundamental ideas struggling for supremacy to-day in the labor world are coöperation and conflict. The spirit of coöperation is neither the older individualism nor the older socialism but a new conception of

[7] This seeming increase in efficiency may have resulted from reversing the process of "dilution" of labor which occurred during the war.

joint responsibility for production. This includes attempts of employers and employees to consider together vital matters of mutual concern; coöperation to decrease industrial hazards in the form of accidents, disease, unemployment or high labor turnover; trade agreements; and combined efforts on the part of management and labor to increase efficiency in industry.

The so-called "American plan" for running a militant non-union shop illustrates the program of conflict. Policies adhered to by certain industries of continuing to operate under conditions no longer considered just, or even efficient, and of fighting union attempts to alter these conditions typify employers' policies inimical to coöperation. The use of the general strike to wrest specific ends from society by paralyzing industry and the exploitation of the public indulged in by certain labor groups also illustrate a retarded social attitude.

During the war the idea of coöperation developed and spread rapidly. Labor's importance as a factor in production was recognized partly, if not largely, because of shortage of man power. There was great demand for workers of ingenuity and ability. Industrial managers began to realize that the machine process as evolved under the present competitive system tended to crush out workers' creative ability, that the long workday with its cumulative fatigue destroyed physical energy and retarded the initiative of labor, and that the inhibition of creative power and resourcefulness of employees was a significant element in industrial waste. Management began to understand that the shorter workday and adequate compensation in wages were good business investments. Labor's good will was found to play effective part in production,[8] not only on the quantitative side but in service to the problem of industrial technique and organization.

In consequence, movements towards coöperation between

[8] Wolf, Robert B., "The Non-Financial Incentives of Workers." Publications, American Society of Mechanical Engineers, No. 1673.

labor and capital were inaugurated during the war. Shop committees were established in many union and non-union factories. Many trade agreements were drawn up, including the cantonment agreement, the ship-building agreement, agreements under the War Labor Board, the leather workers' agreement, the agreement of the Emergency Fleet Corporation with the seamen's union, the organization of the railway shops under the Executive Order of the Railroad Administration, and the extension, a little later, in 1919, of the Hart, Schaffner & Marx plan to other plants in large manufacturing centers in the men's clothing industry. Many gave expression to dawning realization of the fact that production was a joint interest of capital and labor. For example, during this period for the first time the American labor movement officially recognized that standards of living of wage-earners could not be permanently raised without increased production. Declarations were also made officially by the American Federation of Labor, by various large labor groups within its memberships in their national and international unions, and by the Amalgamated Clothing Makers of America, in appreciation of the functions of research and science in the industrial field.[9]

When the armistice was signed, however, largely because no provision had been made on the part of either industrial managers or of labor for the period after the war and no constructive program had been suggested for turning productive efforts of men and plants toward peace-time extension of industry, there came sudden stoppage of activity. The entire machinery of industry suddenly slowed down after having run at full speed. It came to a standstill with a jerk that was quickly reflected in the attitude of capital and labor toward each other. Individualism and the idea of competition

---

[9] These official declarations have been accompanied by evidence of what seems to be a rapprochement between the scientists and technologists and the labor groups. This movement is as yet, however, largely the result of individual efforts.

reasserted themselves. "Garyism," labor's name for the reactionary policies of the Steel Trust and hence for similar tactics in other industries, caused the development in labor's ranks of "Bolshevism," as it was often termed. Reaction in big industries afforded an opportunity for the revolutionary element to gain a hearing among workers engaged in those industries. Strikes were inaugurated by steel, coal, and some railroad workers. The new idea of coöperation was for a time overshadowed by the policy of conflict.[10]

Slowly as the wheels of industry began to revolve, belief in coöperation again asserted itself, though it had not been supplanted in some quarters by the idea of conflict even during the worst of the business depression. The report on "Waste in Industry" of the Federated American Engineering Societies, which marked a distinct new level in industrial thought and action, showed the vast field of known but not practiced efficiency in production which, if exploited, would bring great gains to both worker and employer. Under the direction of Mr. Hoover, the Department of Commerce turned its attention mainly to promotion and intelligent development of industry on the basis of information. By thus concentrating attention upon the constructive side of industry, the Department thereby permitted refocusing of activity and resources along lines which were in marked contrast to wasteful militancy between employer and employed. The public, following the cue, became increasingly intolerant of militant tactics on the part of employers. Revolutionary unions also received scant public sympathy, and predatory labor groups were frankly condemned.

However, the pressure of the public is not yet of such a character as appreciably to diminish industrial strife. There may be recognized two prevailing tendencies on the part of

10 The Plumb Plan of the Railways Brotherhoods was an attempt on the part of those who were not seeking a way out through revolutionary tactics to put into concrete form the newer theory.

outsiders during industrial disputes. There is a healthy desire to secure facts bearing on the matter. This demand for facts coupled with a realization of the power of propaganda during the war has resulted in the establishment of some research bureaus by unions and by employers' organizations. At times of industrial disputes motives underlying the establishment of some of these bureaus may be discovered by a comparison of the findings published on each side. However, aside from investigation carried on to prove a particular thesis, the force of the public's demand for facts may be seen in the establishment of research organizations [11] whose sole motive is the scientific collection of data. The service rendered by gathering material in this way is incalculable; it is the basis of the hope of raising industry to a more efficient level of production out of the jungle of the old *laissez-faire methods* that depend on force and might rather than on intelligent and scientific technique.

THE TENDENCY TOWARD LEGAL AND GOVERNMENTAL REGULATION

There is a tendency on the part of the public, however, to become impatient of industrial strife. It sees no help for the immediate difficulty to be gained from the slow process of scientific investigation, and distrusts much that passes for statistical truth. Statistics are used by each side to bolster up its arguments. Propagandist methods have been abused and overworked. Turning from attempts to arrive at the "facts" of the case, and irritated by loss of service, sometimes in highly essential commodities, the public at present tends to utilize law and the agencies of government and justice in its attempt to secure industrial peace by forcing

[11] For example, the National Bureau of Economic Research, the Institute of Economics, the Coal Fact Finding Commission, and the information gathered by the Interstate Commerce Commission.

the disputants to resume outwardly amicable relations. In its attitude the public is repeating the mistakes made by employees and employers, emphasizing its rights to the exclusion of its responsibilities. Its vision does not extend far beyond a plan to exercise force.

The Kansas Industrial Court, established by law,[12] represents the attempt of one state to exercise repressive control over activities of unions within its boundaries. Another attempt on the part of the government to regulate the activities of specific labor organizations, this time through its administrative branch, may be seen in the Railway Labor Board, established to deal with conditions affecting labor in that vital public service. The fact that these have been rather futile in their attempts to control serious disputes between employer and employee has not yet taught the public that labor problems are too deep-rooted and labor organizations founded on needs too real to be settled or regulated by fiat.

A series of legal decisions carrying the sanction of the highest authorities for justice in the country and of governmental regulations has attempted to curb chiefly the power of labor organizations in industrial disputes. Brief mention of some outstanding cases will suffice to show the trend. In the case of Hitchman Coal and Coke Company *vs.* Mitchell, a permanent injunction restraining the union officers from attempts to unionize the mine was upheld by the Supreme Court.[13] In several recent decisions of the Supreme Court the effectiveness of the Clayton Anti-Trust Act, passed to protect labor organizations against the provisions of the Sherman Act, was practically nullified.[14] In the case of the

---

[12] A recent decision of the Supreme Court has curtailed the power of the Kansas Industrial Court. This does not, however, necessarily modify public opinion concerning the use of force in labor disputes.

[13] See John P. Frey, *The Labor Injunction,* for labor's attitude toward this instrument of law.

[14] "The Clayton Labor Law Provisions," by R. E. Montgomery, *The University Journal of Business,* Vol. I, Nos. 2, 3.

Coronado Coal Company *vs.* the United Mine Workers of America the union was treated as an "unincorporated association" with unlimited liability. The main difference between this decision and that rendered against the Danbury Hatters, which caused the agitation resulting in the Clayton Act of 1914, was the distinction between the local and the national union. In the Coronado Coal Company case only the local union was held responsible for the conspiracy in restraint of trade and therefore liable for assessment of damages.

Further curtailment of the powers and activities of unions was aimed at by the Federal Department of Justice on two different occasions. The injunction secured by the Department of Justice in 1919 restraining the miners from striking under the provisions of the Lever Act was an outstanding example of recourse to that act, which was later declared unconstitutional. A new principle was enunciated at that time, for the injunction restrained the use of union funds during strike. Similar to this but even more drastic was the injunction secured by the Department of Justice against the Railway Department of the American Federation of Labor in 1922. Union officers were enjoined from engaging in any form of activity that might directly or indirectly lead any railway employees to stop work. This tended practically to prevent them from carrying out any of their union duties, inasmuch as the whole effort and power of the organization were focused on the strike. It also enjoined use of union funds for strike purposes. Inasmuch as the strength of labor in times of dispute with the employer lies in its waiting power, tying up its funds seriously hampers its very existence.

Thus at the time when enlargement of the industrial unit is forcing employers together into a contemplation of nation-wide problems facing them and is forcing unions to join hands in attempts to solve their common problems, at the time when these two groups are aligned in greater and

greater array either for broader and more intelligent coöperation or for conflict, the pressure of the machinery of government and of public agencies of law and of justice is being
exerted more and more strongly to outlaw activities essential
to the existence of one of the groups concerned. There has
been little corresponding curtailment of activities of employers except various modifications of application of
anti-trust laws and a recent Supreme Court decision which
outlaws the practice of open prices as developed by one
trade association and leaves other activities of trade bodies
in considerable uncertainty.

UNION FUNCTIONS

With these factors in mind we may now turn to a study
of the way unions are functioning. The first fact to be noted
is the tendency throughout the American labor movement to
enlarge the scope of the old business method of the craft and
to develop what for want of a better name has been called
by some writers "new" unionism. These more inclusive
union groups, looking out upon larger problems than those
faced by the old-time crafts, have reacted differently under
various sorts of conditions. Where the pressure of employing groups or of law and government have been excessive,
endangering the existence of the union itself, the tendency
has been toward "radical" or "revolutionary" measures.
The year 1919 was particularly representative of such a
spirit. Beginning with that year and extending for some
time afterward there occurred widely extended strikes or
labor disturbances among steel workers, miners, railroad men,
printers, and clothing workers, to mention some of the outstanding examples, and general strikes in two cities, Seattle
and Winnipeg. The protracted coal mine, railroad, and
textile strikes of 1922 illustrated the same tendency. Unions
with their backs to the wall, fighting for life against hostile

employers or against governmental regulation, lined up great numbers in bitterly contested strikes.

Another manifestation of the tendency of labor groups to think in terms of larger numbers of workers was shown in increased interest in state control of large public utilities or basic industries. The outstanding examples of such interest were the railway workers' concrete proposal known as the Plumb Plan,[15] for joint operation and control of the railroads by the government, workers, and officials combined into an operating corporation and the United Mine Workers' proposal for nationalization. Indeed, so vital have become such necessities as coal and transportation that consideration of the advisability of providing for state supervision or control have been suggested not only by labor but by some economists, engineers and members of the general public who see danger in the command by individuals of essential commodities.

Still a third result of the tendency of the American labor movement to expand into larger units, paralleling the industrial or capitalistic organization, is increased opportunity for the development of predatory tactics. Given strategic position, as in the building trades, with a quasi-industrial form of organization and highly organized employers' associations in the same field, there is enlarged opportunity for capital and labor allied to exploit the public and to control prices and operations to their mutual benefit. Such exploitation finally may develop such proportions that the machinery of political government must be used to protect society.

Finally the expansion of unions in order to parallel industrial organization shows tendencies toward development of practical coöperation between some labor and some employing groups. The extension of the trade agreement to further industries illustrates this trend. Sometimes an impartial

---

[15] For a discussion of the Plumb Plan see Savel Zimand, "Modern Social Movements," pp. 107-112.

434 TRADE UNIONISM

chairman is called in to exercise administrative functions in deciding cases; sometimes technical experts in the field are asked to give evidence. The final settlement may be arrived at either through an impartial decision or by deliberation on the part of both sides to the agreement.

A slightly different example of the newer ideal of coöperation is found in the recent organization of the American Construction Council, comprising building trades unions, contractors, engineers, and all involved in the process of building. This body, created in what has hitherto been considered one of the most predatory of working and employing groups, gives evidence of growing responsiveness to public opinion in the construction industry and of appreciation of the larger service which it can render. It is of interest to note that this new organization, which aims to preserve voluntary institutions, to foster the interests of all concerned in the industry and to protect the public was promoted by the advisory rather than by the repressive function of the government. The council is, therefore, a step in advance of the Board of Jurisdictional Awards. It looks to the development of industrial standards and practices based upon scientific or factual investigation rather than upon bargaining. The trade agreement, on the other hand, receives its sanction from the relative strength of the parties to the agreement and from the decree of the chairman.

However, heartening as we find such manifestations of progress in American trade unionism, they are not to be counted as the goal or aim of American labor. A pragmatic movement for the betterment of the conditions, not only of their toil, but of their lives, trade unionism is consistently stretching out to include more and more functions. The American labor movement has shown indications of broadening its practices to a conception of production for service. It has passed resolutions recognizing the need of increased production, the high value of creative work, and the function of research. Trade unions are coming to appreciate the value of research, not only for purposes of agreement in labor disputes or for an analysis of the gains of industry with a view to commanding larger wages or to increasing the profits of the business. At times, notably in the clothing industry, it has espoused research for the avowed purpose of producing more largely for general public welfare. The Labor Bureau,[16] a research organization established in 1920 with a policy of service to labor only, in 1921 performed more than four times the volume of service that it did during the eight months of its existence in 1920. Research bureaus or movements, in an embryonic stage, exist in many labor organizations.[17]

Still another example of a broader point of view on the part of labor is the growing belief that unemployment can be corrected or diminished not by curtailing production but by laying it as a burden upon the industry concerned.[18] Such an attitude on the part of labor could not have arisen, however, without a corresponding readiness on the part of the employer to appreciate it as an industrial and not an individual problem. Both employer and worker have in this respect followed the thinking of some economists and humanitarians, and latterly, of some engineers who have attempted to find practical methods of eliminating "unemployment within employment" or in other words of maintaining stability of production organization, a by-product of which would be stabilization of employment for workers.

Another manifestation of the enlarged functions of the American trade union as it faces greater industrial questions

[16] The Labor Bureau, Inc., 1 Union Square, New York City. Directors, Alfred L. Bernheim, Evans Clark, David Saposs, George Soule.
[17] Including the railway unions, the Amalgamated Clothing Workers, the United Mine Workers, the electricians, and the Printing Trades.
[18] See Leo Wolman: The Proposal for an Unemployment Fund in the Men's Clothing Industry. **Amalgamated Clothing Workers of America.**

is the movement, still in its infancy, for workers' education. American trade unions have recently declared for vocational reëducation and rehabilitation. Now they are expanding this vision to include adult education. In the regular courses offered by the International Ladies' Garment Workers' Union, the chief objective in the class room is to teach facts, not arguments or propaganda. Labor's interest in education takes the form in one place of a trade school, in another of a correspondence school, in "labor colleges" in various cities, in the workers' attendance upon classes offered by educational institutions throughout the land from coast to coast. Save, perhaps, for one or two exceptions, this movement is valuable at present from an experimental standpoint mainly rather than because of its actual achievements. It is important, too, because significant of a broadening of labor and of educational interests.

Labor has also been experimenting in the management field in America. During the war workers had a voice in the management of the arsenals. As an outgrowth of the war experience the Plumb Plan, which proposed the operation of the railroads by a tri-partite board composed partly of railway workers was another effort in this direction. There are beginnings, too, of coöperative movements, both in production and in distribution of commodities. Coöperative stores have been run by a few unions for years. Several different kinds of unions run coöperative factories, turning to the field of management in the production of the commodities which they as workers help to manufacture or of totally different products.[19]   More recently, several unions have

---

[19] American labor organizations have in the past experienced serious difficulties in their attempts to manage coöperative enterprises. Able administrators of factories, and stores have been enticed by large salaries over into the field of private business. It has also not always proved easy to maintain the trade-union point of view with reference to the employes hired by the coöperative enterprise. Whether the present efforts, and especially coöperative banking will succeed better, remains to be seen.

entered the field of finance, having established banks or bought large interests in others already in existence. This is undoubtedly a more sound manifestation of the well-known interest of labor in the broader problems of money and finance than some of the earlier political agitations, such as greenbackism or bimetallism. The plan is yet too new, however, to judge of its success.

These plans and policies, some of them still only on paper, show that the American labor movement is beginning to take its place as a responsible factor in the community instead of simply fighting for better wages, hours, and conditions of work. The war, the President's first industrial conference, the General Committee for Disarmament, and Mr. Hoover's conference on unemployment, found labor working with employers and the public, for the solution of general social problems. There are indications that the outcome of this development may be a new functional type, a union characterized by practical idealism, business in its policies of production and of dealing with the employer, using informing methods in record keeping and in production standards, yet considering the needs of the consumer as the prime guide of its activities.

BIBLIOGRAPHY

Historical Review   ..

BEARD, MARY A. *A Short History of the American Labor Movement* (1920).

COMMONS, JOHN R., and Associates. *History of Labour in the United States* (1918).

EVANS, CHRIS. *History of the United Mine Workers, Vol. I* (1918).

PERLMAN, SELIG. *A History of Trade Unionism in the United States* (1922).

Present Union Groups

Constitutions: THE AMALGAMATED CLOTHING WORKERS OF
AMERICA, THE AMALGAMATED TEXTILE WORKERS
OF AMERICA.

Convention Proceedings: DOCUMENTARY HISTORY OF THE
AMALGAMATED CLOTHING WORKERS OF AMERICA,
1914, 1916, 1920; REPORTS OF THE GENERAL EXECU-
TIVE TO THE BIENNIAL CONVENTIONS.

Journals: *Labor*, official weekly of sixteen railroad labor
organizations, Washington, D. C. *Locomotive Engineers' Journal*, published monthly by the Brotherhood
of Locomotive Engineers, Cleveland. *The Advance*.
The New Textile Worker. *The New Majority*, published weekly by the National Farmer-Labor Party,
Chicago, Illinois. *The Seattle Union Record*, daily
paper published by the Seattle, Washington, Federation of Labor.

THE AMALGAMATED CLOTHING WORKERS OF AMERICA:

General Propaganda Leaflets:

The Amalgamated Clothing Workers of America, The
case of the Union as stated by observers:

1. In the Press.
2. In the Court.
3. In a Normal Market (1920).

Amalgamated Illustrated Almanac (1923).

Brief for the Michaels Stern & Co. case *vs*. The Amalgamated Clothing Workers of America.

Schlossberg, Joseph. *Problems of Labor Organization*.
—The Rise of the Clothing Workers.

Soule, George. *Recent Developments in Trade
Unionism*.

Blanshard, Paul. *The Open Shop Movement*.

Wolman, Leo. *The Proposal for an Unemployment
Fund in the Men's Clothing Industry*.

Hillman, Sidney. *Reconstruction of Russia and the Task of Labor.*
Documentary History of the Amalgamated Clothing Workers of America, 1916-1922.

THE AMERICAN FEDERATION OF LABOR:

General Propaganda Books and Leaflets:
American Federation of Labor History, Encyclopedia, Reference Book (1919).
American Federation of Labor Reconstruction Program.
American Labor's Position in Peace or War.
The Challenge Accepted—Labor Will Not Be Outlawed or Enslaved.
Clayton Anti-Trust Law.
Collective Bargaining.
Education for All.
An Eight Hour Decision.
Eight Hours; the Workers and the Eight Hour Workday and the Shorter Workday; Its Philosophy.
Essence of Labor's Contention on the Injunction Abuse.
Forty Years of Action. Non-Partisan Political Policy American Federation of Labor.
Industrial Education.
Industrial Unionism in Its Relation to Trade Unionism.
Initiative, Referendum and Recall.
Involuntary Servitude in Colorado.
Justice Wright's Denial of Free Speech and Free Press.
Kansas Court of Industrial Relations.
Labor and Its Attitude Toward Trusts.
Labor, Its Grievances, Protest and Demands.
Labor—The Courts and the Law.
Legislative Achievements of the American Federation of Labor.
Letters to a Bishop.

National Association of Manufacturers Exposed; Revelations of Senate Lobby Investigation.
No Compulsory Arbitration.
An Open Letter to Ministers of the Gospel.
The Philosophy of the Eight Hour Movement.
Philosophy of Trade Unions.
Real Farmers vs. Professional Farmers.
Report of Labor Mission to Great Britain and France, 1918.
Socialist Methods vs. Trade Union Methods.
Should a Political Labor Party Be Formed?
Trade Union Epigrams.
Trade Unions To Be Smashed Again.
The Truth About Soviet Russia and Bolshevism.
Tuberculosis Movement Inaugural and Plan Adopted by the A. F. of L. to War on Consumption.
The Union Shop and Its Antithesis.
Universal Education.
What Does Labor Want?
What Labor Could Do.
Why the Peace Treaty Should Be Ratified.
Gompers, Samuel. "American Labor and the War."
———. "Labor and the Common Welfare" (compiled and edited by Hayes Robbins).
———. "Labor and the Employer" (compiled and edited by Hayes Robbins).
———. "Labor in Europe and America."
———. "Out of Their Own Mouths."
Ralston, Jackson H. "Judicial Control Over Legislatures as to Constitutional Questions."
Robbins, Hayes. "The Labour Movement and the Farmer" (1922).
Sullivan, J. W., and Robbins, Hayes. "Socialism as an Incubus on the American Labor Movement."
Trant, Wm. "History of Trade Unions."

General:

American Labor Year Book, The. 1916—

ANDREWS, JOHN B. *Labor Problems and Labor Legislation.* Completely Revised (1922).

ARCHBALD, HUGH. *The Four Hour Day in Coal* (1922).

BLOCH, LOUIS. *Coal Miners' Insecurity. Russell Sage Foundation, Department of Industrial Studies* (1922).

BRUERE, ROBERT W. *The Coming of Coal* (1922).

BUDISH, J. M., and SOULE, GEORGE. *The New Unionism* (1920).

CARLTON, FRANK T. *The History and Problems of Organized Labor.* 2d ed. (1920).

CARROLL, MOLLIE RAY. *Labor and Politics, the Attitude of the American Federation of Labor Toward Legislation and Politics* (1923).

COHN, FANNIA. The Educational work of the International Ladies' Garment Workers' Union (1921). Report submitted to the Conference of the Workers' Education Bureau of America.

COMMONS, JOHN R. "Tendencies in Trade Union Development in the United States," *International Labor Review,* June, 1922, pp. 855-887. 2d ed. (1921).

——. *Trade Unionism and Labour Problems,* 2d series (1921).

EVANS, CHRIS. *History of the United Mine Workers,* vols. 1, 2 (1918).

Federated American Engineering Society, "The Twelve-Hour Shift in Industry" (1922).

FOSTER, WM. Z. *The Great Steel Strike* (1920).

FREY, JOHN P. *The Labor Injunction* (1923).

HAMILTON, WALTER HALE. *The Control of Wages* (1923).

HOWARD, EARL DEAN. *The Hart, Schaffner & Marx Labor Agreement Industrial Law in the Clothing Industry* (1920).

HUNTER, ROBERT. *Labor in Politics* (1915).

Inter-Church World Movement of North America, "The Steel Strike of 1919" (1919).

Inter-Church World Movement of North America, "Public Opinion and the Steel Strike" (1921).

Investigation of Wages and Labor Conditions in Coal Mining, Hearings Before the Committee on Labor, House of Representatives, 64th Congress, 2d Sess. (1917).

JANES, GEORGE M. *American Trade Unionism* (1922).

LANE, WINTHROP D. *Civil Car in West Virginia,* 1921.

LAUCK, W. JETT. *The Industrial Code* (1922).

——, and SYDENSTRICKER, EDGAR. *Conditions of Labor in American Industries* (1917).

LOVESTONE, J. *The Government Strike Breaker* (1923).

MURRAY, PHILIP. *The Case of the Anthracite Coal Mine Workers.* Opening statement and closing argument before the U. S. Anthracite Coal Commission (1920).

PERLMAN, SELIG A. *A History of Trade Unionism in the United States* (1920).

PLUMB, GLENN E. *Industrial Democracy* (1923).

POUND, ARTHUR. *Iron Man in Industry* (1922).

Railway Employees Department, American Federation of Labor, before the Railroad Labor Board, Chicago, Ill., 1921, in Reply to the Objections of the Railroads as presented by the Conference Committee of Managers of the Federated Shop Crafts (1921).

ROBBINS, EDWIN CLYDE. "RAILWAY CONDUCTORS; A STUDY IN ORGANIZED LABOR," *Columbia University Studies* (1914).

ROBINSON, JESSE S. "THE AMALGAMATED ASSOCIATION OF IRON, STEEL AND TIN WORKERS," *Johns Hopkins University Studies* (1920).

SAVAGE, MARION D. *Industrial Unionism in America* (1922).

SCHLUTER, HERMANN. *The Brewing Industry and the Brewery Workers' Movement in America* (1910).

Socialist Party, comp. "THE DOUBLE EDGE OF LABOR'S SWORD." Discussion and Testimony on Socialism and Trade Unionism before the Commission on Industrial Relations by Morris Hilquit, Samuel Gompers and Max J. Hayes.

STOCKTON, FRANK T. "THE INTERNATIONAL MOLDERS' UNION OF NORTH AMERICA," *Johns Hopkins University Studies* (1921).

STOWELL, C. J. "THE JOURNEYMEN TAILORS' UNION OF AMERICA": A Study in Trade Union Policy, *University of Illinois Studies* (1918).

Survey Graphic, The, vol. 1, pp. 975-1045. "COAL; MINES, MINERS AND THE PUBLIC" (1922).

TANNENBAUM, FRANK. *Labor Movement, Its Conservative Functions and Social Consequences* (1921).

THOMPSON, LAURA A. "BIBLIOGRAPHY ON WORKERS' EDUCATION," *The Monthly Review, The U. S. Bureau of Labor Statistics,* June, 1922, pp. 181-198.

TRACY, GEORGE. *History of the Typographical Union.*

United Mine Workers of America before the Anthracite Coal Commission, Employees' Exhibits Presented by W. Jett Lauck (1920).

Exhibits:

Vol. 1. Irregularity of Employment in the Anthracite Industry.

Vol. 2. Comparison of Earnings and Wage Rates in the Anthracite and Bituminous Mines of Pennsylvania.

Vol. 3. The Relationship Between Rates of Pay and Earnings and the Cost of Living in the Anthracite Industry in Pennsylvania.

Vol. 4. The Sanctions for a Living Wage.

Vol. 5. What a Living Wage Should Be.

Vol. 6. The Trade Union as the Basis for Collective Bargaining.

Vol. 7. The Sanction for the Eight Hour Day.

Vol. 8. Occupation Hazard of Anthracite Miners.

Vol. 9. Combination in the Anthracite Industry.

Vol. 10. Freight Rates on Anthracite Coal.

Vol. 11. Operating and Financial Performance of Anthracite Railroads.

Vol. 12. Profits of Anthracite Operators.

Vol. 13. The Relations Between Wages and Production, Costs, Prices, and Profits in the Anthracite Mining Industry.

Vol. 14. Summary, Analysis and Statement.

Vol. 15. Wholesale and Retail Prices of Anthracite Coal, 1913 to 1920.

United Mine Workers of America: The Case of the Bituminous Coal Mine Workers' as presented by the United Mine Workers of America to the President's Coal Commission (1920).

United Mine Workers of America, Nationalization Research Committee:

"Compulsory Information in Coal" (1922).
"How to Run Coal" (1922).

Report of the U. S. Commission on Industrial Relations (1915).

U. S. Coal Commission. Report on the Anthracite Industry. Also supplementary report on "Industrial Relations in the Anthracite Industry" (1923).

U. S. Department of Labor, Bureau of Labor Statistics: Series of Bulletins on "Wages and Hours of Labor."

WALKER, CHARLES R. *Steel, the Diary of a Furnace Worker* (1922).

WARNE, FRANK J. "The Railway Employes' Reply to the Railroads." Hearings Before the Committee on Interstate Commerce, U. S. Senate, 67th Congress, 1st Sess. (1920).

WATKINS, GORDON S. *An Introduction to the Study of Labor Problems* (1922).

WOLMAN, LEO; MACK, ELEANOR; WANDER, PAUL. *The Clothing Workers of Chicago* (1922).

"Workers' Education in the United States," Reports of the Proceedings of the First and Second National Conferences of the Workers' Education Bureau of America, 1922 and 1923.

ZIMAND, SAVEL. *Modern Social Movements*: Descriptive Summaries, and Bibliographies, pp. 7-112 (1921).

Revolutionary Unionism

ANDERSON, NELS. *The Hobo; the Sociology of the Homeless Man* (1923).

BEARD, MARY A. *Short History of the American Labor Movement*, chap. XI (1920).

BRISSENDEN, PAUL F. "The I. W. W.: A Study of American Syndicalism," *Columbia University Studies* (1919). See this book for a comprehensive bibliography on the subject.

PARKER, CARLTON H. *Casual Laborer and Other Essays* (1920).

SAVAGE, MARION D. *Industrial Unionism in America* (1922).

ZIMAND, SAVEL. *Modern Social Movements*: Descriptive Summaries and Bibliographies, pp. 207-226 (1921).

Employers' Associations

Annals of the American Academy of Political and Social Science, vol. 91, No. 180 (1920). "LABOR, MANAGEMENT AND PRODUCTION."

446 TRADE UNIONISM

American Federation of Labor Convention Proceedings, 1915, pp. 77-86, on "Strike-Breaking Agencies."

American Trade Index. Gives names of members of National Association of Manufacturers.

Bonnett, C. E. *Employers' Associations in the United States* (1921).

Brissenden, Paul F., and Frankel, Emil: *Labor Turnover in Industry.*

Commons, John R. *Industrial Good Will* (1919).

Federated American Engineering Societies, "Waste in Industry" (1921).

Leitch, John. "Man to Man" (1919).

National Association of Manufacturers of the United States of America, "National Trade Associations" (1922).

National Industrial Conference Board Bulletins.

Naylor, Emmett H. *Trade Associations, Their Organization and Management* (1921).

Howard, Sidney, and Dunn, Robert. *The Labor Spy.* A Survey of Industrial Espionage (1921).

The New York Chamber of Commerce, "Trade and Allied Associations and Publications in New York City Classified."

President's Conference on Unemployment: "Business Cycles and Unemployment," Reports and Recommendations including an Investigation made under the *National Bureau of Economic Research* (1923).

Slichter, Sumner. *The Turnover of Factory Labor* (1919).

U. S. Department of Commerce, Bureau of Foreign and Domestic Commerce, "Commercial and Industrial Organizations of the United States" (1922).

U. S. Department of Labor, Bureau of Labor Statistics, Bulletins.

Nos. 216, 234, 298. Accident Prevention.

No. 235. Employment System of the Lake Carriers' Association.

No. 263. Housing by Employers in the United States.

No. 299. Personnel Research Agencies.

Nos. 196, 202, 227, 247. Proceedings of the Employment Managers' Conferences.

No. 208. Profit Sharing in the United States.

No. 159. Short Unit Courses for Wage Earners, a Factory School Experiment.

Nos. 123, 250. Welfare Work.

LEISERSON, WM. M. *U. S. Department of Labor, Working Conditions Service,* "Employment Management, Employee Representation and Industrial Democracy."

WILLIAMS, WHITING. *What is on the Workers' Mind?* (1920).

The Law in Relation to Labor

ALLEN, HENRY J. *The Party of the Third Part;* the Story of the Kansas Industrial Relations Court (1921).

The American Labor Legislation Review.

CARLTON, FRANK T. *History and Problems of Organized Labor,* chap XI.

CARROLL, MOLLIE RAY. *Labor and Politics, the Attitude of the American Federation of Labor Toward Legislation and Politics,* chap. VII.

COMMONS, JOHN R., and ANDREWS, JOHN B. *Principles of Labor Legislation,* 2d ed. (1920).

FREY, JOHN P. *The Labor Injunction* (1923).

HUGGINS, WILLIAM L. *Labor and Democracy* (1922).

POUND, ROSCOE. *Introduction to the Philosophy of Law* (1922).

——. *The Spirit of the Common Law* (1921).

POWELL, T. R. "Constitutional Law in 1917-18"; "Constitutional Law in 1918-19," *American Political Science Review*, 13: 47-77, 607-633; 14: 53-73.

SAYRE, F. B. *Selection of Cases and Other Authorities on Labor Law* (1922).

U. S. *Department of Labor, Bureau of Labor Statistics Bulletins*:

Nos. 152, 169, 189, 224, 246, 290. "Decisions of Courts Affecting Labor," 1913-1920.

Nos. 111, 112, 148, 168, 186, 211, 213, 229, 244, 257, 277, 285, 292, 308, 309. Series, "Labor Laws of the United States."

No. 303. "Use of Federal Power in Settlement of Railway Labor Disputes."

No. 321. "Labor Laws That Have Been Declared Unconstitutional."

No. 322. "The Kansas Court of Industrial Relations," containing a Bibliography by Laura A. Thompson.

University Journal of Business:
"The Clayton Labor Law Provisions," by R. E. Montgomery, vol. I, Nos. 2, 3.

Collective Bargaining and the Trade Union Program

BARNETT, GEORGE E., and McCABE, D. A. *"Mediation, Investigation and Arbitration in Industrial Disputes"* (1916).

CARLTON, FRANK T. *History and Problems of Organized Labor,* chap. X.

FREY, JOHN P. "Thirty Years' Experience with Industrial Democracy," *International Labor Review,* April, 1922. pp. 539-552.

HOAGLAND, HENRY ELMER. "Collective Bargaining in the Lithograph Industry," *Columbia University Studies* (1917).

HOWARD, EARL DEAN. *The Hart, Schaffner & Marx Agreement, Industrial Law in the Clothing Industry* (1920).
LAUCK, W. JETT. "Railroad Boards of Labor Adjustment," *Railway Employes' Department of the American Federation of Labor.*
U. S. Department of Labor, Bureau of Labor Statistics, Bulletins:
  Nos. 124, 133, 139, 144, 145, 191, 198, 233, 283, 287, 303. "Conciliation and Arbitration."
U. S. Department of Labor Library, Thompson, Laura A., "Recent Literature on Collective Bargaining."
WALKER, CHARLES R. "A National Council for the Printing Trades" (1921). Reprinted from the *Monthly Labor Review*, Feb., 1921.

Scientific Management

Amos Tuck School, *Conference on Scientific Management* (1912).
BABCOCK, GEORGE D. *Taylor System in Franklin Management* (1917).
Bulletin of the Taylor Society, New York.
CANNONS, H. G. T. *Bibliography of Industrial Efficiency and Factory Management* (1920).
Federated American Engineering Societies: "Waste in Industry," 1921.
GANTT, HENRY L. *Work, Wages and Profits* (1919).
LICHTNER, WILLIAM O. *Time Study and Job Analysis* (1921).
MERRICK, DWIGHT V. *Time Studies for Rate Setting* (1921)
National Bureau of Economic Research: "Employment, Hours and Earnings in Prosperity and Depression" (1923).
PARKHURST, FREDERICK A. *Applied Methods of Scientific Management* (1912).

450   TRADE UNIONISM

President's Conference on Unemployment: "Business Cycles
and Unemployment." Report and Recommendations,
including an Investigation made under the *National
Bureau of Economic Research* (1923).

TAYLOR, F. W. "On the Art of Cutting Metals," American
Society of Mechanical Engineers. Paper No. 1119.
New York.

TAYLOR, F. W. *Shop Management* (1911).

THOMPSON, C. BERTRAND. *Theory and Practice of Scientific
Management* (1917).

INDEX

(13)

THE END